Robert L. Ebel
Michigan State University

ESSENTIALS OF EDUCATIONAL

MEASUREMENT

Third Edition

PRENTICE-HALL INC, ENGLEWOOD CLIFFS, NEW JERSEY 07632

Library of Congress Cataloging in Publication Data

Ebel, Robert L.
 Essentials of educational measurement.

 Includes index.
 1. Educational tests and measurements. 2. Prediction of scholastic success. I. Title.
LB3051.E22   1979 371.2'6 78-13392
ISBN 0-13-286013-9

Essentials of Educational Measurement
is the third edition of the book
formerly titled *Measuring Educational Achievement*.

Printed in the United States of America

10 9 8 7 6 5 4 3 2 1

Editorial/production supervision and interior design:
Serena Hoffman and Jeanne Hoeting
Cover design: Edsal Enterprises
Manufacturing buyers: Gordon Osbourne and John Hall

PRENTICE-HALL INTERNATIONAL, INC., *LONDON*
PRENTICE-HALL OF AUSTRALIA PTY. LIMITED, *SYDNEY*
PRENTICE-HALL OF CANADA, LTD., *TORONTO*
PRENTICE-HALL OF INDIA PRIVATE LIMITED, *NEW DELHI*
PRENTICE-HALL OF JAPAN, INC., *TOKYO*
PRENTICE-HALL OF SOUTHEAST ASIA PTE. LTD., *SINGAPORE*
WHITEHALL BOOKS LIMITED, *WELLINGTON, NEW ZEALAND*

To the teachers in my family:

> *my father, Louis*
> *my mother, Lillian*
> *my wife, Hazel June*
> *my sisters, Louise and Ethel*
> *my brother, Marvin*
> *my daughters, Mary Ellen and*
>   *Margaret Louise*

whose examples, support, instruction, and approval have contributed so much to my own satisfaction in being a teacher.

Contents

18   INTELLIGENCE AND APTITUDE TESTS   344

The Nature of Intelligence 344. Kinds of Tasks Used to Test Intelligence 345. Operational and Analytic Definitions of Intelligence 349. Designing Intelligence Tests 349. Tests of Special Aptitudes 352. The Inheritance of Intelligence 356.

Summary 360.

19   PERSONALITY, ATTITUDES, AND INTERESTS   362

Personality Tests 362. What are Attitudes? 366. How are Interests Measured? 372.

Summary 373.

Glossary of Terms Used in Educational Measurement   374.

Author Index   381.

Subject Index   384.

*For myself, I know that, as far as my modest abilities have permitted,
I have presented plainly and simply,
for the instruction of any who wished to learn,
such lessons as I have gained from my own experience,
and all else that I have been able to find
out for the purpose of the present work.
And it is enough for a good man
to have taught what he knows.*

QUINTILIAN
INSTITUTIO ORATIONEM
A.D. 100

Preface

Essentials of Educational Measurement has been designed to serve as a textbook for an introductory course in educational measurement. It can also be used as a reference book by classroom teachers and by those in government and business who are responsible for making and using tests of abilities. The author has undertaken to produce a book that is technically sound, practically useful and clearly written.

This Third Edition has been made more concise and somewhat simpler than the Second. The chapter on Historical Perspectives has been replaced by one on the current status of measurement in education. A new chapter describes the construction of short answer, matching, numerical problems and other objective item types. Chapter 15 treats validity as a problem primarily of test use, not test content. It suggests that attempts to "validate" a test by relating real test items to hypothetical abilities or traits are likely to be no more productive in the future than they have been in the past.

All of the ideas expressed in these pages reflect the author's understandings and values developed over more than forty years of study, teaching and advising. Some may reflect bits of creative originality, but most have been borrowed from others; my teachers, my fellow professionals, and my students. For their competence and their kindnesses, I am most grateful.

R. L. E.
East Lansing, Michigan

1

Educational Measurement:
Current Developments

THE PARADOX

There is a paradox in educational measurement today. While assessments of achievement and competence are being more urgently called for and more widely employed than ever before, at the same time, tests are being more sharply criticized and more strongly opposed.[1] Perhaps these apparent inconsistencies are, in fact, wholly consistent. If demands for more measurement of educational outcomes arise out of dissatisfaction with how much is being learned, those responsible for the teaching are likely to feel threatened by possible public exposure of educational shortcomings. In any case, despite its expanding role in education, measurement is under attack. Let us look briefly at contemporary demands for more evidence of achievement and competence, and then let us consider the arguments being made against the expansion, or indeed even the continued use of, measurement in education.

---

[1] William A. Mehrens, "Evaluators, Educators, and the Publics: A Detente?" *N.C.M.E. Measurement in Education,* Vol. 5, No. 3, Summer, 1974; Thomas J. Fitzgibbon, "Dear Mama: Why Don't They Love Me Anymore?" *N.C.M.E. Measurement in Education,* Vol. 6, No. 4, Fall, 1976.

ARE THEY LEARNING ENOUGH?

Criticism of schools and teaching is not new. It did not begin with Horace Mann, though he was one of the more prominent critics of American schools in the first half of the nineteenth century. He was also one of the first educators to make significant use of educational measurements to assess the effectiveness of schooling. Quite predictably, the written examinations he advocated were strongly opposed by the Boston schoolmasters whose pupils were to be examined.

In the decade of the 1970s, concern for the effectiveness of American schools became much stronger and more widespread than it had been before. Part of this concern arose from evidence, incidental and systematic, of deficiencies in learning. Some pupils given high school diplomas were able to read only with difficulty, or not at all. Incompetence in arithmetic, spelling, composition, geography, science, and other subjects of study was commonly reported. A sharp decline in the college admission test scores of high school students received wide publicity. It became apparent that in many schools the environment for learning had deteriorated badly. Discipline and vandalism became major problems. Hard study, with homework and rigorous grading of assignments, was no longer fashionable. Frustrated and angry because their children seemed to be learning so little, several parents filed suit charging school officials with educational malpractice.

Coupled with declining pupil achievements were sharply increased school costs. Per pupil expenditures for instruction rose much faster than the general rate of inflation. Salaries for teachers in most states increased more rapidly than the average of all wages and salaries. No doubt, some of the increase in teachers' salaries was well warranted for a previously underpaid profession. No doubt, the growing strength and militancy of teachers' associations (unions) had much to do with the increase in salaries and the resultant increase in school costs. But the net effect of these increases was a correspondingly sharp increase in school taxes. It is not surprising that citizens, grumbling about taxes, began to ask for evidence that these tax dollars were doing some good. How much, they asked, are we getting for our money?

MANDATED ASSESSMENT

In response to citizen concern over the quality of student learning and the costs of providing instruction, a number of state legislatures passed laws that required tests to be given to assess the educational achievements of pupils in the public schools. Statewide educational testing began long ago. In the 1930s optional testing programs, often operated by state universities

2

but sometimes by state departments of education, were available to schools in many of the states. But these programs were voluntary. Their stated purpose was to help schools teach better, not to check up on how well they were doing. School administrators and school teachers are much more favorably inclined toward tests used to help them to do a better job than toward tests used to determine how well they have done it.

Some states have mandated programs of testing to determine the competencies of their high school graduates. The intent is to use this information to provide diplomas that will show specifically what the graduate has learned or can do as a result of schooling. This is a move in the direction of the British system of certifying A-level (advanced) or O-level (ordinary) passes on examinations in specific subject areas.

Accountability

The move toward mandated assessment is motivated by contemporary concerns for accountability. Hopeful parents and hard pressed taxpayers believe that it is necessary and proper to hold school board members, school administrators, teachers, and pupils accountable for their successes or failures in the promotion of learning. For their part, school officials tend to be wary of accountability. They fear, not without justification, that they may be held responsible for disappointing outcomes which were not their fault, for failures they could not prevent. However, should this exempt them from accountability? Political leaders, business managers, football coaches, surgeons, and battlefield commanders are all exposed to similar hazards. They may hope to be judged fairly, but they can not escape judgment. Neither can educators. Surely their pupils' educational achievements are part of the evidence required to make a fair judgment.

Instructional Testing

Several recent developments in systematic instruction call for increased use of tests. Competency-based education, directed toward attainment of specific, behaviorally defined objectives of instruction, requires separate tests of attainment for each competency. Programmed instruction requires repeated testing to determine whether a pupil is ready to advance to the next phase of the program or needs to repeat the preceding phase, either in toto or via remedial instruction. Indeed, in many programs for instruction, testing is not separate from but is imbedded in the instructional program. Individually guided education requires pretests to determine initial status and individually administered unit tests at each step along the way.

Good teachers have always used tests to measure the achievements of individual pupils in learning and the effectiveness of instructional programs. Good students have always tested themselves for understanding and for recall as part of their methods of study. What has happened recently is that testing has become a more prominent, more systematically organized element of the instructional process. Such testing is obviously essential. There have been no calls for a moratorium on instructional testing, as there have been on standardized testing. But the same skills of test planning, question formulation, scoring, and score interpretation are basic to both.

Occupational Competency

Tests have long been used as part of the basis for certifying the competence of lawyers (bar exams), of doctors (medical boards), of accountants (CPA exams), of clinical psychologists, of nurses, of policemen and firemen, of real estate brokers, of barbers and hairdressers, and of other professional practitioners and tradesmen. The list is constantly expanding. Dissatisfaction with the quality of some automobile repairs led to a recent proposal to examine and certify auto mechanics.

City, state, and national civil service boards and commissions prepare, administer, and score enormous numbers of competitive examinations to help them select the best-qualified government employees. In England an agency known as The City and Guilds of London Institute examines applicants for certification of competence in a wide range of occupational specialties. Possession of a City and Guilds certificate is a considerable asset, if not a prerequisite to employment in many fields.

What these tests of occupational competence primarily measure is an applicant's knowledge of how a job *ought* to be done. Although this aspect of competence is surely important, clearly it does not guarantee success in the practice of the profession or the trade. That will depend on the practitioner's hard work, personality, good luck, and possibly other factors. In most occupations scores on tests of competence correlate highly with success in practice. That the scores are not infallible predictors of success may be due in part to shortcomings of the tests. But other factors are undoubtedly involved in success, elements that remain untested and probably untestable.

As occupations become more specialized, as demands for competence grow in our complex society, tests of occupational competency will be used more and more. Good tests are urgently needed, and competent test specialists must be produced to supply them.

CRITICISMS OF TESTS AND TESTING

No one who is well acquainted with the tests currently used to assess educational achievement is likely to claim that they are above criticism. The process of assessing achievement in learning is much more complicated than it may seem to be at first glance. The naive view is that all one has to do is to give a test. Each student either passes or fails. The proportion who pass indicates the effectiveness of the educational program. Where the test comes from, what it actually measures, how good it is, what the scores mean, how the passing score is determined—these and many other hard questions that trouble test specialists a great deal trouble the general public hardly at all.

In fact, very little of the criticism of tests and testing comes from the general public. Most of it comes from members of three special interest groups:

1. Professional educators who are uneasy about the accountability associated with standardized tests and external testing in general.
2. Reformers who regard testing as part of an unsuccessful and out-moded instructional process.
3. Free-lance writers whose best sellers purport to expose scandals in important human institutions.

From none of these groups of critics is one likely to get a constructive criticism of tests and testing. What they want is not to improve the tests, to correct their faults, to make them more useful educational tools—it is rather to discredit tests, to minimize their influence, or to get rid of them altogether.

Nonetheless, the criticisms need to be taken seriously. If they are repeated often enough and loudly enough with no response, they will come to be accepted as true, no matter how little evidence there is to support them.

Here are some of the most frequently mentioned criticisms of tests and testing.

1. That the tests are *invalid*, measuring only superficial, unimportant aspects of achievement.
2. That *objective tests* are used mainly because they can be easily scored, regardless of serious shortcomings of triviality, ambiguity, and guessing.
3. That IQ *testing* has led to the labeling of particular pupils as bright or dull, in both cases distorting their expectations and diminishing their efforts.
4. That external testing programs impose *external controls* on the curriculum and lead teachers to give up sound, long-range instruction in order to "teach to the test."
5. That testing places students under harmful *stress* and exposes them to unnecessary experiences of failure, destroying their self-confidence and killing the joy of learning.

6. That the tests carry a white, middle-class *bias*, misrepresenting the achievements and the potential of cultural minorities.
7. That conventional single-score, norm-referenced, standardized tests should be replaced by *criterion-referenced tests* that indicate, not whether Johnny knows more than Mary, but exactly which objectives of instruction have been achieved and which have not.

RESPONSES TO THE CRITICISMS

The matter of test validity is dealt with extensively in the chapters on what educational tests should measure and on test validity. Here it need only be said that tests provide the best information teachers and pupils can get on the success of efforts to teach and to learn.

The values and limitations of objective tests are dealt with in the chapters on test planning, on essay testing, and on types of objective test items. With very few exceptions, whatever can be tested at all can be tested with objective tests, usually with greater precision and often with greater convenience.

Some of the sharpest attacks on the tests used in education have been directed at intelligence, or IQ, tests. The focus of recent controversy has been on whether or not there are racial differences in intelligence. This is part of the larger question of the extent to which a person's mental abilities are the result of heredity. This issue will be examined in some detail in the chapter on intelligence testing.

Two observations may suffice for present purposes. The first is that IQ testing is probably more vulnerable to informed criticism than are most other forms of educational testing. The nature of intelligence is commonly misunderstood, and IQs are commonly misinterpreted. They can be and have been used to discourage some pupils from trying to learn, and to excuse teachers from trying to teach them.

The second observation is that there are important differences between intelligence tests and standardized tests of achievement in what is to be measured, how well it can be measured, and what effect its measurement will have on the progress of learning. Thus it is not true, as critics of testing sometimes imply, that the deficiencies and abuses of the one are necessarily also characteristic of the other.

External Control of Curricula

Standardized tests of achievement are sometimes attacked because of their supposed effect on the curricula of local schools. It is charged that they enforce curricular conformity, that they fail to test what local schools or particular teachers have been trying to teach, that they hamper curricular innovations or the use of open curricula. There is substance to these charges, but the effects are neither so overpowering nor so harmful as the critics imply.

If a school wants its pupils to score high on certain tests, it must of course see to it that they receive instruction in those achievements sampled by the tests. Yet these are areas that panels of expert teachers have identified as important for most pupils to learn. Local schools or individual teachers who decide to concentrate on achievements other than these should be prepared to do two things: (1) to argue convincingly to the public that what they are trying to teach is indeed more important for these pupils to know than the things the standardized test is testing; and (2) to prepare, give, validate, and report the results on a local test that does measure what they have been trying to teach. Few of those who complain about the curricular restrictions of standardized testing are prepared to do either of these things.

A school that is teaching what the tests examine will surely teach many other things as well. Even in the basic skill or core areas that the test does sample, there will be class time and teacher time to venture into interesting and useful areas of learning not covered by the standardized tests. Standardized tests can dominate local curricula only to the extent that school administrators and school teachers allow them to.

In some programs of open education there are covert goals for learning, and classroom activities are covertly manipulated so that pupils make systematic progress toward these goals. In such programs, standardized tests of achievement may be not only appropriate, but essential. Other programs have no particular goals for pupil learning, and are satisfied merely with maximum pupil freedom, trusting nature alone to do the job that others employ the art and science of teaching to help nature to do. That standardized tests of achievement are inappropriate for such programs may imply more criticism of the program than of the tests.

Teaching to the Test

If the effectiveness of instruction is to be assessed on the basis of student performance on a test, the temptation is strong for the instructor to prepare students to handle the specific questions that will be included in the test. This is often called *teaching to the test*. Obviously, it is not an educationally beneficial procedure. It also tends to spoil the test as a measure of general achievement in the subject area. But if the test is a readily available, published test, an insecure or short-sighted teacher is quite likely to undertake to teach to the test. Even a test specially constructed for a particular assessment task is, in effect, a "published" test once it has been used. If teachers care enough, they can find out a great deal about the particular questions included in it. So it too may invite teaching to the test.

Several things can be done to lessen the likelihood of teaching to the test. Teachers can be warned to avoid it and informed that their supervisors will be alert to notice it if it occurs. Pupils can be advised of its undesirability and asked to report its occurrence. Of course, the surest but most expensive way to forestall it is to prepare a new test for each new assessment effort.

Before leaving this subject, let us make an important distinction between teaching to the test (attempting to fix in pupils' minds the answers to particular test questions) and teaching material *covered* by the test (attempting to give pupils the capability of answering questions *like* those in the test on topics covered by the test). The first is thoroughly reprehensible. The second reflects purposeful teaching. Just as there is no warrant for giving away the answers to particular questions, so there is no warrant for testing performance on tasks pupils were never taught to perform. A teacher or school whose work is to be assessed is entitled to know what the pupils will be expected to do. This calls for close cooperation and clear communication between teachers on the one hand and test constructors on the other. An assessment test must be thoroughly relevant to the instruction it is intended to assess. Since a test can never elicit more than a sample of performance, much more will usually be taught than can be tested. However, the test should never go beyond what has been taught.

DOES TESTING HARM PUPILS?

Several claims are made to support the charge that standardized testing harms pupils: that such tests threaten and upset pupils; that some pupils even break down and cry when faced with a test; that if pupils get a low score on a test, they will become discouraged and quit trying; that their self-concept will be seriously damaged; that standardized testing is incompatible with educational procedures designed to support the child.

There is, no doubt, anecdotal evidence to support some of these claims. Common sense suggests, however, that the majority of pupils are not harmed by testing. There are no substantial survey data that would contradict common sense on this matter. Teachers seem much more often concerned with pupils who don't care enough how well or how poorly they do on such tests, than with the relatively exceptional instances of pupils who seem to care too much.

It is normal and biologically helpful to be somewhat anxious when facing any real testing in life. But it is also a necessary part of growing up to learn to cope with the kind of tests that life inevitably brings. Of the many challenges to a child's peace of mind caused by such things as angry parents, playground bullies, bad dogs, shots from the doctor, and things that go bump in the night, standardized tests must surely be among the least fearsome for most children. Unwise'parental pressure can in some cases elevate anxiety to harmful levels. But usually the child who breaks down in tears at the prospect of a test has problems of security, adjustment, and maturity which testing did not create, and which cannot be solved by eliminating tests. Indeed, more frequent testing might help to solve the problem.

A pupil who consistently gets low test scores on material that pupil has tried hard to learn is indeed likely to become discouraged. If this does happen, the school cannot claim to be offering a good educational program, and the teacher cannot claim to be doing a good job of teaching. Most low test scores, however, go to pupils who, for one reason or another, have not tried very hard to learn. In the opinion of the teachers of such pupils it is the trying rather than the testing that is most in need of correction.

Pupils do indeed deserve support from their teachers. But what needs to be supported is the pupils' person and potential, not their mistakes or shortcomings. If teachers support ignorance or wrongdoing, they betray their profession. In the area of school achievement, what teachers need to support is progress toward the goals of learning. Standardized tests can help them to provide that support.

THE PROBLEM OF TEST BIAS

Standardized tests of educational achievement have also been attacked for their alleged bias against cultural minorities and against pupils with poor reading skills. The reason for the attack, at least in part, is that such pupils tend to score lower on standardized tests. But surely lower scores alone do not signify bias. If they did, every spelling test would be biased against poor spellers, and every typing test against persons who never learned to type. A test is biased only if it yields measures that are consistently lower than they should be.

That pupils who do poorly on a particular test in English might do better if the test were in Spanish, or if the questions were presented orally, does not mean that the original test is biased against them. It simply means that they have not learned much of what that particular test measures. Its linguistic context is part of the test. The particularity of what the test measures does not constitute bias.

The score of a pupil on an achievement test indicates how successfully the test questions were answered under the conditions of the test. The reasonable assumption is usually made that the pupil would be equally successful with other tasks requiring the same knowledge or ability. But if the pupil is frightened of being tested, the test score may not be an accurate indication of his/her knowledge or ability. Experimental studies have shown that the scores of some pupils can be raised somewhat by changing the conditions of testing. But the increase is usually rather small, too small to support the hypothesis that it is the conditions of testing which accounts for the lower test scores of minority pupils.

What of the pupil who is offended by being asked to take a test at all? Surely, in this case the test score is not an accurate indication of knowledge. But is this the fault of the test or of the student? Should we say that the test is biased against the pupil? Or is it the pupil who is biased against the test?

The possibility of bias in intelligence tests is much greater than it is in achievement tests. Scores on a test of general intelligence are supposed to indicate a person's ability to learn many different kinds of things from success in having learned a few other things. If the examinees all had nearly equal opportunity to learn what the intelligence test requires, the indications of general intelligence may be reasonably accurate. If not, the test may yield seriously biased indications of intelligence.

CRITERION-REFERENCED TESTS

In the 1960s a new term entered the vocabularies of measurement specialists—*criterion-referenced test*.[2] It referred to a particular kind of test and an unconventional approach to the measurement of educational achievement. Tests of this kind were also referred to as *objectives-referenced* or *domain-referenced,* and were contrasted with the more conventional standardized or teacher-made tests, which were referred to as *norm-referenced tests.*

Strong advocates of the new tests, who were usually rather critical of conventional tests, claimed that criterion-referenced tests constituted a significant and generally applicable improvement in the conception and methodology of achievement testing. They suggested that norm-referenced tests be abandoned as quickly as possible in favor of the new type. An alternative view, which we support, is that neither type is superior to the other for *all* measurement purposes. Each has special characteristics that make it uniquely well suited to particular situations and uses.

One way of becoming familiar with the characteristics of criterion-referenced tests is to consider some of the ways in which they differ from, or are similar to, norm-referenced tests. Comparisons of this kind are bound to involve some oversimplifications and inaccuracies, since there are many different forms of each type of test. Nevertheless, the forms have

[2] Peter W. Airasian and George F. Madaus, "Criterion-Referenced Testing in the Classroom," *N.C.M.E. Measurement in Education,* Vol. 3, No. 4, May 1972.

enough features in common to make the comparisons useful, even if not always completely accurate.

One difference is in the kind of information they are intended to provide. Criterion-referenced tests are used to determine which of certain specified objectives of instruction a particular pupil has attained. Norm-referenced tests are used to determine how much overall knowledge of some subject a particular pupil has achieved. The basic report of results from a criterion-referenced test is a descriptive list of objectives which were or were not attained. The basic report for a norm-referenced test is a count of the number of test questions that were answered correctly.

A second difference is in the basis for interpreting the information provided. The "criterion" in a criterion-referenced test is the attainment of all instructional objectives. The excellence or deficiency of a particular student's achievement in learning is judged by the proportion of the pre-scribed objectives the student has attained. The "norm" in a norm-refer-enced test is the achievement of some specified group of students on the test. The excellence or deficiency of a particular student's achievement in learning is judged by that student's standing among those in the specified group.

A third difference is in the distribution of items over the domain of achievement sampled by the test. The items in a criterion-referenced test cluster around a limited number of specific objectives. For example, a criterion-referenced test might focus on 20 distinct objectives, using five items for each objective in order to determine whether or not the student had attained it. The result would be a 100-item criterion-referenced test. The items in a norm-referenced test would be diffused more widely across the domain of learning. Each of the 100 items would involve a separate aspect of achievement.

A fourth difference is in the use made of the test information. The purpose of a norm-referenced test score is simply to *indicate* a student's degree of success in learning. A criterion-referenced test, on the other hand, is often used with instructional procedures intended to *insure* that certain things will be learned.[3]

Despite these major differences, there are substantial similarities be-tween criterion-referenced and norm-referenced tests. Both have essen-tially the same job to do; that is, to measure achievement in learning. The items in both must be related to the objectives of instruction. Elements of quality are essentially the same for both. The individual test question used in the two are indistinguishable.

For what uses is each form of test most appropriate? In general, criterion-referenced tests are best adapted to assist in categorical pass-fail

[3] Samuel T. Mayo, "Mastery Learning and Mastery Testing," *N.C.M.E. Measurement in Education*, Vol. 1, No. 3, March 1970.

decisions with respect to separate specific tasks or competencies. Can this child tell time from a clock? Can she multiply two three-digit numbers or add two common fractions with different denominators? Can he pick out the nouns, adjectives, verbs, adverbs, and prepositions in a sentence? Can he tell from a map which roads to follow to get from Town A to Town B?

The tests used to certify the competence of a craftsman or a professional—a plumber, an auto mechanic, a radio engineer, accountant, or physician—have one characteristic of the criterion-referenced form. They result in categorical pass-fail decisions. The applicant is either certified or rejected. But the basis for the decision is usually a survey-type test similar to most norm-referenced tests. The test is intended to assess the applicant's general level of competence, not his achievements in each of a list of specific competencies.

The norm-referenced form is useful in measuring a person's general level of knowledge or understanding of a subject. While categorical decisions are sometimes made on the basis of scores on norm-referenced tests, as in the case of certification examinations just mentioned, the purpose of such tests is to *measure* in quantitative terms. Progress toward most educational goals is a matter of more or less, not a matter of all or none. Students are more or less familiar with the history of the United States, with the poetry of Robert Frost, with the logic of statistical inference. They are not either informed or ignorant. For this reason norm-referenced, survey-type tests have very wide uses in the measurement of educational achievement.

Proponents of criterion-referenced tests sometimes criticize standardized tests (norm-referenced) for their lack of specific relevance to what is being taught in a particular unit of study in a given local school system. What they say about lack of specific relevance is true, but it does not justify a criticism of standardized tests. A hammer should not be criticized on the grounds that it makes a poor screwdriver. Surveys of broad areas of achievement, such as standardized tests provide, are educationally useful. More detailed assessments of achievement in narrow units of study are also useful. Whether the more specific unit tests should be norm-referenced or criterion-referenced depends on whether the instruction aimed to develop particular abilities or more general understandings.

Proponents of criterion-referenced tests have performed a valuable service in emphasizing the importance of clearly defining test goals. Those who make survey tests (norm-referenced) have not always been as explicit and detailed with this definition as they should have been. But the proponents of criterion-referenced tests are mistaken when they suggest that their tests avoid the comparison of one pupil's achievement with that of other pupils—when they imply that such comparisons are unnecessary or evil. Judgments of excellence or deficiency in learning cannot be based on anything other than comparisons.

Some technical issues that have arisen in the dialog over criterion versus norm-referenced testing will be discussed in subsequent chapters on school marks, item analysis, and reliability. Most of what is said in the remaining chapters of this book applies equally to criterion-referenced and norm-referenced tests. Let us end this discussion by repeating and reemphasizing the point made at the outset. Neither form of test is superior to the other for *all* educational measurement needs. Each has characteristics that make it uniquely advantageous for particular measurement needs. The question is not "Which is better?" but "When is it better?"

CONCLUDING COMMENTS

The need for good tests of achievement in learning or of competence to practice a profession is not likely to diminish. It is likely to grow. Nor are criticisms of tests and testing likely to disappear. The tests we currently use are not as good, on the whole, as they need to be. Informed criticism can help to make them better. But critics who urge that testing be limited or abandoned advise our schools and our society badly. Even the imperfect tests we now use serve us far better, in general, than no tests would do. Educators should work to improve, not to destroy testing.

SUMMARY

The principal ideas developed in this chapter can be summarized by the statements:

1. As tests of educational achievement have become increasingly important they have been increasingly criticized, particularly by those who may be affected adversely by their use.
2. Concern for the quality of education pupils are receiving, in relation to the money being spent on education, has been a major factor in the current demand for "accountability."
3. State testing programs required by law are intended to assess the general quality of education pupils are receiving, or to identify specific competencies they possess on graduation from high school.
4. Procedures for holding educators accountable for effective educational programs tend to be supported by citizens but to be opposed by educators.
5. Testing plays a prominent role in systematic instructional procedures such as programmed instruction, individually guided instruction, and competency-based education.

6. Tests are widely and increasingly used to certify occupational competency.
7. Most criticisms of educational testing from professional educators, educational reformers, and free-lance writers are intended to discredit tests and reduce their use, rather than to make the tests better.
8. Tests provide the best information teachers and pupils ordinarily can get of the success of their efforts to teach and to learn.
9. Objective tests can provide valid, precise, and convenient measures of the most important outcomes of education.
10. Attacks on IQ testing have some justification, but should not be generalized to apply equally to standardized tests of achievement.
11. The influence standardized tests have on local school curricula is likely to be more beneficial than harmful.
12. External testing can lead teachers to "teach to the test." This is bad if it involves giving the pupils answers to the particular questions that appear on the test. It is good if it involves helping students to learn what they must know to answer questions like those on the test.
13. Claims that testing harms pupils tend to be exaggerated, and are seldom based on substantial evidence.
14. Test bias may exist to some degree, but it cannot account for substantial differences in test scores between different cultural groups.
15. Criterion- or objectives-referenced tests have become popular. They are especially useful in some instructional programs, particularly in the early grades. It is unlikely, however, that they will become part of a radical, sweeping revolution in educational measurement.
16. The need for good tests of educational achievement will in all probability become more intense.
17. The imperfect tests we now use serve us far better than we would be served by no tests at all.

PROJECTS AND PROBLEMS

Project: A Survey of Experience with Tests and Grades

Answer each of the following questions as carefully and as honestly as you can. A summary of the results in your class will be reported to you. If time permits, they will be used as a basis for class discussion. Mark your answers on a machine-scorable answer sheet or as your instructor directs.

1. In your high school experience, about what percent of the tests you took were objective tests (that is, multiple-choice, true-false, short-answer, matching, and so forth) as opposed to essay or problem tests?
   1) Less than 25%
   2) From 25% to 50%
   3) From 50% to 75%
   4) From 75% to 90%
   5) More than 90%
2. In your college experience, about what percent of the tests you have taken have been objective tests?
   1) Less than 25%
   2) From 25% to 50%
   3) From 50% to 75%
   4) From 75% to 90%
   5) More than 90%
3. How often have you, personally, cheated on examinations you have taken?
   1) Never
   2) Once or twice
   3) Three to six times
   4) Seven or more times
   5) I'd rather not say
4. How often have you helped someone else to cheat on an examination?
   1) Never
   2) Once or twice
   3) Three to six times
   4) Seven or more times
   5) I'd rather not say
5. A student caught cheating on an examination should
   1) Fail the course.
   2) Fail that examination.
   3) Receive a grade one unit lower than his score would justify on that examination.
   4) Be required to take another examination.
   5) Be counseled but not punished.
6. How many courses that you wanted to take, and felt that you could have taken with benefit and satisfaction, have you avoided for fear of getting a low grade?
   1) None
   2) One
   3) Two
   4) Three
   5) Four or more
7. When, if ever, did you start to worry about the marks you might get in your school work?
   1) Almost as soon as I started to school
   2) In the early elementary grades
   3) In the upper elementary grades
   4) In high school
   5) In college
8. How severely have you been scolded or punished by your parents for low marks in school?
   1) I never got marks low enough to give cause for scolding or punishment.
   2) I was never blamed by my parents for the low marks I got.
   3) I was scolded for low marks but never punished.
   4) I was punished for low marks by the loss of privilege.
   5) I have been punished by a spanking or a whipping for low marks.

9. If you were to rank low marks as a cause of anxiety and unhappiness in your life among these other four common causes—illness, unpopularity with schoolmates, conflicts in the home, self-criticism over conduct or morals—where would low marks rank?
   1) At the top (the greatest cause of anxiety and unhappiness)
   2) Next to the top
   3) In the middle
   4) Next to the bottom
   5) At the bottom (the least cause of anxiety and unhappiness)

10. Which of these types of test do you personally prefer to take?
    1) An essay test or problems test
    2) A short-answer or completion test
    3) A true-false test
    4) A multiple-choice test
    5) A combination test including several types of items.

11. Which of these types of test do you personally prefer to take?
    1) A supervised in-class test
    2) An unsupervised (honor system) in-class test
    3) An open book in-class test
    4) A take-home test
    5) An oral examination

12. Which of the following grading systems comes closest to the one you would regard as preferable for high school and college courses?
    1) Pass-fail in all courses
    2) The common A–B–C–D–F system
    3) A–B–C–D–F grades with + or − refinements
    4) A nine-point numerical scale (stanines)
    5) A system of percent grades, with 100 percent perfect and 70 percent passing

13. Ideally, what proportion of a student's grade should depend on examination scores?
    1) All of it
    2) Most of it
    3) About half of it
    4) Less than half of it
    5) None of it

14. Who should determine the goals of education in a particular course?
    1) Mainly the teacher
    2) Mainly the individual student
    3) Teacher and student jointly and equally
    4) The class as a group
    5) Each student for himself or herself.

15. Who is primarily and ultimately responsible for the success of the process of education?
    1) The student
    2) The teacher
    3) The parents
    4) The school
    5) The society

16. Which statement below comes closest to expressing your view of the essence of educational achievement?

1) Learning how to learn
2) Gaining command of useful verbal knowledge
3) Cultivating the higher mental processes of reason, judgment, imagination and creativity
4) Developing a favorable self-concept
5) Learning to work effectively with others

17. What do you regard as the best justification for testing by a classroom teacher?
    1) To motivate study
    2) To diagnose difficulties in learning
    3) To provide a basis for more accurate grades
    4) To conform to traditional but largely ineffectual practices
    5) To provide students additional opportunities to learn

If measurement is to continue to play an increasingly important role in education, measurement workers must be much more than technicians. Unless their efforts are directed by a sound educational philosophy, unless they accept and welcome a greater share of responsibility for the selection and clarification of educational objectives, unless they show much more concern with what they measure as well as with how they measure it, much of their work will prove futile or ineffective.

E. F. LINDQUIST

2

Measurement and

the Process of Education

WHAT IS THE PRINCIPAL TASK OF THE SCHOOL?

When one considers the reasons why schools were built, the reasons why children and adults attend them, and the activities that go on inside them, it seems clear that the principal task of the school is to facilitate cognitive learning. Indeed, this answer may seem too obviously true to require any supporting argument. Yet learning has been challenged by some who argue that schools should be concerned primarily with one of the following:

    a. moral character[1]
    b. adjustment to life[2]
    c. reconstruction of society[3]
    d. self-confidence[4]

[1] Ernest M. Ligon, "Education for Moral Character," in *Philosophies of Education,* ed. Philip H. Phenix (New York: John Wiley & Sons, Inc., 1961).

[2] *Life Adjustment Education for Every Youth* (Washington D.C.: U.S. Office of Education, 1951).

[3] George S. Counts, *Dare the School Build a New Social Order?* (New York: The John Day Company, 1932).

[4] Earl C. Kelley, "The Fully Functioning Self," in *Perceiving, Behaving, Becoming,* 1962 Yearbook, Association for Supervision and Curriculum Development (Washington, D.C.: The Association, 1962).

Clearly all of these things are good. Since learning can contribute to each of them, they are not so much alternatives to learning as they are reasons for learning. But should they be given primary emphasis in defining the task of the school? Do they not have more to do with the ends of living than with the means the school should use to help pupils toward those ends?

Those who define the task of the school in terms of character, adjustment, self-confidence, or the good society tend to be critical of emphasis on learning in conventional schools. Loving does more than learning to make people happy, they say, and faith is better than reason as a guide to the good life. They tend to oppose structured learning situations, the setting of specific goals, the objective assessment of attainments, and the use of marks to report and record those attainments. They say that a teacher's primary concern should be to send pupils home in the afternoon thinking better of themselves than when they came to school in the morning. A child's happiness, they say, is more important to society than the ability to read. By thus denying the central role of learning in the activity of the school, they find it easy to excuse themselves from teaching, or their pupils from learning, anything very specific.

Many teachers, however, do not agree with those who set "higher" goals than learning for education. While they acknowledge the ultimate importance of character, adjustment, self-confidence, and the good society, they cite at least two reasons why none of them should replace learning as the school's primary focus of attention.

The first reason is that the school is a special purpose social institution. It was designed and developed to do a specific task: that is, to facilitate learning. Other agencies are responsible for other parts of the complex task of helping people to live good lives together. There are familes and churches, legislative assemblies and courts, publishers and libraries, factories and unions, markets and moneylenders. To believe that the whole responsibility for ethical character, life adjustment, social reconstruction, or happiness must rest on the schools is as presumptuous as it is foolish.

Let us never doubt the power of education for human betterment. But let us not make the mistake, either, of assuming that the schools can and should undertake to solve directly all the world's problems—war, oppression, poverty, exploitation, inflation, unemployment, anxiety, despair, underdevelopment, or overpopulation. If the schools take the burdens of the world on their shoulders, they are likely to neglect the specific tasks of training, instruction, and education that are their special responsibility. The task of facilitating learning is challenging enough, and important enough, to occupy all of a school's time and to consume all of its energy and resources.

The second reason for believing that the schools should continue to emphasize learning is the basic, instrumental importance of learning to all human affairs. With their gift of language, human beings are specially equipped for learning. Cognitive excellence is their unique excellence. The more they know and understand, the better, more effective, and happier they are likely to be.

How better can school help children toward happiness than by increasing their knowledge and understanding of themselves and the world in which they live? By what other means can adjustment be facilitated, character developed, or ability to contribute to society increased? Is not cognitive learning effective in reaching all these goals? And is there any other means?

Yes, there is one. It is the psychological process called conditioning.[5] It makes use of rewards and punishments to establish specific, habitual responses to certain specific conditions. Much of our behavior was molded, especially during our first years of life, by processes of conditioning. Even as adults we are still subject to its influences. If the school is concerned solely with training, if its sole mission is to establish certain specific, unvarying responses or behavior patterns; then it should depend heavily on conditioning, for conditioning can probably get that job done faster and more effectively than cognitive learning. But what conditioning cannot do is give a person flexibility and freedom. Conditioning is better suited to the training of horses or dogs than to the education of human beings to live happy, useful lives as free men and women.

Those who object to emphasis on learning as the school's primary task may do so because they think of learning as academic specialization, designed mainly to prepare a person for further learning, and remote from the practical concerns of living. No doubt some of what all schools have taught warrants this judgment. But learning need not be, and ought not be, the learning of useless things. It can and should be the student's main road to effective living. When it is, it merits recognition as the primary task of the school.

CAN EDUCATIONAL ACHIEVEMENT BE MEASURED?

Education is an extensive, diverse, complex enterprise, not only in terms of the achievements it seeks to develop, but also in terms of the means by which it seeks to develop them. Our understanding of the nature and process of education is far from perfect. Hence it is easy to agree that we do not now know how to measure all important educational outcomes. But in principle, all important outcomes of education are measurable. They may not be measurable with the tests currently available. They may not

---

[5] Ernest R. Hilgard and Donald G. Marquis, *Conditioning and Learning* (New York: Appleton-Century-Crofts, 1940).

even be measurable in principle, using only paper-and-pencil tests. But if they are known to be important, they must be measurable.

To be important, an outcome of education must make an observable difference. That is, at some time, under some circumstances, a person who has more of it must behave differently from a person who has less of it. If different degrees or amounts of an educational achievement never make any observable difference, what evidence can be found to show that it is in fact important?

But if such differences can be observed, then the achievement is measurable, for all measurement requires is verifiable observation of a more-less relationship. Can integrity be measured? It can if verifiable differences in integrity can be observed among individuals. Can mother love be measured? If observers can agree that a hen shows more mother love than a female trout, or that Mrs. A shows more love for her children than Mrs. B, then mother love can be measured.

The argument, then, is this: *To be important an educational outcome must make a difference. If it makes a difference, the basis for measurement exists.*

To say that A shows more of trait X than B may not seem like much of a measurement. Where are the numbers? Yet out of a series of such more-less comparisons, a scale for measuring the trait or property can be constructed. The Ayres scale for measuring the quality of handwriting is a familiar example of this.[6] If a sequence of numbers is assigned to the sequence of steps or intervals that make up the scale, then the scale can yield quantitative measurements. If used carefully by a skilled judge, it yields measurements that are reasonably objective (that is, free from errors associated with specific judges) and reliable (that is, free from errors associated with use of a particular set of test items or tasks).

Are some outcomes of education essentially qualitative rather than quantitative? If so, is it reasonable to expect that these qualitative outcomes can be measured?

It is certainly true that some differences between persons are not usually thought of as more-less differences. This person is a man; that one is a woman. This person has blue eyes; that one has brown. This person speaks only French; that one speaks only German. But we can express these qualitative differences in quantitative terms. This person has more of the characteristics of a man; that one has less. This person has more eye-blueness; that one has less. This person has more ability to speak French; that one has less.

We may think of the weight of a man, his age, or the size of his bank account as quantities, while regarding his health, his friendliness, or his honesty as qualities. But it is also possible to regard all of them—weight,

[6] L. P. Ayres, *A Scale for Measuring the Quality of Handwriting of School Children,* Division of Education, Bulletin 113 (New York: Russell Sage Foundation, 1912).

age, savings, health, friendliness, and honesty—as qualities. And if they serve to differentiate him from other men because he exhibits more or less of them than other men, they become quantitative qualities. It is difficult to think of any quality that interests us that cannot also be quantified, "Whatever exists at all exists in some amount," said E. L. Thorndike.[7] And William A. McCall has added, "Anything that exists in amount can be measured."[8]

WHAT ARE THE FUNCTIONS OF ACHIEVEMENT TESTS?

There are good reasons to believe that the measurement of educational achievement is essential to effective formal education. Formal education is a complex process, requiring a great deal of time and money and the cooperative efforts of many people. Efforts must be directed toward the attainment of specific goals. Education is not automatically or uniformly successful. Some methods are more effective than others. Efficient use of learning resources often requires special motivation, guidance, and assistance. All of those concerned with the process of education—students, teachers, parents, and school officials—need to know periodically how successful their efforts have been, so that they can decide which practices to continue and which to change. It is the function of educational measurement to provide them with this knowledge.

To teach without evaluating the results of teaching would be foolish. Those who suggest that schools do not need tests, or might even do a better job of educating students if tests were prohibited, seldom go so far as to argue that evaluation is not needed. They seldom suggest that learning can be promoted effectively by teachers and students who have no particular goals in view, and who pay no attention to the results of their efforts. If tests were abandoned, some other means of assessing educational achievement would have to be used in their place. No other means that is as efficient, as dependable, and as beneficial to the process of education has yet been discovered.

The major function of a classroom test is to measure student achievement and thus to contribute to the evaluation of educational progress and attainments. This is a matter of considerable importance. To say, as some critics of testing have said, that what students know and can do is more important than their scores on a test or grades in a course implies, quite incorrectly in most cases, that knowledge and scores are independent or unrelated. To say that testing solely to measure achievement has no educational value also implies, and again quite incorrectly in most cases, that

[7] E. L. Thorndike, *The Seventeenth Yearbook of the National Society for Study of Education,* Part II (Bloomington, Ill.: Public School Publishing Co., 1918), p. 16.
[8] William A. McCall, *Measurement* (New York: Macmillan Publishing Co., 1939), p. 18.

test scores are unrelated to educational efforts, that they do not reward and reinforce effective study, that they do not penalize unproductive efforts or tend to discourage lack of effort.

Tests can, and often do, help teachers and professors to give more valid, reliable grades. Because these grades are intended to summarize concisely a comprehensive evaluation of student achievement, because they are reported to the students and their parents to indicate the effectiveness of their efforts, because they are entered in the school record and may help to determine honors and opportunities for further education or future employment, it is important that teachers and professors take seriously their responsibilities for assigning accurate, meaningful grades. Students are urged, quite properly, not to study *merely* to earn high grades. But, in terms of the students' present self-perceptions and future opportunities, there is nothing "mere" about the grades they receive.

A second major function of classroom tests is to motivate and direct student learning. The experience of almost all students and teachers supports the view that students do tend to study harder when they expect an examination than when they do not, and that they emphasize in studying those things on which they expect to be tested. If the students know in advance they will be tested, if they know what the test will require, and if the test does a good job of measuring the achievement of essential course objectives, then its motivating and guiding influence will be most wholesome.

Anticipated tests are sometimes regarded as extrinsic motivators of learning efforts, less desirable or effective than intrinsic motivators would be. Learning should be its own reward, it is said. Fortunately, no choice need be made between extrinsic and intrinsic motivation. Both contribute to learning. Withdrawal of either would be likely to lessen the learning of most students. For a fortunate few, intrinsic motivation may be strong enough to stimulate all the effort to learn that the student ought to put forth. For the great majority, however, the motivation provided by tests and other influential factors is indispensable.

Classroom tests have other useful educational functions. Constructing them should cause instructors to think carefully about the goals of instruction in a course. It should lead them to define those goals operationally in terms of the kind of tasks a student must be able to handle to demonstrate achievement of the goals. On the students' part, the process of taking a classroom test and discussing the scoring of it afterward can be a richly rewarding learning experience. As Stroud has said,

> It is probably not extravagant to say that the contribution made to a student's store of knowledge by the taking of an examination is as great, minute for minute, as any other enterprise he engages in.[9]

[9] James B. Stroud, *Psychology in Education* (New York: David McKay Company, Inc., 1946), p. 476.

Hence, testing and teaching need not be considered as mutually exclusive, as competitors for valuable class time. They are intimately related parts of the total educational process.

USING TESTS TO PROMOTE LEARNING

Most classroom tests are used only once, at the end of a unit of instruction to measure the relative achievements of all class members. If the instructor can retrieve all copies of the test each time it is used, he or she may feel secure in reusing the same test with successive classes year after year. This procedure has the great advantage of saving the time-consuming preparation of a new test for each new class.

When used in this way, and it is a perfectly sound educational use, the test functions almost exclusively as a measuring instrument. Students have little or no opportunity to learn from the mistakes they made on it. They cannot review the questions critically or question the instructor's judgment concerning the correct answers to any of them. Some instructors whose objective tests are of marginal quality find it easy to live with these limitations.

However, it is also possible to use a test more than once with the same class, and to do so in a way that not only makes the test much more of a learning exercise, but also improves the reliability of the scores it yields. The catch is that these procedures require a new test, or at least a substantially new test, for each new class. However, it is possible to create new forms of a test in a way that keeps the task properly manageable.

The dual or triple use of the same test can be arranged in this way. The first use is as a supervised, secure classroom test that differs from usual testing practice in only two small ways. One is that the students are allowed to keep their copy of the test. The second is that they are encouraged to mark the answers they have chosen not only on the separate answer sheet that is to be turned in, but also on the test.

The second use, immediately following the first, is as an unsupervised take-home test. The students are given a second answer sheet that is due to be turned in several days after the in-class test. They are encouraged to meet in small groups with other students to compare answers and, when the answers differ, to discuss justifications for the alternate answers. Of course, they are free to consult textbooks, class notes, and other references. Their aim should be to turn in perfect or near-perfect answer sheets for the take-home test. Each student's score on the take-home answer sheet is added to his or her score on the in-class answer sheet to give a score for the entire test.

Experience indicates that most students (excepting those few who are overburdened with other duties or who are low in motivation) work hard on the take-home test and learn a considerable amount in the process. As might be expected, the sums of scores on in-class and take-home tests are much more reliable than scores on either test by itself. Somewhat surprisingly, it often happens that scores on the take-home test are actually more reliable than those on the in-class test. Although the items are identical, the two tests clearly measure somewhat different aspects of achievement. Quickness of intellect probably counts more on the in-class test. Persistence of effort counts more on the take-home. It seems reasonable to claim that the composite provides a more valid measure of achievement than either alone.

The third use of the same test is as a pretest for the succeeding class. This pretest serves three functions. It tells the students what kind of test to expect. Since they are allowed to keep copies of the pretest, it gives them some practice problems against which to test their developing knowledge. Finally, after an item analysis, it tells the instructor which of his questions were too easy to function as proper measures of achievement.

This multiple use of a test, with the attendant requirement of a new test form for each new class, is likely to seem attractive only to instructors who can develop a system for creating new test forms easily. One instructor manages it this way: The first four times he taught the course he built four new test forms with no common test items. After that, the test for each succeeding class has been a revision of one of the earlier forms. From one-third to one-half of the items in each revised form are new or are revised (hopefully improved) items from the earlier test. He uses item analysis from in-class, take-home, and pre-test administrations to identify the items most in need of revision or replacement.

To use each test form three times and to create a substantially new test for each class undeniably requires both instructor and students to spend more than the usual amount of time on testing. The system may appeal only to measurement specialists, but it does what nonspecialists often urge teachers to do—use measurements to promote learning, not just to assess it. And it results in better tests and better measurements of achievement.

LIMITATIONS OF ACHIEVEMENT TESTS

It is easy to show that mental measurement falls far short of the standards of logical soundness that have been set for physical measurement.[10] Ordinarily the best it can do is provide an approximate rank ordering of individuals in terms of their ability to perform a more or less well defined

---

[10] B. Othanel Smith, *Logical Aspects of Educational Measurement* (New York: Columbia University Press, 1938).

set of tasks. The units used in measuring this ability cannot be shown to be equal. The zero point on the ability scale is not clearly defined.

Because of these limitations, some of the things we often do with test scores, such as finding means, standard deviations, and correlation coefficients, ought not to be done if strict mathematical logic holds sway. Nonetheless we often find it practically useful to do them. When strict logic conflicts with practical utility, it is the utility that usually wins, as it probably should.

On the other hand, the logical limitations of test scores mean that they are unlikely to contribute to the formulation of psychological laws that can compare in precision with, say, the laws of motion. But then, development of precise laws of human behavior is unlikely on other, more fundamental grounds. Deficiencies in the scales of measurement are not the only, nor the most serious, problems in this area.

It is well for us to recognize the logical limitations of the units and scales used in educational measurement. But it is also important not to be so impressed by these limitations that we stop doing the useful things we can legitimately do. One of those useful things is to measure educational achievement.

Are some outcomes of education too intangible to be measured? No doubt there are some that we speak of often, like critical thinking or good citizenship, that are so difficult to define satisfactorily that we have given up trying. To this extent they are intangible, hard to measure, and hard to teach purposefully. We may feel intuitively that critical thinking and good citizenship are immensely important. But if we are unable to state objectively what they consist of, it is hard to show that the concepts they might stand for are, in fact, important.

The processes of education that a particular student experiences probably have subtle and wholly unforeseen effects on that individual, and possibly on no one else. Some of these effects may not become apparent until long after the student has left school. These, too, could be regarded as intangible outcomes. It is unlikely that any current tests, or any that could conceivably be built, would measure these intangibles satisfactorily. In individual instances they might be crucially important. But since they may be largely accidental, subtle, and quite possibly long delayed in their influence, the practical need to measure them may be no greater than the practical possibility of measuring them.

The belief that certain important outcomes of education are difficult to measure may stem in part from a confusion between measurement and prediction. For example, most people agree that it is quite difficult at present to measure motivation or creativity. But those who want to measure motivation or creativity are interested mainly in future prospects, not in present status or past achievements. They are less interested in the motivation or the creative achievements individuals have shown in the past than in how hard they will work and how successfully they will create in the future.

Difficult as the problems of measuring some complex human traits are, they are much simpler than the problems of predicting future success, especially if that success requires a fortunate coincidence of many influences. To help keep our thinking straight, we probably should not charge those difficulties to the limitations of educational measurement. We might charge them in part to the somewhat indefinite generality of the concepts (motivation, creativity, and so on), in part to the complexity of human behavior, and in part to our cherished, if partly imaginary, freedom of choice and action.

Finally, it should be recognized that paper-and-pencil tests do have some limitations. They are well adapted to testing verbal knowledge and understanding and ability to solve verbal and numerical problems. These are important educational outcomes, but they are not all. One would not expect to get far using a paper-and-pencil test to measure children's physical development. Perhaps such a test could be made to yield somewhat better measures of the social effectiveness of adults, but even here the paper-and-pencil test is likely to be seriously limited. Both performance tests of physical development and controlled observations of behavior in social situations would be expected to offer more promise than a paper-and-pencil test.

However, it is important to remember that the use of alternative measures of achievement does not in any way lessen the need for objectivity, relevance, reliability, and validity. To achieve these qualities of excellence in measurement may well be even more difficult in performance testing and observational rating than it is in paper-and-pencil testing. But the usefulness of the measurements depends on them.

HOW IMPORTANT IS MEASUREMENT OF EDUCATIONAL ACHIEVEMENT?

The view that classroom tests are important and that they could be, and ought to be, much better than they often are is shared by most school teachers and college professors. Occasionally one hears the suggestion that education could get on perfectly well, perhaps even better than it has, if tests and testing were abolished. Others accept tests grudgingly as a "necessary evil" in education. But the view of the great majority of teachers at all levels is that periodic assessment of educational progress is essential to effective education and that good tests afford very useful assistance to teachers in making those assessments.

One would have difficulty in finding a teacher or professor who is not concerned about quality in education—about the achievements of his students, the adequacy of their previous preparation, his own success as a teacher, and the effectiveness of the whole enterprise of education. But quality is a matter of degree. Unless some means exist for measuring it, for distinguishing between higher and lower quality, between better and poorer achievement, concern for quality will not mean very much. If tests are abandoned, it must be on the ground that better means are available for measuring educational achievement.

It is easy to understand why tests are sometimes characterized as a "necessary evil" in education. Almost all students, but especially students of average or inferior ability, approach a test with apprehension. Those who do less well than they had expected can easily find some basis for regarding the examination as unfair. Cheating on examinations is reported often enough to cast some shadows of disrepute over the whole enterprise.

Instructors, too, sometimes dislike to assume the role of examiners. Most prefer to be helpful rather than critical. There is something inconsiderate about probing the minds of other human beings and passing judgment on their shortcomings. There is even something presumptuous in assuming the right to set the standards by which others will be judged. And if instructors have learned that they are not infallible examiners, if they have experienced the critical retaliation of students who have been unfairly judged, their wishful dreams of education freed from the torments of examining and evaluating are also easy to understand. No doubt they sometimes feel like the Sergeant of Police in *The Pirates of Penzance*, who sings, "Taking one consideration with another, a policeman's lot is not a happy one."

Unfortunately, there is no effective substitute for tests or examinations in most classrooms. Even in a leaflet generally critical of contemporary testing in the public schools, the authors say:

> To teach without testing is unthinkable. Appraisal of outcomes is an essential feedback of teaching. The evaluation process enables those involved to get their bearings, to know in which direction they are going.[11]

Anxiety, unfairness, dishonesty, humiliation, and presumptuousness can and should be minimized, but the process of examining and evaluating cannot be dispensed with if education is to proceed effectively.

Those who would abolish tests or who regard them as a necessary evil usually do not mean to imply that good education is possible without any assessment of student achievement whatsoever. What they sometimes do suggest is that a good teacher, working with a class of reasonable size, has

---

[11] Joint Committee of the American Association of School Administrators, *Testing, Testing, Testing* (Washington, D.C.: American Association of School Administrators, 1962), p. 9.

no need for tests in order to make sufficiently accurate judgments of student achievement. They may also suggest that the tests they have seen or even have used themselves leave so much to be desired that a teacher is better off without the kind of "help" such tests are likely to give. In some cases they may indeed be right in this judgment. No doubt some bad tests have actually been worse than no tests at all.

But again, the majority of teachers and professors are keenly aware of the limited and unsatisfactory bases they ordinarily have for judging the relative achievement of various students, and of the fallibility of subjective judgments based on irregular, uncontrolled observations in their classroom or office. They welcome the help that tests can give in providing a more extensive and objective basis for judgment, for testing is not really an alternative to teacher observation of student behavior. It is simply a specialized technique for extending, refining, efficiently recording, and summarizing those observations.

Some people who know little about mental measurement have been led to expect something close to magic to result from it. They are sure to be disappointed. Test scores are powerful educational tools, but they are only tools. They will not give direct, complete answers to the practical educational questions that bother teachers and students. They will not point unequivocally to a specific course of action in a given set of circumstances. They may indicate that something needs to be done. They may provide data that will help in deciding what to do. But they will not make the decision.

Those who expect tests to do more than they can do may overreact to the disappointment in store for them. In their frustration, they may assert that all tests are worthless. This is not true. If properly used, tests can be worth a great deal. It is not the fault of the tests that too much is sometimes expected of them.

The tendency to expect too much is encouraged by a few test specialists who have cloaked the process of testing and the interpretation of test scores in mystery. It is too complex, they imply, to be dealt with by any but the fully initiated. Test scores should never be reported directly, they say, to anyone who has not been specially trained to interpret them.

Now it is quite true that the meaning of some test scores is obscure, but this is due more often to the test constructor's own confusion than to any technical complexity in the scores. It is also true that test scores have been misinterpreted by those who do not understand fully how they were derived and the limits of their meaning. But openness and explanation would seem to be a better cure for this fault than secrecy and mystery.

There is nothing inherently complex or technical about the processes of measuring educational achievement. First, a field of knowledge is defined, then a class of tasks appropriate for testing command of that knowledge is defined. Test items are written and administered, and answers are scored as correct or incorrect. The number answered correctly is then reported as a proportion of the total number presented, or as a comparison with the score of some reference group of students.

In general the best test scores are the most straightforward and the easiest to interpret. One should be skeptical of the meaning of any test score that cannot be explained to a layman in a paragraph or two, or in ten minutes. Few specialists in educational measurement are so much brighter than their fellow men that they need to withhold what they know in order to protect others from error. Education is a public concern that involves the cooperative efforts of many people; secrecy and mystery have no place in it.

SUMMARY

The main ideas of this chapter can be summarized in the following propositions:

1. There are good reasons for believing that the principal task of the school is to facilitate cognitive learning.
2. There are two means that schools can use to help children become effective, happy adults: cultivating their cognitive abilities, and molding their behavior by processes of conditioning.
3. Cognitive competence provides a better basis for the good life of a free people than does conditioned behavior.
4. Any important outcome of education is necessarily measurable, but not necessarily by means of a paper-and-pencil test.
5. It is a mistake to believe that qualities cannot be measured.
6. The measurement of educational achievement is essential to effective formal education.
7. The primary function of a classroom test is to measure student achievement.
8. Classroom tests can help motivate and direct student achievement and can provide learning exercises.
9. The development of a good classroom test requires the instructor to define the course objectives in specific, operational terms.
10. By using the same test twice in the same class—first as a supervised test in class and then as an open-book, freely discussed take-home test—instructors can enhance the reliability of its scores and its value as a learning exercise.
11. The fact that educational measurements fail to meet high standards of mathematical soundness does not destroy their educational value.
12. Educational outcomes that are said to be intangible because they

are not clearly defined are as difficult to attain through purposeful teaching as they are to measure through achievement tests.

13. Any measurement of an educational achievement should be relevant, reliable, and objective, regardless of whether it is a paper-and-pencil test or some other technique, such as a performance test or a rating of observed behavior.
14. Good achievement in education is fostered by the use of good tests of educational achievement.
15. Most teachers recognize the essential role of measurement in education.
16. There is no magic in educational measurement, and there should be no mystery about it.

PROJECTS AND PROBLEMS

Project: A Survey of Opinions About Tests and Grades

Answer each of the following 33 questions as honestly as you can. If you are directed to mark your answers on a machine-scorable sheet, use response number:

1) if you agree or tend to agree
2) if you disagree or tend to disagree
3) if you have no opinion, or agree about as much as you disagree

A summary of the results in your class will be reported to you. If time permits, they will be used as a basis for class discussion.

1. Students tend to learn more in classes that emphasize student participation in discussion than in classes where the teacher does most of the talking.
2. Intelligence is more a developed than an inherited ability.
3. The elimination of failure from the educational experience is a desirable and an attainable educational goal.
4. Individual instruction tends to be more effective than group instruction.
5. The typical teacher's responsibilities for motivating student learning are greater than his/her responsibilities for directing the process of learning.
6. The relation between success in school and success on the job is very low.
7. The goal of teaching and of learning should be mastery, even when attaining mastery takes some pupils much longer than others.
8. Schools have in the past paid too much attention to the pupils' intellectual development and too little to their social and emotional development.

9. Progress in education has been slowed by the reluctance of teachers to try out new ideas.
10. Discipline problems in class are usually the fault of the teacher.
11. Present emphasis on tests and grades in American education is excessive.
12. Giving an hour test as often as once a month would more likely impede rather than to promote effective learning in most high school subjects.
13. In order to properly evaluate a student's educational achievement, it is necessary to know his/her I.Q.
14. A nationwide test of secondary school achievement would provide useful information to supplement the diploma of high school graduation.
15. College students should be permitted to earn credit toward graduation by passing examinations in certain courses, without enrolling or attending classes in them.
16. Pupils' standardized test scores provide information that is useful in judging the competence of the pupils' teacher.
17. In some college courses a term paper provides a better basis than any examination for determining how much a pupil has learned.
18. The use of extrinsic rewards (grades, honors, credits, degrees, and so forth) to motivate learning is educationally undesirable.
19. Student achievement should be measured and expressed in terms of the amount of knowledge gained and the nature of abilities developed, not in terms of relative standing among the student's classmates.
20. The achievement of every important educational objective can be measured.
21. Educational objectives should be defined in terms of desired behavior.
22. The possibility of correct response by guessing is a serious weakness of objective tests.
23. A teacher should be able to determine the passing score on any of her tests before the test is given.
24. In essay testing, effective use can be made of questions that have no right answer, but which show how a student thinks and what evidence he has available to use.
25. The widespread use of objective tests has encouraged a great deal of superficial rote learning.
26. Some students suffer so badly from test anxiety that they seldom do justice to themselves on a test.
27. The main cause of cheating on examinations is overemphasis on grades.
28. Hard questions should count more than easy questions in determining a student's score on an examination.
29. The questions in a good test range widely in difficulty.
30. A test that is low in reliability can be made more reliable simply by making it longer.

31. The statistical validity of most educational tests can be, and should be, determined.
32. Most students would do a better job of getting an education if the "system" did not force them to work for high grades.
33. Instructors should be free to determine for themselves what the overall distribution of grades in their course should be.

Project: A Survey of Educational Values

The 20 statements listed below each contrast two alternative aims or methods of teaching. While both may be desirable, they are also competing alternatives in most cases. The teacher cannot give more emphasis to one without giving less to the other. Your opinion is sought on two questions relative to each of the statements in the list.

1. *Is it in fact true* that the typical elementary school teacher in the United States today is more concerned with what is mentioned first in the statement than with what is mentioned second?
2. *Should* a good elementary school teacher be more concerned with the first than with the second?

In each case your answer can be either *yes, no,* or *I don't know.* If you use a machine-scorable answer sheet, mark the first response position if you mean yes, the second if you mean no, and the third to indicate that you don't know or can't say.

The first time you react to the 20 statements below, do so in relation to the first of the two questions above; that is, ask yourself whether typical elementary school teachers today *actually do* emphasize the first more than the second. Enter this first set of responses in positions 1 through 20 on the answer sheet.

The second time through, react to the 20 statements in terms of the second question above; that is, ask yourself whether elementary school teachers *really should* emphasize the first more than the second. Enter this second set of responses in positions 21 through 40 on the answer sheet.

Does (should) the typical elementary school teacher pay more attention to:

1. The intellectual development of her pupils than their adjustment to life?
2. Her pupils' thoughts than their feelings?
3. The thoughts of her pupils than their actions?
4. Her pupils as learners than as persons?
5. The future welfare of her pupils than their present enjoyment of living?
6. The needs of society for loyal, cooperative members than the needs of individuals for freedom and independence?
7. Encouraging conformity than individuality?
8. Using competition rather than cooperation as a motivator?

9. Encouraging convergent rather than divergent thinking?
10. Teaching subjects effectively than understanding pupils thoroughly?
11. The product rather than the process of learning?
12. Helping pupils learn what others have discovered than helping them discover things for themselves?
13. Instructing pupils who want to learn than motivating those who don't?
14. Directing the learning process rather than participating in it?
15. Initiating learning activities than responding to pupil questions and suggestions?
16. Her class as a group of similar children than as a collection of different individuals?
17. The common needs of all children than the unique needs of particular children?
18. Using tests to evaluate learning rather than to produce it?
19. Encouraging pupils to evaluate their achievements relative to those of other pupils rather than relative to their own past achievements?
20. Making accurate evaluations of pupil achievement herself than helping pupils make their own self-evaluations?

*Education is for learning things, and teaching is
the teaching of what you learn. All the rest comes by the way
if it comes at all.*

GEORGE BOAZ

3

What Should

Achievement Tests Measure?

THE DUAL PROBLEMS OF TEST CONSTRUCTION

The test constructor faces two major problems. The first is to determine what to measure, and the second is to decide how to measure it. In general, books and articles on educational testing offer more help in solving the second problem than the first. But the quality of an educational achievement test depends on how well *both* problems have been solved. How well the first problem is solved largely determines what is sometimes called the *relevance* of the test. By "relevance" we mean the apparent or obvious logical relationship between what the process of testing requires students to do and what the process of education attempted to teach them. How well the second problem is solved has a great deal to do with the *reliability* of the test and its practicality. By "reliability" we mean consistency in the measurement of a particular achievement from time to time or from test to test. To the degree that a test has this kind of relevance and yields reliable scores, it can claim to be a *valid* test. A valid test of educational achievement is one composed of relevant tasks and yielding reliable scores.

If the test constructor has sound and specific ideas about what constitutes educational achievement in the area of the test, he knows what to measure. But these sound and specific ideas are sometimes hard to get. For one thing, there is far more knowledge, ability, skill, and effective behavior available for us to learn in the world than any one person could possibly learn. Teachers and students are constantly faced with the need to make choices between many varied things to be taught and to be learned. We keep asking ourselves and others the question Herbert Spencer asked and tried to answer a century ago. "What knowledge is of most worth?"[1] Benjamin Franklin recognized the same problem. "It would be well if they could be taught everything that is useful and everything that is ornamental: but art is long and their time is short. It is therefore proposed that they learn those things that are likely to be most useful and most ornamental."[2]

The problems of the test constructor are thus in essence not much different from those of the curriculum maker, the textbook writer, or the classroom teacher. Test constructors, however, can borrow ideas from all of the other three. If they accept guidance from professionals who are themselves well educated and have thought long and carefully about what achievements are most valuable, test constructors may be able to build good tests. But the problem is not a simple one. In the foreseeable future educators will probably have to get along as best they can with somewhat imperfect, uncertain answers to the question of what to test. This, of course, is no excuse for not trying to define educational objectives to the best of one's ability.

THE USES AND LIMITATIONS OF EDUCATIONAL OBJECTIVES IN TEST DEVELOPMENT

An educational achievement test should seek to measure what the process of education has sought to achieve. Hence test constructors need to be concerned with educational objectives, both those that relate to the total process of education and those that relate to a specific course or subject. The tests they build ought to be as consistent as possible with their own educational objectives, those of the school, and of society as a whole.

One of the uses of any statement of educational objectives is to remind all concerned that education should be a purposeful activity, not simply a meaningless ritual. The steady influx of pupils to be educated and the organization of these pupils into a succession of annual class groups, each of which follows much the same program of studies as it advances through the institution, give the process of education a repetitive characteristic that could easily become a fixed routine. Often the educational needs of a society seem to change faster than its educational institutions can devise new programs. Indeed, some educators seem to make a virtue of the

---

[1] Herbert Spencer, *Education: Intellectual, Moral and Physical* (New York: A. L. Burt, 1861), p. 5.

[2] Thomas Woody, *Educational Views of Benjamin Franklin* (New York: McGraw-Hill Book Company, 1931), p. 158.

traditional in education, regardless of the educational needs of contemporary society. It is occasionally useful to ask of any subject of study or method of instruction the simple question, "Why?" and to insist on an answer that makes sense. The formulation of educational objectives can be the occasion for asking this question. Another use of educational objectives, related to the first, is to redirect educational emphases. Often the motivation for this redirection is the observation that instruction in the schools is not adequately meeting the needs of the day. Herbert Spencer's essay on the purposes of education begins by deploring the overemphasis on the *ornamental* in education, to the neglect of the useful.[3]

General statements of educational objectives are useful to test constructors as guides to content and the direction of emphasis within a test. Highly specific statements may be useful in suggesting particular questions or types of questions to ask. But statements of objectives have limitations too.

Sometimes instead of aiming to be directive, general statements aim to be inclusive. Instead of suggesting that the schools or the teacher of a particular course do this *instead* of that, they seem to suggest that the schools do both this *and* that, as well as everything that anyone has suggested it might also be good to do. Frequently they include such highly attractive terms as "critical thinking," "creative productivity," or "good citizenship," which everyone can endorse but few can define. Such all-inclusive statements of objectives may be of some use as systems of grouping or classification, but they have little directive value.

Another limitation of statements of educational objectives grows out of the very large number of things to be learned and abilities to be acquired. To attempt to list them all would be an enormous task. The task of getting agreement on some order of priority would be even greater. And if the job were ever completed, the list would be so long and so subject to criticism that few would ever bother to read it. The alternative of a comprehensive listing in detail of all objectives is to list names or descriptions of only the major categories of objectives. This is the alternative ordinarily chosen. It gives some indication of coverage and emphasis but is usually too general and indefinite to be of much direct help to the test constructor.

A serious effort to take some of the vagueness out of statements of educational objectives has been made by Bloom, Krathwohl, and their co-workers. They have divided all objectives into three domains: cognitive, affective, and psychomotor. Systematic outlines or taxonomies of objectives in the first two of these domains have been published.[4] The major categories are:

---

[3] Spencer, *Education*, p. 5.
[4] Benjamin S. Bloom et al., *Taxonomy of Educational Objectives, Handbook I: Cognitive Domain* (New York: David McKay Company, Inc., 1956); David R. Krathwohl et al., *Taxonomy of Educational Objectives, Handbook II: Affective Domain* (New York: David McKay Company, Inc., 1964).

Cognitive	**Affective**
1. Knowledge	1. Receiving
2. Comprehension	2. Responding
3. Application	3. Valuing
4. Analysis	4. Organization
5. Synthesis	5. Characterization
6. Evaluation	

Thus far, the cognitive taxonomy has had a much greater influence on test constructors. It has been available longer, and it is relevant to the kinds of abilities most items are intended to test. Under its influence, many test constructors have tried to write fewer items testing "knowledge" and more testing higher level mental processes. However, as we point out later in this chapter, in the section on mental abilities, it is very difficult to pinpoint the mental processes involved in answering a particular test question.

It may be worth mentioning in passing that the term *knowledge* is given a somewhat broader meaning in this book than it is apparently given in the Bloom taxonomy. Here knowledge will be distinguished from information; and the claim will be argued that to possess knowledge, one must not only comprehend the information received but also be able to apply it. Whether anything more than comprehension and application is required for analysis, synthesis, or evaluation may be open to question.

Insofar as the Bloom taxonomy has encouraged test constructors to probe comprehension and to require application, no doubt its influence has been good. Insofar as it has encouraged the writing of long, complex test items, its influence may have been less desirable.

But the taxonomy does attack one of the major limitations of some statements of objectives—that is, indefiniteness—for accompanying each description of a subclass of objectives are illustrative items taken from actual tests. Even where the subclasses are not clearly distinct, and the appropriateness of a stated objective or test item to one rather than another subclass is not clearly apparent, the items do help to reduce the uncertainty regarding what a particular objective or set of objectives means. The taxonomy also provides a collection of illustrative test items that can be most useful to the test constructor.

In summary, test constructors need to be informed about and interested in the educational objectives of their field of study. A good statement of objectives can help extend and balance the test content and check on the appropriateness of its emphasis. But even the best such statement is likely to leave the individual constructor with many item ideas to discover and many value judgments to make. Ordinarily examiners will need considerable help from course outlines, textbooks, and even other tests in deciding on a final test content.

BEHAVIORAL GOALS OF EDUCATION

The history of education indicates that most subjects of study were introduced into the educational program in response to real and immediate needs. With changing times these needs sometimes disappeared, but successive generations of teachers tended to continue teaching those same things they had been taught. Partly in response to the persistence of irrelevant knowledge in the curriculum and partly in reaction to the vagueness of many statements of objectives, some educators like Ralph Tyler began to urge that objectives be redefined in terms of desired behavior.[5] The purpose of education, they suggest, is not to accumulate knowledge but to change behavior. Their suggestions have borne fruit in two volumes setting forth the goals of education in behavioral terms.[6] The efforts of a great many carefully selected educators went into the production of these reports, whose progress was closely supervised by the Educational Testing Service, with financial support from the Russell Sage Foundation.

The defects in education that led to this development are real and need to be corrected. All knowledge is not of equal worth, as Herbert Spencer argued a century ago. The knowledge that we ask teachers to teach and students to acquire needs to be reviewed frequently in terms of its efficacy and relevance to contemporary needs. Educational objectives that are so vaguely stated as to be useless in determining through observation whether the student has attained them are not likely to provide useful guides to either teaching or testing.[7]

But the remedy proposed, that of defining educational objectives in terms of desired behavior, also has shortcomings.[8] It appears to assume that despite the highly complex and rapidly changing world in which we live, a teacher can know years ahead of time how students ought to behave in a given set of circumstances. It also seems to assume that the teacher is entitled to prescribe student behavior. Both of these assumptions may be open to serious question. An alternative to defining educational objectives as descriptions of specific acts or general patterns of desired behavior is to define them in terms of relevant and powerful knowledge, the command of which seems well calculated to give students the capacity to adapt their behavior effectively in varied, changing situations.

[5] Ralph W. Tyler, "A Generalized Technique for Constructing Achievement Tests," *Educational Research Bulletin* (Columbus, O.: Ohio State University, 1931), 10, 199–208.

[6] Nolan C. Kearney, *Elementary School Objectives* (New York: Russell Sage Foundation, 1953); and Will French et al., *Behavioral Goals of General Education in High School* (New York: Russell Sage Foundation, 1957).

[7] Robert F. Mager, *Preparing Instructional Objectives* (Palo Alto, Calif.: Fearon Publishers, 1962).

[8] Robert L. Ebel, "Behavioral Objectives: A Close Look," *Phi Delta Kappan,* 52 (1970), 171–73.

The power of knowledge as a tool for the attainment of human aspirations can hardly be doubted. But knowledge is not all-powerful. It cannot guarantee the results we seek. This leads to the question of what other means might be used to attain our goals. What alternative to reason based on knowledge might the schools cultivate in order to help human beings live better?

One alternative to knowledge and reason as a basis for behavior is simple conditioning. Much of the behavior we exhibit is conditioned behavior. Human beings are almost as adept as other animals at learning to do the things their environment rewards and to avoid the things it punishes. In the case of very young children, conditioning may be the only effective means of education. As our experiences accumulate, as our awareness develops, reflective thought becomes available as a means of problem solving and of education. But the adult remains susceptible to conditioning, however rationally he may seek to behave. Fortunate success or unfortunate failure can encourage or discourage future efforts along the same line. The attitudes and values a person holds, even his beliefs, are attributable to conditioning as well as to reflective thought.

No doubt a case could be made in favor of conditioning as the exclusive means of education in a static society dedicated to the strength and stability of the group. But that is not the kind of a society in which we live nor the ideal to which we are dedicated. We respect the worth and dignity of the individual and seek to facilitate each person's optimal development. This means that we must be concerned with the cultivation of human reasoning. Quoting the Educational Policies Commission:

> To be free, a man must be capable of basing his choices and actions on understandings which he himself achieves and on values which he examines for himself. . . . The free man, in short, has a rational grasp of himself, his surroundings, and the relation between them.[9]

Emphasis on desired behavior as an educational outcome has encouraged test builders to write items that describe specific situations and call for the examinee to choose the most appropriate or effective behavior in that situation. Here is an example.

Jim has a movie date for Saturday night but is short on cash. His brother Bob has $5.00 that he is willing to loan for a week at 5 percent interest, provided Jim will give him some security. Jim offers any one of the following items. Which should Bob accept if he is a prudent businessman?

1. Jim's class ring
2. Jim's new sweater
*3. Jim's car keys
4. Jim's football

[9] National Education Association Educational Policies Commission, *The Central Purpose of American Education* (Washington, D.C.: National Education Association, 1961), p. 4.

Items such as this one test ability to behave effectively in a particular situation. They seem to emphasize *doing* the right thing rather than *knowing* why it is the right thing. An item asking why the car keys provide the best security would emphasize understanding, which in our society is a generally accepted educational goal.

Items like that cited above are subject to two other weaknesses. They tend to require lengthy descriptions of the problem setting and thus to become time-consuming and inefficient sources of information on achievement. Because of the difficulty of communicating fully and clearly all the factors that might be relevant to the choice of an answer, they also tend to become somewhat ambiguous. Taken together these weaknesses may account for the rather lower reliability of tests of this type than of more direct measures of knowledge. There is little evidence that the situational tests are more valid measures of command of substantive knowledge than are simpler, more direct tests. The test constructor may wish to experiment with items of this type, but in the absence of empirical evidence of their superiority there are no compelling reasons for insisting on their use.

Those who have urged that educational goals be expressed in terms of desired behavior have wisely sought emphasis on meaningful statements of useful educational outcomes. They have not advocated conditioning as the primary means of human education. They have not tried to promote a static society. The aim they have been pursuing may not be significantly different from that expressed by the phrase "command of substantive knowledge." If so, the foregoing paragraphs may seem more concerned with the use of particular words than about the purposes and means of education.

At this juncture, it should perhaps be stressed that the proper starting point of educational planning in a democracy is not the kind of behaviors present adults desire future adults to exhibit, but rather the kind of equipment that will enable youngsters to choose their own behavior intelligently. A major problem of education is to identify the elements of knowledge whose command will be most useful to students in fulfilling themselves within a society that encourages each to give his/her best. From this point of view educational achievement should be judged more in terms of what students *can* do than in terms of what they may *actually* do. If there is any sizable discrepancy in the long run between the two, something must be wrong either with what education has taught pupils how to do or with what society rewards them for doing.

THE COGNITIVE OUTCOMES OF EDUCATION

If we look at what actually goes on in our school and college classrooms and laboratories, libraries and lecture halls, it seems reasonable to conclude that the major goal of education is to develop in students a *command of substantive knowledge.* Achievement of this kind of cognitive mastery is clearly not the only concern of educators and students, but it is, and ought to be, the central concern of education.

Our knowledge is based on the information we get, either directly from our own experiences or indirectly from the reports of others. Thus everything we have experienced *can* become a part of our knowledge, but will become knowledge only if we reflect on it, and thus analyze and synthesize it into a coherent whole. Knowledge is a structure built out of information by processes of thought.

Information by itself is not knowledge. Teachers can convey information; they cannot give knowledge, for knowledge is a private, personal possession. We must create it for ourselves. If our information on important matters is abundant and accurate, and if we think about it clearly and persistently, the structure of knowledge we build will be substantial and useful. But if some of these essentials are lacking, our house of intellect is likely to be only a shanty.

Pursuit of knowledge is clearly the business of scholarship. The power of knowledge has been so generally acknowledged, from ancient to modern times, that it may seem surprising for anyone to challenge cognitive mastery as the central purpose of education. Yet all around us we hear it being challenged. Knowledge alone is not enough, says the businessman. It does not guarantee financial success. Knowledge alone is not enough, says the college president. It does not guarantee scholarly achievement. Knowledge alone is not enough, says the religious leader. It does not guarantee virtue. Knowledge alone is not enough, says the philosopher. It does not guarantee happiness.

They are all right, of course. Knowledge alone is *not* enough. But in this complex world of chance and change, no one thing nor any combination of things ever will be enough to *guarantee* financial success or scholarly achievement or virtue or happiness. Few would deny that the command of substantive knowledge does contribute mightily to the attainment of these other, more ultimate goals. Further, it is difficult to name any other developed human ability that is likely to contribute more than, or as much as, knowledge to the attainment of these goals. It is even more difficult to describe what sorts of things the schools ought to be doing to develop the alleged noncognitive ingredients of success, achievement, virtue, or happiness.

Our knowledge includes everything we have experienced as a result of perceiving the external environment and reflecting upon our relationship to it. Our entire history of living becomes a part of this knowledge. Psychologists suggest that nothing a person has experienced is ever completely and permanently forgotten. It all remains somewhere, however deeply buried and overlaid with other experiences. The problem of learning, in the modern view, is not so much how to get things into the mind as it is how to get them out again when they are needed. The problem is less one of storage than it is of ready access.

The kind of knowledge that schools and colleges are most concerned with is verbal knowledge. To the degree that our experiences of external affairs and internal thoughts can be expressed in words, they become part of our verbal knowledge. Because verbal knowledge can be recorded, thought about, and communicated so conveniently, it is a very powerful form of knowledge. Possession of skills in using verbal knowledge may be the source of, and certainly provides the clearest evidence of, human superiority over the lower animals.

Schools are sometimes criticized for excessive concern with verbal knowledge, at the expense of nonverbal knowledge growing out of direct, firsthand experiences in the laboratory, the shop, or outside the schoolroom altogether. Such directly obtained knowledge, it is pointed out, provides the foundation on which the truth and usefulness of all verbal knowledge must rest. For some students, that foundation appears to be none too broad and none too firm. To strengthen and extend it is to add important new dimensions to an otherwise empty understanding of words and sentences.

All this can be granted without abandoning the proposition that development of a student's command of useful verbal knowledge is the principal function of formal education. Direct experience is essential as a foundation, but it provides little more than the foundation. It is the verbal knowledge through which those experiences are integrated, interpreted, and communicated that makes possible the intelligent behavior of a human being and the culture of a human society.

There is already a great store of recorded human verbal knowledge in the world. Day by day it increases. Indeed it seems to some observers to be increasing so rapidly that they speak frighteningly of an "explosion of knowledge." In some fields, notably medicine, computer technology, and electronics, the vast amount of knowledge that is accumulated yearly makes constant study imperative.

Not all the items in this store of knowledge—the names, dates, events, concepts, ideas, and propositions—are of equal value. Some are of limited, temporary interest. Some are indefinite and inaccurate. One of the most important and most difficult tasks of the educator is to sort out the more valuable from the less valuable. The task of selecting specific items from specific subject areas is not easy, but it is essential. Whether in curriculum construction, test development, or any other activity concerned with the content of education, the educator's first problem is to make a sound decision about the potential usefulness of various kinds and items of knowledge. Teachers must guide pupils toward the development of structures of *substantive knowledge*, that is, knowledge of enduring importance and usefulness.

The second major problem of the educator is to manage the learning process so as to develop the student's *command* of knowledge. To have command of knowledge is to have ready access to it and full comprehension of its scope, limitations, and implications—hence to develop relationships between words and things, between instances and generalizations, between concepts and principles. The more of these relationships students know, the better their command of discrete items and the more likely they are to recall them in a given situation. Only when items of information are related to each other do they become parts of a structure of knowledge.

Relating is understanding. Thunder is understood better when it is related to lightning. Fermentation is understood better when it is related to bacteria. Fluid pressure is understood better when it is related to depth and density. In general, the understanding of any separate thing involves seeing its relations to other things. This is what we mean when we say that understanding is command of knowledge.

Command of knowledge obviously involves thinking, which both requires and produces it. Thus while knowledge and thinking are not identical, they are closely related. To say that the purpose of education is not to acquire knowledge but to develop the ability to think is to establish a false antithesis. Knowledge and thinking are not mutually exclusive or even alternative goals of education. Each demands the other. One cannot be in favor of thinking but opposed to knowledge. Nor can the power to think be increased appreciably except by increasing the store of knowledge at the command of the thinker. Faulty thinking usually reflects limited or erroneous knowledge, or failure to make careful and unbiased use of it.

Thus knowledge is a very extensive and important aspect of a person's mental development. But is it all? Surely not. There are also feelings and habits. There are attitudes and values. There are the behavior patterns that constitute a person's character and personality. These other characteristics may be influenced by a person's knowledge, but they are not part of it. Clearly, not all of the goals of education have to do with command of useful verbal knowledge.

The Role of Propositions

Objective tests, composed as they are of many separate, independent items, are sometimes supposed to be useful only for measuring isolated bits of factual information. This supposition involves several questionable assumptions:

1. Whatever characterizes a test must also characterize the thing it tests.
2. Information can be, and often is, stored in the form of isolated bits.
3. The questions on objective tests are familiar questions, to which pat answers can be recalled if they ever were learned.

Yet if the test is good, and if the teaching that preceded it was good, such assumptions are unjustified. Test constructors can build novel problems that require students to apply previously learned information, and they can phrase their questions so as to make students draw upon an integrated body of knowledge. In this way discrete items will test command of knowledge rather than mere recall of facts.

Cohen and Nagel have made two comments about knowledge that seem particularly useful in this context.[10] They say (1) that knowledge is of propositions and (2) that a proposition is anything that can be said to be true or false. Propositions are expressed in sentences, but not all sentences are propositions. Those expressing questions or commands cannot be said to be true or false, nor can those that report purely subjective wishes or feelings. Propositions are always declarative sentences about objects or events in the external world. For example:

The earth is a planet in the solar system.

A body immersed in a fluid is buoyed up by a force equal to the weight of fluid displaced.

As we consume or acquire additional units of any commodity, the satisfaction derived from each additional installment tends to diminish.

William J. Bryan failed in his bid for election to the presidency of the United States in the campaign of 1896.

The relation of propositions such as these to objective test items of the true-false type is direct and simple. Less obvious, but no less true, is the fact that propositions like those above are implicit in most other types of objective test items—multiple-choice, matching, short-answer, or completion. What we test, beyond students' ability to understand the language used in the test item, is their knowledge of the proposition that makes one answer correct and others incorrect. All of the propositions cited above appear to deserve a place in the "information conserved by civilization." Contrast them with the group of propositions that follows:

Rain fell in New York City on December 6, 1962.

The cost of living in Canada advanced two-fifths of a point during October 1962.

Work-limit tests are mentioned on page 366 of *Educational Measurement,* edited by E. F. Lindquist.

Objective test items ought not to be based on propositions such as these but sometimes, unfortunately, they may be.

<hr>

[10] Morris R. Cohen and Ernest Nagel, *An Introduction to Logic and Scientific Method* (New York: Harcourt Brace Jovanovich, 1934), p. 27.

The closeness of this relation between the propositions that constitute our knowledge and the items needed for our objective tests may suggest a convenient source of good test items. Simply pick out of a good textbook or reference work a number of sentences expressing important propositions and use these as the basis for test items in the desired form. Basically this is an excellent idea, but it does involve some problems.

Relatively few of the sentences encountered in even a good text or reference work are intended to express propositions about the external world. Many are quite indefinite. Many are offered modestly as tentative hypotheses. Many depend heavily on the context for their meaningfulness or accuracy. Many are in the nature of explanatory comments to help the reader follow the author's line of thought. Sometimes the basic proposition implicit in a paragraph or section of a text is never stated succinctly and explicitly by the author. Finally, many of the declarative sentences that seem important and necessary in an extended discourse on a topic do not seem important enough in isolation to be selected in the limited sampling of propositions that must constitute a test.

Thus, despite the fact that the major goal of education is to develop in students a command of substantive knowledge and despite the fact that all knowledge is knowledge of propositions, it is not easy to discover ready-made propositions that are suitable as bases for objective test items. To be suitable, propositions need to meet at least four requirements:

1. They must be worded as accurately and unambiguously as the precision of knowledge and language allow in a reasonably concise statement.
2. They must be acceptable as established truth by a preponderance of experts in the field.
3. They must be regarded as the propositions most worthy of knowing and remembering by the majority of experts in the field.
4. They must express principles and ideas not generally known by those who have not studied in the field.

The difficulty of finding or creating propositions that meet these standards in some areas of study may raise questions about the value of study in that field. If good examinations are difficult to build, it may be because the supporting structure of substantive knowledge is weak.

PROBLEMS IN MEASURING COGNITIVE KNOWLEDGE

Rote Learning

Do objective tests encourage rote learning? Do they reward students for memorizing pat answers to a few standard questions? Do they require little more than recognition or recall of isolated factual details? No doubt the answers to all of these questions could be "yes." However, it is quite possible to construct tests that do not encourage or reward rote learning.

The phrase *rote learning* refers to both a process and a product. The process is one of repetition of the same sequence of words, as in learning a poem or the lines of a play or the basic facts of addition or multiplication. The product is a ready recall of the exact word or number sequences that were learned.

Now clearly rote learning is sometimes useful and necessary, as in the examples just given. It is an effective means of storing information. But just as clearly it has little to do with knowledge as defined in this chapter: with understanding and application, or with thought and intellect. It is not only meaningless—psychologists often use nonsense syllables to study this phenomenon—it is also mechanical learning. A tape recorder can beat the human mind hands down at rote learning.

Hence rote learning has only limited and special applications in an educational program. Good instruction in most areas of learning will not rely on it or even tolerate it. Good tests of achievement in most subjects will award low scores to students who have used it as their primary means of learning. All the test constructor needs to do to defeat the rote learner is to ask questions that the examinee has never seen before; questions whose answers could not possibly have been learned by rote; questions that require reflective thought so that knowledge can be applied correctly. If a test encourages or rewards rote learning, it is not because of the form of the item (multiple-choice, true-false, or whatever) but because it includes questions to which pat answers were or could have been learned previously by rote.

How prevalent is rote learning in the schools of today? From all indications, not very prevalent. Educational leaders and practicing teachers seldom recommend it. Those who are alarmed at the extent of rote learning and the harm it has done have probably been misinformed.

One source of overconcern with rote learning may be failure to distinguish clearly between incomplete understanding, on the one hand, and rote learning on the other. Students, and adults too, sometimes reveal a woeful lack of understanding in certain subject areas. But it may not be quite correct to charge these deficiencies to an excess of rote learning in the schools. Perhaps the trouble is not rote learning, but no learning. Instead of too much learning of the wrong kind, the deficiencies we exhibit may imply too little learning of any kind.

There is another factor that limits somewhat the danger of rote learning. From the point of view of the learner, rote learning is seldom a very attractive occupation. It is dull, hard work, with no promise of any long-term value. A student may engage in it, out of desperation, in the hope of getting by on a quiz or examination, but it seldom leaves any sense of permanent achievement.

Finally, rote learning is relatively inefficient and ineffective. Even if we aim solely at temporary recall of the answers to a set of questions given in advance, we will ordinarily find *understanding,* even limited understanding, a better ally than rote learning. For understanding involves the sifting out, from a variety of aspects and details, of those structural unities which aid memory and recall. A student who chooses to rely on rote learning is seldom likely to do as well on a test as one who seeks the aid of understanding, even when the questions in the test call for nothing more than the recall of isolated factual details.

In summary, because rote learning may be far less common than our fears of it imply and because it is generally unattractive and ineffective, the danger that tests of factual knowledge will reward and encourage rote learning may not be serious.

Meaningless Verbalization

There is, however, a related danger that may deserve to be taken more seriously. It is the danger of confusing verbal facility and fluency, on the one hand, with command of substantive knowledge on the other. To the degree that test questions demand only acquaintance with verbal stereotypes, with oft-repeated word sequences or associations, to the degree that they may be answered successfully on the basis of word-word associations alone, without clear perceptions of word-thing relationships, to that degree the tests may be measuring superficial verbal facility instead of command of substantive knowledge.

Written tests depend heavily upon words. Words are versatile and essential instruments for thinking and communicating, but they represent the means, not the ends, of learning. Their usefulness to us depends upon our nonverbal knowledge of what they symbolize.

It is possible, indeed it is not uncommon, for speakers or writers to use words with more concern for fluency and grace in expression than for the accuracy of the ideas being expressed. Most students, and most adults as well, recognize and use more words, phrases, even stereotyped sentences than they understand clearly. One of the main responsibilities of test makers in working with words in test questions or with students' verbal responses is to make sure that mere verbal facility does not pass for substantive knowledge. To do this they must seek original expressions for ideas, simple and accurate but unconventional. If they use familiar textbook language, it should be done in such a way that a student who merely recognizes the phrase but does not understand it will be attracted to a wrong answer. Test makers must invent novel questions and novel problem situations so that recognition alone will not provide the answer.

Forgetting

The acquisition of knowledge as an educational goal is sometimes discounted on the grounds that (1) most of what is learned is quickly forgotten and (2) it is wasteful of time and effort to "stuff the mind" with facts that are readily available in a set of good reference works. There is some truth in both of these contentions, but they do not argue so strongly as they may seem to against the pursuit of knowledge as the primary goal of education.

Forgetting does occur, of course, but what is forgotten, and how much, depends largely on how strong the students' command of the knowledge actually was and how well selected (that is, how useful) the knowledge was to them. The greater command students achieve, the more they understand a unifying structure in the knowledge, the less likely they are to forget. Then too, the more useful the knowledge, the more likely they are to practice and thus maintain command over it.

Reference works are valuable accessories to the effective use of knowledge, but they are poor substitutes for command of knowledge. How effectively they can be used depends to a considerable degree on how much the user already knows. Further, those students who must constantly refer to texts for facts that could be part of a personal store of knowledge generally exhibit extremely slow progress in learning. The "ready availability" of facts in good reference works is something of an illusion. Finding the specific fact one needs can be a frustrating, time-consuming enterprise.

DEVELOPMENT OF MENTAL ABILITIES AS AN EDUCATIONAL GOAL

The development of mental abilities is sometimes proposed as the primary purpose and goal of education. Stroud, for example, has said, "All education is in large measure a cultivation of the higher mental processes, even instruction in the basic skills or so-called tool subjects."[11] Later, in the same passage he explains, "By the cultivation of the higher mental processes is usually meant instruction in reflective, relational and inferential thinking." C. H. Judd has compiled a book on the subject.[12] Yet others are convinced that educators err seriously when they seek to develop general mental abilities rather than to cultivate command of knowledge.[13]

[11] James B. Stroud, *Psychology in Education* (New York: David McKay Company, Inc., 1946), p. 198.
[12] C. H. Judd, *Education as Cultivation of the Higher Mental Processes* (New York: The Macmillan Company, 1936).
[13] Edward L. Thorndike, "In Defense of Facts," *Journal of Adult Education*, 7 (1935), 381–88; Ben D. Wood and F. S. Beers, "Knowledge Versus Thinking?" *Teachers College Record*, 37 (1936), 487–99; Robert L. Ebel, "Knowledge Versus Ability in Achievement Testing," *Proceedings of the 1969 Invitational Conference on Testing Problems* (Princeton, N.J.: Educational Testing Service, 1970).

It is not always clear what the term *mental ability* is intended to mean. It could mean no more nor less than "development of ability to think," to use the words of the Educational Policies Commission. Perhaps it is simply intended to emphasize the use of knowledge, as opposed to its possession. If so, development of mental abilities is not so much an alternative to acquisition of knowledge as an extension to include assimilation of knowledge, which is essentially the same extension as that implied by the phrase "command of substantive knowledge." It is hard to see how mental abilities can be developed or can exist apart from knowledge.

The use of the plural term "mental abilities" suggests that several separate abilities are involved. Presumably these are not intended to refer to the so-called mental faculties of attention, memory, imagination, reason, will, temperament, and character that were thought to be independent, general powers of the mind in the nineteenth century. Studies of transfer of training do not support the belief that such abstract mental faculties or abilities exist or that developing and strengthening them by study in one area of knowledge will make them available for use in any other area. Presumably a mental ability is something more general than, for example, ability to spell the word *Constantinople,* ability to add 7 and 9, or ability to complete and balance the chemical equation for the preparation of oxygen from potassium chlorate.

Thus it would seem that the concept of mental abilities or processes is quite indefinite. No generally recognized catalog of mental processes with titles and definitions for distinctly different mental processes seems to exist. There is no reliable classification of such processes into higher and lower levels. Even if we agree that the term *mental process* means no more nor less than the term *thinking,* we have no very clear notions of what processes may be involved or of how the "higher" processes may differ from the "lower." Daydreaming seems different from problem solving, but at present we can only guess in what way and to what extent different mental processes may be involved.

The indefiniteness of mental abilities is a problem that plagued the authors of the *Taxonomy* from the beginning of their labors. They solved it as well as may be humanly possible, after years of deliberation. But they would be the last to claim that they succeeded in discovering an underlying simple structure in mental abilities.

To demonstrate the complexity of the problem of identifying and classifying mental abilities, the reader is invited to take a little test. In each of the triads below two of the abilities were put in the same major class in the condensed version of the *Taxonomy.*[14] The third was put in a different major class. Your task is to identify this third (dissimilar) ability. Answers appear at the end of the chapter.

[14] Bloom et al., *Taxonomy of Educational Objectives,* condensed version, pp. 201–7.

1a. Ability to interpret various types of social data
1b. Ability to predict continuation of a trend
1c. Ability to predict the probable effect of a change

2a. Ability to distinguish facts from hypotheses
2b. Ability to indicate logical fallacies in arguments
2c. Ability to recognize unstated assumptions

3a. Ability to comprehend the relationship among the ideas of a passage
3b. Ability to grasp the thought of a work as a whole
3c. Ability to recognize the techniques used in propaganda

It may be apparent after this test that different mental abilities do not fall obviously and neatly into a small number of distinct categories. Like people, mental abilities vary continuously, and probably on many dimensions as well. But it seems unlikely that any small number of distinct, coherent mental processes will ever be discovered to account for any substantial part of the wide range of intellectual achievements human beings show.

Most educational psychologists now seem to agree that the mind does not consist of separate faculties that can be cultivated independently. It functions as a unit, and all aspects of its functioning—attention, perception, memory, volition, emotion, and so forth—are likely to be involved whenever the mind is active. The objects of thought may be more or less complex and the procession of thoughts may be more or less purposefully directed and controlled, but so far as we now know, the mind probably functions in essentially the same way regardless of its task. It must certainly need different kinds of knowledge to cope effectively with different kinds of problems, knowledge of processes as well as knowledge of content, but there seems to be no good basis for suggesting that different, whether higher or lower, types of mental functions need to be involved.

Attempts to write test items that will require examinees to use higher level mental processes involve several hazards. One is that they may demand more than the average examinee is capable of delivering and thus contribute little to effective measurement. Another is that they may involve fairly complex situations; a wordy description may present the examinee with problems of comprehension and interpretation that are irrelevant to the main purpose of the examination. Characteristics of this kind are likely to lower the precision and the efficiency of the test question.

In order to describe the items in a test adequately, it seems necessary to specify more than the areas or topics of subject matter with which they deal. Categories of mental abilities or processes have sometimes been used to provide a second dimension to the test outline. But in view of the difficulty of distinguishing clearly between different mental abilities and processes, it may be advisable to avoid this approach as much as possible.

One alternative is to describe test items in terms of the kind of task they present, rather than in terms of the somewhat hypothetical processes that may be involved in their solution. For example, different kinds of questions used in typical classroom tests may:

1. Ask what a particular term means
2. Ask for a particular fact or principle
3. Ask the explanation of something
4. Ask the solution to a problem.

By including a variety of tasks like these, the test can probably cover adequately most of the outcomes of instruction in most courses without becoming involved with the intangibles of mental processes or abilities.

One of the propositions advanced by Richardson and Stalnaker in their "Comments on Achievement Examinations" was this: "Proposition III. The form of a test gives no certain indication of the ability tested." In discussing this proposition they said:

> We wish to digress enough to point out that psychologists do not know what abilities are involved in procedures such as writing examinations. The nature of these mental operations had best be left alone when discussing test form.[15]

This advice was given in 1935, but it would still appear to be sound.

AFFECTIVE OUTCOMES AS EDUCATIONAL GOALS

Those who teach and those who test are sometimes charged with over-emphasis on cognitive learning, with consequent neglect of the affective determiners of behavior. Teachers, it is said, are preoccupied with what their pupils know or do not know; pupils, on the other hand, are more concerned with what they like or dislike, and how they feel. Thus teachers and students may find themselves living in separate worlds. Further, say the critics, the most profound challenges in our society are not cognitive. They are challenges to our social unity and to our individual righteousness, to our ethical standards and to our moral values, to our courage and to our compassion. If the schools focus too much on cognitive learning, they will fail to contribute as they should to meeting those challenges.[16]

These charges and criticisms are not without foundation. Feeling is as

---

[15] M. W. Richardson and J. M. Stalnaker, "Comments on Achievement Examinations," *Journal of Educational Research,* 28 (1935), 425–32.
[16] Ralph W. Tyler, "Assessing Educational Achievement in the Affective Domain," *N.C.M.E. Measurement in Education,* Vol. 4, No. 3, Spring 1974.

real and as important a part of human nature as is knowning. How we feel is almost always more important to us than what we know and how we behave is a paramount concern of those whose lives we share. And since behavior is sometimes determined more by how we feel about a situation than by what we know about it, clearly the affective dimension will play a most important role in meeting the challenges of society.

Well, then, should not the school transfer some of its concern from cognitive outcomes and place it on affective outcomes? Probably not, and for two reasons. The first is that many affective goals can be reached at least in part through cognitive means. Affect and cognition are not independent aspects of the personality: How we feel about a problem or an event depends in part on what we know about it. Wisdom doesn't guarantee happiness, but the lack of it often entails great unhappiness. Our affective failures among students—the alienated, the dropouts, even the bright revolutionaries—can almost always be traced to some prior cognitive failure of theirs or ours. Psychologists who try to help people with problems of affect usually employ cognitive means. The psychotherapy they practice is essentially a cognitive process of fostering self-knowledge in the patient.

The second reason why the schools should not put more stress on affective outcomes is that the only noncognitive means a school can use to attain its affective ends is the process of conditioning. When a school adopts and enforces (with rewards and punishments) certain rules of behavior, it conditions its students to regularly exhibit that kind of behavior. What students initially accept as "the way things are done around here" is gradually transformed into the belief that things ought to be done that way.

When a basketball coach insists that players behave in a sportsmanlike manner on the court and off, that their speech, dress, and actions be at all times decent and in good taste, the coach is using conditioning, and most of us applaud both the end and the means. But Hitler used the same process to solidify popular support for his evil purposes, and most effectively, be it noted, to gain support from the German youth.

No teacher can afford to ignore the affective side effects of efforts to promote cognitive learning. But teachers should not use their concern for affective outcomes as an excuse for paying less attention to the cognitive outcomes.

Our schools and colleges were established primarily to develop cognitive competence, in the well-founded belief that this was the best the state could do to help young people become effective and happy men and women.

KEY TO ABILITIES CLASSIFICATION TEST (PAGE 51)

1a. Comprehension	2a. Analysis	3a. Analysis
1b. Comprehension	2b. Evaluation	3b. Comprehension
1c. Application	2c. Analysis	3c. Analysis

SUMMARY

Some of the main ideas developed in this chapter may be summarized in the following 19 statements:

1. Determination of what to measure is a critical, difficult problem in achievement test construction.
2. Statements of educational objectives are useful in redirecting educational emphases from past to present needs.
3. Guidance in determining what to measure may be obtained from a statement of educational objectives.
4. Objectives defined in terms of desired behavior are concretely meaningful but may emphasize specific end products at the expense of more general means toward those ends.
5. The use of conditioning as a means for improving the effectiveness of human behavior is more appropriate in the early years of life than it is after formal schooling has begun.
6. A major goal of education is to develop in the student a command of substantive knowledge.
7. A person's knowledge consists of everything that he or she has experienced as a result of perceptions of external stimuli or internal thought processes.
8. Knowledge is a structure built out of information by processes of thought.
9. Verbal knowledge is a very powerful, uniquely human form of knowledge.
10. The first problem of the educator is to decide what kinds and items of knowledge will be most useful to the student. The second task is to manage the learning process so that the student develops a command of this body of knowledge.
11. All knowledge can be expressed in propositions.
12. Propositions provide the basis for most good objective achievement test items.
13. Rote learning is a process of information storage. It has little to contribute to the cultivation of knowledge.
14. Rote learning cannot lead to command of knowledge and is unlikely to be used extensively by students.
15. Uncritical acceptance of words of vague or uncertain meaning interferes with development of command of knowledge.
16. The greater a student's command of a body of knowledge, the less likely that individual will be to forget it.
17. General mental abilities are difficult to identify and to define clearly.

18. Items designed to test the higher mental processes tend to be unsatisfactory.
19. The school should seek to attain affective ends through cognitive means.

PROJECTS AND PROBLEMS

Project: Article Report

Read and report on five recent journal articles on testing. Choose articles that interest you and that you can understand. Locate the articles by consulting the *Education Index*. Write a report on each article, following the form and style of the example on this page. Limit your report to a single page. The references you submit will not be returned to you.

SAMPLE ARTICLE REPORT

AUTHOR: Betts, Gilbert L.

POSITION: Editor, Educational Test Bureau, Minneapolis, Minnesota.

TITLE OF ARTICLE: "Suggestions for a Better Interpretation and Use of Standardized Achievement Tests."

REFERENCE: *Education*, vol. 71 (December 1950), 217–21.

THESIS: In order to get a meaningful measurement, achievement should be graded in relation to ability to achieve.

DEVELOPMENT: The intelligence test should be used as a measure of ability to achieve, and the achievement test score should be used as a measure of achievement. The two scores should then be compared for purposes of judging achievement. The use of grade norms leads to mediocrity because the more capable students are not motivated. If they are rated against themselves, they will receive more equal motivation. Improved use of tests begins with selection. Each test should be selected to cover the area the tester desires to cover and to measure what he desires to measure.

CONCLUSION: Achievement and intelligence should be compared by percentile ranks to see if the students are working up to their ability. All students should learn at their own rates but each should receive proper motivation in regard to his or her abilities.

EVALUATION: The author presents a very good argument in that good students are not properly motivated when achievement is judged solely on the basis of grade norms, as is many times done. One trouble with his suggested remedy is that when the poor students are motivated on the basis of their own intelligence scores, which correlate very highly with achievement scores, they will tend to become somewhat more satisfied with their performances as they are.

GLEN A. STEPHENSON
May 27, 1964
Ed. 465

We have faith that whatever people now measure crudely by mere descriptive words, helped out by comparative and superlative forms, can be measured more precisely and conveniently if ingenuity and labor are set at the task. We have faith also that the objective products produced, rather than the inner condition of the person whence they spring, are the proper point of attack for the measurer, at least in our day and generation.

EDWARD L. THORNDIKE

4

How Should Achievement Be Measured?

ALTERNATIVE TYPES OF TESTS

The most commonly used types of tests are the essay (or discussion) type, the objective (or short-answer) type, the mathematical problem type, and the oral examination type. We now undertake a brief comparison of the characteristics of these major test forms.

To begin, let us dispose of some common misconceptions. It is not true that one type tests real understanding whereas another tests only superficial knowledge. As Richardson and Stalnaker have said, "The form of a test gives no certain indication of the ability tested."[1] It is not true that luck is a large element in scores on one type and nearly or totally absent in another. On the contrary, all three types can require much the same kind and level of ability, and if carefully handled can yield results of satisfactory reliability and validity, as Stalnaker[2] and Coffman[3] have shown. A good essay test or a good objective test could be constructed so that it would rank a group of students in nearly the same order as that resulting

[1] M. W. Richardson and J. M. Stalnaker, "Comments on Achievement Examinations," *Journal of Educational Research*, 28 (1935), 425–32.

[2] John M. Stalnaker, "Essay Examinations Reliably Read," *School and Society*, 46 (1937), 671–72.

[3] William E. Coffman, "On the Validity of Essay Tests of Achievement," *Journal of Educational Measurement*, 3 (1966), 151–56.

from a good problem test. But this is not to say that all three types can be used interchangeably with equal ease and effectiveness.

Vernon has called attention to evidence that

> while . . . tests of the same objectives employing different forms tend to give discrepant results (e.g., essay and new-type), tests in the same form which are aimed at different school subjects or different intellectual functions inter-correlate very highly. For many purposes the simpler tests show superior validity, and it is doubtful how far the more complex ones do bring in the "higher" intellectual functions at which they are aimed.[4]

Both essay and problem tests are easier to prepare than objective tests. But the objective test can be scored more rapidly and more reliably (unless very special and unusual pains are taken) than either of the other types, particularly the essay type. Where very large groups of students must be tested, the use of objective tests generally permits a gain in efficiency with little if any loss in validity. But where classes are small, the efficiency advantage is in the opposite direction, and essay or problem tests should be preferred.

The problem type has the advantage of greater intrinsic relevance—of greater identity with on-the-job requirements—than either of the other types. Many superficial or purely academic questions have been included in essay and objective tests. But this fault could and should be avoided.

Because of the length and complexity of the answers they require and because these answers must be written by hand, neither essay nor problem-type tests can sample as widely as is possible in an objective test. Writing is a much slower process than the reading on which objective tests depend. It is sometimes claimed that ability to choose an answer is different from, and less significant than, ability to produce an answer. But most of the evidence indicates that these abilities are highly related.

In considering the relative merits of essay, problem, and objective tests, it is important to remember that the only useful component of any test score is the objectively verifiable component of it, regardless of the type of test from which it was derived. To the degree that a test score reflects the private, subjective, unverifiable impressions and values of one particular scorer, it is deficient in meaning and hence in usefulness to the student who received it or to anyone else who is interested in this ability or achievement.

In objective tests and problem tests there is often a good deal more objectivity than in essay tests. The student usually has a more definite task, and the reasons for giving or withholding credit are more obvious to all

---

[4] Philip E. Vernon, *Educational Testing and Test Form Factors*, Research Bulletin 58–3 (Princeton, N.J.: Educational Testing Service, February, 1958).

concerned. But it is well to remember that even the objective test is based on many subjective decisions as to what to test and how to test it. For the problem test there is an additional element of subjectivity in scoring that is not present in the objective test. How much credit to give for an imperfect answer and which elements to consider in judging degree of perfection are often spur-of-the-moment, subjective decisions.

Whatever test form examiners use, they should seek to make measurements as objective as possible. A measurement is objective to the extent that it can be independently verified by other competent measurers. It is entirely conceivable that measurements obtained from a good essay test could be more objective in this sense than measurements obtained from a poor multiple-choice test. On the other hand, it is fair to say that those who use essay tests tend to worry less about the objectivity of their measurements and evaluations than those who use multiple-choice tests.

Since all of us have had our own unique history of experiences, it is not surprising that we sometimes find it difficult to agree on perceptions, meanings, and values. Yet the harmony of our relationships and the effectiveness of our common enterprises depends on agreement, so it is important for us to establish as much identity as possible among ourselves in these perceptions, meanings, and values. This is only another way of saying we need to be as objective as possible in all things, including the measurement of achievement.

In most cases teachers have chosen to use the type of question that seems most useful to them, or which they feel most competent to use effectively. However, it is possible that force of habit and some unwarranted assumptions may have prevented some teachers from trying other types that would prove more advantageous to them. The classroom testing practices of many school and college faculties probably could be improved by a periodic review of the types of tests being used.

Oral Examinations

In essence the oral examination involves two persons, examiner and examinee, face to face. The examiner asks questions. The examinee attempts to answer them. The examiner probes with further questions or accepts the answer. Finally he judges the quality of the answers and grades the examinee accordingly. Often the grade is either pass or fail.

Sometimes, to improve the objectivity of the examination more than one examiner is present. Or to improve the efficiency of the process and the fairness of the judgments, several examinees might be interviewed simultaneously, giving each a chance to respond to the same questions and to comment on answers given by the other examinees. Sometimes the examinees are directed to question each other, with the examiners acting only as judges, or even with the judging left to the examinees themselves.

Brody and Powell[5] have described in detail some of these variations on the basic oral examination.

Employment interviews often include a kind of oral examination, and there is some similarity in the principles of good practice for both. The oral examination can be properly regarded as one kind of performance test, but since very special circumstances surround it—the stress of being under observation, the unequal status of the participants, the importance of what hangs in the balance—the performance can seldom be regarded as typical behavior.

Obviously the oral examination does involve direct contact and interaction between examiner and examinee. This makes it, if not less threatening, at least more personal, and possibly more humane than written examinations. Some even regard an oral examination as an enjoyable experience.

Personal characteristics that would be impossible to assess on a written test can be evaluated in the face-to-face situation—the candidate's appearance, manner, personality, alertness, forthrightness, stress tolerance, and speech pattern and quality. One can judge the impression the examinee would probably make on others.

When the purpose of the examination is to assess the examinee's knowledge or intellectual abilities, the oral approach permits a flexibility that the written examination usually lacks. The examinee can be asked to expand, clarify, or justify an answer. An important point can be probed in depth. A competent examiner may thus be able to get a clear picture of the examinee's abilities and limitations. Also, the problem of cheating can hardly arise in an oral examination; even bluffing may be harder to manage effectively in spur-of-the-moment responses to oral questions than on a written exam. Finally, like all good examinations, an oral examination can be a learning experience.

However, it is easy for oral examination enthusiasts to claim too much. An oral examination does no better than a written one in assessing intangible, poorly defined traits such as character, creativity, or "general fitness." Those who claim it tests examinees' ability to think on their feet, that is, to think effectively under stress, ignore the fact that most people do their best thinking while not under stress. Resistance to "choking up" under stress is probably not a very good indicator of overall effectiveness. Above all, advocates of oral examinations should avoid claiming that they measure abilities such as loyalty to the organization, honesty, industry, integrity, or even ability to get along with others, for these are characteristics that examinees have little opportunity to show, or examiners to observe, in the oral examination situation.

[5] William Brody and Norman J. Powell, "A New Approach to Oral Testing," *Educational and Psychological Measurement,* 7 (Summer 1947), 289–98.

Oral examinations are subject to serious limitations, which account for their virtual disappearance as tools for educational evaluation. Because the oral examination is essentially an individual process, it is very time-consuming. In fact, to yield a fair sample of the examinee's abilities, it should last at least 30 minutes, and often more than one examiner must be used to obtain an objective assessment. Obviously, these qualities make oral examinations costly and complex to administer.

The personal contact and interaction between examiner and examinee that is one of the assets of the oral examination is also a liability. It opens the door to prejudice, partiality, and discrimination on grounds other than the relevant traits and abilities. Other influences lower the validity of the examination. For some, as has been suggested above, the stress of the confrontation may upset normally effective mental processes. For others, glibness and pleasantness may help to conceal genuine deficiencies.

But the major limitation of the oral examination is the difficulty of obtaining reasonably reliable scores in reasonable amounts of time. Studies by Hartog,[6] Barnes and Pressey,[7] and others support this conclusion. However, Trimble[8] showed in another study that it is possible to obtain reliable evaluations under certain conditions. Oral examination scores can be both reliable and valid *if* several raters are used, *if* they are all looking for the same things, and *if* the examination is long enough and structured so that examinees can present a fair picture of overall traits and abilities. Usually, however, this calls for more care, skill, and time than most examiners can dedicate to the task.

THE VALUE OF CONTROLLED CONDITIONS

Precise measurement requires careful control, or standardization, of the conditions surrounding it. Obviously this control renders the behavior being measured to some degree artificial, but artificiality is a price that scientists and engineers, as well as psychologists and teachers, have usually found worth paying to achieve precision. For tests intended to measure typical behavior, such as personality, attitude, or interest, the price may sometimes be too high. That is, the behavior in the artificial test situation may be so poorly related to typical behavior in a natural situation that precise measurement is wasted effort. But for tests of educational aptitude or achievement, the gain in precision resulting from the controlled con-

[6] Sir Philip Hartog and E. C. Rhodes, "A Viva Voce (Interview) Examination," in *The Marks of Examiners* (London: Macmillan and Company, 1936), pp. 168–78.

[7] Elinor J. Barnes and S. L. Pressey, "The Reliability and Validity of Oral Examinations," *School and Society*, 30 (November 23, 1929), 719–22.

[8] Otis C. Trimble, "The Oral Examination: Its Validity and Reliability," *School and Society*, 39 (April 28, 1934), 550–52.

ditions that formal testing can afford usually far outweighs the slight loss in relevance of behavior.

Perhaps an illustration from physical ability testing may be helpful. Judges watching a group of children at play (the natural situation) could make rough estimates of the relative abilities of the students to run fast, jump high, or throw some object far. But the precision of the estimates obtained in such an uncontrolled, unstandardized situation would probably be quite low. Individual judges would not be likely to agree with each other, or even with themselves on different occasions, in the estimates they would report. If precise estimates are desired, the judges, the children, and everyone else concerned would probably prefer to see them made under the standardized and controlled conditions of a regular track meet. No one would worry much about the possibility that the ones who performed best in the track and field events might perform less well on the playground.

Because all pupils in a class usually take the same test of achievement under the same conditions, some critics have concluded that uniform written tests, particularly objective tests, disregard individual differences and even tend to suppress individuality. The fact that some classroom tests are graded by machines has served to strengthen this misconception. Mass testing and machine grading suggest a standardized uniformity in education that seems inconsistent with concern for individual students and their unique needs and potentials.

However, although the tests and the processes of testing are as nearly alike for all students of a given class as we can make them, test scores differ markedly. Those who score high on one test reflect superior ability and achievement in that area. Those who score low reveal deficiencies. Tests tend to reveal differences among students, not to suppress or conceal them. In fact, uniformity in the conditions of testing is a prerequisite to unequivocal indication of individual differences. If the tests are not identical for all students, not all of the differences in their scores can be attributed to differences among them in ability or achievement. The kind of information about individual differences that uniform tests reveal so clearly is essential to identifying and meeting the unique needs of individual students.

The emphasis in this chapter on the value of written tests in confirming and refining a teacher's observations of student behavior is not intended to suggest that tests should be the sole means used in judging students' educational achievement. Sometimes teachers are concerned mainly with the development of physical skills or social behavior, in which case direct observation is a much better basis for assessment. Nor should teachers and professors ignore their own direct observations, in the classroom or elsewhere, of a student's level of understanding or ability to use knowledge. The broader the basis of observations on which evaluation rests, the better, provided only that each observation carries no more weight in determining the final result than its appropriateness and accuracy warrant.

THE NEED FOR OBJECTIVITY

Regardless of the type of test used, it must yield objective measurements in order to be a useful tool. A measurement is objective if it can be verified by another independent evaluator. Any assessment that depends more on the subjective judgment of the evaluator than on the objective performance of the examinee is unlikely to be very dependable or useful, and there would be little point in reporting it to anyone else.

By this definition of objectivity, it is clear that objective tests do not necessarily yield objective measures and do not provide the only source of such measures. What is "objective" about an objective test is mainly the scoring. Even that is not likely to be perfectly objective if several scorers make up their own answer keys. And if two examiners start from scratch in building, administering, and scoring independent "objective" tests of the same achievement in the same group of students, it is likely that their measures will be substantially different from one another.

It is usually rather difficult to obtain objective measures from an essay test, but it can be done if sufficient care is taken in defining what is to be measured, and in building and using a test that conforms to that definition. The point is that objectivity is a characteristic of the measures obtained, not of the process by which they are obtained.

The objectivity of a set of measures is obviously a matter of degree. Not even measures of such physical characteristics as height or weight are likely to be perfectly objective. On the other hand, most measuring devices are built with the idea of objectivity in mind, though their usefulness and value will depend on the degree of objectivity they exhibit. If they are largely the products of chance or whimsy, they will have little value to anyone other than the examiner. On the other hand, if the knowledge being measured has been defined clearly, and if the process of measuring is adequate and competently carried out, it is likely that objective measures, of some value, will be obtained.

Other Requirements for Effective Testing

If all teachers and prospective teachers were skilled in the arts of test development and use, there would be little need for professional training in test construction. However, on their own testimony and on that of their sometimes suffering students—not to mention the reports of specialists called in to advise them on their testing problems—teachers do reveal shortcomings in their use of tests.

In order to ask significant, novel questions, to express them properly and plainly, and to provide acceptable model answers, test constructors must be thoroughly familiar with the material to be tested. They must be accurately aware of the examinees' level and range of understanding and ability so that they can choose problems of appropriate intrinsic difficulty and present them so that they will have appropriate functional difficulty. And only by understanding the thought processes of the students and the misconceptions the less capable ones are likely to have can test builders make wrong answers attractive to those of low achievement.

Skill in written expression is also required to communicate clearly and concisely the information and instructions that make up the test and the test items. A mastery of the techniques of item writing entails acquaintance with the most useful forms of test items, with their unique virtues, limitations, and pitfalls. And no less important is the desire to spend the time and make the effort necessary to do a competent, workmanlike job.

The traits just enumerated either contribute to good teaching as well as good testing, or contribute uniquely to good testing. More of the shortcomings observed in classroom tests probably result from deficiencies in teaching technique rather than in testing procedure. But the correction of deficiencies in command of subject matter, and skill in teaching, is beyond the scope of this book. Nothing that can be said about the techniques of test construction and use will enable an incompetent teacher to make a good test. What a book on classroom testing may do is to help good teachers make better tests than they would otherwise.

A point worth mentioning in passing is that some instructors, outstanding in their scholarship and teaching ability, possess rather naive notions about the requirements for effective measurement of educational achievement. The nuclear physicist, the economic theorist, the Shakespearean scholar, and many of their expert colleagues may practice rather primitive and untrustworthy techniques of testing and grading.

The gap between what we know about how educational achievement ought to be measured and what we actually do is sometimes explained away as a failure in communication, which it almost certainly is. Test specialists are blamed for having developed highly abstruse concepts and highly technical jargon that place their special knowledge beyond the reach of the typical teacher. No doubt there is some justification for this charge. But some of the responsibility may also belong to the teachers. They may have expected that their own native good sense, plus some effortless sleight of hand, could qualify them as experts in educational measurement. The matter is not quite that simple, as Henry Dyer has pointed out.

> I don't think the business of educational measurement is inherently simple, and I don't think it is something that can be wrapped up in a do-it-yourself kit. Any way you look at it, the measurement of human behavior is bound to be a terribly complex process, since the phenomena of human behavior are themselves as complex as anything in the universe.[9]

[9] Henry S. Dyer, "What Point of View Should Teachers Have Concerning the Role of Measurement in Education?" *The Fifteenth Yearbook of the National Council on Measurements Used in Education* (East Lansing, Mich.: Michigan State University, 1958).

COMMON MISTAKES OF TEACHERS IN TESTING

What are some of the mistakes that even expert teachers and eminent professors make in measuring educational achievement? What are some of their unsound practices in classroom testing?

First, they tend to rely too much on their own subjective judgments, on fortuitous observations, and on unverified inferences. The wide difference among different judges in their evaluations of the same evidence of student achievement—that is, the unreliability of those judgments—has been demonstrated over and over again, yet many teachers have never checked on the reliability of any of their tests and may not even have planned those tests purposely to make them as reliable as possible.

Second, some teachers feel obliged to use absolute standards in judging educational achievement, rather than more fair and consistent relative terms. If most of the students in a class get A's on one test and most of the same students fail another, some teachers prefer to blame the students rather than the test. They believe, contrary to much evidence, that a teacher can set a reasonable passing score on a test simply by looking at it, without reviewing any student answers. They believe that "grading on the curve" permits the students to set the (relative and presumably fallible) standards, instead of permitting the teacher (whose standards are presumed to be absolute and infallible) to set them.

Third, both teachers and professors tend to put off test preparation to the last minute and then to do it on a catch-as-catch-can basis. A last minute test is likely to be a poor test. Further, such a test cannot possibly have the constructive influence in motivating and directing student learning that a good test of educational achievement ought to have and that a test planned and described to students early in the course would have.

Fourth, many teachers use tests that are too inefficient and too short to sample adequately the whole area of understanding and abilities that the course has attempted to develop. Essay tests have many virtues, but efficiency, adequacy of sampling, and reliability of scoring are not among them.

Fifth, teachers often overemphasize trivial or ephemeral details in their tests, to the neglect of understanding of basic principles and ability to make practical applications. To illustrate, it is probably far more important to understand the forces that brought Henry VIII into conflict with the pope than to know the name of his second wife. Yet some teachers are more inclined to ask about the specific, incidental details than about the important general principles.

Sixth, the test questions that teachers and professors write, both essay and objective, often suffer from lowered effectiveness due to unintentional ambiguity in the wording of the question or to inclusion of irrelevant clues to the correct response. Too few teachers avoid these hazards by asking a competent colleague to review the tests beforehand.

Seventh, the inevitable fact that test scores are affected by the questions or tasks included in them tends to be ignored, and the magnitude of the resulting errors (called *sampling errors*) tends to be underestimated. Many classroom teachers believe that a test score will be perfectly accurate and reliable if no error has been made in scoring the individual items or in adding these to get a total score. Differences as small as one score unit are often taken to indicate significant differences in attainment.

Finally, many teachers and professors do not use the relatively simple techniques of statistical analysis to check on the effectiveness of their tests. A mean score can show whether or not the general level of difficulty was appropriate for the group tested. A standard deviation can show how well or how poorly the test differentiated among students at different levels of attainment. A reliability coefficient can show how much or how little the scores on this test are likely to differ from those the same students would get on an independent, equivalent test.

An analysis of the responses of good and poor students to individual test items can show whether the items discriminate well or poorly and, if poorly, can suggest why and what needs to be done to improve the item. The calculation of these statistics is quite simple. There is no better way for teachers and professors to continue to improve their skill in testing, and the quality of the tests they use, than to analyze test results systematically and to compare the finding of these analyses with ideal standards of test quality, such as those discussed in Chapter 13.

SUMMARY

The main conclusions to be drawn from the discussions presented in this chapter can be summarized in the following 11 propositions:

1. The form of a test gives no certain indication of the ability tested.
2. Whatever form of test or type of item is used, examiners should seek to make their measurements as objective as possible. A measurement is objective if it can be verified by another independent measurement.
3. The oral examination allows for personal contact between examiner and examinee and also allows considerable flexibility in the examining process, but it does not allow for accurate assessment of intangible traits or on-the-job performance characteristics.
4. Oral examinations tend to be time-consuming, to be subject to personal bias, and to yield unreliable measurements.
5. Achievement tests are given under specially devised and carefully controlled conditions to improve the precision of measurement without impairing seriously its validity.

6. Written tests provide an important basis, but not the only basis for evaluating student achievement.

7. A measurement must be objective to be useful.

8. Objective test scores are not always objective measurements, and they are not the only source of such measurements.

9. Competence in teaching is a necessary, but not a sufficient, condition for expert test construction.

10. Construction of a good objective test requires special knowledge of testing techniques and special skill in the use of language.

11. Some common weaknesses of teacher-made tests are attributable to: (a) reliance on subjective judgments, (b) reliance on absolute standards of judgment, (c) hasty test preparation, (d) use of short, inefficient tests, (e) testing trivia, (f) careless wording of questions, (g) neglect of sampling errors, and (h) failure to analyze the quality of the test.

PROJECTS AND PROBLEMS

Project: Data on a Measurement Problem

Using a reference located through the *Education Index, Psychological Abstracts, Review of Educational Research*, or simply by leafing through issues of *Educational and Psychological Measurement, The Journal of Educational Measurement*, or other periodicals, find an article that presents solid data on a measurement problem that interests you. Data of this kind are almost certain to be numerical: numbers, proportions, averages, ratios, differences, standard deviations, correlation coefficients, significance levels, and so forth.

Write a brief summary of the study reported in the article, following the form illustrated below.

GUESSING ON OBJECTIVE TESTS

Problem:

How much guessing do students do on objective tests?

Procedure:

College students taking true-false tests in a course on educational testing were asked to check any questions on their test copies to which their answers were no better than blind guesses. The answers they gave to these questions were then marked on a separate "Guesses" answer sheet. The inducement to report these guesses and to report them accurately was the promise that the students would be given credit for as many right answers as the laws of chance would predict, even if their actual guesses were not that good.

Data:

		Midterm	Final	Midterm	Final
1.	Test	Midterm	Final	Midterm	Final
2.	Date	7-7-67	7-25-67	10-23-67	12-4-67
3.	Number of items	98	89	108	116
4.	Number of students	158	158	121	121
5.	Responses	15,484	14,062	13,068	14,036
6.	Percent Correct	76	72	76	71
7.	Guesses	486	905	620	1,108
8.	Percent of Responses	3.1	6.4	4.7	7.9
9.	Guesses Correct	271	494	336	575
10.	Percent Correct	56	55	54	52
11.	Test Reliability	0.79	0.89	0.79	0.81

Conclusion:

Students like these taking tests like these do relatively little blind guessing.

Reference:

Ebel, Robert L. "Blind Guessing on Objective Achievement Tests," *Journal of Educational Measurement* vol. 5 (Winter 1968), 321–25.

Here are some measurement problems for which you might want to collect data:

I. Functions
   A. Measurement of motivation
   B. Measurement of vocabulary
   C. Measurement of writing ability
   D. Prediction of success in college
   E. Credit by examinations
   G. Wide-scale testing programs

II. Construction
   A. Types of objective test items
   B. Free response vs. choice-type tests

      C. Number of multiple-choice options
      D. Effects of position of correct response among multiple-choice options.
      E. Specific determiners
      F. Negative suggestions effects of true-false test items

III. Administration
      A. Methods of presenting test items
      B. Open-book examinations
      C. Confidence weighting of objective test responses
      D. Testwiseness
      E. Effects of practice
      F. Effects of special coaching
      G. Response sets and objective test responses
      H. Test anxiety
      I. Persistence on objective tests
      J. Correctness of first impressions on objective test answers
      K. Test time limits
      L. Rate of work scores
      M. Correction for guessing
      N. Accuracy of objective test scoring

IV. Evaluation
      A. Determination of the difficulty of objective test items
      B. Item difficulty distributions
      C. Indices of item discrimination
      D. Reliability of essay test grades
      E. Validity of the Spearman-Brown formula
      F. Methods of scaling test scores

5

Planning the Test

TEST SPECIFICATIONS

The firmest basis for the construction of a good test is a set of explicit specifications that indicate the following:

forms of test items to be used
number of items of each form
kinds of tasks the items will present
number of tasks of each kind
areas of content to be sampled
number of items in each area
level and distribution of item difficulty

Test specifications of this kind are useful not only in guiding the constructor of the test, but also in informing students what they may expect to find on the examination and how they can best prepare to do well on it. That information is likely to enhance the value of the test as an incentive to learning. If it is not provided, the examinees may claim, with some justice, that the test was unfair.

One of the devices that has been used to outline the coverage of a test, as part of the test specifications, is the two-way grid, sometimes called a "test blueprint." The several major areas of content to be covered by the test are assigned to the several rows (or columns) of the grid. The several major kinds of abilities to be developed are assigned to the columns (or rows). Each item may then be classified in one of the cells of the grid. Various numbers of items are assigned to each of the rows and columns. Knowing the proportion of items specified for a particular row and for a particular column, one can ideally determine the proportion of items appropriate for the cell formed by that row and that column.

The two-way grid is a good first step toward balance in a test. But it has limitations. For some tests a one-dimensional classification of items may be entirely adequate. Others may require three or four. There is some tendency for content to be related to goals or abilities. Hence the assumption that every cell should be represented by at least one item can be unwarranted. Since the number of cells in the chart equals the number of content areas multiplied by the number of educational goals, there is often a fairly large number of such cells. This leads to a more refined classification of items and a more difficult task of classifying them than may actually be necessary to produce a balanced test.

Another problem in using this device arises from difficulty in providing clear definitions of the categories involved, particularly the goal or ability categories. Content categories, on the other hand, are usually simpler to deal with. In a test for a course in consumer mathematics, for example, it is quite easy to tell whether a given item deals mainly with insurance or with taxation. It is much more difficult to decide whether it deals more with the ability to weigh values than it does with the ability to spend money wisely. Experience suggests that the reliability of a classification of test items in the usual two-way grid may be quite low, especially along the goal or ability dimension.

One way of reducing this difficulty is to classify test items in terms of their overt characteristics as verbal objects instead of on the basis of educational goals to which they seem to relate or mental abilities they presumably require. Another step toward making the measurement of balance more workable is to forego the fine detail in classification demanded by the two-way grid. Instead, one could settle for separate specifications of the desired weighting on each basis for classifying the items, such as item type or content area.

To guide test construction effectively and to inform prospective examinees adequately, the specifications need to be fairly detailed. To answer the question, How detailed? we might pose another question: If they were followed exactly by a competent item writer, would they be likely to produce an acceptable test? Obviously, specifications should be detailed enough to indicate what kinds of items should be written on what general areas of learning; but they should not be so detailed as to give away the actual questions that will appear on the test.

Two examples of explicit specifications follow. Exhibit 5-1 specifies

EXHIBIT 5–1. SPECIFICATIONS FOR A COLLEGE-LEVEL TEST OF UNDERSTANDING OF EDUCATIONAL MEASUREMENTS

Form of Item	Number
Multiple choice	50

Kinds of Tasks	Items
Terminology	5
Factual information	10
Generalization	10
Explanation	10
Calculation	5
Prediction	5
Recommended action	5
	—
	50

Content Areas	Items
Nature of educational measurement	2
History of educational measurement	2
Statistical techniques	7
Finding and selecting tests	3
Tests and objectives	3
Teacher-made tests	4
Test tryout and analysis	2
Elementary school testing	5
Secondary school testing	4
Educational aptitude	5
Personality and adjustment	2
Observational techniques	2
School testing programs	5
Using the results of measurement	4
	—
	50

Item Difficulty	
Intended average percent incorrect	30%
Range of percents incorrect	10%–60%

the item forms, kinds of tasks, areas of content, and item difficulties. Exhibit 5–2 illustrates the kinds of tasks that will make up the test. Each of these test characteristics will be discussed in greater detail in the pages that follow.

FORMS OF OBJECTIVE TEST ITEMS

The most commonly used kinds of objective test items are multiple-choice, true-false, matching, classification, and short-answer. Many other varieties have been described in more comprehensive catalogs of objective test items.[1] However, most of these special varieties have limited merit and

[1] A. G. Wesman "Writing the Test Item," in *Educational Measurement*, ed. Robert L. Thorndike (Washington, D.C.: American Council on Education, 1976).

EXHIBIT 5–2. EXAMPLES OF KINDS OF TASKS

1. *Terminology* (statistical techniques)
   What is meant by the term ''error of measurement'' as it is used by technically trained specialists?
   - a. Any error in test construction, administration, scoring, or interpretation that causes a person to receive different scores on two tests of the same trait.
   - b. A test score that is unreliable or invalid as a result of (1) sampling errors in test construction, (2) performance errors on the part of the examinee, or (3) evaluation errors on the part of the scorer.
   - *c. The difference between a given measurement and an estimate of the theoretical true value of the quantity measured.
   - d. The difference between the obtained score and the predicted score on a trait for a person.

2. *Factual information* (educational aptitude)
   How does one determine a child's mental age on the Stanford-Binet Scale?
   - a. By dividing the number of tests passed by the child's age in years.
   - *b. By giving a specified number of months of credit for each test passed.
   - c. By noting the highest level at which the child answers all tests correctly.
   - d. By noting the highest level at which the child answers *any* test correctly.

3. *Generalization* (educational aptitude)
   Expert opinion today assigns how much weight to heredity as a determiner of intelligence?
   - *a. Less weight than in 1900
   - b. More weight than in 1900
   - c. All of the weight
   - d. None of the weight

4. *Explanation* (personality and adjustment)
   Why is the Rorschach Test regarded as a projective test?
   - a. Because scores on the test provide accurate projections of future performance.
   - *b. Because the examinee unintentionally reveals aspects of his own personality in the responses he makes.
   - c. Because the stimulus material is ordinarily carried on slides that must be projected for viewing.
   - d. Because the test is still in an experimental, developmental phase.

5. *Calculation* (educational aptitude)
   What is the I.Q. of an eight-year-old child whose mental age is 10 years?
   - a. 80
   - b. 90
   - *c. 125
   - d. The answer cannot be determined from the data given.

6. *Prediction* (test tryout and analysis)
   If two forms of a 50-item, 30-minute test are combined to produce a single 100-item, 60-minute test, how variable and reliable will scores from the combined test be (in comparison with those from a single short form)?
   - *a. More variable and more reliable
   - b. More variable but less reliable
   - c. Less variable but more reliable
   - d. Less variable and less reliable

7. *Recommended action* (teacher-made tests)
   In drafting a multiple-choice test item which of these should be written *second*?
   - a. The stem question
   - *b. A good answer
   - c. A good distracter
   - d. An absurd distracter

applicability. Their unique features do more to change the appearance of the item, and often to increase the difficulty of using it, than to improve the item as a measuring instrument.

Two special item types that have achieved some popularity, the true-false with correction and the multiple-response variation of the multiple-choice item, are displayed in Exhibit 5-3. The disadvantages of both appear to outweigh their advantages. Presumably the corrected true-false item is less subject to guessing than the ordinary true-false item and tests recall as well as recognition. However, the added difficulty and uncertainty involved in scoring student responses to it more than offsets whatever slight reduction in guessing or slight increase in recall testing the item might produce. The multiple-response item is essentially a collection of true-false statements. If the statements were presented and scored as independent true-false statements, they would yield more detailed and reliable information concerning the state of the examinee's knowledge than they can do in multiple-response form. Those critics who urge test makers to abandon the "traditional" multiple-choice and true-false forms and to invent new forms to measure a more varied and more significant array of educational achievement have failed to grasp two important points:

1. *Any* aspect of cognitive educational achievement can be tested by either the multiple-choice or the true-false form.
2. What a multiple-choice or true-false item measures is determined much more by its content than by its form.

Multiple-choice and true-false test items are widely applicable to a great variety of tasks. Because of this, and because of the importance of

EXHIBIT 5–3. SPECIAL ITEM TYPES

---

1. **True-false with correction**
   Directions: If the statement is true as given, write the word "true" on the blank following the item. If it is false, find a substitute for the underlined word or phrase that would make it true. Then, write the substitute on the blank following the item.

Example:	*Answer*
0. The use of steam revolutionized transportation in the 17th century.	0. *19th*

2. **Multiple-response**
   Directions: Choose the most nearly correct set of responses from among those listed.

   Example: *Responses*
   0.   Our present constitution   1. *a*

   - a. Was the outgrowth of a previous failure   2. *a, b*
   - b. Was drafted in Philadelphia during the summer (May to September) of 1787   3. *a, b, c*
   - c. Was submitted by the Congress to the states for adoption   4. *b, c, d*
   - d. Was adopted by the required number of states and put into effect in 1789.   *5. *a, b, c, d*

developing skill in using each form effectively, separate chapters are devoted to true-false and multiple-choice item forms later in this text.

The multiple-choice form of test item is relatively high in ability to discriminate between better and poorer students. It is somewhat more difficult to write than some other item types, but its advantages seem so apparent that it has become the type most widely used in tests constructed by specialists. Theoretically, and this has been verified in practice, a multiple-choice test with a given number of items can be expected to show as much reliability in its scores as a typical true-false test with almost twice that number of items. Here is an example of the multiple-choice type.

Directions: Write the number of the best answer to the question on the line at the right of the question.

Example: Which is the most appropriate designation for a government in which control is in the hands of a few men?

1. Autonomy   **4**
2. Bureaucracy
3. Feudalism
4. Oligarchy

The true-false item is the simplest to prepare and is also quite widely adaptable. It tends to be less discriminating, item for item, than the multiple-choice type, and somewhat more subject to ambiguity and misinterpretation. Although theoretically a high proportion of true-false items could be answered correctly by blind guessing, in practice the error introduced into true-false test scores by blind guessing tends to be small. This is true because well-motivated examinees taking a reasonable test do very little blind guessing. They almost always find it possible to give a rational answer and much more advantageous to do so than to guess blindly. The problem of guessing on true-false test questions will be discussed in greater detail in Chapter 7. Here is an example of the true-false form.

Directions: If the sentence is essentially true, encircle the letter "T" at the right of the sentence. If it is essentially false, encircle the letter "F."

Example: A substance that serves as a catalyst in a chemical reaction may be recovered unaltered at the end of the reaction.

                                                         Ⓣ   **F**

The matching type is efficient in that an entire set of responses can be used with a cluster of related stimulus words. But this is also a limitation since it is sometimes difficult to get clusters of questions or stimulus words that are sufficiently similar to make use of the same set of responses. Further, questions whose answers can be no more than a word or a phrase tend to be somewhat superficial and to place a premium on purely verbalistic learning. An example of the matching type is given here.

Directions: On the blank before the title of each literary work place the letter that precedes the name of the person who wrote it.

Literary Works		Authors	
b	1. *Paradise Lost*	a.	Matthew Arnold
		b.	John Milton
e	2. *The Innocents Abroad*	c.	William Shakespeare
		d.	Robert Louis Stevenson
d	3. *Treasure Island*	e.	Mark Twain

The classification type is less familiar than the matching type, but possibly more useful in certain situations. Like the matching type, it uses a single set of responses but applies these to a large number of stimulus situations. An example of the classification type is the following.

Directions: In the following items you are to express the effects of exercise on various body processes and substances. Assume that the organism undergoes no change except those due to exercise. For each item blacken answer space.

1. If the effect of exercise is to *increase* the quantity described in the item
2. If the effect of exercise is to *decrease* the quantity described in the item
3. If exercise should have no *appreciable effect*, or *an unpredictable effect* on quantity described in the item

27. Rate of heart beat	■	☐2	☐3
28. Blood pressure	■	☐2	☐3
29. Amount of glucose in the blood	☐1	■	☐3
30. Amount of residual air in the lungs	☐1	■	☐3

The short-answer item, in which students must supply a word, phrase, number, or other symbol is inordinately popular and tends to be used excessively in classroom tests. It is easy to prepare. In the early grades, where emphasis is on the development of vocabulary and the formation of concepts, it can serve a useful function. It has the apparent advantage of requiring the examinee to think of the answer, but this advantage may be more apparent than real. Some studies have shown a very high correlation between scores on tests composed of parallel short-answer and multiple-choice items, when both members of each pair of parallel items are intended to test the same knowledge or ability.[2]

This means that students who are best at *producing* correct answers tend also to be best at *identifying* them among several alternatives. Accurate measures of how well students can identify correct answers tend to be somewhat easier to get than accurate measures of their ability to produce

---

[2] Alvin C. Eurich, "Four Types of Examinations Compared and Evaluated," *Journal of Educational Psychology*, 22 (1931), 268–78; and Desmond L. Cook, "An Investigation of Three Aspects of Free-response and Choice-type Tests at the College Level," *Dissertation Abstracts*, 15 (1955), 1351.

them. There may be special situations, of course, where the correlation would be much lower.

The disadvantages of the short-answer form are that it is limited to questions that can be answered by a word, phrase, symbol, or number and that its scoring tends to be subjective and tedious. Item writers often find it difficult to phrase good questions on principles, explanations, applications, or predictions that can be answered by one specific word or phrase. Here are some examples of short-answer items.

Directions: On the blank following each of the following questions, partial statements, or words, write the word or number that seems most appropriate.

Examples:

What is the valence of oxygen? **-2**

The middle section of the body of an insect is called the **thorax**.

What major river flows through or near each of these cities?

Cairo	**Nile**
Calcutta	**Ganges**
New Orleans	**Mississippi**
Paris	**Seine**
Quebec	**St. Lawrence**

Some authorities suggest that a variety of item types be used in each examination in order to diversify the tasks presented to the examinee. They imply that this will improve the validity of the test or make it more interesting. Others suggest that test constructors should choose the particular item type that is best suited to the material they wish to examine. There is more merit in the second of these suggestions than in the first, but even suitability of item form should not be accepted as an absolute imperative. Several item forms are quite widely adaptable. A test constructor can safely decide to use primarily a single item type, such as multiple-choice, and to turn to one of the other forms only when it becomes clearly more efficient to do so. The quality of a classroom test depends much more on giving proper weight to various aspects of achievement, and on writing good items of whatever type, than on choice of this or that type of item.

THE NUMBER OF ITEMS

The number of questions to include in a test is determined largely by the amount of time available for it. Many tests are limited to 50 minutes, more or less, because that is the scheduled length of the class period. Special examination schedules may provide periods of two hours or longer. In general, the longer the period and the examination, the more reliable the scores obtained from it. However, it is seldom practical or desirable to prepare a classroom test that will require more than three hours.

For various reasons there is a growing trend to make tests include few enough questions so that most students have time to attempt all of them when working at their own normal rates. One reason for this is that speed of response is not a primary objective of instruction in most high school and college courses and hence is not a valid indication of achievement. In many areas of proficiency, speed and accuracy are not highly correlated. Consider the data in Table 5–1. The sum of the scores for the first 10 students who finished the test was 965. The highest score in that group was 105. The lowest was 71. Thus, the range of scores in that group was 35 score units. Note that though the range of scores varies somewhat from group to group, there is no clear tendency for students to do better or worse depending on the amount of time spent. One can conclude from these data that on this test there was almost no relation between time spent in taking the test and the number of correct answers given.

A second reason for giving students ample time to work on a test is that examination anxiety, severe enough even in untimed tests, is accentuated when pressure to work rapidly as well as accurately is applied. A third is that efficient use of an instructor's painstakingly produced test requires that most students respond to all of it.[3] In some situations speed tests may be appropriate and valuable, but these situations seem to be the exception, not the rule.

The number of questions that an examinee can answer per minute depends on the kind of questions used, the complexity of the thought

TABLE 5–1. *THE RELATION BETWEEN RATE AND ACCURACY*

Order of Finish	Sum of Scores	Range of Scores
1–10	965	35
11–20	956	32
21–30	940	31
31–40	964	32
41–50	948	52
51–60	955	25
61–70	965	27
71–80	1010	30
81–90	942	24
91–100	968	40

* Based on a test in educational measurement composed of 125 true-false test items taken by 100 students on November 3, 1969. The mean score on the test was 96.1. The tenth student finished the test after working on it for 50 minutes. The 100th student used 120 minutes.

[3] Robert L. Ebel, "Maximizing Test Validity in Fixed Time Limits," *Educational and Psychological Measurement*, 13 (1953), 347–57.

processes required to answer them, and the examinee's work habits. The fastest student in a class may finish a test in half the time required by the slowest. For these reasons it is difficult to specify precisely how many items to include in a given test. Experience with similar tests in similar classes is the best guide. Lacking that, test constructors might assume that typical multiple-choice items can be answered by even the slower students at the rate of one per minute, and that true-false items can be answered similarly at the rate of two per minute. If the proposed items are longer or more complex than usual, these estimates may need to be revised. The time required by an essay question or a problem depends on the nature of the question or problem. Sometimes it is helpful for test constructors to specify how much time they wish the examinee to spend on each question or problem.

Sampling Errors in Test Scores

If the amount of time available for testing does not determine the length of a test, the accuracy desired in the scores should determine it. In general, the larger the number of items included in a test, the more reliable the scores will be as measures of achievement in the field. In statistical terminology, the items that make up a test constitute a *sample* from a much larger collection, or *population,* of items that might have been used in that test. A 100-word spelling test might be constructed by selecting every fifth word from a list of the 500 words studied during the term. The 500 words constitute the population from which the 100-word sample was selected.

Consider now a pupil who, asked to spell all 500 words, spells 325 (65 percent) of them correctly. Of the 100 words in the sample, he spells 69 (69 percent) correctly. The difference between the 65 percent for the population and the 69 percent for the sample is known as a *sampling error.* Statisticians refer to the population quantity, 65 percent in this case, as a parameter. The sample quantity, 69 percent in this case, they refer to as a statistic. A statistician, or anyone else for that matter, can use a statistic obtained from a sample to estimate the parameter of a population.

For example, if a teacher wishes to estimate the average weight of 30 students in a second grade, she or he might weigh five of them and find the average of their weights. That sample statistic would probably be close to but not identical with the average that would have been obtained if all 30 students had been weighed to find the population parameter. The difference would be a sampling error.

In the case of the spelling test just cited, the population of possible questions is real and definite. But for most tests it is not. That is, there is almost no limit to the number of problems that could be invented for use in an algebra test, or to the number of questions that could be formulated for a history test. Constructors of tests in these subjects, as in most other subjects, have no predetermined, limited list from which to draw a representative sample of questions. But their tests are samples, nevertheless, because they include only a fraction of the questions that could be asked in each case. A major problem of test constructors is thus to make their samples fairly represent a theoretical total population of questions on the topic.

The more extensive the area of subject matter or abilities a test is intended to cover, the larger the population of potential questions. The size of this population places an upper limit on the size of the sample that can be drawn from it; that is, the sample cannot be larger than the population. But population size does not place a *lower* limit on the size of the sample. A population of 1,000 potential items can be sampled by a test of 10, 50, or 100 items. So can a population of 100,000 potential items. The larger the population, the more likely it is to be heterogeneous, that is, to include diverse and semi-independent areas of knowledge or ability. To achieve equally accurate results, a somewhat larger sample is required in a heterogeneous than in a homogeneous field. And, as we have already noted, generally a larger sample will yield a sample statistic closer to the population parameter than a more limited sample.

Now since any test is a sample of tasks, every test score is subject to sampling errors. If test scores are expressed as percent correct, the larger the sample, the smaller the sampling errors are likely to be. Posey has shown that examinees' luck, or lack of it, in being asked what they happen to know is a much greater factor in the grade they receive in a 10-question test than in one of 100 questions.[4] His charts, reproduced in Figure 5-1, show the distributions of expected scores for three students on three tests. One student is assumed to be able to answer 90 percent of all the questions that might possibly be written on the subject of the test. Another is assumed to be able to answer 70 percent of such questions, and the third is assumed capable of answering only 50 percent of them. Of the three tests, one includes 10 questions, the second 20, and the third 100.

Now, suppose each of these three students took not just one 10-item test but 100 of them, with each test made up of 10 questions drawn at random from a supply of 1,000 questions, all different, but all on the same general subject. The 50 percent student is assumed to be able to give acceptable answers to 500 of the 1,000 questions. However, as the dotted line on the top chart shows, he could *not* expect to answer exactly 5 questions out of 10 acceptably on each of the 100 tests, because in the process of sampling some tests would include more, some fewer, of the questions he could answer.

The number of tests on which each of the three students could expect

---

[4] Chesley Posey, "Luck and Examination Grades," *Journal of Engineering Education*, 23 (1932), 292–96.

FIGURE 5–1. *Relation of the Number of Questions in an Examination to the Sharpness of Discrimination of Different Levels of Ability*

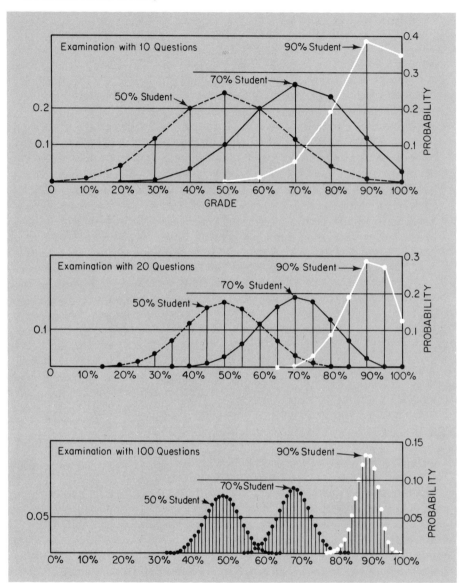

SOURCE: Chesley Posey, "Luck and Examination Grades," *Journal of Engineering Education*, 23 (1932), 292–96. Reproduced by permission of Chesley Posey and the *Journal of Engineering Education*.

to make each of the 11 possible scores (zero to 10) is shown in Table 5–2. Note that the 50 percent student could not expect a single score of 10 in all of the 100 tests: he could expect one score of 9, four of 8, and so on. Columns for the other two students can be interpreted similarly.[5]

The variations in scores for these students on equivalent tests, which differ only in the samples of questions used, are a direct result of sampling errors. To reiterate, the sampling error is the difference between the score a student gets on a specific sample of questions and the average score he or she should expect to get in the long run on tests of that kind. Thus, the 50 percent student, whose long-run expectation is for a score of 5 on the 10-item tests, benefits from a sampling error of +4(9 − 5) on one test and suffers from a sampling error of −4(1 − 5) on another. There is zero sampling error (5 − 5) in the scores this student receives on 24 of the tests. These kinds of sampling errors are present in practically all educational test scores. However, it is important to understand that they are not caused by mistakes in sampling. A perfectly chosen random sample will still be subject to sampling errors simply because it is a random sample.

The point of Posey's charts is that these sampling errors have less serious consequences when the samples are large (100-item tests) than

TABLE 5–2. SCORES OF THREE STUDENTS ON 100 10-QUESTION TESTS

Score	Number of Tests Yielding This Score for		
	50 Percent Student	70 Percent Student	90 Percent Student
10	0	3	35
9	1	12	38
8	4	23	20
7	12	27	6
6	21	20	1
5	24	10	0
4	21	4	0
3	12	1	0
2	4	0	0
1	1	0	0
0	0	0	0
	100	100	100
Average Score	5	7	9

[5] Those who are mathematically inclined may know, or may be interested in learning, that the three "Number of tests" columns in Table 5-2 can be obtained

for the 50 percent student by expanding the binomial $(.5R + .5W)^{10}$
for the 70 percent student by expanding the binomial $(.7R + .3W)^{10}$
for the 90 percent student by expanding the binomial $(.9R + .1W)^{10}$

and reducing the coefficient of each term to a percent of the sum of all coefficients for the expanded binomial. The letters R and W refer to right and wrong answers, and their coefficients to the probability of giving a right or wrong answer.

when the samples are small (10-item tests). This is because the spread of scores, expressed as percents, becomes less as the number of questions in the test increases. With less spread there is less overlap in scores for students at different levels of ability. With less overlap, there is a smaller probability that the poorer student will get a higher test score than the better student. In the examination with 100 questions, there is very little chance that a 50 percent student will score higher than a 70 percent student, and almost no chance that the 70 percent student will outperform the 90 percent student. In the 10-question examination, both these chances are much greater.

ASPECTS OF ACHIEVEMENT

Educational achievement in most courses consists in acquiring command of a fund of usable knowledge and in developing the ability to perform certain tasks. Knowledge can be conveniently divided into verbal facility and practical know-how. Abilities usually include ability to explain and ability to apply knowledge to the taking of appropriate action in practical situations. Some courses aim to develop other abilities, such as ability to calculate or ability to predict.

A rather detailed analysis of educational objectives for student achievement has been published by Bloom and his associates.[6] Their taxonomy includes test items appropriate for each objective or category of achievement. Dressel and his colleagues have published outlines of test content in terms of subject matter and pupil achievements, and also have presented illustrative items.[7] These are instructive guides for the test constructor to decide what to test and how to test it.

Some of the words used to identify achievements are more impressionistic than objectively meaningful, however. Some categories of educational achievement are based on hypothetical mental functions, such as comprehension, analysis, synthesis, scientific thinking, or recognition, whose functional independence is open to question. Those who currently attempt to describe mental processes and functions may be a little, but not significantly, better off than sixteenth-century map makers.

> So geographers in Afric maps
> With savage pictures fill their gaps
> And o'er unhabitable downs
> Place elephants for want of towns.[8]

[6] Benjamin S. Bloom et al., *Taxonomy of Educational Objectives* (New York: David McKay Company, Inc., 1956).

[7] Paul L. Dressel, *Comprehensive Examinations in a Program of General Education* (East Lansing, Mich.: Michigan State College Press, 1949).

[8] Jonathan Swift, "On Poetry, A Rhapsody," *The Portable Swift* (New York: The Viking Press, Inc., 1948), p. 571.

Unless mental processes are directly related to obvious characteristics of different kinds of test questions, it is somewhat difficult to use them confidently in planning a test or analyzing its contents. As Thorndike put it, "We have faith also that the objective products produced, rather than the inner condition of the person whence they spring, are the proper point of attack for the measurer, at least in our day and generation."[9] Occasionally, too, the specified areas of achievement are so closely related to specific units of instruction that it is difficult to regard them as pervasive educational goals.

Most of the questions used in many good classroom tests can be classified with reasonable ease and certainty into one or another of the following seven categories:

1. Understanding of terminology (or vocabulary)
2. Understanding of fact and principle (or generalization)
3. Ability to explain or illustrate (understanding of relationships)
4. Ability to calculate (numerical problems)
5. Ability to predict (what is likely to happen under specified conditions)
6. Ability to recommend appropriate action (in some specific practical problem situation)
7. Ability to make an evaluative judgment

Multiple-choice test items illustrating each of these categories are presented in Exhibit 5–4.

Items belonging to the first category always designate a term to be defined or otherwise identified. Items dealing with facts and principles are based on descriptive statements of the way things are. If the question asks, Who? What? When? or Where? it tests a person's factual information. Items testing explanations usually involve the words *why* or *because*, while items belonging to the fourth category require the student to use mathematical processes to get from the given to the required quantities. Items that belong in both categories 5 and 6 are based on descriptions of specific situations. "Prediction" items specify all of the conditions and ask for the future result, whereas "action" items specify some of the conditions and ask what other conditions (or actions) will lead to a specified result. In judgment items the response options are statements whose appropriateness or quality is to be judged on the basis of criteria specified in the item stem.

The usefulness of these categories in the classification of items testing various aspects of achievement depends on the fact that they are defined mainly in terms of overt item characteristics rather than in terms of pre-

[9] Edward L. Thorndike, "The Nature, Purposes, and General Methods of Measurement of Educational Products," in *The Measurement of Educational Products*, part II, Seventeenth Yearbook of the National Society for the Study of Education (1918), p. 160.

EXHIBIT 5–4. MULTIPLE-CHOICE ITEMS INTENDED TO TEST VARIOUS ASPECTS OF ACHIEVEMENT

I. *Understanding of terminology*
   A. The term *fringe benefits* has been used frequently in recent years in connection with labor contracts. What does the term mean?
      1. Incentive payments for above-average output
      2. Rights of employees to draw overtime pay at higher rates
      3. Rights of employers to share in the profits from inventions of their employees
      *4. Such considerations as paid vacations, retirement plans, and health insurance
   B. What is the technical definition of the term *production*?
      1. Any natural process producing food or other raw materials
      *2. The creation of economic values
      3. The manufacture of finished products
      4. The operation of a profit-making enterprise

II. *Knowledge of fact and principle*
   A. What principle is utilized in radar?
      1. Faint electronic radiations of far-off objects can be detected by supersensitive receivers.
      *2. High-frequency radio waves are reflected by distant objects.
      3. All objects emit infrared rays, even in darkness.
      4. High-frequency radio waves are not transmitted equally by all substances.
   B. The most frequent source of conflict between the western and eastern parts of the United States during the course of the nineteenth century was:
      *1. The issue of currency inflation
      2. The regulation of monopolies
      3. Internal improvements
      4. Isolationism vs. internationalism
      5. Immigration

III. *Ability to explain or illustrate*
   A. If a piece of lead suspended from one arm of a beam balance is balanced with a piece of wood suspended from the other arm, why is the balance lost if the system is placed in a vacuum?
      1. The mass of the wood exceeds the mass of the lead.
      2. The air exerts a greater buoyant force on the lead than on the wood.
      3. The attraction of gravity is greater for the lead than for the wood when both are in a vacuum.
      *4. The wood displaces more air than the lead.
   B. Should merchants and middlemen be classified as producers or nonproducers? Why?
      1. As nonproducers, because they make their living off producers and consumers
      2. As producers, because they are regulators and determiners of price
      *3. As producers, because they aid in the distribution of goods and bring producer and consumer together
      4. As producers, because they assist in the circulation of money

IV. *Ability to calculate*
   A. If the radius of the earth were increased by three feet, its circumference at the equator would be increased by about how much?
      1. 9 feet   *3. 19 feet
      2. 12 feet   4. 28 feet
   B. What is the standard deviation of this set of five measures—1, 2, 3, 4, 5?
      1. 1   4. $\sqrt{10}$
      *2. $\sqrt{2}$ 5. None of these
      3. 9

EXHIBIT 5–4. (Continued)

V. Ability to predict

   A. If an electric refrigerator is operated with the door open in a perfectly insulated sealed room, what will happen to the temperature of the room?
     *1. It will rise slowly.
     2. It will remain constant.
     3. It will drop slowly.
     4. It will drop rapidly.

   B. What would happen if the terminals of an ordinary household light bulb were connected to the terminals of an automobile storage battery?
     1. The bulb would light to its natural brilliance.
     *2. The bulb would not glow, though some current would flow through it.
     3. The bulb would explode.
     4. The battery would go dead in a few minutes.

VI. Ability to recommend appropriate action

   A. Which of these practices would probably contribute *least* to reliable grades from essay examinations?
     *1. Weighting the items so that the student receives more credit for answering correctly more difficult items.
     2. Advance preparation by the rater of a correct answer to each question.
     3. Correction of one question at a time through all papers.
     4. Concealment of student names from the rater.

   B. "None of these" is an appropriate response for a multiple-choice test item in cases where:
     1. The number of possible responses is limited to two or three.
     *2. The responses provide absolutely correct or incorrect answers.
     3. A large variety of possible responses might be given.
     4. Guessing is apt to be a serious problem.

VII. Ability to make an evaluative judgment

   A. Which one of the following sentences is most appropriately worded for inclusion in an impartial report resulting from an investigation of a wage policy in a certain locality?
     1. The wages of the working people are fixed by the one businessman who is the only large employer in the locality.
     2. Since one employer provides a livelihood for the entire population in the locality, he properly determines the wage policy for the locality.
     3. Since one employer controls the labor market in the locality, his policy may not be challenged.
     *4. In this locality, where there is only one large employer of labor, the wage policy of this employer is really the wage policy of the locality.

   B. Which of the following quotations has most of the characteristics of conventional poetry?
     1. "I never saw a purple cow;
        I never hope to see one."
     *2. "Announced by all the trumpets of the sky
        Arrives the snow and blasts his ramparts high."
     3. "Thou art blind and confined,
        While I am free for I can see."
     4. "In purple prose his passion he betrayed
        For verse was difficult.
        Here he never strayed."

sumed mental processes required for successful response. The appropriate proportion of questions in each category will vary from course to course, but the better tests tend to be those with heavier emphasis on application of knowledge than on mere ability to reproduce its verbal representations. But since it is more difficult to write good application questions than reproduction questions, unless test constructors decide in advance what proportion of the questions should relate to each specified aspect of achievement, and carry out this decision, they may produce unbalanced tests.

COMPLEX OR EFFICIENT TASKS?

In recent years achievement tests have tended toward the use of complex tasks, often based on descriptions of real or imagined situations or requiring the interpretation of data, diagrams, or background information. A variety of complex test items is illustrated in a publication of the Educational Testing Service[10] as well as in the *Taxonomy of Educational Objectives*.[11] Some examples of complex items of this type are described in Exhibit 5–5.

There are several reasons for this trend. Since these tasks obviously call for the *use* of knowledge, they provide an answer to critics who assert that objective questions test only recognition of isolated factual details. Further, since the situations and background materials used in the tasks are complex, the items presumably require the examinee to use higher

EXHIBIT 5–5. DESCRIPTIONS OF COMPLEX ITEMS

---

1. The item begins with a description of a dispute among baseball players, team owners, and Social Security officials over off-season unemployment compensation for the players. Examinees are asked whether the players are justified in their demands, not justified, or whether they need more information before deciding. Then, they are asked whether each one of a series of statements about the case supports their judgment, opposes it, or leaves them unable to say.

    (Taxonomy, pp. 196–97)

2. An unusual chemical reaction is described. Examinees are asked to consider which of a series of possible hypotheses about the reaction is tenable and how the tenable hypotheses might be tested.

    (Taxonomy, pp. 183–84)

3. Examinees are given a chart on which the expenditures of a state for various purposes over a period of years have been graphed. Then, given a series of statements about the chart, they are asked to judge how much truth there is in each.

    (Taxonomy, pp. 118–19)

---

[10] Test Development Division, ETS, *Multiple-Choice Questions: A Close Look* (Princeton, N.J.: Educational Testing Service, 1963).
[11] Bloom et al., *Taxonomy of Educational Objectives, Handbook I: Cognitive Domain*.

mental processes. Finally, the items are attractive to those who believe that education should be concerned with developing a student's ability to think rather than mere command of knowledge (as if knowledge and thinking were independent attainments!).

However, these complex tasks have some undesirable features as test items. Because they tend to be bulky and time-consuming, they limit the number of responses examinees can make per hour of testing time, that is, the size of the sample of observable behaviors. Hence, because of reduced reliability, tests composed of complex tasks tend to be inefficient in terms of accuracy of measurement per hour of testing.

Further, the more complex the situation, and the higher the level of mental process required to make some judgment about it, the more difficult it becomes to defend any one answer as the best answer. Complex test items tend to discriminate poorly. They also tend to be inordinately difficult, unless the examiner manages to ask a very easy question about a complex problem situation. Even the strongest advocates of complex situational or interpretive test items do not claim that good items of this type are easy to write.

The inefficiency of these items, the uncertainty of the best answer, and the difficulty of writing good ones could all be tolerated if the complex items did, in fact, measure more important aspects of achievement than can be measured by simpler types. However, there is no good evidence that this is the case. A simple question like, "Will you marry me?" can have the most profound consequences. It can provide a lifetime's crucial test of the wisdom of the man who asks it and of the woman who answers.

It would be a mistake in testing to pursue efficiency wherever it may lead, for it may lead to testing only vocabulary and simple word associations, and these are inadequate for testing all the dimensions of command of knowledge. It is equally a mistake to value the appearance of complexity for its own sake. If the complex item tests a genuinely important achievement that is within the grasp of most students and that cannot be tested in any simpler way, then retain it. If not, seek some other important achievement or seek to test it more simply.

CONTENT TO BE COVERED BY THE TEST

An area of information or an ability is appropriate to use as the basis for an objective test item in a classroom test if it has been given specific attention in instruction. Emphasis in an achievement test on things that were not taught or assigned for learning is hard to justify.

One approach to defining the appropriate universe for sampling is to list as topics, in as much detail as seems reasonable, the areas of knowledge and abilities toward which instruction was directed. In the simplest case, where instruction is based on a single text, section headings in the textbook may provide a satisfactory list of such topics. If sections are regarded as about equal in importance, and if there are n times as many of them as of items needed for the test, the instructor might systematically sample every nth topic as the basis for a test item.

If the various sections of the text are not reasonably equal in importance or if no single text provided the basis for teaching, instructors may wish to create their own list of topics. Perhaps separate lists of vocabulary items, items of information, and topics involving explanation, applications, calculation, or prediction may be required. This last approach may make it easier to maintain the desired balance among the several aspects of achievement. Illustrative portions of lists of topics for various aspects of achievement are shown in Exhibit 5-6.

LEVEL AND DISTRIBUTION OF DIFFICULTY

There are two ways in which this problem can be approached. One is to include in the test only those problems or questions that any student who has studied successfully should be able to answer. If this is done, most of the students can be expected to answer the majority of the questions correctly. Put somewhat differently, so many correct answers are likely to be given that many of the questions will not be very effective in discrimi-

EXHIBIT 5–6. ILLUSTRATIVE PORTIONS OF TOPIC LISTS FOR A TEST ON CLASSROOM TESTING*

List A—Vocabulary
1. Aptitude test
2. Bimodal distribution
3. Composite score
4. Expectancy table
5. Factor analysis

List B—Knowledge
1. Achievement quotients
2. Types of test items
3. Essay tests
4. Kuder-Richardson formulas
5. Educational uses of tests

List C—Explanation
1. Correction for attenuation
2. Use of standard scores
3. Cross validation
4. Separate answer sheet
5. Guessing correction formula

List D—Application
1. Reporting scores
2. Test selection
3. Sources of information
4. Judging test quality
5. Item writing

List E—Calculation
1. Mean
2. Index of item difficulty
3. Index of item discrimination
4. Percentile rank
5. Reliability coefficient

* All of these lists are merely illustrative; each could include many more items.

nating among various levels of achievement—best, good, average, weak, and poor.

The other approach is to choose questions on the basis of their ability to reveal different levels of achievement among the students tested. This requires preference for somewhat harder questions. The ideal difficulty for these items would be at a point on the difficulty scale midway between zero difficulty (100 percent correct response) and chance level difficulty (50 percent correct for true-false items, 25 percent correct for four-alternative multiple-choice items). This means that the proportion of correct responses to an ideal true-false item would be about 75 percent and to an ideal multiple-choice item about 62.5 percent. This second approach will generally yield more reliable scores for the same amount of testing time, but it may be viewed with apprehension by the majority of students. Also, such a procedure does not readily yield a minimum standard of competence (passing score).

Some instructors believe that a good test includes some difficult questions to "test" the better students and some easy questions for the poorer students. This belief might be easier to justify if each new unit of study in a course or each new idea required the mastery of all preceding units and ideas presented in the course. In such a course students would differ in how far they had successfully progressed through it rather than in how many separate ideas they had grasped.

However, few courses illustrate such perfect sequences of units and ideas. A student who has missed some of the early ideas or done poorly in the first units of study will usually be handicapped in later study, but the sequence of development is seldom so rigidly fixed that early lapses or deficiencies preclude later progress. Foreign language courses and courses in some branches of mathematics and engineering show more sequential dependence than those in other areas, but even here the dependence is far from absolute.

In most courses of study, the difference between good and poor students is less in how far they have gone than in how many things they have learned to know and to do. Unless the class is extremely heterogeneous and the test extremely reliable, there is no need to vary the difficulty of the questions on purpose. Theoretical analyses and experimental studies demonstrate quite convincingly that in most situations questions that are neither very difficult nor very easy are best. Richardson, for example, found that

> . . . a test composed of items of 50 percent difficulty has a general validity which is higher than tests composed of items of any other degree of difficulty.[12]

---

[12] Marion W. Richardson, "The Relation Between the Difficulty and the Differential Validity of a Test," *Psychometrika*, 1 (1936), 33–49.

And Gulliksen concluded on the basis of a theoretical analysis that

> in order to maximize the reliability and variance of a test the items should have high intercorrelations, all items should be of the same difficulty level, and the level should be as near 50 percent as possible.[13]

PRESENTING THE TEST TO THE STUDENTS

Objective tests are almost always presented to students in printed booklets. Some careful attention to legibility and attractiveness in the arrangement and typing of the copy is usually well worthwhile. The use of separate answer sheets greatly simplifies scoring without adding seriously to the student's problem of response.

As illustrated in Exhibit 5–7, listing responses to multiple-choice items rather than arranging them in tandem makes the student's task easier. Considerable space can be saved if multiple-choice items are printed in double columns rather than across the page. Designation of alternatives by number is simple and convenient, unless many items include small-digit responses that might be confused with response numbers. In this case letters probably should be used.

If time limits for the test are generous, as they usually should be for achievement tests, the order of presentation of the items has little effect on student scores, as shown by Sax and Cromack.[14] If time is restricted, the items probably should be arranged in order of increasing difficulty. It is reasonable to suppose that to begin a test with one or two easy questions would help to lessen excessive test anxiety. It also seems reasonable to group together items that deal with the same area of subject matter. However, empirical evidence that these practices improve the validity of the test scores is difficult to obtain.

EXHIBIT 5–7. A COMPARISON OF LISTED AND TANDEM RESPONSES

Listed	Tandem
What does religious tolerance mean?	What does religious tolerance mean? (1) Making
1. Making all people belong to one church	all people belong to one church. (2) Believing
2. Believing everything in the Bible	everything in the Bible. (3) Believing in science
3. Believing in science instead of the church	instead of the church. (4) Allowing people to be-
*4. Allowing people to believe what they wish	lieve what they wish.

[13] Harold Gulliksen, "The Relation of Item Difficulty and Inter-item Correlation to Test Variance and Reliability," *Psychometrika*, 10 (1945), 79–91.

[14] Gilbert Sax and Theodore R. Cromack, "The Effects of Various Forms of Item Arrangements on Test Performance," *Journal of Educational Measurement*, 3 (1966), 309–11.

Oral presentation of true-false items can be reasonably satisfactory, but other item forms may be too complex for this means. Some instructors have been well satisfied with the projection of objective test items on a screen in a partly darkened room. The cost of slides or filmstrips may be less than that of paper and printing, and they may be more convenient to prepare. Further, problems associated with differences among students in rate of work will be largely eliminated. Experiments have shown that most students can be paced to respond to objective test items more quickly than they do when working at their own rates, with no decrease in accuracy of response.

On the other hand, there are some obvious drawbacks to test administration by visual projection. Students' attention is not so firmly fixed on their own answer sheet. The job of the test administrator is more tedious and limiting. There must be enough light to facilitate marking the answer sheets, but not so much as to make reading the projected test item difficult. Finally, make-up examinations present a serious problem with projected tests. Hence it seems likely that most objective tests will continue to be presented in printed form.

Open-book examinations, in which the examinees are permitted to bring and use textbooks, references, and class notes, have attracted some interest and attention from instructors and educational research workers. Instructors have seen in them a strong incentive for students to study for ability to use knowledge rather than for ability simply to remember it. Such examinations also encourage instructors to eschew recall-type test questions in favor of interpretation and application types. In this light there is much to be said in favor of the open-book examination. On the other hand, students soon learn that the books and notes they bring with them to class are likely to provide more moral than informational support. Looking up facts or formulas may take away from valuable problem-solving time.

Stalnaker and Stalnaker reported favorably on experiences with open-book examinations in Chicago.[15] Tussing, at El Camino College, listed a number of reasons in support of this type of examination:[16]

1. Open-book tests can be constructed and used in all the traditional test forms—essay, multiple-choice, true-false, and so forth.
2. Fear and emotional blocking are reduced.
3. There is less emphasis on memory of facts than on practical problems and reasoning.
4. Cheating is eliminated.
5. The approach is adaptable to the measurement of student attitudes.

[15] John M. Stalnaker and Ruth C. Stalnaker, "Open Book Examinations: Results," *Journal of Higher Education*, 6 (1935), 214–16.
[16] Lyle Tussing, "A Consideration of the Open-Book Examination," *Educational and Psychological Measurement*, 11 (1951), 597–602.

An experimental comparison of scores on the same multiple-choice examination, administered as an open-book test in one section and as a closed-book test in another section of the same course in child psychology, was reported by Kalish.[17] He concluded that although "the group average scores are not affected by the examination approach, the two types of examinations measure significantly different abilities." Kalish also suggested some possible disadvantages of the open-book examination:

1. Study efforts may be reduced.
2. Efforts to overlearn sufficiently to achieve full understanding may be discouraged.
3. Note-passing and copying from other students are less obvious.
4. More superficial knowledge is encouraged.

The take-home test has some of the same characteristics as the open-book test, with two important differences. On the pro side is removal of the pressure of time, which often defeats the very purpose of a classroom open-book test. The disadvantage is the loss of assurance that the answers students submit represent their own achievements. For this reason the take-home test often functions better as a learning exercise than as an achievement test. Students may be permitted, even encouraged, to collaborate in seeking answers in which they have confidence. The efforts they sometimes put forth and the learning they sometimes achieve under these conditions can be a pleasant surprise to the instructor. But the take-home test must be scored and the scores must count in order to achieve this result. And, as with any effective testing procedure, the correct answers should be reported to the students, with opportunity for them to question and discuss. One precaution: it is especially hazardous to use a take-home test of low or unknown quality. Student cross-examination can be devastating.

SUMMARY

The principal ideas developed in this chapter may be summarized in 13 statements:

1. The form of a test gives no certain indication of the ability tested.
2. Multiple-choice and true-false items can be used to measure any aspect of cognitive educational achievement.
3. Other item types have more limited usefulness, but may be advantageous in certain circumstances.

[17] Richard A. Kalish, "An Experimental Evaluation of the Open-Book Examination," *Journal of Educational Psychology*, 49 (1958), 200–204.

4. Whatever form of test or type of item is chosen, test constructors should seek to make their measurements as objective as possible.
5. Most classroom tests of achievement should be short enough, in relation to the time available, so that virtually all students have time to attempt all items.
6. All questions that ask Who? What? When? or Where? are properly classified as factual information questions.
7. Most good true-false items are tests of ability to apply information.
8. Items intended to test various aspects of achievement can ordinarily be classified more reliably on the basis of overt item characteristics than on the basis of the mental processes they presumably require.
9. Situational or interpretive test items tend to be inefficient, difficult to write, sometimes hard to defend, and unconvincing as measures of the higher mental processes.
10. An outline of topics dealt with in instruction provides a useful basis for developing test items that will sample the desired achievement representatively.
11. In most tests of achievement, the items that contribute the greatest amount of useful information are those on which the proportion of correct response is halfway between 100 percent and the expected chance proportion.
12. Objective classroom tests usually are, and should be, presented in printed test booklets.
13. The most crucial decision the test constructor must make is what to test.

PROJECTS AND PROBLEMS

Project: Development of a Test Plan

Draw up detailed plans for an important test, such as an hour-long final test, or an important series of shorter tests in elementary reading or arithmetic in a substantial paper (1000-1500 words). Organize the paper around the following headings:

1. *Identity of the Test.* Give the proposed test title, so as to indicate the subject, grade level, and type of test (for example, achievement, aptitude, diagnosis).
2. *Purpose of the Test.* Here state the purpose of the test and defend its educational value. Do not attempt the impossible or even the unlikely of attainment, but show some commitment to excellence in education.
3. *Type and Number of Test Questions.* Identify the type or types of

questions (for example, essay, short answer, true-false, multiple-choice) to be used, and the number of each. Defend your choices on the basis of item characteristics in relation to the purposes of the test and the time available.

4. *Abilities to be Measured.* What will be your criteria of relevance for the test items? What item content will you approve (understanding, problem solving, explanation, application, and so forth) or disapprove (rote memory, verbal recall, general intelligence, testwiseness). Defend your decisions. Provide one or two illustrations of each of the various kinds of items you plan to use.

5. *Content to be Covered.* Present a content outline and justify it.

This assignment will be graded for completeness and quality. Instructors will not second-guess your decisions unless they are clearly wrong. They are more interested in the value of this activity as a learning exercise—in the questions it causes you to ask and answer—than in its limited values as a measure of your competence. However, since it involves a substantial amount of work, do not let sloppy appearance detract from its apparent worth.

The teacher who, without experience or technical training, has endeavored to use objective tests for his own class has often been dissatisfied with the results and rightly so.... Nearly every teacher, however, considers himself fully capable of setting a satisfactory essay test in his own course or subject, and of reading the answers at least to his own satisfaction.... Norms, correlations, reader or test reliability, and validity do not worry the teacher. If he knows what they are, he ignores them in dealing with his own classroom situation. The popularity of the essay question should not, therefore, be misinterpreted to indicate that it is the most suitable form for many purposes, that it is in a "healthy" condition, or that improvements are not needed.

JOHN M. STALNAKER

6

Essay Tests

POPULARITY OF ESSAY TESTS

Essay tests continue to be a very popular form, especially among scholars and at the higher levels of education. Their history of usage dates back earlier than 2300 B.C. in ancient China, and until the turn of the century they were about the only form of written examination in wide use. Thus they have the sanction of tradition.[1]

However, there are other reasons for their popularity. One is convenience. In contrast with objective tests, essay tests are relatively easy to prepare—the difficult part of the job is usually grading students' answers. Another is the security they provide to the examiner. Writers of essay questions are seldom required, as are composers of objective test items, to defend the "correct" answer or to demonstrate that none of the "wrong" answers is as good as the correct answer. Essay questions require the student to create an explicit answer that the scorer can rate without describing the basis of any rating scale or producing his or her own version of an ideal answer. Thus the deficiencies of an essay question are seldom so readily available for observation as are those of an objective test item.

It is also quite easy for the grader of an essay test to control the

---

[1] William E. Coffman, "Essay Examinations," in *Educational Measurement*, ed. Robert L. Thorndike (Washington, D.C.: American Council on Education, 1971).

general level and distribution of scores. Whether the examiner allows no points, five points, or even seven points for a seriously inadequate answer is a matter of personal decision. Thus, no matter how inappropriate the level of difficulty of an essay test, the grader can adjust the standards so some—but not too many—will receive scores below some preset minimum passing score. The fact that test item difficulty is not a crucial factor contributes in no small measure to the popularity of the essay test.

VALUE OF ESSAY TESTS

Those who argue for essay tests and against objective tests usually do so on the ground that essay tests provide a better indication of students' real achievements in learning. Students are not given ready-made answers but must have command of an ample store of knowledge that enables them to relate facts and principles, to organize them into a coherent and logical progression, and then to do justice to these ideas in written expression. Recall is, of course, involved in the composition of an answer to an essay test question, but it would be a gross oversimplification to characterize an essay test as simply a measure of recall.

Further, the answers given to an essay test question can often provide clues to the nature and quality of students' thought processes. Some writers of essay test questions occasionally deliberately choose indeterminate issues as the basis for their questions. What the student concludes, they say, is unimportant. The evidence on which the examinee bases the conclusion and the cogency of his or her arguments in support of it are said to be all-important.

Many of the traits that essay tests have been said to measure, such as critical thinking, originality, and ability to organize and integrate, are not at all clearly defined. Those characteristics of the answers that serve to indicate which students have more and which have less of these traits are seldom set forth explicitly. When the scores awarded to essay test answers are explained or defended, deductions from a maximum possible score are usually attributed to some combination of these deficiencies:

1. Incorrect statements were included in the answer.
2. Important ideas necessary to an adequate answer were omitted.
3. Correct statements having little or no relation to the question were included.
4. Unsound conclusions were reached, either because of mistakes in reasoning or because of misapplication of principles.
5. Bad writing obscured the development and exposition of the student's ideas.

6. There were egregious errors in spelling and the mechanics of correct writing.

Mistakes in the first four categories can be attributed either to weaknesses in the student's command of knowledge or to lack of clarity and specificity in the examiner's question. Mistakes in the last two categories either indicate a weakness in written self-expression or reflect the difficulties of the hand in keeping up with a mind racing ahead under the pressure of a time limit. As essay tests are typically used, the unique functions they have that are beyond the scope of objective tests seem somewhat limited and indefinite. Odell's scales for rating essay test answers suggest strongly that the length of a student's answer may be closely related to the score it receives.[2] Longer answers tend to receive higher ratings.

Effect on Study

That the nature of the examination expected affects the preparation students make for it is attested by experience, reason, and research.[3] Surveys of student opinion conducted about 30 years ago suggest that students then studied more thoroughly in preparation for essay examinations than for objective examinations. More recent evidence is scanty and inconclusive.

With respect to the influence of examinations on study, the really important question is not how students say they study for examinations of different kinds—or even how they actually do study—but how these differences affect their achievement. In the absence of adequate research, we venture to make the following inferences:

1. The kind of study and achievement that a test stimulates is probably more a function of the kind of questions asked than of the mode of student response.
2. To the degree that tests in different forms measure the same kinds or aspects of achievement, they should stimulate the same kind of study and have the same effect on achievement.

Many potent factors other than examinations affect how and with what success students study. These factors interact in complex ways to

[2] Charles W. Odell, *Scales for Rating Pupils' Answers to Nine Types of Thought Questions in English Literature* (Urbana, Ill.: University of Illinois, Bureau of Educational Research, 1927).

[3] George Meyer, "An Experimental Study of the Old and New Types of Examination: II, Methods of Study," *Journal of Educational Psychology*, 26 (1935), 30–40; and Paul W. Terry, "How Students Review for Objective and Essay Tests," *Elementary School Journal*, 33 (1933), 592–603.

facilitate or to inhibit learning. The chances are small, therefore, that research will ever demonstrate clearly which form of examination, essay or objective, has the more beneficial influence on study and learning.

Essay Tests and Writing Ability

Essay tests are also valued for the emphasis they place on writing. However, this is both an advantage and a disadvantage. Written expression is an important skill that essay tests do encourage. However, the practice that essay tests give in writing may be practice in *bad* writing—hasty, ill considered, and unpolished. Worse, skill in writing, or lack of it, may influence the scorer's judgment regarding the content of the answer. Uniform, legible handwriting and fluent, graceful sentences can compensate for some deficiencies in content. On the other hand, flaws in spelling, grammar, or usage can detract from the scorer's evaluation of the content.

Students occasionally use writing skill to compensate for lack of knowledge. Students who are hard put to answer adequately the question asked can transform it subtly into a related question that is easier for them to answer. If they perform well on the substitute task, the reader may not even notice the substitution. Or the student may concentrate on form rather than on content, on elegant presentation of a few rather simple ideas, in the hope that this may divert the reader's attention from the lack of substantial content.

Not all readers of essay examinations are easy to bluff. Then, too, students likely to be most in need of the kind of assistance that bluffing might give them are usually the least able to use such techniques. For this reason, bluffing on essay tests is hardly more serious a problem than guessing one's way to success on an objective test.

Reliability

The most serious limitation of essay tests as measures of achievement in classroom settings is the low reliability of the scores they typically yield. Low reliability means that there is a good deal of inconsistency between scores obtained from successive administrations of the same test or equivalent tests, or from independent scorings of the same test. On the whole, three conditions are responsible for this low reliability: (1) the limited sampling of the content covered by the test; (2) the indefiniteness of the tasks set by the essay questions; and (3) the subjectivity of the scoring of essay answers.

In general, the larger the number of independent elements in the sample of tasks chosen for an achievement test, the more accurately performance on those tasks will reflect overall achievement in the field. It is true that the answer to a complex essay test question often involves many separate elements of achievement. Yet they are dealt with as a more or less integrated whole by both the student and the grader, not as independent elements.

Few, if any, experimental studies of the sampling reliability of essay tests relative to that of objective tests have been made. The difficulty of obtaining sufficiently objective scoring of essay test answers may be part of the reason. But there have been some theoretical analyses of the problem. Ruch has proven a direct relation between the extensiveness of the sample of tasks in a test and the precision with which different levels of achievement can be differentiated.[4] Posey's charts (p. xxx) show that examinees' luck, or lack of it, in being asked what they happen to know is a much greater factor in the grade they receive in a 10-question test than in one of 100 questions.[5]

On many essay test questions, the task, and the basis for judging an examinee's success in completing it are not clearly specified. Essay questions *can* be explicit, they can guide students to produce those answers that will signify achievements. Often, however, they do not. Similarly, scoring directions can be written in a concise, easy-to-follow manner. Again, they often fall short of the mark. The more detailed and explicit the directions to both student and scorer, the more objective and reliable the measurements obtainable from an essay test question.

The classic studies of Starch and Elliott exposed the appallingly wide variations in the grades that typical teachers assigned to the same student's answers to questions in geometry, literature, and history.[6] Later studies confirmed these findings in other contexts.[7] Thus, although it has been elsewhere shown that essay test answers can be graded reliably when the job is done under careful supervision, the fact that essay tests typically yield highly subjective and unreliable measures of achievement was established beyond dispute.

The score on any test is a means of communicating and recording a measurement or an evaluation. It is useful only insofar as it is meaningful. It must mean something to the person who determined it, not only at the moment of determination, but days or weeks later. It must mean as nearly as possible the same thing to the student who receives it as it did to the teacher who assigned it. To the degree that other qualified observers would

---

[4] G. M. Ruch, *The Objective or New-type Examination* (Glenview, Ill.: Scott, Foresman and Company, 1929), p. 56.

[5] Chesley Posey, "Luck and Examination Grades," *Journal of Engineering Education,* 23 (1932), 292–96.

[6] Daniel Starch and E. C. Elliott, "Reliability of Grading High School Work in English," *School Review,* 20 (September 1912), 442–57; ". . . in Mathematics," *School Review,* 21 (April 1913), 254–59; ". . . in History," *School Review,* 21 (December 1913), 676–81.

[7] D. S. Finlayson, "The Reliability of the Marking of Essays," *British Journal of Educational Psychology,* 21 (1951) 126–34; and P. E. Vernon and G. D. Millican, "A Further Study of the Reliability of English Essays," *British Journal of Statistical Psychology,* 7 (1954) 65–74.

assign different scores, the measurement lacks objectivity and hence utility. Measurements of school achievement, like other reports, must be trustworthy in order to be useful. To be trustworthy means that they are capable of independent verification. If the same teacher were to assign totally different scores to the same essay test answer on different occasions—or if different teachers were to disagree in the same way—our confidence in the scores would be shaken and their usefulness seriously diminished.

COMPARISON OF ESSAY AND OBJECTIVE TESTS

The following statements summarize some of the similarities and differences of essay and objective tests.

1. Either an essay or an objective test can be used to measure almost any important educational achievement that any written test can measure.
2. Either an essay or an objective test can be used to encourage students to study for understanding of principles, organization and integration of ideas, and application of knowledge to the solution of problems.
3. The use of either type necessarily involves the exercise of subjective judgment.
4. The value of scores from either type of test is dependent on their objectivity and reliability.
5. An essay test question requires students to plan their own answers and to express them in their own words. An objective test item requires examinees to choose among several designated alternatives.
6. An essay test consists of relatively few, more general questions that call for rather extended answers. An objective test ordinarily consists of many rather specific questions requiring only brief answers.
7. Students spend most of their time in thinking and writing when taking an essay test. They spend most of their time reading and thinking when taking an objective test.
8. The quality of an objective test is determined largely by the skill of the test constructor. The quality of an essay test is determined largely by the skill of the test scorer.
9. An essay examination is relatively easy to prepare but rather tedious and difficult to score accurately. A good objective examination is relatively tedious and difficult to prepare but comparatively easy to score.

10. An essay examination affords students much freedom to express their individuality in the answers they give and much freedom for the examiner to be guided by his or her individual preferences in scoring the answer. An objective examination affords much freedom for the test constructor to express personal knowledge and values but allows students only the freedom to show, by the proportion of correct answers they give, how much or how little they know or can do.
11. In objective test items the student's task and the basis on which the examiner will judge the degree to which it has been accomplished are stated more clearly than they are in essay tests.
12. An objective test permits, and occasionally encourages, guessing. An essay test permits, and occasionally encourages, bluffing.
13. The distribution of numerical scores obtained from an essay test can be controlled to a considerable degree by the grader; that from an objective test is determined almost entirely by the examination itself.

When to Use Essay Tests

Use essay tests in the measurement of educational achievement when:

1. The group to be tested is small, and the test will not be reused.
2. The instructor wishes to encourage to the fullest the development of student skill in written expression.
3. The instructor is more interested in exploring student attitudes than in measuring achievements. (Whether instructors *should* be more interested in attitudes than achievement and whether they should expect an honest expression of attitudes in a test situation seem open to question.)
4. The instructor is more confident of his or her proficiency as a critical reader than as an imaginative writer of good objective test items.
5. Time available for test preparation is shorter than time available for test grading.

Essay tests have important uses in educational measurement. They also have serious limitations. It would be well for all teachers to be on guard against unsubstantiated claims that essay tests can measure undefined and only vaguely perceived "higher-order mental abilities." They ought also to question the propriety of using essay tests to determine how well students can do what the instructor has not really tried to teach them to do—to analyze, to synthesize, to organize, to develop original ideas and to express them with clarity, grace, wit, and correctness. Above all, they ought to avoid using an essay test when an objective test could do the job better and more easily.

SUGGESTIONS FOR PREPARING ESSAY TESTS

Implicit in what has been said in this chapter about the values and limitations of essay tests are a number of suggestions for improving essay-type questions.

1. Ask questions or set tasks that will require the student to demonstrate a command of essential knowledge.

Such questions will not simply call for reproduction of materials presented in the textbook or classroom. Instead of looking exclusively backward to the past course of instruction, they will also look forward to future applications of the things learned. The questions will be based on novel situations or problems, not on the same ones used for instructional purposes.

Many different types of questions may be used as the basis for essay test questions. An outline of types of thought questions found in science textbooks has been prepared by Curtis.[8] Similar lists in other subject areas have been prepared by Wesley[9] and by Monroe and Carter.[10]

2. Ask questions that are determinate, in the sense that experts could agree that one answer is better than another.

Indeterminate questions are likely to function in some measure as exercises in exposition, whose relation to effective behavior may be quite remote. Such questions will probably not be especially relevant to the measurement of a student's useful command of essential knowledge. Further, and most importantly, the absence of a good best answer may make it much more difficult for a reader to judge a given student's level of achievement. On controversial questions, which many indeterminate questions are, the reader's opinions and biases may considerably influence any evaluation of the student's answer.

[8] Francis D. Curtis, "Types of Thought Questions in Textbooks of Science," *Science Edu cation,* 27 (1943), 60–67.

[9] Edgar B. Wesley and Stanley P. Wronski, *Teaching Social Studies in High Schools* (4th ed.; Boston: D. C. Heath & Company, 1958), pp. 356–57.

[10] Walter S. Monroe and Ralph E. Carter, *The Use of Different Types of Thought Questions in Secondary Schools and Their Relative Difficulty for Students,* University of Illinois Bulletin, Vol. 20, No. 34 (April 13, 1923).

3. Define the examinee's task as completely and specifically as possible without interfering with measurement of the achievement intended.

The question should be carefully phrased so that examinees fully understand what they are expected to do. If the task is not clearly evident in the question itself, add an explanation of the basis on which answers will be evaluated. Do not allow students more freedom than is necessary to measure the desired achievement. If the question permits variation in the extent and detail of the answer given but this is not a relevant variable, specify about how long the answer is expected to be.

4. In general, give preference to more specific questions that can be answered more briefly.

The larger the number of independently scorable questions, the higher the sampling reliability of the test is likely to be. Narrower questions are likely to be less ambiguous to the examinee and easier for scorers to grade reliably. Occasionally an instructor may find it necessary to base an essay test on only a few very broad questions. These occasions are not frequent, however, and the instructor should be sure that the need for extended answers is sufficient to warrant the probable loss in score reliability.

5. Avoid giving the examinee a choice among optional questions unless special circumstances make such options necessary.

If different examinees answer different questions, the basis for comparing their scores is weakened. Clearly, when students choose the questions they can answer best, the range of test scores is likely to be narrower— hence the reliability of the scores would be expected to be somewhat less. Research indicates that this expectation is justified.

When college students in psychology were given the choice of omitting one of five essay questions, Meyer found surprisingly that only 58 percent of them omitted the question on which they would do least well. He "suggested that unless the various questions are weighted in some suitable fashion the choice form of essay examination be discontinued."[11] Stalnaker concluded a survey of the problems involved in the use of optional questions with these words:

No experimental evidence has been published to show that skills and

---

[11] George Meyer, "The Choice of Questions on Essay Examinations," *Journal of Educational Psychology,* 30 (1939), 161–71.

abilities can be adequately sampled by the use of optional questions; on the other hand, several studies have shown that optional questions complicate measurement and introduce factors of judgment which are extraneous to the ability being measured. For sound sampling, it is recommended that optional questions be avoided and that all examinees be asked to run the same race.[12]

Optional questions are sometimes justified on the ground that giving students a choice among the questions they are to answer makes the test "fairer." But if all the questions involve essential aspects of achievement in a course (as they ordinarily might), it is not unfair to any student to require answers to all of them. Furthermore, an opportunity to choose among optional questions may help the poorer student considerably, but may actually distract the well-prepared student.

Optional questions may be justifiable when a test of educational achievement must cover a broad area, and when the students who take it have received unequal training in different areas. Even in such a situation, however, the advantage of using optional questions are highly dubious. Optional tests, separately scored, might be preferable to a common test, yielding a single score, based on different sets of questions.

6. Test the question by writing an ideal answer to it.

Writing the ideal answer at the time a question is drafted serves an immediate purpose. It gives the test constructor a check on the reasonableness of the questions and on the adequacy of his/her own understanding. Perhaps some change in the question could make it easier, if that seems desirable, or more discriminating, which is always desirable. Also useful, if it can be arranged, is to have a colleague in the same field try to answer it. Comparison of such ideal answers might shed additional light on the question's suitability and might suggest additional ways of improving it.

The deferred purpose served by drafting an ideal answer to each essay test question is to provide guidance, and a point of reference, for the later scoring of students' answers. If someone other than the instructor is to grade the questions or to help with the grading, the ideal answer is almost indispensable to uniformity in grading.

SUGGESTIONS FOR GRADING ESSAY TESTS

As has been mentioned, the efficacy of essay tests as measures of educational achievement depends primarily on the quality of the grading process. The competence of the grader is crucial to the quality of this process, yet

---

[12] John M. Stalnaker, "The Essay Type of Examination," in *Educational Measurement*, ed. E. F. Lindquist (Washington, D.C.: American Council on Education, 1951), p. 506.

even competent graders may inadvertently do things that make the results less reliable than they ought to be. Here are some suggestions for graders of essay test answers to consider if they are anxious to make their work as precise as possible.

1. Use either analytic scoring or global-quality scaling.

In analytic scoring, crucial elements of the ideal answer are identified and scored more or less separately. The higher the proportion of these crucial elements appearing in the student's answer and the less they are contaminated by inaccuracies or irrelevancies, the higher the student's score. Analytic scoring can pay attention not only to the elements of an ideal answer, but also to relations between these elements, that is, to the organization and integration of the answer. But if these relationships are complex and subtle, analytic scoring may prove to be too cumbersome and tedious to be effective.

An alternative is global-quality scaling. Scorers using this method simply read the answer for a general impression of its adequacy, then transform that impression into a numerical grade, record the grade, and go on to the next answer. A better procedure, which allows the grader to check the consistency of grading standards as applied to different papers, involves the sorting of answers into several piles corresponding to different levels of quality. Sorting before marking permits, even encourages, graders to reconsider their decisions in the light of experience with all the students' answers. It lessens the possibility of giving a higher score to one of two answers which, on rereading, seem to be of equal quality.

As a general rule, global-quality scaling is simpler and faster than analytic scoring. In some situations it may be more reliable. But it does not provide any clear justification of the grade assigned, nor does it give students any indication how their answers fell short of the mark. Analytic scoring can provide such indications. It is well suited to questions that are likely to elicit detailed, uniformly structured answers.

2. Grade the answers question by question rather than student by student.

This means that the grader will read the answers to one question on all students' papers before going on the next question. Such a procedure is obviously required in the global-quality scaling just described. It is also advantageous in analytic scoring, since concentration of attention on one question at a time helps to develop specialized skill and to foster independent judgment in scoring it.[13]

[13] Loyde Hales and Edward Tokar, "The Effect of the Quality of Preceding Responses on the Grades Assigned to Subsequent Responses to an Essay Question," *Journal of Educational Measurement,* 12 (Summer 1975), 115–18.

3. If possible, conceal from the grader the identity of the student whose answer he or she is grading.

The purpose of this procedure is to reduce the possibility that biases or halo effects will influence the scores assigned. Ideally, the answers to different questions would be written on separate sheets of paper, identified only by a code number. These sheets would be arranged into groups by question for the grading process and then recombined by the student for totaling and recording. By this process one can reduce not only the halo effect associated with the student's name and reputation, but also that which might result from high or low scores on preceding answers.

4. If possible, arrange for independent grading of the answers, or at least a sample of them.

Independent grading is the only real check on the objectivity, and hence the reliability, of the grading. Since it is troublesome to arrange and time-consuming to carry out, however, it is seldom likely to be utilized by the classroom teacher. But if a school or college were to undertake a serious program for the improvement of essay examinations, such a study of the reliability of essay test grading would be an excellent way to begin.

To get independent grades, at least two competent readers would have to grade each question, without consulting each other and without knowing what grades the other had assigned. At least 100, preferably 300, answers should be given this double, independent reading. (The answers need not all be to the same question. Reading the answers of 30 students to each of 10 questions would be quite satisfactory.) The correlation between pairs of grades on individual questions would indicate the reliability of the grading procedure. Then the Spearman-Brown formula could be applied to estimate the reliability of grading for the test as a whole (see Chapter 14).

SUMMARY

The main conclusions we can draw from the findings presented in this chapter are summarized in the following 19 propositions:

1. Essay tests have been in use for more than 4,000 years.
2. The popularity of essay tests is partly due to their convenience, the security they provide the examiner, and the control they afford over score distributions.
3. Essay test questions are less vulnerable to criticism than are objective test questions.
4. It is easier for the examiner to control the distribution of essay than of objective test scores.

5. Because an essay question requires the examinee to produce the answer, not just to choose it, some teachers regard it as a better measure of real achievement.

6. An essay test may permit the examiner to assess students' thought processes.

7. Essay tests usually do not provide valid measures of complex mental processes such as critical thinking, originality, or ability to organize and integrate.

8. It is unlikely that students study more effectively in preparation for an essay than for an objective test.

9. The emphasis essay tests place on ability to write is both advantageous and disadvantageous.

10. Essay test questions are vulnerable to student bluffing, but the actual harm this can do is likely to be small.

11. Essay test scores tend to be low in reliability because of limited sampling, indefinite tasks, and subjective scoring.

12. To be useful, essay test scores must possess objective meaning.

13. Essay tests save time when the group to be tested is small.

14. Good essay test questions require the student to demonstrate command of essential knowledge.

15. The reliability of essay test scores can be improved by making the questions specific enough so that all good answers must be nearly identical.

16. Reliability can also usually be improved by asking more questions that call for short answers than by asking fewer questions that call for long answers.

17. Optional questions should be avoided in essay testing.

18. The quality of an essay question can be tested and reliable scoring facilitated by attempting to write an ideal answer to it.

19. The reliability of scoring essay answers can be improved by grading them question by question, by concealing the name of the examinee, and by arranging for several independent gradings.

PROJECTS AND PROBLEMS

Problem: Grading Essay Test Answers

This activity is based on the essay test question, the model answer to that question, and five student answers to the question. Your task is to assign a numerical grade to each student answer, using the scale of grades defined below:

9. Much better than the model
8. Slightly better than the model

7. As good as the model
6. Not quite as good as the model
5. A little more than half as good as the model
4. Half as good as the model
3. Not quite half as good as the model
2. Only slightly correct or relevant
1. Totally incorrect or irrelevant

Make an initial grade decision, paying attention only to the completeness and correctness of the statements made and the absence of irrelevant statements. Then lower the initial grade by a point if ideas are poorly expressed or if there are serious errors in sentence structure, spelling, or punctuation. Write a brief statement explaining the grades you give to each answer. Do not confer with any other student in this class in deciding on these grades. Do not change your grade if you discover that others disagree with you.

A committee will collate the grades and report the distribution of grades assigned to each question. Results may be discussed in class. Later, data from this assignment may be used to demonstrate how the reliability of these grades can be calculated.

A. *The Question:*

Identify and comment on the misconceptions (there are at least five) that surround the problem of guessing on objective tests.

B. *Model Answer:*

A number of misconceptions surround the problem of guessing on objective tests. One is that students are likely to do extensive blind guessing on objective tests. The fact is that well-motivated students taking an examination that is appropriate for them do relatively little blind guessing. Another is that students who guess may, if they are lucky, make a high score on an objective test by blind guessing alone. The fact is that the odds against a high score on a reasonably long objective test are astronomical.

A third misconception is that if an objective test score is corrected for guessing, the effect of luck in guessing is removed or neutralized. The fact is that a correction for guessing hurts the lucky guesser far less than it hurts the unlucky guesser. Another misconception is that students should avoid guessing if the score is to be corrected for guessing. Actually they have the best chance of making a high score by offering an answer to every question, even when the correction is to be applied. Usually an answer will be better than a blind guess. Even if it is not, the penalty is not likely to hurt more than an omission would.

Finally there is the common misconception that guessing involves an element of cheating, with the students trying to get credit for answers they are not sure of. But since the purpose of the test is to measure amount of knowledge, students ought to use all of it they possess to give the best answers they can, even if they are quite uncertain of the correctness of some of them.

C. *Student Answers:*

1. There are many misconceptions that surround the problem of guessing on objective tests. It is some of these misconceptions that will be discussed in this paper.

   One common misconception that surrounds guessing on objective tests is that guessing is not helpful to maintaining a higher grade. We can see that this is truly a misconception because any answer is better than none and the guessed answer could be a right answer.

   Another misconception in this same idea is the view that correction for guessing makes a difference in the score. This is not true because the score is usually the same.

   Another is the psychological advantage.

2. First the chances of doing well on a test by blindly guessing alone are very slim, contrary to popular belief. Secondly, very few guesses are really blind guesses. Uncertainty may exist but some basis exists for the choice. Third, it is not undesirable to encourage students to make educated guesses. Life is full of uncertainties we must learn to cope with. We must often make decisions before all the needed information is available. Fourth, tests corrected for guessing yield results almost identical to those not corrected. Why waste valuable time, unless it be for public relation purposes? Fifth, objective tests are no more subject to "guessing" than are essay tests to "bluffing." Sixth, the better students receive the higher grades regardless of whether the test is corrected for guessing or not.

3. Test-wiseness is one problem surrounding guessing on objective tests. Students who know "how" to take a test can do well even when they aren't familiar with the material being tested if the questions contain specific determiners which give away the answer.

   Rote learning also promotes guessing on exams when application of knowledge is required.

4. One misconception surrounding the problem of guessing on objective tests is that students really do guess blindly. If a student has any information at all about the subject matter, he is not really guessing blindly; he only does that if he marks answers without any regard to the question.

   A second misconception is that guessing (with some information for background) is harmful. A student will often have to make decisions in life on things of which he is not certain. He will often have to use whatever resources he has available to make choices. This is not a harmful thing.

   A third misconception is that one can get a high score by guessing blindly. The longer the test, the smaller the probability that the student will get a high score by true blind guessing.

   A fourth misconception is that a guessing correction really corrects for guessing. When the formula $R - [W/(k - 1)]$ is used, subtractions are being made for all the questions a student missed, even if he was positive the answer was right; in other words, even though the answer was not a guess.

A fifth misconception is that guessing is a large problem in objective tests, making luck more important than knowledge. A student with even a moderate command of the material has a better chance on the questions he must guess on because he is not guessing blindly.

Guessing does not seem to have much of an effect on the reliability of objective test scores.

5. The first misconception surrounding the problem of guessing on objective tests deals with a false assumption. Critics suggest that a correction for guessing assumes that incorrectly answered questions are guessed at blindly by the examinee; this not only is incorrect but it also has no relevance in the use of correction for guessing.

The second misconception deals with the correction for guessing. It is assumed (and sometimes so because of false representation) that guessing on a test—or at least its effects—is eliminated by this correction. Again—not true. Corrected and uncorrected tests correlate highly.

The third misconception assumes that if corrected and uncorrected tests correlate highly then correction for guessing does no good. Perhaps that is so with the correction per se but it has been shown that by telling a class a test will be corrected for guessing (but not necessarily doing this correction) the reliability of the test scores increased. In this sense some good has been done.

The fourth misconception deals with testwiseness. It is assumed that two people knowing absolutely nothing about a subject should both perform at about a chance level. However, a testwise student can pick out specific determiners and irrelevant clues and quite possibly function above the chance level.

The fifth (but not necessarily the last) misconception is that students should never just guess—because it is immoral, or lying, or misrepresentation, etc. Not true! A student might make a good guess based on his basic understanding of the material and justly score better. Actually, not guessing would probably give a less accurate measure of his ability.

7

True-False Test Items

From one point of view, as Linus has observed, true-false tests are easier than they ought to be. From another, as many students would testify, they tend to be unnecessarily, irrelevantly, and frustratingly difficult. Both groups would agree that there are better ways of measuring achievement than by using true-false questions. Yet this attitude of disapproval is not universally shared in educational circles. A few, including the author of this book, regard true-false test items much more favorably.[1]

THE QUALITY OF TRUE-FALSE TEST ITEMS

The basic reason for using true-false test items is that they provide a simple and direct means of measuring the essential outcome of formal education. The argument for the value of true-false items as measures of educational achievement can be summarized in four statements:

1. The essence of educational achievement is the command of useful verbal knowledge.
2. All verbal knowledge can be expressed in propositions.

---

* Text from PEANUTS by Charles M. Schulz © 1968 United Features Syndicate, Inc.
[1] Robert L. Ebel, "Can Teachers Write Good True-False Test Items?" *Journal of Educational Measurement*, 12 (Spring 1975), 31–36.

3. A proposition is any sentence that can be said to be true or false.
4. The extent of students' command of a particular area of knowledge is indicated by their success in judging the truth or falsity of propositions related to it.

We considered and defended the first of these statements in Chapter 3 (see pp. 41–44). The second is almost self-evident. Is it possible to imagine an element of verbal knowledge that could not be expressed as a proposition? The third is a generally accepted definition. The fourth seems to be a logical consequence of the first three. It may, of course, be challenged on the basis of technical weaknesses in true-false items, but it is not likely to be rejected in principle.

To test a person's command of an idea or element of knowledge is to test his or her understanding of it. A student who can recognize an idea only when it is expressed in some particular set of words does not have command of it. Neither does the student who knows the idea only as an isolated fact, without seeing how it is related to other ideas. Knowledge one has command of is not a miscellaneous collection of separate elements, but an integrated structure that one can use to make decisions, draw logical inferences, or solve problems. It is usable knowledge.

Consider how one might test a student's command of Archimedes' Principle. Clearly, to offer the student the usual expression of the principle as a true statement, or some slight alteration of it as a false statement, as has been done in items 1 and 2, is to misunderstand the true nature of knowledge.

(1) A body immersed in a fluid is buoyed up by a force equal to the weight of the fluid displaced.   (T)
(2) A body immersed in a fluid is buoyed up by a force equal to half the weight of the fluid displaced.   (F)

Instead the student might be asked to recognize the principle in some alternative statement of it, as in items 3 and 4 below.

(3) If an object having a certain volume is surrounded by a liquid or gas, the upward force on it equals the weight of that volume of the liquid or gas.   (T)
(4) The upward force on an object surrounded by a liquid or gas is equal to the surface area of the object multiplied by the pressure of the liquid or gas surrounding it.   (F)

Or the student might be required to apply the principle in specific situations such as those described in items 5 and 6 below.

(5) The buoyant force on a one-centimeter cube of aluminum is exactly the same as that on a one-centimeter cube of iron when both are immersed in water.   (T)

(6) If an insoluble object is immersed successively in several fluids of different density, the buoyant force upon it in each case will vary inversely with the density of the fluids. (F)

Sometimes the use of an unconventional example can serve to test understanding of a concept.

(7) Distilled water is soft water. (T)

It is a popular misconception that true-false test items are limited to testing for simple factual recall. On the contrary, complex and difficult problems can be presented quite effectively in this form.

(8) The next term in the series 3, 4, 7, 11, 18 is 29. (T)
(9) If the sides of a quadrilateral having two adjacent right angles are consecutive whole numbers, and if the shortest side is one of the two parallel sides, then the area of the trapezoid is 18 square units. (T)

The reason why true-false tests are often held in low esteem is not that there is anything inherently wrong with the item form. It is rather that the form is often used ineptly by unskilled item writers. It has also been alleged that true-false tests are especially susceptible to guessing and that they have harmful effects on student learning, beliefs that have not been checked against experimental data. These alleged weaknesses of true-false items will be dealt with more fully later in the chapter.

The Efficiency of True-False Tests

In addition to providing intrinsically relevant measures of the essence of educational achievement, true-false test items have the advantage of being quite efficient. The number of independently scorable responses per thousand words of test or per hour of testing time tends to be considerably higher than that for multiple-choice test items. Offsetting this advantage in efficiency is a disadvantage in individual item discriminating power. A single true-false item is likely to reveal somewhat less about educational achievement than a single multiple-choice item. In sum, a good one-hour true-false test is likely to be about as effective as a good one-hour multiple-choice test.

Compared with other item forms, true-false test items are relatively easy to write. They are simple declarative sentences of the kind that make up most oral and written communications. It is true that the ideas they affirm or deny must be judiciously chosen. It is also true that the ideas chosen must be worded carefully, with a view to maximum precision and clarity, since they stand and must be judged in isolation. For this reason they must be self-contained in meaning, depending wholly on internal content, not on external context. But the basic skill involved in true-false item writing is no different from that required in any written communication situation. Those who have difficulty in writing good true-false test items probably have trouble expressing themselves clearly and accurately in writing.

EQUIVALENCE OF TRUE-FALSE AND MULTIPLE-CHOICE ITEMS

An obvious difference between true-false and multiple-choice items is in the number of alternative answer choices offered to the examinee. Another difference is in the definiteness or specificity of the task presented. It may

EXHIBIT 7–1. CORRESPONDING MULTIPLE-CHOICE AND TRUE-FALSE TEST ITEMS

Multiple-Choice Version	True-False Version

1. James wants to put a fence around a garden that is 60 feet long and 45 feet wide. How many feet of fencing will he need?
   a. 90 feet   *c.* 120 feet
   b. 105 feet   **d.* 210 feet
	1*a.* It will take 105 feet of fencing to put a fence around a garden that is 60 feet long and 45 feet wide. (F)
	1*b.* It will take 210 feet of fencing to put a fence around a garden that is 60 feet long and 45 feet wide. (T)

2. The equation $X^2 + Y^2 = 4$ is represented graphically by
  *a. a circle
   b. an ellipse
   c. a parabola with its base on the *X*-axis
	2*a.* The graph of $X^2 + Y^2 = 4$ is a circle. (T)
	2*b.* The graph of $X^2 + Y^2 = 9$ is an ellipse. (F)
	2*c.* The graph of $X^2 + Y^2 = 1$ is a parabola with its base on the *Y*-axis. (F)

3. How can one generate enough electric current to light a flashlight bulb?
   a. By rubbing two good conductors of electricity together
   b. By dipping two strips of zinc in dilute sulphuric acid
   c. By connecting the north pole of a magnet to the south pole, using a coil of wire
  *d. By rotating a coil of wire rapidly near a strong magnet
	3*a.* One can generate enough electric current to light a flashlight bulb by dipping two strips of zinc in dilute sulphuric acid. (F)
	3*b.* One can generate enough electric current to light a flashlight bulb by rotating a coil of wire rapidly near a strong magnet. (T)

4. What does religious tolerance mean?
   a. Admitting everyone to the same church
   b. Accepting religious teachings on faith
   c. Altering religious belief so that it does not conflict with science
  *d. Allowing people to believe what they wish
	4*a.* Religioustolerancemeansadmittingeveryone to the same church. (F)
	4*b.* Religious tolerance means allowing people to believe what they wish. (T)
	4*c.* Religious tolerance means altering religious beliefs so that they do not conflict with science. (F)

be more difficult to judge whether a statement should be called true or false than to judge which of several alternatives is the best answer to a particular question. Apart from these differences, however, there are substantial similarities between true-false and multiple-choice items.

Implicit in most multiple-choice test items are one true statement and several false statements. Like true-false items, multiple-choice items also test knowledge and are based on propositions. When expertly written multiple-choice items are converted to true-false items, and both forms administered to the same large group of examinees, the scores obtained correlate as closely as their reliabilities allow.[2] Exhibit 7–1 displays items testing essentially the same propositions in both multiple-choice and true-false form.

While most multiple-choice test items are based on propositions, a few, like the example which follows, are not.

Which of the following sentences is stated most emphatically?
a. If my understanding of the question is correct, this principle is one we cannot afford to accept.
b. One principle we cannot afford to accept is this one, if my understanding of the question is correct.
c. This principle, if my understanding of the question is correct, is one we cannot afford to accept.
d. This principle is one we cannot afford to accept, if my understanding of the question is correct.

Items of this kind, which involve some degree of personal judgment, are not derived directly from propositions and cannot easily be converted to true-false form.

There are also questions which are much easier to present as true-false than as multiple-choice items, because only two answers are plausible. For example, when one wishes to ask whether two variables are related, or about the effect of increasing one variable on the size of the other, it is almost impossible to find more than two reasonable alternatives. Here are some examples.

(1) Changing the temperature of a mass of air will change its relative humidity. (T)
(2) More amendments were added to the U.S. Constitution during the first ten years after ratification than during the next one hundred years. (T)
(3) An eclipse of the sun can occur only when the moon is full. (F)
(4) Increasing the length of a test is likely to decrease its standard error of measurement. (F)

Commitment to the multiple-choice item form has led some item

---

[2] David A. Frisbie, "Multiple-Choice Versus True-False: A Comparison of Reliabilities and Concurrent Validities," *Journal of Educational Measurement*, 10 (Winter 1973), 297–304.

EXHIBIT 7–2. ITEMS BETTER SUITED TO TRUE-FALSE THAN TO MULTIPLE-CHOICE FORM

Multiple-Choice Version	True-False Version	
1. Which of these is *not* characteristic of a virus?		
a. It can live only in plant and animal cells.	1a. A virus can live only in plant and animal cells.	(T)
b. It can reproduce itself.	1b. A virus can reproduce itself.	(T)
*c. It is composed of very large living cells.	1c. A virus is composed of very large living cells.	(F)
d. It can cause disease.	1d. A virus can cause disease.	(T)
2. Given $\triangle PQR$ with median RS. Which of the following must be true?		
a. RS is prependicular to PQ.	2a. The median of a triangle is perpendicular to the side it intersects.	(F)
b. *RS* bisects ⟨QRP.	2b. The median of a triangle bisects the angle from which it is drawn.	(F)
c. △PQR is a right triangle.	2c. A triangle with a median is a right triangle.	(F)
*d. None of the above.	2d. The median of a triangle divides it into two triangles of equal area.	(T)

writers to present what is essentially a collection of true-false statements as a multiple-choice item. Exhibit 7–2 provides some examples.

Logic suggests and experiment has confirmed that more reliable measures of achievement can be obtained from independently scored true-false items than from multiple-choice items obtained by grouping one true statement with three that are false or by grouping one that is false with three that are true.

GUESSING ON TRUE-FALSE ITEMS

A charge against true-false tests that many take quite seriously is that they are subject to gross error introduced by guessing. Several things can be said in response to this charge.

The first is that a distinction needs to be made between blind guessing and informed guessing. Blind guessing adds nothing but error to the test scores. Informed guesses, on the other hand, provide valid indications of achievement. The more a student knows, the more likely that informed guesses will be correct.

The second is that well-motivated students, taking a test of appropriate difficulty with a generous time limit, are likely to do very little blind guessing on true-false tests. They know that thinking is a surer basis than guessing for determining the correct answer. In a recent study, college students reported an average of only one response in 20 that was equivalent, in their opinion, to a blind guess.[3] Hills and Gladney have shown that scores in the chance range are not significantly different from above-chance scores as predictors of college grades.[4] This suggests that scores in the chance range were not in fact the results of pure chance (blind guessing).

The third is that the influence of blind guessing on the scores of a test diminishes as the test increases in length. On a one-item true-false test a student has a 50 percent chance of getting a perfect score, but on a 2-item test it drops to 25 percent, on a 5-item test to 3 percent, and on a 10-item test to 0.1 percent. On a 100-item test it becomes less than one chance in a million trillion trillion! The chance of getting even a moderately good score, say 70, on a 100-item true-false test by blind guessing alone is less than one in 1,000.

The fourth and most significant response that can be made to this charge is that reliable scores could not be obtained from true-false tests if they were seriously affected by blind guessing. But in fact they are: True-false classroom tests of 100 items have shown reliability coefficients of 0.85 to 0.95. These values are about as high as can be expected for any classroom test, regardless of the form of test item used. They support the conclusion that good true-false tests need not be vitiated by guessing.

Some persons who are somewhat familiar with objective testing believe that the problem of guessing can best be dealt with by "correcting the scores for guessing." This is a misconception. The announcement that test scores will be corrected for guessing may deter *some* students from guessing, but it only magnifies the differences between the scores of lucky and unlucky guessers. In fact, its effect on the validity of the test scores is negligible. If guessing on a true-false test were to be extensive enough to affect the test scores seriously, there is almost nothing that a guessing correction could do to improve the accuracy of the scores.

Are True-False Items Necessarily Trivial?

One of the common criticisms of true-false test items is that they are limited to testing for specific, often trivial, factual details. As a result, the critics say, students are encouraged and rewarded for rote learning of bits of factual information rather than for critical thinking and understanding. In support of this criticism, items like these are cited as typical of true-false tests:

The author of Don Quixote was Cervantes.   (T)

The chemical formula for water is H_2O.   (T)

---

[3] Robert L. Ebel, "Blind Guessing on Objective Achievement Tests," *Journal of Educational Measurement*, 5 (1968), 321–25.

[4] John R. Hills and Marilyn B. Gladney, "Predicting Grades from Below Chance Test Scores," *Journal of Educational Measurement*, 5 (1968), 45–53.

The Battle of Hastings was fought in 1066. (T)
Christopher Columbus was born in Spain. (F)
There are six planets in the solar system. (F)

If these were indeed the only kinds of questions that could be asked in true-false form, it would surely be of limited value. However, it is possible to ask questions that not only test students' comprehension of broader principles but also their ability to apply them. For example, one can test understanding of an event or of a process:

King John of England considered the Magna Carta one of his great achievements. (F)

In the laboratory preparation of carbon dioxide one of the essential ingredients is limewater. (F)

One can test knowledge of a functional relationship:

The more widely the items in a test vary in difficulty, the narrower the range of test scores. (T)

If heat is supplied at a constant rate to melt and vaporize a substance, the temperature of the substance will increase at a constant rate also. (F)

One can test the ability to apply principles:

It is easier for a poor student to get a good score (80 percent correct) on a true-false test if the test includes only 50 items than if it includes 100 items. (T)

If an electric refrigerator is operated in a sealed, insulated room with its door open, the temperature of the room will decrease. (F)

The time from moonrise to moonset is usually longer than the time from sunrise to sunset. (T)

Are True-False Items Necessarily Ambiguous?

A second major criticism of true-false test items is that they are frequently ambiguous. Although some do indeed succumb to this charge, ambiguity is not an inherent weakness of the true-false item—especially if the ideas for the items are carefully chosen and if the items themselves are carefully worded. Further, we must make a distinction between intrinsic ambiguity and apparent ambiguity. Students who say, "If I interpret the statement this way, I'd say it is true. But if I interpret it that way, I'd have to say it is false," are complaining about apparent ambiguity. If experts in the field have the same difficulty in interpreting a particular statement, the trouble may be intrinsic ambiguity.

Apparent ambiguity may sometimes be due to inadequacies in the students' knowledge. They have trouble interpreting a statement because the words mean something a little different to them than to the expert, or because the statement fails to evoke the necessary associations that would yield the intended interpretation.

Hence apparent ambiguity is not only unavoidable, it may even be useful. By making the task of responding harder for the poorly prepared than for the well-prepared student, it can help to discriminate between the two. Thus a student's comment that a test question is unclear is not necessarily an indictment of the question. It may be, rather, an unintentional confession of his or her own shortcomings.

Intrinsic ambiguity, on the other hand, the kind of ambiguity that troubles the expert as much as or more than it troubles the novice, is a real concern. It probably can never be totally eliminated, since language is inherently somewhat abstract, general, and imprecise. But in the statements used in true-false test items it should be minimized.

Of course, there is sometimes truth in the charge that true-false test items are ambiguous and lack significance: one reason is that teachers sometimes try to excerpt textbook sentences for use as test items. Even in a well-written text, few of the sentences would actually make good true-false test items. Many statements serve only to keep readers informed of what the author is trying to do or to remind them of the structure and organization of the discussion. Some are so dependent for their meaning on sentences that precede or follow them that they are almost meaningless out of context. Others are intended only to suggest an idea, not to state it positively and precisely. Still others comprise a whole logical argument, involving two or three propositions, in a single sentence. Another category of statements is intended not to describe what is true, but to prescribe what ought to be true. Finally, some are expressed so loosely and so tentatively that there is hardly any possible basis for doubting them. In all the writing we do to preserve the knowledge we have gained and to communicate it to others there seem to be very few naturally occurring nuggets of established knowledge.

For this reason it is seldom possible to find in a text or reference work a sentence that can be copied directly for use as a true statement or transformed by a simple negation for use as a false statement. The task of writing good true-false test items is more a task of creative writing than of copying. This may be a fortunate circumstance, for it helps test constructors avoid the hazard of writing items that would encourage and reward rote learning.

There is a special source of ambiguity in true-false test items that needs to be guarded against. It is uncertainty on the part of the examinee as to the examiner's standards of truth. If the statement is not perfectly true, if it has the slightest flaw, should it be considered false? Probably not; the item writer's task will be easier, and the test will be better, if she/he directs the examinee to consider as true any statement that has more truth than error in it, or any statement that is more true than its contradiction would be. The test builder's task then is to avoid writing statements that fall in the twilight zone between truth and falsehood.

Of course, even the most competent and careful item writer may unintentionally include a few intrinsically ambiguous items. Such items are usually quite easy to identify after the test has been given. The better students who miss these items will call attention to their ambiguity. If the test is analyzed, the ambiguous items are likely to show low discrimination or high difficulty. Post mortems such as this do nothing to correct past failures, but they can help examiners identify items that need to be revised or discarded and make them more sensitive to avoidable sources of ambiguity.

Do True-False Tests Misdirect Efforts to Learn?

Critics of true-false tests sometimes charge that their use has harmful effects on learning: that they encourage students (1) to concentrate on remembering isolated factual details and to rely heavily on rote learning; (2) to accept grossly oversimplified conceptions of truth; and (3) that they expose students undesirably to error. Let us consider these charges.

True-false items need not emphasize memory for isolated factual details. Good ones present novel problems to be solved and thus emphasize understanding and application. Even those that might require recall of factual details do not necessarily reward rote learning, for facts are hard to remember in isolation. They are retained and can be recalled better if they are part of a structure of knowledge.

There is reason to believe that rote learning is something of an educational bogeyman, often warned against and cited as the cause of educational failure, but seldom practiced or observed. Rote learning is not much fun, and it promises few lasting rewards. Most students and teachers properly shun it. Perhaps its supposed prevalence results from an error in inference. It is surely true that rote learning always results in incomplete learning (that is, lack of understanding), but it does not follow that all incomplete learning is the result of too much rote learning. It may simply be the result of too little learning of any sort.

What of the second charge, that the categorical way in which answers are both offered and scored, is likely to give students a false notion about the simplicity of truth? Evidence in support of this argument is seldom presented, and the argument itself is seldom advanced by those who have used true-false tests extensively. Test writers know students will challenge answers that disagree with their own. Often they will point to the complexity of the entire subject and will insist that a case can be made for the alternative answer. Usually the author concedes that the statement in question is neither perfectly true nor totally false. The discussion that normally follows tends to emphasize, rather than to conceal, the complexity, the impurity, the relativity of truth. On occasion it leads to the conclusion that the item in question was simply a bad item, poorly conceived or carelessly stated.

Now consider the third charge, namely that true-false test items are educationally harmful because they expose the student to error. The argument is that the presentation of false statements as if they were true may have a negative suggestion effect, causing students to believe and remember untruths. However, Ruch tentatively concluded that the negative suggestion effect in true-false tests is probably much smaller than is sometimes assumed and is fully offset by the net positive teaching effects.[5] Other experimental studies confirm this conclusion, and as Ross points out:

> Modern psychology recognizes the importance of the total situation or configuration in learning. Whether or not a false statement is dangerous depends largely upon the setting in which it appears. A false statement in the textbook, toward which the characteristic pupil attitude is likely to be one of passive, uncritical acceptance, might easily be serious. But the situation is different with the items in a true-false test. Here the habitual attitude of the modern pupil is one of active, critical challenge.[6]

In the light of these findings, we can only conclude that the answer to our initial question is "no." Well-conceived and well-developed true-false test items can contribute substantially to the educational process. The harm some fear they might do is trivial in comparison.

REQUIREMENTS FOR GOOD TRUE-FALSE TEST ITEMS

There are five general requirements for a good true-false test item.

1. It should test the examinee's knowledge of an important proposition, one that is likely to be significant and useful in coping with a variety of situations and problems. It should say something worth saying.
2. It should require understanding as well as memory. Simple recall of meaningless words, empty phrases, or sentences learned by rote should not be enough to permit a correct answer.

[5] G. M. Ruch, *The Objective or New-type Examination* (Chicago: Scott, Foresman and Company, 1929), p. 368.
[6] C. C. Ross, *Measurement in Today's Schools* (2nd ed.; Englewood Cliffs, N.J.: Prentice-Hall, Inc., 1947), p. 349.

3. The intended correct answer (true or false) should be easy for the item writer to defend to the satisfaction of competent critics. The true statements should be true enough and the false statements false enough so that an expert would have no difficulty distinguishing between them. Any explanation or qualification needed to justify an unconditional answer should be included in the item.

4. On the other hand, the intended correct answer should be obvious only to those who have good command of the knowledge being tested. It should not be a matter of common knowledge. It should not be given away by an unintended clue. The wrong answer should be made attractive to those who lack the desired command.

5. The item should be expressed as simply, as concisely, and above all as clearly as is consistent with the preceding four requirements. It should be based on a single proposition. Common words should be given preference over technical terms. Sentences should be short and simple in structure. Essentially true statements should not be made false by simply inserting the word *not*.

Here are some pairs of true-false test items that illustrate these requirements. The first of each pair is an acceptable item, while the second is poor.

1. *The item tests an important idea.*

(1) President Kennedy attempted to solve the missile crisis by threatening a blockade of Cuba.   (T)
(2) President Kennedy was 12 years older than his wife.   (T)

The difference in the ages between President Kennedy and his wife might be a subject for comment in a casual conversation, but it has little to do with the important events of the time. The Cuban missile crisis, on the other hand, brought the United States and Russia to the brink of war. How this crisis was handled is a far more important element in world history than a difference in ages between a president and his wife.

(3) Words like *some, usually, all,* or *never* should be avoided in writing true-false test items.   (F)
(4) Two pitfalls should be avoided in writing true-false test items.   (F)

Item 4 is the type of textbook sentence that sets the stage for an important pronouncement—but fails to make it. Item 3, on the other hand, tests the examinee's understanding of several important principles. Specific determiners like *some* and *usually* provide irrelevant clues only when used in true statements. If used in false statements they tend to attract wrong answers from the ill-prepared student. Conversely, specific determiners like *all* or *never* should be avoided in false statements, but are useful in attracting wrong answers from the uninformed.

(5) More salt can be dissolved in a pint of warm water than in a pint of cold water. (T)
(6) Some things dissolve in other things. (T)

A statement like that in item 6 is too general to say anything useful. Item 5, on the other hand, provides a test of the understanding of an important relationship.

2. *The item tests understanding. It does not reward recall of a stereotyped phraseology.*

(7) When a hand pushes a door with a certain force, the door pushes back on the hand with the same force. (T)
(8) For every action there is an equal and opposite reaction. (T)
(9) If the hypotenuse of an isosceles right triangle is seven inches long, each of the two equal legs must be more than five inches long. (F)
(10) The square of the hypotenuse of a right triangle equals the sum of the squares of the other two sides. (T)

Both items 8 and 10 are word-for-word statements of important principles that could be learned by rote. To test a student's understanding it is desirable to present specific applications that avoid the stereotyped phrases, as has been done in items 7 and 9.

3. *The correct answer to an item is defensible.*

(11) Moist air is less dense than dry air. (T)
(12) Rain clouds are light in weight. (T)

Since a rain cloud seems to float in the air, it might reasonably be called light in weight. On the other hand, a single rain cloud may weigh more than 100,000 tons. One cubic foot of the cloud probably weighs about the same as a cubic foot of air. Since the cloud contains droplets of water, it could conceivably weigh more per cubic foot than cloudless dry air. On the other hand, moist air alone (item 11) weighs less per cubic foot than does dry air. Should the item also specify "other things being equal," for example, pressure and temperature? It might, but in the absence of mention, a reasonable person is justified in assuming that temperature and pressure should not be taken to be variable factors in this situation.

(13) The proposal that salary schedules for teachers ought to include skill in teaching as one of the determining variables is supported more strongly by teachers' organizations than it is by taxpayers. (F)
(14) Merit is an important factor affecting a teacher's salary. (F)

The first version is much more specific, and much more clearly false than the second. Experts could agree on the answer to the first, but would be troubled by the intrinsic ambiguity of the second. Across the country it is no doubt true that the salaries of good teachers are higher than those of poor teachers. However, it is also true that the salary schedules of many school systems do not include merit as one of the determining factors.

(15) The twinkling of starlight is due to motion in the earth's atmosphere.   (T)
(16) Stars send out light that twinkles.   (T)

The answer to the second, unacceptable version of this item could be challenged by a reasonable, well-informed person on the following grounds. It is not the light sent out by the star that twinkles—that light is relatively steady. But, owing to disturbances in our atmosphere, the light that reaches our eyes from the star often appears to twinkle. That the second version is unacceptable is due either to the limited knowledge or to the carelessness in expression of the person who wrote it.

4. *The answer to a good test item is not obvious to anyone. It tests special knowledge.*

   A. It is not self-evident.

(17) Frozen foods are usually cheaper than canned foods.   (F)
(18) Frozen foods of the highest quality may be ruined in the kitchen.   (T)

(19) Most local insurance agencies are owned and controlled by one of the major national insurance companies.   (F)
(20) Insurance agencies may be either general or specialized.   (T)

Who could doubt the possibility of cooking any kind of food badly? How plausible is the belief that only general or only specialized insurance agencies could be found? The unacceptable versions, items 18 and 20, are too obviously true to discriminate high achievement from low. Both read like introductory sentences lifted from a textbook, sentences that set the stage for an important idea but do not themselves express important ideas.

   B. To one who lacks the knowledge being tested, a wrong answer should appear more plausible than the correct one.

(21) By adding more solute, a saturated solution can be made supersaturated.   (F)
(22) A supersaturated solution contains more solute per unit than a saturated solution.   (T)

It appears reasonable to believe that adding more solute would turn a saturated solution into a supersaturated solution (item 21). But those who understand solutions know that it doesn't work that way. The added solute won't dissolve in a saturated solution. Only by evaporating some of the solvent, or cooling it, can a saturated solution be made supersaturated. The student who tries to use common sense as a substitute for special knowledge is likely to give a wrong answer (which is all his knowledge entitles him to) to the first item. But the same common sense leads the student of low achievement to answer item 22 correctly. Thus the second version fails to function properly as a test of the student's command of knowledge.

5. *The item is expressed clearly.*

  A. *It is based on a single idea.*

(23) The salt dissolved in water can be recovered by evaporation of the solvent. (T)
(24) Salt can be dissolved in water and can be recovered by evaporation of the solvent. (T)[7]
(25) At conception the sex ratio is approximately 3 boys to 2 girls. (T)
(26) Scientists have found that male-producing sperm are stronger and live longer than female-producing sperm, which accounts for the sex ratio at conception of approximately 3 boys to 2 girls. (T)

An item based on a single idea is usually easier to understand than one based on two or more ideas. It is also more efficient. One can obtain a more accurate measurement of a student's achievement by testing separate ideas separately than by lumping them together and scoring one composite answer right or wrong.

(27) Individuals who deliberate before making choices seldom find themselves forced to sacrifice one good thing in order to attain another. (F)
(28) Life is a continuous process of choice making, sacrificing one human value for another, which goes through the following steps: spontaneous mental selections regarding everything we want, conflicting preferences hold each other in check, hesitation becomes deliberation as we weigh and compare values, finally choice or preference emerges. (T)

The strong inclination of some teachers to use their tests as opportunities for teaching, or their misguided attempts to use textbook sentences as test items, may account for the appearance of such items as number 28. But if one looks for the central idea in item 28, and asks what misapprehension it might serve to correct, an item like number 27 may emerge. Item 27 is simpler, clearer, and better in almost every way than item 28.

---

[7] Another unacceptable version that inappropriately combines two ideas might be:
Salt dissolves in hot water; sugar dissolves in cold water. (T)

B. It is concise.

(29) The federal government pays practically the entire cost of constructing and maintaining highways that are part of the interstate highway system.   (F)

(30) When you see a highway with a marker that reads "Interstate 80," you know that the construction and upkeep of that road is built and maintained by the state and federal governments.   (T)

The wording of item 30 is careless and redundant. It is the *highway* that is built and maintained, not its construction and upkeep. The personal touch ("when you see") may give the appearance of practicality, but does not affect what the item really measures at all. Finally, making item 30 true by including state as well as federal governments as supporters of the interstate highway system probably makes the item easier for the uninformed. Item 29 hits the intended mark more clearly because it is more straightforward and concise.

C. It does not include an artificial, tricky negative.

(31) Columbus made only four voyages of exploration to the Western Hemisphere.   (T)

(32) Columbus did not make four voyages of exploration to the Western Hemisphere.   (F)

Some item writers try to turn textbook propositions into false statements for test items simply by inserting the word *not* in the original statement. The result is seldom good. The item usually carries the clear birthmark of its unnatural origin: It reads awkwardly and invites suspicion, which, if the item is indeed false, may give away the answer. Further, these items tend to be tricky. An unobtrusive "not" in an otherwise wholly true statement may be overlooked by even a well-prepared examinee. Such items put students at an unnecessary and undesirable disadvantage.

THE DEVELOPMENT OF TRUE-FALSE TEST ITEMS

The instructor who wishes to write a true-false item for a classroom test should begin by focusing attention on some segment of the knowledge that has been taught. It is assumed that the item writer is in firm command of that segment of knowledge and that it is something any capable student of the subject ought also to understand. This segment of knowledge is, or easily could be, described in a single paragraph such as those found in any good textbook adopted for the class. Accordingly, item writers usually find it easier and more effective to use instructional materials as the source of ideas for test items than to derive those ideas directly from educational objectives.

Suppose now that an item writer singles out a specific paragraph of text intended to help the student develop some segment of knowledge. Take, for example, the paragraph found on pp. 60–61 of Chapter 4 of this book:

> Precise measurement requires careful control or standardization of the conditions surrounding it. Obviously, this control makes the behavior being measured artificial to some degree. Artificiality is a price that usually must be paid to achieve precision. It is a price that scientists and engineers, as well as psychologists and teachers, have usually found worth paying. For tests intended to measure typical behavior, such as personality, attitude, or interest tests, the price may sometimes be too high. That is, the behavior in the artificial test situation may be so poorly related to typical behavior in a natural situation that precise measurement of something hardly worth measuring is so much wasted effort. But for tests of educational aptitude or achievement, the gain in precision resulting from the controlled conditions that formal testing can afford usually far outweighs the slight loss in the relevance of artificial to natural behavior.

The first question the item writer must ask himself or herself is, "What are the most important ideas presented in this paragraph?" There are two possibilities:

1. The controls required for precise measurement make the behavior being measured somewhat artificial.
2. Artificiality is more harmful when personality is being measured than when achievement is being measured.

The next question is how these ideas can be expressed as true-false test items. At this point, a very important suggestion can be offered.

Always think of possible true-false test items in pairs, one true, the other false.

Of course, only one member of the pair is actually used in the test. However, unless a parallel but opposite statement can be made, the proposition is not likely to make a good true-false test item. Here are some item pairs derived from the ideas presented above.

1a. In measurements of behavior, precision and naturalness are directly related.   (F)
1b. In measurements of behavior, precision and naturalness are inversely related.   (T)

2a. To obtain precision in the measurement of behavior, naturalness must be preserved. (F)
2b. To obtain precision in the measurement of behavior, naturalness must be sacrificed. (T)
3a. The purpose of controls in the process of measuring behavior is to make the measurements more precise. (T)
3b. The purpose of controls in the process of measuring behavior is to make the behavior being measured more realistic. (F)
4a. In measurements of achievement it is desirable to emphasize precision at the expense of naturalness. (T)
4b. In measurements of achievement it is undesirable to emphasize precision at the expense of naturalness. (F)
4c. In measurements of personality it is desirable to emphasize precision at the expense of naturalness. (F)
4d. In measurements of personality it is undesirable to emphasize precision at the expense of naturalness. (T)
5a. It is better to measure achievement precisely than to measure it naturally. (T)
5b. It is better to measure achievement naturally than to measure it precisely. (F)
5c. It is better to measure personality precisely than to measure it naturally. (F)
5d. It is better to measure personality naturally than to measure it precisely. (T)

Note how many variations can be developed from the two basic ideas specified. Note that none of the items, nor indeed the basic ideas, is a reproduction of any of the original sentences. All the items are designed to test for understanding, not simply for recall of sentences read or heard.

Items 4a to 4d and 5a to 5d illustrate another trick that sometimes can be employed to reduce ambiguity. It is to write statements that compare two alternatives. Such internal comparison can focus attention on the central presupposition; it also avoids the necessity of using arbitrary standards in judging truth or falsity and the resulting possibility that the examiner's standards might differ significantly from those of the examinee.

To avoid ambiguity, it is important always to express an idea as accurately and as specifically as possible. Instead of saying "a long test," say "a 100-item test." Instead of saying "a test item of moderate difficulty," say "an item that between 40 percent and 60 percent of the examinees answer correctly."

WRITING ITEMS TO DISCRIMINATE

The job of a test item is to discriminate between those who have and those who lack command of some element of knowledge. Those who have achieved command should be able to answer the questions correctly without difficulty. Those who lack it should find the wrong answers attractive. To produce items that will discriminate in this way is one of the arts of item writing. Here are some of the ways in which such items can be produced.

1. *Use more false than true statements in the test.*

When in doubt, students seem more inclined to accept than to challenge propositions presented in a true-false test. Several investigators have found that false statements tend to discriminate somewhat more sharply between students of high and low achievement than do true statements. This may be due to what is called an "acquiescent response set." In the absence of firm knowledge, students seem more likely to accept than to question a declarative statement whose truth or falsity they must judge.

Instructions for preparing true-false tests sometimes suggest including about the same number of false and true statements. But if the false statements tend to be higher in discrimination, it would seem advantageous to include a higher proportion of them, perhaps as many as 67 percent. Even if students come to expect a greater number of false items, the technique still seems to work. In one study students took a test on which two-thirds of the statements were false. After answering the questions and counting how many they had marked true, they were told the correct number of true statements and were given a chance to change any answers they wished. Most of them changed a number of answers, but they improved their scores very little, on the average. They changed about as many of their answers from right to wrong as from wrong to right.

2. *Word the item so that superficial logic suggests a wrong answer.*

(1) A rubber ball weighing 100 grams is floating on the surface of a pool of water exactly half submerged. An additional downward force of 50 grams would be required to submerge it completely. (F)

The ball is half submerged and weighs 100 grams, which gives one-half of 100 considerable plausibility on a superficial basis. The true case is, of course, that if its weight of 100 grams submerges only half of it, another 100 grams would be required to submerge all of it. Superficial logic also would make the incorrect answers to questions 2, 3, and 4 seem plausible.

(2) Since students show a wide range of individual differences, the ideal measurement situation would be achieved if each student could take a different test specially designed to test him. (F)
(3) The output voltage of a transformer is determined in part by the number of turns on the input coil. (T)
(4) A transformer that will increase the voltage of an alternating current can also be used to increase the voltage of a direct current. (F)

3. *Make the wrong answer consistent with a popular misconception or a popular belief irrelevant to the question.*

(5) The effectiveness of tests as tools for measuring achievement is lowered by the apprehension students feel for them. (F)

Many students do experience test anxiety, but for most of them it facilitates rather than impedes maximum performance.

(6) An achievement test should include enough items to keep every student busy during the entire test period. (F)

Keeping students busy at worthy educational tasks is usually commendable, but in this case it would make rate of work count too heavily, in most cases, as a determinant of the test score.

4. *Use specific determiners in reverse to confound testwiseness.*

In true-false test items extreme words like *always* or *never* tend to be used mainly in false statements by unwary item writers, whereas such modifiers as *some, often,* or *generally* tend to be used mainly in true statements. When they are so used they qualify as "specific determiners" that help testwise but uninformed examinees to answer true-false questions correctly. But some *always* or *never* statements are true and some *often* or *generally* statements are false. Thus these specific determiners can be used to attract the student who is merely testwise to a wrong answer.

5. *Use phrases in false statements that give them the "ring of truth."*

(7) The use of better achievement tests will, in itself, contribute little or nothing to better achievement. (F)

The phrases "in itself" and "little or nothing" impart a tone of sincerity and rightness to the statement that conceals its falseness from the uninformed.

(8) To ensure comprehensive measurement of each aspect of achievement, different kinds of items must be specifically written, in due proportions, to test each distinct mental process the course is intended to develop. (F)

As in questions 2, 3, and 4, superficial logic is predominant. But this item also displays the elaborate statement and careful qualifications that testwise individuals associate mainly with true statements.

Are teachers playing fair when they set out deliberately to make it easy for some students to give wrong answers to test items? We contend that if they want valid measures of achievement—that is, measures that correctly distinguish between those who have and those who lack command of a particular element of knowledge—it is the only way they can play fair. The only reason a test constructor sets out to make wrong answers attractive to those who lack command of the knowledge is so that correct answers will truly indicate the achievement they purport to measure.

SUMMARY

Some of the main ideas developed in this chapter are expressed by the following 27 statements:

1. True-false test items provide a simple and direct means of measuring the essential outcome of formal education.
2. The low esteem in which true-false tests are sometimes held is due to inept use, not to inherent limitations.
3. True-false test items provide information on essential achievements more efficiently than other item forms.
4. True-false items are relatively easy to write.
5. Many important aspects of achievement can be tested equally well with either true-false or multiple-choice test items.
6. It is difficult to transform every multiple-choice test item into a true-false test item.
7. It is undesirable to group true-false statements to produce a multiple-choice test item.
8. Unlike blind guesses, informed guesses provide valid indications of achievement.
9. In practice, guessing is not a serious problem on true-false tests, both because students tend to do very little blind guessing and because the probability of their achieving a high score through guessing is extremely low.
10. Correction of true-false test scores for guessing is neither necessary nor beneficial.
11. True-false items can test students' comprehension of important ideas and their ability to use them in solving problems.
12. Good true-false items that appear ambiguous to poor students are actually powerful discriminators, in that knowledgeable students will see beyond such apparent inconsistencies.
13. Few textbook sentences are significant enough, and meaningful enough out of context, to be used as the true statements in a true-false test.

14. Statements that are essentially (but not perfectly) true or essentially (but not totally) false can make good true-false test items.
15. There are no firm empirical data to support the charges that true-false tests encourage rote learning, oversimplified conceptions of the truth, or the learning of false ideas.
16. The answer to a good true-false test item is easy for the item writer to defend, but difficult for those students whose knowledge is superficial to discern.
17. Good true-false statements express single, not multiple, ideas.
18. In general, one cannot create good false statements by inserting the word *not* in a true statement.
19. The materials used in instruction provide better ideas for test items than do statements of course objectives.
20. Test items should be based on important ideas expressed or implied in the instructional materials.
21. True-false test items should always be thought of in pairs, one true, one false.
22. The test maker can reduce ambiguity by writing items that involve an internal comparison of alternatives.
23. False statements tend to make more discriminating test items than true statements.
24. Avoid giveaway modifiers like *sometimes*, *usually*, or *often* in true statements, or *always, never,* or *impossible* in false statements.
25. Using words like *always* or *never* in true statements, and *often* or *usually* in false statements, tends to mislead the student who relies on testwiseness to give him a good score.
26. Make false items plausible by using familiar words and phrases in seemingly straightforward factual statements.

PROJECTS AND PROBLEMS

Project: Writing True-False Test Items

Using the information in the following paragraphs as directly and simply as possible, write ten pairs of parallel statements, one true and one false. Do not try to test for understanding of the information or for applications of it. For example, if the information given had been:

The highest mountain in the fifty states is Mt. McKinley. It is not Pike's Peak.

An appropriate pair of true-false items would be:

(T)   The highest mountain in the fifty states is Mt. McKinley.
(F)   The highest mountain in the fifty states is Pike's Peak.

Treat each of the ten paragraphs below in the same way. Place a (T) before the true statement and an (F) before the false statement.

1. Iron is an element. It is not a compound.
2. Ice is less dense than water. It is not more dense.
3. If two angles of a triangle are equal, it is isosceles. It is not equilateral.
4. The Panama Canal is controlled by the United States. It is not controlled by Panama.
5. One third times one third is one ninth. It is not one sixth.
6. The heart pumps blood into the arteries. It does not pump blood into the veins.
7. Words that name objects are nouns. They are not verbs.
8. The first ten amendments to the United States Constitution are known as the Bill of Rights. They are not known as the Articles of Confederation.
9. The best place to look for an account of the French Revolution would be an encyclopedia. It would not be a dictionary.
10. Temperatures change less from season to season on the equator than in the arctic. They do not change more on the equator.

Problem: Tryout of True-False Test Items

This assignment is based on 20 true-false test items that were intended to test for elements of knowledge that most college students are unlikely to have. Decide how you would answer each question and record your answers on a special answer sheet. Then your instructor will read or show you the 10 paragraphs on which the questions were based. After you have heard or seen the background information you will be asked to respond again to the 20 questions. This time your answers may be recorded in spaces 21 to 40 on the special answer sheet.

A committee from the class or a test-scoring machine will determine the proportion of correct answers given to each question each time it was taken (that is, before and after "instruction"). The difference between *proportion correct after* and *proportion correct before* will indicate how effective the instruction was in giving information and how effective the item was in measuring it. These differences will be reported to you and will form the basis for a discussion of good and poor true-false test items.

1. Napoleon won most of his military campaigns.
2. Napoleon's downfall was his loss of the battle for Spain.
3. Six of the several known species of penguins are found on the Galapagos Islands near the equator.
4. Adult penguins have no natural enemies on the ice.
5. Sugar is often added to wine during fermentation to make it sweeter.
6. Most wines require fairly long aging periods before they reach the peak of their flavor.
7. Scientists have found that male sperm are stronger and live longer than female sperm; this accounts for the sex ratio of males to females—140 to 160 to 100.
8. Human population studies indicate that the general weakness of

the male sperm accounts for the relationship of more birth defects, miscarriages, and death among males than females.

9. Infection was the major cause of death for soldiers in the Civil War.
10. Pneumonia was the most common illness suffered by soldiers in the Civil War.
11. After learning something, you forget more in the next few hours than in the next several days.
12. Lessons learned early in the morning are remembered better than those learned just before going to sleep.
13. In cases of severe shock, the victim's feet should be elevated.
14. Small amounts of an alcoholic beverage can be given to shock victims if they are conscious.
15. When selling a home, realtors must be aware of its individual "sex appeal" to the buyer.
16. A man considers price and location as the most important elements when purchasing a home.
17. Due to the many new techniques that have been developed by psychologists, mental illness is not considered to be one of our biggest problems today.
18. Some forms of mental illness can be inherited.
19. A recent survey indicates that many parents give stock to their children.
20. 6.5 percent of the stockholders in the United States are children.

8

Multiple-Choice Test Items

THE STATUS OF MULTIPLE-CHOICE TEST ITEMS

Multiple-choice test items are currently the most highly regarded and widely used form of objective test item. They are adaptable to the measurement of most important educational outcomes: of knowledge, understanding, and judgment; of ability to solve problems, to recommend appropriate action, to make predictions. Almost any understanding or ability that can be tested by means of any other item form—short answer, completion, true-false, matching, or essay—can also be tested by means of multiple-choice test items.

The form of the multiple-choice item, with the stem asking or implying a direct question, provides a realistic, naturally appropriate setting for testing student achievement. There tends to be less indirectness and artifice in multiple-choice than in some other item forms. Students often find multiple-choice questions less ambiguous than completion or true-false items. Instructors also find it easier to defend correct answers.

Finally, multiple-choice items seem to both instructors and students to be less susceptible to chance errors resulting from guessing than true-false items. It is easy to exaggerate the harm done by guessing, and to place too much emphasis on the need to limit the amount of guessing students do. Yet however little the harm done by guessing, it does less harm in multiple-choice than in true-false tests.

In spite of their virtues, multiple-choice test items have not escaped the attention of critics. Some of the criticisms reflect a general mistrust of all objective testing techniques. These critics allege that objective test questions are inevitably superficial, ambiguous, and conducive to guessing. They say or imply that the only good way to test is the old way they prefer to use—namely, essay testing. Other critics find fault with specific test items, alleging that the questions are ambiguous, the correct answers incorrect, or the distracters as good as or better than the intended correct answer.

Few objective tests or test items are so perfect as to be above reproach from a persistent, perceptive critic. But there are at least two weaknesses in the general indictments that have been issued against all multiple-choice tests and items. First, the criticisms are seldom supported by unbiased experimental data, despite the fact that relevant data would be fairly easy to obtain. Most of the flaws pointed out should lower the discriminating power of the items and the reliability of the test scores, yet by and large they fail to do so. In addition, some of the critics, instead of obtaining or even welcoming experimental evidence, tend to discredit statistical methods of testing the quality of items or tests, without suggesting any replacement procedure—other than their own intuitions (and occasionally those of a few friends) and what seems to them to be plain common sense.

In the second place, the critics seldom attempt seriously to make a good case for a better way of measuring educational achievement. Even the most ardent advocates of objective testing do not claim perfection. They acknowledge that multiple-choice test questions can be subject to serious flaws and that, in general, they are not as clearly meaningful and sharply discriminating as they should be. Users of objective tests agree wholly with the observation that the scores are not as reliable as they might be and ought to be for maximum value, but they are not likely to abandon multiple-choice testing until a substitute can be found whose shortcomings are less serious. The implied alternative, essay testing, is clearly much less convenient to use in many situations. In any case, advocates of objective testing are not likely to consider seriously any recommendations accompanied by expressions of disdain for experimental evidence.

RELATION OF MULTIPLE-CHOICE TO ESSAY QUESTIONS

It is sometimes suggested that objective tests are inevitably more superficial and less realistic tests of a student's knowledge than are essay tests. The reasoning is that in suggesting possible answers to the student the examiner has done the important part of the task. But most good objective test items require the examinee to develop, by creative, original thought, the *basis* for choice among the alternatives. Good objective test items do not permit correct response on the basis of simple recognition, sheer rote memory, or meaningless verbal association. Consider the nature of the thought processes involved in selecting an answer to this question.

A child buys jelly beans which the grocer picks up, without regard for color, from a tray containing a mixture of jelly beans of three different colors. What is the smallest number of jelly beans the child can buy and still be certain of getting at least four jelly beans of the same color?

The answers provided are 4, 7, 10, and 12.

Assume that examinees are seeing this particular problem for the first time, so that they cannot answer it successfully by simply repeating an answer someone else has given them. Assume, too, that problems of this kind are not of sufficient practical importance to have been made the subject of a special unit of study. These assumptions call attention to an important general principle of educational measurement. What a test item measures, that is, what a successful response to it indicates, cannot be determined on the basis of the item alone. Consideration must also be given to the examinee's previous experiences. These may differ significantly for different examinees. But in the case of the foregoing problem, the assumptions mentioned above may be quite reasonable.

How much different would the thought processes be, and how much more difficult would the problem be, if no answers were suggested and the task required production of the answer rather than selection? Producing an answer is not necessarily a more complex or difficult task, or one more indicative of achievement, than choosing the best of the available alternatives.

In Cook's study, where the same questions were presented to college students in two forms, one an essay format, the other a multiple-choice format, the correlation between scores for the same students on the two forms was as high as would be expected if both of them were measuring the same achievement.[1] Table IX of Cook's unpublished dissertation shows a correlation of .97 between the scores for 152 college freshmen on two 60-item tests of knowledge of contemporary affairs, one composed of completion (free-response) items and the other of multiple-choice items. When this correlation was corrected for unreliability of the two tests (.87 for the completion test and .86 for the multiple-choice test), it rose to .99. This means that, within the limits of their accuracy of measurement, the two tests appeared to be measuring identical aspects of achievement. Further, as Sax and Collet report, both types seem equally effective in motivating student learning.[2]

[1] Desmond L. Cook, "An Investigation of Three Aspects of Free-response and Choice-type Tests at the College Level," *Dissertation Abstracts*, 15 (1955), 1351.

[2] Gilbert Sax and LeVerne S. Collet, "An Empirical Comparison of the Effects of Recall and Multiple-Choice Tests on Student Achievement," *Journal of Educational Measurement*, 5 (1968), 169–73.

Paterson, in a similar study conducted 32 years earlier, came to the same conclusion: ". . . there seems to be no escape from the conclusion that the two types of examinations are measuring identical things."[3]

An illustration of the use of essay and objective questions to test essentially the same educational achievement is given in Exhibits 8–1 and 8–2. These tests were devised for use in a dental prosthetics course. The instructor had always used essay questions but was interested in the greater reliability and ease in scoring that objective tests might afford. He was dubious, however, about the prospect of having to write a number of independent objective test items relating to the same complex process without having one question give away the answer to another.

To explore this possibility, the professor of dentistry supplied an essay test question and an ideal answer to it. This is displayed in Exhibit 8–1. Then a series of multiple-choice items was written on the basis of this essay-type answer. Eight of these are shown in Exhibit 8–2. Items 2 and 3 are

EXHIBIT 8–1. ESSAY TEST QUESTION AND ANSWER

Q. Sometimes a bridge will not go in place properly when being tried in the mouth after being soldered. If the operator should consider it advisable or necessary to unsolder, reassemble, and resolder the bridge, describe how this should be done.

A. The operator should first determine which joint or joints are to be unsoldered. The parts of the bridge should never be separated with a saw or disc, as this leaves a wide space to be filled in with solder. Instead, the bridge should be held in a blow-torch flame in such a way that the flame is directed on the joint to be unsoldered. Only enough heat must be used to melt the solder, and care must be used not to melt or distort an abutment piece.

When the parts of the bridge have been separated, they should be pickled in acid to clean them of oxide. It will be necessary to use a disc or stone to smooth and reduce the amount of solder at the joints before the bridge will go into place in the mouth. This must be done till all parts of the bridge can be reassembled in the mouth.

Place some Parr's flux wax on all contact points of the abutment pieces and pontics (this is done while the pieces outside the mouth), then place all pieces back in the mouth. The Parr's flux wax will hold the parts in place, and the wax is soft enough so the pontics can be moved around to a certain extent to get them in the right position. When positioned property, the joints should be reinforced with sticky wax, which is hard and brittle and will hold the parts firmly together. Then to further reinforce and strengthen the bridge so the parts will not be disarranged while taking the impression, a short piece of wire about 16 gauge should be bent and placed along the buccal or labial surface of the bridge and the approximating teeth and held firmly in place with sticky wax. All this waxing must be done with the field perfectly dry because any moisture will positively prevent the wax from holding.

Then a small, shallow impression tray is selected, filled with a fast-setting impression plaster and a shallow occlusal impression (if for a posterior bridge) or lingual and incisal impression (if for an anterior bridge) is secured. The impression is removed from the mouth, the bridge also removed and reassembled in the impression, the joints filled with Parr's flux wax, the plaster impression given a coat of separating medium, and the exposed parts of the bridge covered with soldering investment. When the investment is set, the plaster impression is cut away and more soldering investment applied in the proper manner to provide for correct soldering. The case is now ready to be heated and soldered in the regular way.

[3] Donald G. Paterson, "Do New and Old Type Examinations Measure Different Mental Functions?" *School and Society*, 24 (August 21, 1926), 246–48.

EXHIBIT 8–2. CORRESPONDING MULTIPLE-CHOICE ITEMS

The following eight items deal with the problem of separating, reassembling, and resoldering a bridge that will not go into place properly after being soldered.

(1) Which joint or joints should be separated?
   a. The joint between pontics and smallest abutment piece
   b. Any single joint (the faulty joint must be located by trial and error)
   c. All that were originally soldered
   *d. Only the one or ones which appear responsible for the failure to fit

Note: Only one of the following two items should be used.

(2) Should the joints be separated using a saw or disc rather than heat?
   a. No, because the saw might damage the original castings
   *b. No, because the saw will leave too large a gap to be filled with solder
   c. Yes, because the use of heat might damage the original castings
   d. Yes, because the saw leaves a clean joint ready for resoldering

(3) Should the flame be concentrated on the joint to be unsoldered? Why?
   a. No, because the bridge may crack if heated unevenly
   b. No, because the abutments must be thoroughly heated before the solder will melt
   *c. Yes, to avoid damage to the other pieces
   d. Yes, to avoid delay in separation

(4) After the bridge has been separated what, if anything, needs to be done before reassembling it in the patient's mouth?
   *a. The pieces should be cleaned in acid, and the joints smoothed with a stone
   b. The pieces should be cleaned in acid, but the joints should not be smoothed
   c. The joints should be smoothed, but the pieces need not be cleaned in acid
   d. Reassembling should begin as soon as the bridge has been separated

(5) What is used initially to hold the pieces together on reassembly in the patient's mouth?
   a. Sticky wax
   *b. Parr's flux wax
   c. Impression plaster
   d. Soldering investment

(6) Which of the following materials—flux wax, sticky wax, metal wire, and soldering investment—are used to hold the pieces of the reassembled bridge in place prior to taking the impression?
   a. All of them
   b. All but metal wire
   *c. All but soldering investment
   d. Only flux wax and sticky wax

(7) What precaution is necessary in using sticky wax?
   a. It must not be allowed to touch gum tissues.
   b. It must be applied in separate thin layers to avoid cracking.
   c. The surface to which it is applied must be moist.
   *d. The surface to which it is applied must be dry.

(8) What function does the plaster impression have in the process of resoldering the bridge?
   *a. It holds the parts in place while soldering investment is applied.
   b. It holds the parts in place while they are being soldered.
   c. It permits the resoldered bridge to be checked before insertion in the patient's mouth.
   d. It has no function in resoldering the bridge.

interlocking items; that is, the question asked in item 3 gives some indication as to the best answer to item 2. Hence only one of the two items should be used in any one test.

DEVELOPMENT OF MULTIPLE-CHOICE TEST ITEMS

Like true-false items, multiple-choice items are developed most conveniently and appropriately on the basis of ideas expressed or implied in the instructional materials. In Chapter 7 a paragraph of text material was reproduced and these two ideas were inferred from it.

1. The controls required for precise measurement make the behavior being measured somewhat artificial.
2. Artificiality is more harmful when personality is being measured than when achievement is being measured.

To develop multiple-choice test items on the basis of ideas like these one must:

(a) formulate a question or an incomplete sentence that clearly implies a question (the stem of the item)
(b) provide a good answer to the question in a few well-chosen words
(c) produce several plausible but incorrect answers to the question, termed *distracters*.

Multiple-choice items 1 and 2 that follow were developed on the basis of the first idea from the excerpted paragraph, and items 3 and 4, on the basis of the second.

(1) What is the relation between the naturalness of a test situation and the precision of the resulting measurement?
    a. In general, the more natural the situation, the more precise the measurement.
  b. In general, the more natural the situation, the less precise the measurement.
    c. The nature of the relation depends on what is being tested.
    d. There is no significant relation in general.
(2) Is it possible to measure natural behavior precisely? Explain.
    a. No. Natural behavior can be observed, but it cannot be measured.
  b. No. The controls necessary to achieve precision make the behavior measured somewhat unnatural.
    c. Yes. Precision of measurement does not require artificiality of behavior.
    d. Yes. The degree of precision depends on the process of measurement, not on the thing being measured.

(3) In achievement testing and in personality testing, is precision (in the resulting measurement) more important than naturalness (in the test situation)?
   a. Yes, in both achievement testing and personality testing.
   *b. No, only in achievement testing.
   c. No, only in personality testing.
   d. No, naturalness is more important than precision in both kinds of testing.

(4) Is it desirable to emphasize precision at the expense of naturalness in measurements of both achievement and personality?
   a. Yes.
   *b. No, only in measurements of achievement.
   c. No, only in measurements of personality.
   d. No. It is undesirable to emphasize precision at the expense of naturalness in either case.

In the remainder of this chapter, a number of suggestions will be offered for writing good multiple-choice test items. Most of these reflect conclusions that item writers have reached as a result of their own efforts to produce items that will yield dependable indications of achievement, and many are supported by rational inference. Nonetheless, only a few have been tested in rigorous experiments, and the results have not always clearly supported the suggestions.[4] Rigorous experiments in this area are difficult to manage, and the effect of violating one or a few suggestions is not likely to be great. On the whole, however, item writers are likely to produce better items if they know and follow the suggestions than if they are ignorant of them or disregarded them.

THE MULTIPLE-CHOICE ITEM STEM

The function of the item stem is to acquaint the examinee with the problem that is being posed. Ideally, it should state or imply a specific question. Although one can sometimes save words without loss of clarity by using an incomplete statement as the item stem, a direct question is often better. Not only does a direct question tend to present the student with a more specific problem, it also may focus the item writer's purposes more clearly and help him or her to avoid irrelevance or unrelatedness in the distracters. The two sample questions that follow illustrate two rather poor techniques for beginning the multiple-choice question.

[4] Robert F. McMorris et al., "Effects of Violating Test Construction Principles," *Journal of Educational Measurement*, 9 (Winter 1972), 287–95; and Cynthia Board and Douglas R. Whitney, "The Effect of Selected Poor Item-Writing Practices on Test Difficulty," *Journal of Educational Measurement*, 9 (Fall 1972), 225–34.

Physiology teaches us that
a. The development of vital organs is dependent upon muscular activity.
 b. Strength is independent of muscle size.
 c. The mind and body are not influenced by each other.
 d. Work is not exercise.

Here the subject of a sentence is used as the item stem and its predicate as the correct response. Obviously, the predicate does not *necessarily* follow: Physiology could teach us a variety of things. Even if the stem were rephrased to read, "What does physiology teach us?" the item would be just as bad.

In comparing the period of heterosexual adjustment of our culture with those of other cultures, it must be concluded that
a. There are tremendous differences that can only be explained on a cultural basis.
 b. There are large differences that must be explained by the interaction of biology and the more influential culture.
 c. Although there are some differences, the biological foundation of puberty is fundamental.
 d. In most cultures puberty is the period of heterosexual adjustment.

Here, again, there are any number of conclusions possible on the basis of a study of a particular period of human development. Until the examinee reads all the responses, she or he has no clear idea of what the question is asking. The item as a whole is not focused on any specific problem. This opens the way for confusing multiple interpretations.

Absolute Correctness Versus Best Possible Response

Ideally, the intended answer to a multiple-choice question should be a thoroughly correct answer, admitting no difference of opinion among adequately informed experts. This kind of absolute correctness, however, is difficult to achieve except in formal logical systems or in statements that simply reproduce other statements. Few, if any, inductive truths or experimentally based generalizations can be regarded as absolutely true. Test constructors must base many of their items on propositions that are not absolutely true but are strongly probable. They should, however, guard against basing items on statements whose validity would be challenged by competent scholars.

Another guideline to follow is that the stem of a multiple-choice item should ask a question that has a definite answer. Indeterminate questions may provide interesting topics for discussion, but they do not make good items for testing achievement. For example:

Which event in the following list has been of the greatest importance in American history?
*a. Braddock's defeat
b. Burr's conspiracy
c. The Hayes-Tilden contest
d. The Webster-Hayne debate

It is unlikely that scholars can agree on which of these events is of the greatest importance in American history. The importance of an event depends on the point of view of the person making the judgment and the context in which that individual is thinking of it.

While each multiple-choice item should have a definite answer, it may not always be an absolutely correct answer. Many good items ask the examinee to choose the best answer, as in this example.

Which statement best characterizes the man appointed by President Eisenhower to be Chief Justice of the United States Supreme Court?
a. An associate justice of the Supreme Court who had once been a professor of law at Harvard.
*b. A successful governor who had been an unsuccessful candidate for the Republican presidential nomination.
c. A well-known New York attorney who successfully prosecuted the leaders of the Communist party in the United States.
d. A Democratic senator from a southern state who had supported Eisenhower's campaign for the presidency.

For many of the most important questions that need to be asked, it is impossible to state an absolutely correct answer within the reasonable limits of a multiple-choice test item. Even if space limitation were not a factor, two experts would probably not agree on the precise wording of the best possible answer. Items whose "correct" answer is simply the best among the alternatives offered often permit the item writer to ask much more significant questions and free him or her from the responsibility of stating a correct answer so precisely that all authorities would agree that the particular wording used was the best possible wording.

Opinions in Multiple-Choice Items

What about items that involve expressions of opinion? If it is an opinion on which most experts agree, then a reasonable multiple-choice item can be based on it.

Which of these statements is most consistent with Jefferson's concept of democracy?
a. Democracy is part of the divine plan for mankind.
b. Democracy requires a strong national government.

*c. The purpose of government is to promote the welfare of the people.
 d. The purpose of government is to protect the people from radical or subversive minorities.

The responses to this question represent generalizations on the basis of Jefferson's speeches and writings. No authoritative sanction for one particular generalization is likely to be available. Yet scholars familiar with Jefferson's work would probably agree on a best answer to this item. In such cases the use of an item based on expert opinion is entirely justifiable. However, if the item asks the examinee for a personal opinion, it is subject to criticism. For example:

What do you consider the most important objective of staff meetings?
*a. To establish good working relations with your staff
 b. To handle routine matters
 c. To help teachers improve instruction
 d. To practice and exemplify democracy in administration

There is one sense in which any answer to this item must be considered a correct answer. On the other hand, what the item writer obviously wanted to do was to test the examinee's judgment against that of recognized authorities in the field of interpersonal relations. It would have been better to ask students directly to "choose the most important objective of staff meetings." Their answers will obviously be what *they* consider the most important objective, but all answers will be open to criticism and possible correction should they differ from the judgment of recognized experts.

Content and Presentation of the Item

Good multiple-choice items deal with important, significant ideas, not with incidental details, as does the first item following, nor with particular, unique organizations of subject matter, as does the second.

This question is based on the advertising campaign of Naumkeag Mills to retain the market leadership of Pequot bed linen. What was the competitive position of Pequot products in 1927?
 a. Ahead of all competitors among all customers
*b. Strong with institutional buyers but weak with household consumers
 c. Second only to Wamsutta among all customers
 d. Weak with all groups of consumers

This advertising campaign may indeed provide an excellent illustration of the problems involved and the practices to follow in advertising campaigns. But it seems not entirely appropriate to measure students' ability to handle an advertising campaign by asking them to recall the details of one illustration used in instruction.

The second principle of education is that the individual:
a. Gathers knowledge
b. Makes mistakes
c. Responds to situations
*d. Resents domination

The only person capable of answering this question is one who has studied a particular book or article. Whether a given principle of education is first or second is usually a matter of little importance. Educators have not agreed on any particular list of principles of education or any priority of principles. This item shows an undesirable close tie-up to the organization of subject matter used by a specific instructor or writer.

It is usually desirable to express the stem of the item so that it requests the essential knowledge being tested as directly, accurately, and simply as possible. The following item stem seems needlessly complex:

Considered from an economic viewpoint, which of these proposals to maintain world peace derives the least support from the military potentialities of atomic energy?
a. An international police force should be established.
b. Permanent programs of universal military training should be adopted.
*c. Sizes of standing military forces should be increased.
d. The remaining democratic nations of the world should enter into a military alliance.

Even after repeated careful readings, the meaning of this item stem is not clear. It involves a negative approach and seems to combine two dissimilar bases for judgment, economics and atomic energy. The wording of this item might seem to reflect lack of clarity in the thinking of the person who wrote it.

Informational preambles that serve only as window dressing and do not help the examinee understand the question being asked should ordinarily be avoided. Here are two examples.

While ironing her formal, Jane burned her hand accidentally on the hot iron. This was due to a transfer of heat by
*a. Conduction
b. Radiation
c. Convection
d. Absorption

The introductory sentence suggests that the item involves a practical problem. Actually the question asked calls only for knowledge of technical terminology.

In purifying water for a city water supply, one process is to have the impure water seep through layers of sand and fine and coarse gravel. Here many

impurities are left behind. Below are four terms, one of which will describe this process better than the others. Select the correct one.
  a. Sedimentation
*b. Filtration
  c. Chlorination
  d. Aeration

The primary purpose of a test item is to measure achievement. While much learning may occur during the process of taking a test, deliberate inclusion of instructional materials may reduce its effectiveness as a test more than its instructional value is increased. It might be better to ask the purpose of filtration in purifying city water supplies or the type of filter used.

Novel questions and novel problem situations reward the critical-minded student who has sought to understand what he/she was taught and penalize the superficial learner. Consider this example:

If the radius of the earth were increased by 3 feet, its circumference at the equator would be increased by about how much?
  a. 9 feet
  b. 12 feet
*c. 19 feet
  d. 28 feet

Requiring students to predict what would happen under certain unusual, even impossible, circumstances is a good way to measure their understanding of the principle involved. This type of task does a good job of discriminating between the student who can estimate an answer based on a thorough understanding of the principles and the student who must rely on formula and tedious computations.

It is usually desirable to avoid using the same questions or problems in a test that were used during instruction. In general, bona fide questions such as would be asked by a person honestly seeking information are likely to be more important than quiz-type questions, which would only be asked by someone who already knew the answer. Here is an example of a bona fide question:

J. B. Matthews, one-time employee of Senator McCarthy's subcommittee, charged that a large number of supporters of communism in the United States would be found in which of these groups?
  a. Wall Street bankers
  b. Newspaper editors
  c. Professional gamblers
*d. Protestant clergymen

It sometimes seems desirable to phrase the stem question to ask not for the correct answer, but for the incorrect answer. For example,

In the definition of a mineral, which of the following is incorrect?
    a. It was produced by geologic processes.
    b. It has distinctive physical properties.
    c. It contains one or more elements.
*d. Its chemical composition is variable.

Items that are negatively stated, that is, that require an examinee to pick an answer that is not true or characteristic, tend to be somewhat confusing. They appear unusually attractive to examination writers because so much of the instructional material is organized in terms of parallel subheadings under a main topic. This suggests the easy approach, that of asking for something that is *not* one of those subheadings. However, such questions are rarely encountered outside the classroom and thus lack the practical relevance that is usually desirable.

THE ALTERNATIVE RESPONSES

Each of the alternative answers offered in a multiple-choice test item should be appropriate to the question asked or implied by the item stem. Careless, hasty item writing can sometimes result in the inclusion of inappropriate answer choices as in this example.

The chief difference between the surface features of Europe and North America is that
    a. The area of Europe is larger.
    b. Europe extends more to the south.
    c. The Volga River is longer than the Missouri-Mississippi.
*d. The greater highlands and plains of Europe extend in an east-west direction.

Only the correct answer really describes a surface feature of Europe. Either the question should not be limited to "surface features" or the responses given should all conform to that category.

    Since multiple-choice responses are all intended to be answers to the same question, they should all be parallel (that is, similar) in grammatical structure, in type of content, in length, and in complexity. Unfortunately this is not always the case.

Slavery was first started
*a. At Jamestown settlement
    b. At Plymouth settlement
    c. At the settlement of Rhode Island
    d. A decade before the Civil War

The first three responses to this item are places; the fourth is a time. In questions of this type, it is not difficult to visualize an instance in which two responses would be correct. Use of a direct question stem might help to prevent this type of ambiguity.

Parallel structure sometimes requires that all responses begin with the same word. But if the same group of words is repeated in each response, the possibility of including that phrase only once in the stem should be considered.

Which is the best definition for a vein?
*a. A blood vessel carrying blood going to the heart
 b. A blood vessel carrying blue blood
 c. A blood vessel carrying impure blood
 d. A blood vessel carrying blood away from the heart

This item could probably be improved by using an incomplete statement stem such as, "A vein is a blood vessel carrying. . . ." Occasionally some repetition provides the most convenient way of making the item clear, but in this case, the repetition seems excessive.

Since alternative responses are intended to represent a set of distinct options to the stem question, it is helpful to the examinee and to the effectiveness of the test item if they do indeed present clear choices.

Meat can be preserved in brine due to the fact that:
 a. Salt is a bacterial poison.
*b. Bacteria cannot withstand the osmotic action of the brine.
 c. Salt alters the chemical composition of the food.
 d. Brine protects the meat from contact with air.

Both responses *a* and *b* could be judged correct. Response *b* simply explains why response *a* is correct. In a case like this, it is undesirable to count only one of two almost equally correct responses.

Another problem arises when responses are long and complex so that examinees have difficulty perceiving and keeping in mind the essential differences among the alternatives.

Systematic geography differs from regional geography mainly in that
 a. Systematic geography deals, in the main, with physical geography, whereas regional geography concerns itself essentially with the field of human geography.
 b. Systematic geography studies a region systematically, while regional geography is concerned only with a descriptive account of a region.
*c. Systematic geography studies a single phenomenon in its distribution over the earth in order to supply generalizations for regional geography, which studies the arrangement of phenomena in one given area.
 d. Systematic geography is the modern scientific way of studying differentiation of the earth's surface, while regional geography is the traditional and descriptive way of studying distribution of phenomena in space.

A better question might ask, "What is the characteristic of systematic geography which distinguishes it essentially from regional geography?"

Brevity in the responses simplifies the task for the examinee by removing an irrelevant source of difficulty. Brief responses also tend to focus attention on the essential differences among the alternatives offered. Other things being equal, the multiple-choice test item having shorter responses will be superior. But a test composed largely of items using one-word responses or very short phrases is likely to place more emphasis on vocabulary than on command of knowledge. The item writer should not sacrifice importance and significance in the questions to gain brevity in the responses. By way of illustration, if the purpose of an item is to test understanding of the word *monogamy*, the first of the following items will probably do the job better than the second.

What is monogamy?
 a. Refusal to marry
 b. Marriage of one woman to more than one husband
 c. Marriage of one man to more than one wife
d. Marriage of one man to only one wife

A marriage in which one woman marries one man is called
 a. unicameral
 b. dualism
 c. monotheism
d. monogamy

A common device for adapting multiple-choice items to questions that seem to require several correct answers is to add as a final alternative the response, "all of the above." But use of this response is strictly appropriate only if all the preceding alternatives are *thoroughly correct* answers to the stem question, and even here there is an element of inherent ambiguity. A correct answer should not be wrong simply because there are other correct answers. For these reasons, "all of the above" should be used sparingly as an alternative to multiple-choice test items.

The response "none of the above" is also sometimes used, either as the intended answer or as a distracter. It is particularly useful in multiple-choice arithmetic or spelling items where the distinction between correctness and error is unequivocal. But this response, like "all of the above," should *not* be used unless the best answer is a thoroughly correct answer. Here are examples of correct (first) and incorrect (second) usage of these responses.

Which word is misspelled?
 a. Contrary
b. Tendancy
 c. Extreme
 d. Variable
 e. None of these

What does the term *growth* mean?
a. Maturation
 b. Learning
 c. Development
 d. All of these
 e. None of these

Number and Arrangement of Responses

Common practice in writing multiple-choice tests calls for three or four distracters for each item. If good distracters are available, the larger the number of alternatives, the more highly discriminating the item is likely to be. However, as one seeks to write more distracters each additional one is likely to be somewhat weaker. There is some merit in setting one's goal at three good distracters to each multiple-choice item and in struggling temporarily to reach this goal. Not all good distracters are immediately apparent. Some will emerge only after considerable brain racking.

On the other hand, there is no magic in four alternatives and no real reason why all items in a test should have the same number of alternatives. It is quite possible to write a good multiple-choice test item with only two distracters (three responses), and occasionally with only one distracter, as Smith, and Ebel and Williams have shown.[5] After tryout, one can actually improve some items by dropping those alternatives that don't distract poor students, or that do distract good ones.

Students may sometimes arrive at the correct answer to a multiple-choice test item through a process of elimination. Rejecting responses that seem unsatisfactory, they are finally left with one termed the "right answer," not because they have any basis for choosing it directly, but simply because none of the others will do.

The availability of this process of elimination is sometimes regarded as a weakness of the multiple-choice item form. It is charged that students get credit for knowing something they really don't know. Most specialists in test construction, however, do not disapprove of the process of answering by elimination and do not regard it as a sign of weakness in multiple-choice items in general, or in an item where the process is particularly useful. (It might be noted in passing that an item that uses the response "none of the above" as a correct answer *requires* the student to answer by a process of elimination.) There are two reasons why this process is not generally deplored by test specialists.

In the first place, the function of achievement test items is primarily

[5] Kendon Smith, "An Investigation of the Use of 'Double Choice' Items in Testing Achievement," *Journal of Educational Research*, 51 (1958), 387–89; and Robert L. Ebel and Bob J. Williams, "The Effect of Varying the Number of Alternatives per Item on Multiple-choice Vocabulary Test Items," *The 14th Yearbook of the National Council on Measurements Used in Education* (East Lansing, Mich.: Michigan State University, 1957), pp. 63–65.

to contribute to a measure of general achievement in an area of study. They are not intended primarily to provide an inventory of which particular bits of knowledge or skills a student has. The achievement of a student who answers items 1, 3, and 5 correctly but misses 2 and 4 is regarded as equal to the achievement of another student who answers items 2, 3, and 4 correctly but misses 1 and 5. Identifying exactly which things a student has achieved or failed to achieve is a matter of secondary importance in an achievement test.

In the second place, the knowledge and ability required to properly eliminate incorrect alternatives can be, and usually is, closely related to the knowledge or ability that would be required to select the correct alternative. If education does not consist in the accumulation of unrelated bits of information, if the development of a meaningful network of related facts and concepts is essential, then the fact that a student responds in a reflective, problem-solving manner, choosing the best answer by rational processes (including the process of elimination), should be applauded rather than deplored.

In practice, few multiple-choice test items are likely to be answered correctly merely by eliminating incorrect choices. Far more often the process of choice will involve comparative judgments of this alternative against that. It is unlikely that an examinee who is totally ignorant of the correct answer would have knowledge enough to eliminate with certainty the incorrect alternatives. This is especially likely to be true if the item is well enough constructed so that all the available alternatives, correct and incorrect, have some obvious basic similarity. For these reasons, it seems safe to conclude that the problem of answer choice by a process of distracter elimination need not be regarded as a serious one.

It is usually desirable to list the responses to a multiple-choice item rather than to arrange them in tandem, as in this example.

The balance sheet report for the Ajax Canning Company would reveal (a) The company's profit for the previous fiscal year *(b) The amount of money owed to its creditors (c) The amount of income tax paid (d) The amount of sales for the previous fiscal period.

Responses in tandem save some space but are much more difficult to compare than those placed in list form. Another good rule is that whenever the alternatives form a quantitative or qualitative scale, they normally should be arranged in order of magnitude from smallest to largest or largest to smallest. This may avoid some confusion on the part of the examinee and eliminate an irrelevant source of error.

The population of Denmark is about
  a. 2 million
*b. 4 million
  c. 7 million
  d. 15 million

THE DISTRACTERS

The purpose of a distracter (incorrect response) in a multiple-choice test item is to discriminate between those students who have command of a specific body of knowledge and those who lack it. To do this, the distracter must be a plausible alternative. One way of obtaining plausible distracters is to use true statements which do not correctly answer the stem question. For example:

What is the principal advantage of a battery of lead storage cells over a battery of dry cells for automobile starting and lighting?
   a. The storage cell furnishes direct current.
   b. The voltage of the storage cell is higher.
 c. The current from the storage cell is stronger.
   d. The initial cost of the storage cell is less.

Lead storage cells do furnish direct current, and at a higher voltage than dry cells, but this is not the reason why the storage cell is preferred. Judgments concerning the relevance of knowledge may be as important as judgments concerning its truth. Multiple-choice items should make frequent use of this device for testing an achievement that is sometimes thought to be testable only by using essay examinations.

    Another source of plausible distracters are familiar expressions, phrases that have been used in common parlance and this may seem attractive to students whose knowledge is merely superficial.

Which of these has effected the greatest change in domestic plants and animals?
   a. Influence of environment on heredity
   b. Organic evolution
 c. Selective breeding
   d. Survival of the fittest

Phrases like "organic evolution" or "survival of the fittest," which a student may have heard without understanding, provide excellent distracters at the elementary level of discrimination for which this item is intended.
    Obscure distracters, on the other hand, are usually undesirable.

A *chaotic* condition is
   a. Asymptotic
 b. Confused
   c. Gauche
   d. Permutable

If the words *chaotic* and *confused* represent an appropriate level of difficulty for this vocabulary test, then the remaining terms used as distracters are obviously too difficult. It is unreasonable to expect the examinee to know for sure that one of them might not be a better synonym for "chaotic" than the intended correct answer. The use of distracters that are less difficult than the correct answer is sometimes criticized because it permits a student to respond successfully by eliminating incorrect responses. However, students who can respond successfully on this basis usually possess more knowledge than those who cannot. Hence the discriminating power of an item is not impaired by this characteristic. Of course, a distracter which is absurd or highly implausible will contribute little or nothing to the effectiveness of a test item.

Which of the following has helped most to increase the average length of human life?
  a. Fast driving
  b. Avoidance of overeating
  c. Wider use of vitamins
*d. Wider use of inoculations

Some teachers may feel that the abilities of some of their students cannot possibly be underestimated, but they should not let this feeling of frustration lead them to employ such an unreasonable distracter as response *a*.

The search for plausible distracters may sometimes induce an item writer to resort to trickery, as in this item.

Horace Greeley is known for his
  a. Advice to young men not to go West
  b. Discovery of anesthetics
*c. Editorship of the *New York Tribune*
  d. Humorous anecdotes

Insertion of the "not" in the first response spoils what would otherwise be the best answer to the question and thus makes the item more a test of students' alertness than of their knowledge of Horace Greeley. Trickery of this kind reflects badly on the ethics of the item writer, and is likely to spoil the discriminating power of the item.

It has occurred to a number of item writers that they might use as distracters the wrong answers students give when they are asked to complete short-answer tests.[6] Some useful ideas are quite likely to be obtained in this way, but the gain in quality of items or ease of item writing seldom seems to justify the labor of obtaining the student responses.[7] An item writer's own unaided ideas are likely to be about as good as those he or she would get from the student responses.

[6] M. R. Loree, "A Study of a Technique for Improving Tests." Unpublished doctoral dissertation, University of Chicago, 1948.

[7] Richard E. Owens, Gerald S. Hanna, and Floyd L. Coppedge, "Comparison of Multiple-Choice Tests Using Different Types of Distracter Selection Techniques," *Journal of Educational Measurement*, 7 (1970), 87–90.

Obtaining Good Distracters

Here are some tactics that the item writer may find helpful in developing good distracters for a multiple-choice test item.

1. *Define the class of things to which all the alternative answers must belong.*

For example, if the question asks what cools an electric refrigerator, the class of possible answers is defined as "things that can cause cooling," such as ice, moving air, expansion of gas, and so forth.

2. *Think of things that have some association with terms used in the question.*

For the electric refrigerator question, these might be such things as "flow of electricity through a compressed gas," or "electromagnetic absorption of heat energy."

3. *If the item calls for a quantitative answer, make the responses distinctly different points along the same scale.*

For example, in response to the question, "How many questions should the average student answer correctly on a good multiple-choice test?" the alternative answers might be 40 percent, 60 percent, 80 percent, and 90 percent. Such a scale is illustrated in this item.

How did (A) the estimated amount of petroleum discovered in new fields in 1953 compare with (B) the amount extracted from producing fields in the same year?
  a. A was practically zero.
  b. A was about half of B.
  c. A just about equaled B.
*d. A was greater than B.

In many situations the precise value of a quantitative answer is less important than knowledge of a general level or relationship. One systematic approach to testing in quantitative situations is to categorize the responses to represent intervals on a scale of quantities. The use of code letters for the two quantities to be compared shortens the response options and probably adds to their clarity.

Sometimes it is possible to establish a qualitative scale of responses, as in this item.

Some cases of lung cancer have been attributed to smoking. What was the status of this idea in 1953?[8]
 a. The theory had been clearly established by medical evidence.
b. It was a controversial matter and some experts considered the evidence to be inconclusive.
 c. The theory had been clearly disproved by surveys of smokers.
 d. The theory was such a recent development that no tests of it had been completed.

The responses to this item represent a scale of values from complete establishment to complete indefiniteness. The use of a qualitative scale of responses helps to systematize the process of test construction and to suggest desirable responses.

4. *Phrase the question so that it calls for a "yes" or "no" answer plus an explanation.*

Here is an example.

Has the average size of farms in the United States tended to increase in recent years? Why?
 a. Yes, because as the soil loses its natural fertility more land must be cultivated to maintain the same output
b. Yes, because the use of farm machinery has made large farms more efficient than small farms
 c. No, because the difficulty in securing farm labor has forced many farmers to limit their operations
 d. No, because large family farms tend to be subdivided to provide smaller farms for the children

5. *Use various combinations of two elements as the alternatives.*

Thus four responses might occasionally assume this form:

1. Only A
2. Only B
3. Both A and B
4. Neither A nor B

[8] This item and others used as illustrations in this chapter were collected from a variety of sources. Some were written originally for use in tests of understanding of contemporary affairs in the early 1950s. Although the item content may be out of date, the principles of item writing are still valid.

An item illustrating this tactic is:

What was the general policy of the Eisenhower administration during 1953 with respect to government expenditures and taxes?
  a. Reduction of both expenditures and taxes
*b. Reduction of expenditures, no change in taxes
  c. Reduction in taxes, no change in expenditures
  d. No change in either expenditures or taxes

If the two elements each have two different values, for example rise-fall, rapidly-slowly, they can be combined in this way to give four alternatives.

1. It rises rapidly
2. It rises slowly
3. It falls slowly
4. It falls rapidly

6. *Finally, if alternatives still remain elusive, consider using a different approach in the item stem.*

It is also useful sometimes to back off from the writing job and to ask just what the item is supposed to be testing. If the proposition on which it is based is self-evident, or if a plausible false alternative to it does not exist, the idea may just as well be discarded, and a new start made with a better idea.

WORDING THE ITEM

The purpose of the words and syntax chosen in writing a multiple-choice test item is to communicate explicit meaning as efficiently as possible. Habits of colorful, picturesque, imaginative, creative writing may serve the item writer badly by impairing the precision and definiteness of a communication. Few written words are read with such careful attention to meaning, expressed and implied, as those in objective test items. Item writing makes rigorous demands on the vocabulary and writing skill of test constructors as well as on their mastery of the subject matter and their familiarity with the caliber of the students to be tested. Simple carelessness in grammar, usage, punctuation, or spelling may interfere with the effectiveness of an item and will certainly reflect no credit on the item writer. Skill in expository writing and careful exercise of that skill are essential to the production of good objective test items.

It is well to specify all conditions and qualifications necessary to make the intended response definitely the best of the available alternatives. Consider this example.

What change occurs in the composition of the air in a lighted airtight room in which the only living things are growing green plants?
   a. Carbon dioxide increases and oxygen decreases.
b. Carbon dioxide decreases and oxygen increases.
   c. Both carbon dioxide and oxygen increase.
   d. Both carbon dioxide and oxygen decrease.

As originally worded this item simply asked, "What change occurs in the composition of the air in a room in which green plants are growing?" Only if one specifies that the room is lighted, so that photosynthesis can take place; that it is airtight, so that changes in air composition will not be neutralized by ventilation; and that there are no other living things that might consume the oxygen faster than it is produced, is it possible to give a firm answer to this question.

Sometimes when item writers seek to limit a question in order to elicit a definitely correct answer, they reduce its dimensions to the point that the question itself becomes inconsequential. For example, it is important to know why the armed forces of the United States were ordered into combat in Korea in 1950, but it is difficult to give a thoroughly correct answer to such a question. On the other hand, it is quite easy to give an unequivocally truthful answer to the question, "What explanation for U. S. military action in Korea was given in an editorial in the *Chicago Tribune* on Friday, June 30, 1950?" But the knowledge this question tests is of dubious value.

Item writers should never settle for a best answer when a correct answer to the same question is available. They should be sure that, in the eyes of competent experts, the best alternative is clearly superior to all the others. At the same time, however, they should not avoid important questions simply because there is no absolutely and completely correct answer. If many descriptive or qualifying ideas are required, the clearest expression may be achieved by placing them in separate introductory sentences.

The term *creeping socialism* appeared frequently in political discussions in the early 1950s. Which of these is most often used to illustrate creeping socialism?
a. Generation and distribution of electric power by the federal government
   b. Communist infiltration of labor unions
   c. Gradual increase in sales and excise taxes
   d. Participation of the United States in international organizations such as the United Nations

The use of two sentences—one to present background information and the other to ask the question—frequently adds to the clarity of the item stem. Combining these two elements into a single-question sentence probably would make it considerably more complex.

Clues to the Correct Response

Multiple-choice items sometimes provide unintended clues to the correct answer that offer considerable help to a poorly prepared examinee. One indication of the correct response is a lack of parallelism in the alternatives offered. There is a tendency for item writers to express the correct answer more carefully and at greater length than the other alternatives. Sometimes key words from the item stem, or their synonyms, are repeated in the correct answer. Sometimes the correct response is more consistent grammatically or semantically with the item stem than are the other responses. Or perhaps the correct response is more general and inclusive than any distracter. At other times a familiar verbal stereotype is used as the correct answer, so that students can respond successfully simply by recalling vaguely that they had encountered those same words before. Finally, it occasionally happens that the stem of one item will inadvertently suggest the answer to another item. Here are some examples of items that provide irrelevant clues:

When used in conjunction with the T-square, the left vertical edge of a triangle is used to draw:
a. Vertical lines
  b. Slant lines
  c. Horizontal lines
  d. Inclined lines

The use of the word *vertical* in both the stem and the correct response of this item provides an obvious clue.

Minor differences among organisms of the same kind are known as:
  a. Heredity
b. Variations
  c. Adaptation
  d. Natural selection

The plural term *differences* in the stem calls for a plural response, which can only be response *b*.

The major weakness of our government under the Articles of Confederation was that:
  a. There were no high officials.
b. It lacked power.
  c. It was very difficult to amend.
  d. There was only one house in Congress.

There is an obvious relation between lack of power and weakness of government. If a person knew nothing about the Articles of Confederation, common sense would nonetheless dictate the correct response.

How did styles in women's clothing in 1950 differ most from those in 1900?
  a. They showed more beauty.
  b. They showed more variety.
  c. They were easier to clean.
d. They were easier to live in, to work in, to move in, and were generally less restrictive.

The greater detail used in stating the correct response makes it undesirably obvious.

History tells us that all nations have enjoyed participation in:
  a. Gymnastics
  b. Football
c. Physical training of some sort
  d. Baseball

Response 3 obviously provides a more reasonable completion to the stem than any of the other responses. It represents a consistent style of expression. This is one of the dangers inherent in the use of incomplete statement item stems.

All of these irrelevant clues to the correct answer are undesirable, of course, and should be avoided. It is entirely appropriate to plant such clues deliberately in the distracters to mislead the testwise but poorly prepared student. To give all of the relevant clues—those useful to well-prepared examinees—while avoiding the irrelevant clues is an important skill in writing multiple-choice test items.

Adjusting Item Difficulty

Any test item that is either much too easy or much too difficult for a group of examinees cannot provide much useful information about their relative levels of achievement. If on inspection or after tryout an item is found to be inappropriate in difficulty, some corrective action may be needed.

To some extent the difficulty of a multiple-choice test item is inherent in the idea on which it rests. There are, however, techniques that give the writers of multiple-choice test items some control over the difficulty of the items they produce on a given topic. In general, stem questions can be made easier by making them more general or harder by making them more specific. The following pair of items is illustrative.

A tariff is a tax on:
  a. Gifts of money
b. Goods brought into a country
  c. Income of immigrants
  d. Real estate

Only the most general notions about a tariff are required to respond successfully to this item, which is thus suitable for use at the lowest level of achievement. Much more knowledge of tariffs is required to respond successfully to the following item.

A high protective tariff on Swiss watches in the United States is intended to most directly benefit:
a. Swiss watchmakers
b. United States citizens who buy Swiss watches
c. United States government officials
*d. United States watchmakers

This pair of items illustrates how the generality or specificity of a question can be used to help control its difficulty.

Item writers can also make the correct response easier to select by making the alternatives more heterogeneous or harder to select by making them more homogeneous. Compare the responses of the first item that follows with those of the second.

An embargo is
*a. A law or regulation
b. A kind of boat
c. An embankment
d. A foolish adventure

Because the responses to this item vary widely, only an elementary knowledge of embargoes is required for successful response.

An embargo is
a. A tariff
b. A customs duty
*c. The stoppage of goods from entry and departure
d. An admission of goods free of duty

The homogeneity of responses in this second question make it considerably more difficult.

Another means of making an item easier is to provide more than one basis for choosing the correct answer, as in this item.

Which of the following are outstanding contemporary pianists?
*a. Robert Casadesus and Rudolph Serkin
b. Patrice Munsel and Marian Anderson
c. Claude Debussy and Ignace Paderewski
d. Alan Paton and Alec Guinness

The use of the names of two individuals fitting the specification in the item stem makes it somewhat easier. The examinee need only know one of the contemporary pianists—or know one in each of the three distracters is not a contemporary pianist—to respond successfully.

SUMMARY

Some of the main ideas developed in this chapter are expressed in the following 26 statements:

1. The most highly regarded and widely used form of objective test at present is the multiple-choice test.
2. Critics of multiple-choice test items tend to exaggerate the number of faulty items that appear in tests and the seriousness of the consequences of those faults. They seldom offer evidence in support of their charges or better alternatives for testing.
3. Multiple-choice test items should be based on sound, significant ideas that can be expressed as independently meaningful propositions.
4. The important aspects of educational achievement that can be measured by objective tests are largely identical with those that can be measured by essay tests.
5. The use of compound responses, including an answer plus an explanation, or some combination of two elements, sometimes solves the problem of providing four good alternative answers to a multiple-choice test question.
6. The stem of a multiple-choice item should state or clearly imply a specific direct question.
7. The wording of a multiple-choice item should not follow familiar textbook phraseology so closely that verbal memory without comprehension will provide an adequate basis for response.
8. Item stems including the word *not* and asking in effect for an incorrect answer tend to be superficial in content and confusing to the examinee.
9. Some of the most effective multiple-choice test questions call for a best answer rather than an absolutely correct answer.
10. Good multiple-choice test items can be based on matters of opinion if most experts share that opinion.
11. The item writer should avoid asking the examinee for a personal opinion.
12. Items testing recall of incidental details of instruction or special organizations of subject matter are ordinarily undesirable.
13. The item stem should pose the essence of its question as simply and accurately as possible.

14. The stem of a multiple-choice item should be expressed as concisely as possible without sacrificing clarity or omitting essential qualifications.
15. To function properly a multiple-choice item must be expressed in carefully chosen words and critically edited phrases.
16. All of the responses to a multiple-choice test item should be parallel in point of view, grammatical structure, and general appearance.
17. Brevity is desirable in multiple-choice item responses, but it should not be achieved at the expense of importance and significance in the question asked.
18. The responses "none of the above" and "all of the above" are appropriate only when the answers given to a question are absolutely correct or incorrect (as in spelling or arithmetic problems).
19. The responses to a multiple-choice item should be expressed simply enough to make clear the essential differences among them.
20. While most multiple-choice items provide at least four alternative answers, good questions can be written with only two or three alternatives.
21. The responses to a multiple-choice item should be listed rather than written one after another in a compact paragraph.
22. A student who selects the correct response to a multiple-choice item by eliminating the incorrect responses demonstrates useful achievement.
23. The distracters in a multiple-choice item should be definitely less correct than the answer, but plausibly attractive to the uninformed.
24. True statements that do not provide good answers to the stem question often make good distracters.
25. The intended answer should be clear, concise, correct, and free of clues.
26. Test constructors can make some multiple-choice items easier by making the stem more general and the responses more diverse; they can make items harder by making the stem more specific and the responses more similar.

PROJECTS AND PROBLEMS

Project: Writing Multiple-Choice Test Items

Using the information in the following paragraphs as directly and simply as possible, write ten good multiple-choice items. Do not try to test for understanding of the information or for applications of it. For example, if the information given had been:

The national government of Great Britain is located in London. It is not located in Birmingham, Paris, or Berlin.

An appropriate multiple-choice item would be:

Where is the national government of Great Britain located?
  a) Berlin
  b) Birmingham
*c) London
  d) Paris

Treat each of the ten paragraphs below in the same way. Indicate the correct response with an asterisk.

1. A magnet attracts pieces of iron. It does not attract pieces of glass or wood or copper.
2. When heat is applied to a liquid, the molecules of the liquid move faster. The molecules do not expand, or decompose, or combine.
3. A major cause of lung cancer is smoking. Pneumonia, high blood pressure, or excessive use of alcohol are not major causes of lung cancer.
4. If the sides of a rectangle are 5 inches and 12 inches, the diagonal is 13 inches. It is not 17 inches, or 7 inches, or 34 inches.
5. The intelligence quotient involves measures of mental ability. It does not involve measures of physical development, years of schooling, or social maturity.
6. The Elizabethan Age is notable for the amount of great literature produced. It is not notable for improvements in agriculture, for revolutionary uprisings in Europe, or for popular democracy in government.
7. The purpose of the judicial branch of the United States Government is to interpret laws. It is not to make the laws, or to enforce the laws, or to investigate violations of laws.
8. The increasing size of farms in the United States is due mainly to the use of farm machinery. It is not due mainly to the development of farm cooperatives, or high yield varieties, or mortgage foreclosures on small farms.
9. The area of land that was located north of the Ohio River, east of the Mississippi River, and south of Canada was known as the Northwest Territory. It was not known as the Louisiana Purchase, the Gadsden Purchase, or the Old Dominion.
10. Knowing what force operates through what distance, you can calculate how much work has been done. You cannot calculate how much horsepower was used, or how great was the mechanical advantage, or the velocity of motion.

Problem: Writing Items to Discriminate

Write or copy a short paragraph of from three to seven sentences expressing ideas you think few, if any, of the other members of this class already know. On another sheet, write three different independent items—two true-false and one four-alternative multiple-choice—designed to test the knowledge of these ideas. None of the items should refer directly to the paragraph.

Your items and the paragraph on which they are based will be tried out by your classmates in one of the class meetings. The class will be divided into tryout groups of 6 to 10 members. The items written by members of the group will be circulated within the group to obtain pre-information responses. Each person, except the author of the item, will record his or her responses independently, guarding against being influenced by the responses others may have given. Then the items will be circulated again along with the paragraphs to obtain post-information responses.

When all this has been done and the responses have been returned to the author of the items, he/she must do these four things:

1. Enter the key (correct response) for each item.
2. Calculate an index of discrimination for each item using this arithmetic:
   a. Number of post-information correct responses, minus
   b. Number of pre-information correct responses, divided by
   c. Number of total responses, pre or post (that is, one less than the number of members of the group).
3. Add the three indices of discrimination, taking account of signs (that is, subtracting the negative indices).
4. Fasten paragraph, items, responses, and calculations together and turn them in. Be sure your name is on each sheet.

Your instructor may supply you with special forms on which you may write the items. The other side of the form will provide spaces for recording the responses and calculating the discrimination indices.

Tests should use whatever testing technique
is most relevant to the trait and group
being measured.

WILLIAM A. McCALL

9

Short-Answer, Matching, and Other Objective Test Items

SHORT-ANSWER ITEMS[1]

A short-answer test item aims to test knowledge by asking examinees to supply a word, phrase, or number that answers a question or completes a sentence. Here are several examples.

(1) Who discovered the insulin treatment of diabetes?	Banting
(2) The holy city of Islam is	Mecca
(3) When was the battle of Hastings fought?	1066 A.D.

What is the common name of each of these chemical substances?

(4) $CaCO_3$	limestone
(5) NaCL	salt
(6) $C_{12}H_{22}O_{11}$	sugar
(7) NaOH	lye
(8) NH_3	ammonia

Items 4 through 8 constitute a cluster of similar short-answer items based on the same question.

[1] This section owes much to the work of Alexander G. Wesman, "Writing the Test Item," in *Educational Measurement*, ed. Robert L. Thorndike (Washington, D.C.: American Council on Education, 1971).

Short-answer items deal mainly with words and numbers. They ask for names of persons, places, things, processes, colors, and so forth. They may also ask for English words, foreign equivalents, or symbols that represent words in shorthand, mathematics, chemistry, music, or logic. Common responses also include numbers representing dates, distances, costs, and populations. If they call for a phrase, it is usually something short, specific, and familiar, such as "spontaneous combustion" or "discovery of America." An item that calls for a collection of somewhat longer responses, for example, "Give three reasons why . . ." or "List the traits of . . ." is more correctly classified as a short essay question than a short-answer item.

This means that short-answer items test mainly for factual information. As the foundation of all reliable knowledge, facts constitute an important substratum. But there is much, much more to knowledge than the facts that can be reported in single words, short phrases, or numbers. What short-answer items can test is much more limited than what true-false or multiple-choice items can test. Thus, while any short-answer item can be converted to a true-false or multiple-choice item, only a few true-false or multiple-choice items can be converted to the short-answer form.

Short-answer items are very much less affected by guessing than are true-false or multiple-choice items. They also are supposed to test recall rather than recognition, which in the eyes of some instructors makes them more demanding and more valid as tests of achievement. However, as we have already seen, blind guessing is not only a rather rare phenomenon; the harm that it can do to the score on a reasonably good, reasonably long test is actually rather slight. And in response to the contention that recall is a more strenuous mental process than recognition, it may be said that good choice-type items seldom can be answered by simple recognition. In fact, they are more likely than are short-answer items to test understanding and to require reflective thinking.

Despite these limitations, short-answer items have a place in educational measurement. They are reasonably easy to write. They are efficient, providing many separate scorable responses per page or per unit of testing time. And if the group to be tested is reasonably small, the scoring which must be done by the teacher or a competent aide is not unreasonably burdensome.

Short-answer tests are widely and justifiably popular in the elementary grades where basic vocabularies are being built in subjects like spelling, shorthand, and arithmetic, and in those parts of science where names of structures, substances and symbols must be learned.

Writing Short-Answer Items

1. *Word the question or incomplete statement carefully enough to require a single, unique answer.*

A common problem with short-answer items is that a question which the item writer thought would call for answer A elicits from some of the examinees equally defensible answers B, C, or D. For example, the question, "What is coal?", to which the intended answer was "a fuel," might also elicit such answers as "petrified vegetable matter," "a burning ember," or "impure carbon." To prevent this dual ambiguity—indefiniteness in what is tested and consequent difficulty in scoring—the question should be reworded so as to elicit a more specific answer.

For what purpose is most coal used?
From what substance was coal formed?
What name is applied to a glowing coal in a fire?
Coal consists mainly of what chemical element?

2. *Think of the intended answer first. Then write a question to which that answer is the only appropriate response.*

The focus of a short-answer question should be on the intended answer. If item writers keep that answer in mind and word their questions accordingly, they will probably succeed in avoiding indefiniteness and multiple correct answers. An alternative, but inferior, method of obtaining short-answer items is to find a textbook sentence from which a word can be deleted to make a short-answer item. For example:

Thunderstorms form when columns of _____ air rise to cooler altitudes.

Possible correct answers to this item include "warmer," "lower," and "moist." This example also serves to illustrate the next three suggestions for writing short-answer items.

3. *If the item is an incomplete sentence, try to word it so the blank comes at the end of the sentence.*

This will often make the intent of the item clearer and avoid some of the indefiniteness and possibility of multiple answers.

4. *Use a direct question, unless the incomplete sentence permits a more concise or clearly defined correct answer.*

When an incomplete sentence is arranged so the blank comes at the end, it will often be apparent that a direct question would be just as easy to write and possibly a shade easier to understand. For example:

The holy city of Islam is _____.

versus

What is the holy city of Islam? _____.

However, answers to the question:

Why did the United States declare war on Japan in 1941?

are likely to be more variable and somewhat longer than completions of the sentence:

The immediate cause for the U.S. declaration of war on Japan in 1941 was the bombing of Pearl Harbor.

5. *Avoid unintended clues to the correct answer.*

The word *cooler* in the item on thunderstorms suggests that the air before it rose must have been warmer. Or consider this item:

Steamboats are moved by engines that run on the pressure of _____.

It takes little knowledge or insight to guess that the correct answer to this item must be "steam." For what purpose is a question like this one being asked at all? Focusing on the answer before writing the question is likely to result in more important questions that have more specifically unique answers. It is also important to remember that questions written with a specific answer in mind are likely to be more relevant and more concise than sentences lifted from text material:

6. *Word the item as concisely as possible without losing specificity of response.*

Clear ideas are expressed in concise statements or questions. Excess words waste the examinee's time and may confuse the idea to be expressed.

7. *Arrange space for recording answers on the right margin of the question page.*

This practice not only makes the items easier to score, which is its main justification, but also encourages the use of direct questions or placement of blanks at the end of incomplete sentences.

8. *Avoid using the conventional wording of an important idea as the basis for a short-answer item.*

Use of the usual wording may encourage and reward study to memorize rather than to understand. For example:

Gain or loss divided by the cost equals the gain or loss in _____.
Two lines perpendicular to the same line in the same plane are _____ to each other.

Better versions of these items would be:

To determine the percent of gain on a transaction, by what must the actual gain be divided? _____
If two lines are drawn perpendicular to the same line on a sheet of paper, they are _____.

Paragraph-Completion Items

In the early years of objective testing, item writers sometimes used paragraph-completion items as a convenient device to yield a large number of answers on any one test page. A paragraph of text was selected and key words were replaced by blanks. The student's task was to fill in the blanks.

Items of this kind are no longer in favor. In addition to the general limitations of short-answer items and the particular limitations of such items when based on textbook sentences, the paragraph-completion items had two other shortcomings. One was that item writers tended to mutilate the paragraphs by removing so many key words that what remained might best be described as a skeletal guessing game. Consider this example:

A ray of _____ entering a _____ of _____ is bent _____, which makes the _____ appear _____ than it really is.

Students who guess that the sentence is talking about rays of light entering a body of water may, if they know about refraction, understand that the ray will be bent downward, making the water appear shallower than it really is. But to fill these blanks correctly requires either a photographic memory for textbook sentences or considerable luck and cleverness.

The foregoing illustration points to the second shortcoming of paragraph-completion items. The student responses to be scored tend to be concentrated on relatively narrow aspects of the subject being studied. Further, they are highly interrelated, so that success in filling an earlier blank may be a prerequisite for completing later items. Since the separate responses do not provide independent indications of achievement, sampling of achievements is restricted. When this happens, the reliability and validity of the scores will suffer.

NUMERICAL PROBLEMS

While numerical problems can be presented as multiple-choice test items, they are most often presented in short-answer form. Numerical problems provide the basis for a wide variety of test items in arithmetic and other branches of mathematics, in the sciences, in bookkeeping, and accounting, and in any fields of study where exact quantitative relationships have been developed.

Numerical problems provide good measures of achievement in learning. They are performance tests that assess application of knowledge. Many novel problems can easily be produced by changing the given quantities and the ways in which they are presented; and these novel problems are an excellent way to test understanding in contrast to mere recall. The answers are usually concise and hence easy to score, even in short-answer form. All these are virtues of numerical problems as short-answer test items. But sometimes there are minor difficulties in using them.

The problem of avoiding a number of correct responses, which plagues other short-answer items, takes a somewhat different form in numerical problems. How precisely correct must the answer be to receive credit? How much partial credit should be given if the process is correct but the answer incorrect because of computational errors? No blanket answer can be given to these questions, but the following suggestions may help to avoid serious difficulties on these points.

1. *Use the simplest numbers possible.*

The purpose of the item is to test understanding of a process, not computational accuracy. If accuracy needs to be tested, test it in separate items, using numbers as complex as may be necessary.

2. *If possible, choose the given quantities so that the answer will be a whole number.*

To do this will help to avoid uncertainty about how far a decimal fraction should be carried out.

3. *Specify the degree of precision expected in the answer.*

If students are uncertain about what they are being asked to do, and if they guess wrongly, the measurement of what they are able to do will be made less accurate.

4. *If a fully correct answer must specify the unit of measure in which it is expressed, tell the examinee this as part of the problem.*

It is easy for a distracted examinee to forget to write the units in which an answer is expressed. If knowing what the units should be is an important part of the problem, ask for them separately, thus:

What number expresses the intensity of illumination on this surface?
_____

In what units is this illumination intensity expressed? <u>foot candles</u>

5. *If possible, divide a single complex multiple-step problem into a number of simpler single-step problems.*

It is a mistake to believe that the more complex the problem, the better it will test the examinees' ability. Just the reverse is usually true. Any complex problem involves a number of procedural choices, as well as a number of quantitative calculations. Each of these can be made the basis of a separate test item. Success in solving the whole problem involves nothing more than success in making the separate choices and calculations.

To handle later phases of the problem, the examinee will need to be given numerical values for answers obtained in earlier phases, but these need not be the correct values. Breaking down a complex problem in this way will minimize the problem of partial credit. It will result in more independent indications of achievement or lack of it. That will improve the reliability of the test scores.

6. *Express the numerical problem clearly and as concisely as possible.*

Clarity requires full information and simple direct statements. Conciseness, the elimination of unnecessary words or distracting comments, also aids in achieving clarity. A study was made some years ago to test the hypothesis that inclusion of irrelevant data would improve the measuring characteristics of physics test problems.[2] This hypothesis was based on the assumption that giving the examinee only the numerical information needed was not true to life and might help students who lacked understanding to stumble onto the correct answer. But the inclusion of complicating irrelevant data did not improve the items. Evidently they were quite complicated enough without it.

MATCHING-TEST ITEMS

Matching test items occur in clusters composed of a list of premises, a list of responses, and directions for matching the two. In many clusters the distinction between premises and responses is simply in the names given

[2] Robert L. Ebel, "Some Effects of Irrelevant Data in Physics Test Problems," *School Science and Mathematics* 37 (1937), 327–330.

to them. The two lists can be interchanged without difficulty. In other clusters, such as the following example, it is convenient to use descriptive phrases as the premises and shorter names as responses.

Directions: On the blank before each of the following contributions to educational measurement, place the letter that precedes the name of the person responsible for it.

Premises

___ 16. Developed the Board of Examiners at the University of Chicago

___ 17. Developed high-speed electronic test-processing equipment

___ 18. Published the first textbook on educational measurement

Responses

a. Alfred Binet
b. Arthur Otis
c. E. F. Lindquist
d. E. L. Thorndike
e. L. L. Thurstone

A wide variety of premise-response combinations can be used as the basis for matching test items: dates and events; terms and definitions; writers and quotations; quantities and formulas; color samples and names of colors; and so on. Names of an animal's organs or structures can be matched to parts shown on a sketch of the animal.

Closely related to the matching-test item is the classification or key-list item. Responses for this item consist of a list of classes such as the parts of speech, periods of history, classes of plants or animals, types of chemical reactions, cause-effect sequences, branches of government, nations or states, and so on. The premises consist of names, descriptions, or examples that are to be classified among the responses provided. Here is an illustration.

Directions: After each event in the list below, put the number
  1. if it happened before the birth of Christ (4 B.C.)
  2. if it happened after the birth of Christ but before the Magna Carta was signed (1215 A.D.)
  3. if it happened after the Magna Carta was signed but before Columbus arrived in America (1492)
  4. if it happened after Columbus arrived in America but before the Declaration of Independence (1775)
  5. if it happened after the Declaration of Independence (1775)

36. Battle of Hastings		2
37. Eruption of Mt. Vesuvius		2
38 Gutenberg Bible printed		3
39. Pilgrims landed at Plymouth		4
40. William Shakespeare was born		4

Apart from the use of classes or categories as responses (the key list), classification items differ from typical matching items in that the same response is "matched" to more than one premise, and the number of premises is usually greater than the number of responses. In typical matching items there are more responses than premises.

Matching items have something in common with multiple-choice items in offering explicit alternative answers. They also have something in common with short-answer items. They are usually limited to specific factual information—names, dates, labels, and so on. They are poorly suited for testing understanding. They are also poorly adapted for testing unique ideas, since a cluster of related items is a prerequisite to the writing of such items. Clustering can reduce the breadth of sampling of questions in a test, concentrating attention on particular narrow aspects of achievement.

There are, on the other hand, some attractive features of matching test items. They are efficient in that they yield many independent scorable responses per test page or per unit of testing time. They may also motivate students to cross-reference and integrate their knowledge and to consider relations among the items in the lists of responses and premises. Yet seldom can a whole test be composed of matching or classification-test items. Some aspects of achievement may, however, be ideally suited to this item form. Here are some suggestions for using it effectively.

1. *Choose homogeneous premises and responses for any matching cluster.*

The premises and responses in the list that follows are not homogeneous.

_ 13. dark, hard wood	*a.*	board foot
_ 14. tool for smoothing	*b.*	drawing
_ 15. 12″ × 12″ × 1″	*c.*	plane
	d.	shellac
	e.	walnut

Is it necessary to supply a key for the correct answers to the items in this cluster? As this example illustrates, if the lists are not homogeneous, the items are likely to test only the simplest associations and to provide many commonsensical clues to the correct answer.

2. *Make the lists of premises and responses relatively short.*

It is easier to keep short lists homogeneous. The task involves less irrelevant difficulty if examinees do not have to hunt through long lists for a match. Adding responses beyond four or five reduces the chance of successful guessing only a very little. The difference in probability of correct answer by chance between a five- and a six-response item is only about .03. Common practice among expert item writers is to use a list of three premises to be matched by one of five responses.

3. *Do not attempt "perfect" matching, in which each response is matched once and only once to each of the premises.*

In perfect matching, the final match may be given away by the other matches. Or if an error is made in one match, there is certain to be an error in another. Thus the items are not wholly independent. Using more responses than premises eliminates these potential dangers of perfect matching.

4. *Provide directions that clearly explain the intended basis for matching.*

While the intended basis may be self-evident in simple matching clusters, in most cases it should be made explicit to avoid any misunderstandings. Classification items usually require fairly detailed directions.

5. *Arranging responses or premises or both in alphabetical order, usually prevents give-away clues that can occur in item writing.*

Item writers are likely to think of a premise and its responses together. If they are written down just as they are thought of, their sequence may make the task of matching easier than it should be. Rearranging one or both lists in alphabetical order will eliminate such clues. However, if any logical order exists among the responses (for example, quantities or dates) preserving that order will remove an irrelevant difficulty from the examinees' task.

6. *If the responses are numerical quantities, arrange them in order from low to high.*

7. *Use the longer phrases as premises, the shorter as responses.*

Both of these actions will tend to simplify the examinees' task in finding the correct match, and may eliminate irrelevant difficulty.

TESTING FOR APPLICATION OF KNOWLEDGE

Any good item tests application of knowledge. Good multiple-choice items require more than recall. Yet many of the items discussed in this and the two preceding chapters test for knowledge directly by asking for factual knowledge. There are also items that test for knowledge indirectly by giving the examinee a task that requires knowledge.

Numerical problems, discussed earlier in this chapter, test for application of knowledge. So do dictation or error recognition, spelling tests, tests that require the examinee to add or correct punctuation or capitalization, to edit or proofread copy, or to diagram a sentence. Examinees can be asked to provide all or parts of the proof of a proposition in geometry;

to write or to complete the equation for a chemical reaction. They can be asked to interpret the meaning of a table, a graph, a musical score, a cartoon, a poem, or a passage of literary, scientific, or other test material.

Items that require interpretations of these kinds are sometimes referred to as context-dependent items. They are widely used in tests of general educational development, whose purpose is to measure fairly the abilities of students with widely different educational backgrounds. In this they succeed quite well. They are less appropriate, convenient, and efficient in testing for achievement in learning specific subject matter. One should be skeptical of claims that context-dependent items measure *abilities* rather than *knowledge*, for the abilities they measure are almost wholly the results of knowledge.

Many of these indirect tests of knowledge via special applications of that knowledge can be presented in true-false, multiple-choice, short-answer, or matching forms. Some are more conveniently presented for response in other ways, such as by directing the examinee to produce the required diagram, sketch, or corrections. The main point to be made here is that while achievement in learning can usually be tested most conveniently in one of the common forms of test items, there are occasions when other means may be more convenient and satisfactory. Gerberich has compiled an excellent collection of specimen objective-test items.[3]

SUMMARY

The principal ideas developed in this chapter are summarized in these 24 statements:

1. Short-answer items are used mainly to test for factual information.
2. A much wider range of educational achievements can be tested with true-false or multiple-choice items than with short-answer items.
3. The difficulty examinees have in producing the correct answer to a short-answer item is an advantage of limited value.
4. Short-answer items do not provide more valid measures of real achievement than do choice-type items.
5. Short-answer items are efficient and relatively easy to write.
6. Short-answer items need to be conceived and written carefully to avoid the possibility of multiple correct answers.
7. In writing short-answer items, it is advantageous to think first of the answer and then write the question that elicits it.

---

[3] J. Raymond Gerberich, *Specimen Objective-Test Items* (New York: Longmans, Green and Company, 1956).

8. A direct question tends to make a better short-answer item than does an incomplete sentence.

9. It is easy to include unintentional clues to the correct answer of a short-answer item.

10. Item writers should avoid "lifting" intact sentences from textual materials as the basis for short-answer items.

11. Paragraph-completion items have lost favor because of their tendency to triviality, ambiguity, and over-concentration on narrow aspects of achievement.

12. When functional, numerical problems provide valid and convenient measurements of achievement.

13. Two difficulties sometimes encountered in test items based on numerical problems center on defining the required accuracy of the answer and deciding how much credit to give for partially correct answers.

14. If a complex, multiple-step problem is broken down into a number of simpler, single-step problems, better measurements of ability will ordinarily be obtained.

15. To test for understanding of a process, it is best to use the simplest possible numerical calculations.

16. While many bases can be found for constructing matching-test items, they, like short-answer items, are usually limited to testing for factual information.

17. Matching-test items are efficient and useful in emphasizing relationships.

18. Short, homogeneous lists should be used in any matching cluster.

19. Perfect matching of the two lists on a one-to-one basis is undesirable.

20. Directions should explain the basis for matching.

21. After the lists for a matching cluster have been prepared, the order of responses should be scrambled to avoid give-away clues.

22. All good items test for application of knowledge. Some test it directly by asking questions. Others test it indirectly, by presenting tasks to be performed.

23. Context-dependent items calling for interpretations are mainly useful in testing for general educational development.

24. Conventional item forms are the most generally useful but not the only available means for testing achievement in learning.

10

How to Administer and Score an Achievement Test

Unless the class is very large, unless the classroom is poorly suited for test administration, or unless other special problems are encountered, test administration usually is the simplest phase of the whole testing process. In the administration of external, standardized tests, the golden rule for the test administrator is: *Follow the directions in the manual precisely.* In classroom testing there is usually no such manual, and the need for rigidly standardized conditions of test administration is much less. Nevertheless, here, as in most other areas, advanced planning usually pays dividends. Also there are some persistent problems associated with test administration, such as the questions of time limits, of guessing on objective tests, and of cheating. These topics, together with the problems of efficient scoring of objective tests, will provide the subject matter of this chapter.

TEST PRESENTATION

The questions for essay or problem tests are sometimes written on the chalkboard as the test period begins. This saves duplication costs and helps to maintain the secrecy of the questions, but it gives the teacher the double responsibility of copying the questions and of getting the students started to work on them, at a time when minutes are precious and when everyone

EXHIBIT 10–1. SAMPLE LAYOUTS OF OBJECTIVE TEST ITEMS

A. True-False Test Items
1. The indirect influence of a test on student learning is greater than its direct influence.
2. Most teachers are quite unaware of the fallibility of their subjective judgments.
3. For assessing a student's typical behavior, informal observation is more effective than formal testing.
4. Since pupils differ in ability, the tests used to measure their achievements should, ideally, also differ in difficulty.
5. It is a good thing for students to study with an eye to doing well on the kind of tests they will have to take.

B. Multiple-Choice Test Items
1. In what part of the process of preparing, giving, and scoring an objective test in American history would the help of another history teacher be most valuable?
   a. In planning the test
   b. In writing the original item drafts
   c. In reviewing and revising the original item drafts
   d. In scoring the answer sheets

2. How important is the assignment of marks as a function of educational achievement tests?
   a. It has ceased to be important enough to deserve special attention.
   b. It is definitely less important than the diagnostic values of taking such tests.
   c. It is important enough to justify special efforts to construct valid and reliable tests.
   d. It is the only important function of such tests.

3. What is the chief weakness of many achievement tests constructed by classroom teachers?
   a. They are speed tests rather than power tests.
   b. They are too difficult.
   c. They are too long.
   d. They test memory of details rather than achievement of objectives.

4. Is it desirable for classroom teachers themselves to construct most of the tests they use? Why?
   a. Yes, because the process of test construction helps the teacher to diagnose student difficulties.
   b. Yes, because teacher-made tests permit instructors to fit the tests to their own program of instruction.
   c. No, because teachers lack the time to do an acceptable job of test construction.
   d. No, because test construction requires special knowledge and skill that few teachers possess.

is likely to be somewhat tense. Then, too, when the blackboard has been erased, no one has a valid record of exactly what the questions were.

Oral dictation of test questions, especially short-answer or true-false questions, has been tried with some success, but most students prefer to be able to look at the question while they are trying to decide on an answer to it. Putting the questions on slides and projecting them in a semi-darkened room has also been tried.[1] It enables the examiner to pace the students and ensures that each examinee will give at least brief consideration to

[1] H. A. Curtis and Russell P. Kropp, "A Comparison of Scores Obtained by Administering a Test Normally and Visually," *Journal of Experimental Education*, 24 (1961), 249–60; see also their follow-up work, *Experimental Analyses of the Effects of Various Modes of Item Presentation on the Scores and Factorial Content of Tests Administered by Visual and Audio-visual Means*, Department of Educational Research and Testing, Florida State University, Tallahassee, Florida, 1962, p. 83; and the later research by Robert W. Heckman, Joseph Tiffin, and Richard E. Snow, "Effects of Controlling Item Exposure in Achievement Testing," *Educational and Psychological Measurement*, 27 (1967), 113–25.

print and of format are prime consid...
duplicated unskillfully, on inadequate equipment. Questions may be crowded too closely together. Instead of being listed in a column, the response options to multiple-choice questions may be written in tandem to form a continuous, hard-to-read paragraph. Testers can avoid faults like these by taking pains with the layout and duplication of test copy. Examples of good layouts for true-false and multiple-choice test items are shown in Exhibit 10–1. Some duplication processes permit the use of both sides of the paper. This is economical and, if the papers are stapled only once in the upper lefthand corner, causes the examinees no problems. The use of a separate cover page on which the directions are printed helps to empha-

EXHIBIT 10–2. SAMPLE TEST DIRECTIONS

A. For a True-False Test

This test consists of 102 statements. You are to decide whether each statement is true or false, and to record your decision on the answer sheet provided. Your score will be the number of correct decisions you make. It is to your advantage to mark an answer to each item, and to record the answer you give in the test booklet beside the question.

Please use the special pencil provided, and mark each response carefully so that the scoring machine will be able to determine your score accurately.

Identify your answer sheet with your name and the date (July 9, 1978). The name of the test is "465 Midterm." The form is "In Class." No other identifying information is required.

When you finish, turn in your answer sheets and the special pencil. Keep your copy of the test, and be prepared to turn in a revised answer sheet next Monday (July 13, 1978).

B. For a Multiple-Choice Test

Please Read These Directions Carefully

REMOVE the answer sheet that is loosely inserted in this booklet and fill in the information called for on the top margin. Then finish reading these directions, but do not open the test booklet until the instructor tells you to do so.

INDICATE your choice of the one best answer to each question by making one solid black pencil mark in the proper space on the answer sheet. If you change your mind, erase the first mark completely. Do not carelessly or intentionally make any other marks on the answer sheet.

IMPROPER marks will reduce your score on this test.

  a. If mismarking (light marks, double marks, stray marks, or improper erasures) causes the test to score differently on two machines, the lower score will be recorded.

  b. If mismarking causes the total number of marks registered by the machine to be greater than the total number of questions in the test, the excess will be subtracted from the score.

DO NOT waste time on difficult questions. You may answer questions even when you are not perfectly sure your answers are correct, but you should avoid wild guessing.

size those directions and to keep the students from seeing the questions prematurely. Sample test directions are shown in Exhibit 10–2.

PREPARING THE STUDENTS

In addition to preparing the test for the students, it is important to prepare the students for the test. To begin with, they usually should know that a test is coming. Any important test should be announced well in advance. If a test is to have a desirable effect in motivating and directing efforts to learn, the students need to know not only that a test is coming but what kinds of achievement the test will require them to demonstrate. This means that the instructor should plan tests *before* the course begins, as part of the overall planning for the course.

Some instructors favor surprise tests in the belief that such tests keep the students studying regularly and discourage cramming. In some situations these tactics may be necessary and effective. Most instructors, however, see some elements of unfairness in surprise tests. Further, cramming is unlikely to be effective with, or to be encouraged by, a test of a student's command of knowledge. Such command cannot be achieved in a few short sessions of intensive cramming. Cramming is most essential and effective if the test requires no more than superficial memory for prominent details. Advance announcement and description of a good test is likely to do more to encourage effective study than the surprise administration of a test, especially if its nature has been kept secret from the students.

DEVELOPING SKILL IN TEST TAKING

In addition to knowing that a test is coming, and to having a good general idea of what to expect in it, the students need to know how to give a good account of themselves on the test. The measurement of achievement requires active cooperation from the students. If they lack skill in test taking, their scores may fall short of their true achievements. Test taking is not a highly specialized skill nor is it difficult to master. But almost anyone who has taken more than a few tests can testify from personal experience how easy it is to go astray on an examination, how failure to heed all directions, carelessness, unwarranted assumptions, or ignorance of some crucial rule of the game has marred an otherwise creditable test performance.

What are some of the legitimate and essential test-taking skills that examinees ought to possess?

1. They ought to be aware of the danger of failing to read or listen attentively when directions for taking the test are presented and of the danger of failing to follow those directions exactly.

4. They should p... shape for taking the test. Fatigue induced by an all-night cram session, even when partially offset by stimulants, is a heavy handicap. Examinees should realize that last-minute cramming is a poor substitute for consistent effort throughout the course, particularly if the test they are facing is likely to be a well-constructed measure of their command of knowledge. Some anxiety is useful in motivating examinees to do their best, but jitters are even less helpful than fatigue.

5. Students should pace themselves so as to have time to consider and respond to all the test questions. This means that they must not puzzle too long over a difficult question or problem, or write too extensively on an essay test question, even when a long answer seems easy to write.

6. They should know that ordinary guessing corrections really do not penalize even blind guessing, but simply seek not to reward it. Hence, students should act in their own best interest by attempting to answer all questions, even those that they have only a slight basis for answering.

7. In answering an essay question, students should take time to reflect, to plan, and to organize their answer before starting to write. They should decide how much they can afford to write in the time available. And in all cases they should write something, however flimsy it may seem to be, as an answer.

8. If they are making responses on a separate answer sheet, students should check frequently to be sure their mark actually indicates the response they intended and that it is marked in the spaces provided for that question.

9. If possible, examinees should take time to reread their answers, to detect and correct any careless mistakes.[2]

Since examinations do count, students and their teachers are well advised to spend some time considering how to cope with them most

[2] Daniel J. Muller and Virginia Wasser, "Implications of Changing Answers on Objective Test Items," *Journal of Educational Measurement,* 14 (Spring 1977), 9–14.

skillfully. Some good books on the subject, giving more detailed help than we have suggested here, are available.[3]

Skill in test taking is sometimes called testwiseness. Students who are richly endowed with this attribute are supposed to be able to score well on any test, whether they know anything about the subject or not. Further, it is supposed by some that objective tests inevitably are better measures of students' testwiseness than of their real achievements.

There is some basis for this concern. Certain tests, especially some kinds of intelligence tests, include novel, unique, and highly specialized tasks, for example, figure analogies or number series. For test items of this nature the main problem of the examinee is to "get the hang of" solving them. They do not reflect previous learning, nor is the skill developed in solving these test problems likely to be practically useful in other settings. Their use in intelligence testing is justified on the grounds that brighter students will get the hang of solving novel problems sooner, and more fully, than duller students.

Items of this type are seldom used in classroom tests. But there are common faults in item writing that may allow an examinee to substitute testwiseness for knowledge. Some of these, involving unintended clues to the correct answer, were discussed in the chapters on true-false and multiple-choice test items. They are outlined and discussed in greater detail in an article by Millman and his colleagues.[4] In a good test, however, the item writer will avoid dropping very many clues of this or any other kind. Given a test that measures command of knowledge and is free of technical flaws, error in measurement is likely to be due to too little, rather than too much, testwiseness.

The Problem of Test Anxiety

The problem of test anxiety was mentioned in the preceding section. Anxiety is a frequent side effect of testing, whether that testing occurs in the classroom, on the athletic field, in the art exhibit hall, in the courtroom, in the conference room where a crucial business decision is being discussed, or in the legislative chamber where a bill is being debated. Test anxiety in the classroom is not something unique. It is a part, though hopefully not too large a part, of life itself.

Because human beings are complex and the situations in which they

---

[3] Joseph C. Heston, *How to Take a Test* (Chicago: Science Research Associates, 1953); Herschel Manuel, *Taking a Test* (New York: Harcourt Brace Jovanovich, 1956); Jason Millman and Walter Pauk, *How To Take Tests* (New York: McGraw-Hill Book Company, 1969).

[4] Jason Millman, Carol H. Bishop, and Robert Ebel, "An Analysis of Testwiseness," *Educational and Psychological Measurement,* vol. 25 (1965), 707–26.

1. There is a negative correlation between ~~~~~~~~ ~~~~~~~ ~~.
   test anxiety.[5] Those who are most capable tend to be least anxious
   when facing a test.
2. There is a positive correlation between level of anxiety and level of
   aspiration. Those who are most anxious when facing a test tend to
   be those who have the greatest need or desire to do well on it.
3. Mild degrees of anxiety facilitate and enhance test performance.
   More extreme degrees are likely to interfere with and depress test
   performance.
4. The more frequent a student's contact with tests of a specific type
   given for a specific purpose, the less likely he or she is to be the
   victim of extreme anxiety.
5. Test anxiety can be educationally useful if it is distributed, at a
   relatively low level, throughout the course of instruction, instead of
   being concentrated at a relatively high level just prior to and during
   an examination. Skillful teaching involves the controlled release of
   the energy stimulated by test anxiety.

Evidence to support the belief that some students of good or superior
achievement characteristically go to pieces and do poorly on every examination is hard to find. Since individuals differ in many respects, it is
reasonable to suppose that they may differ also in their tolerance of the
kind of stress that tests generate. On the other hand, it is conceivable that
apparent instances of underachievement on tests may actually be instances
of overrated ability in non-test situations. In other words, a student whose
achievement is really quite modest may have cultivated the poise, the ready
response, the verbal facility, and the pleasing manners that would ordinarily
mark the person as an accomplished and promising scholar. All things
considered, a teacher is well advised to take with several grains of salt any
claim that a student's test performances never do justice to her/his real
achievements.

[5] Irwin G. Sarason, "Empirical Findings and Theoretical Problems in the Use of Anxiety
Scales," *Psychological Bulletin* (1960), pp. 403–15.

ADMINISTERING THE TEST

As we have stated earlier, the actual administration of most tests involves relatively few and simple problems. Since the time available for the test is usually limited, and seldom as long as some of the students wish, every available minute should be used to good advantage. By giving preliminary instructions the day before the test, by organizing test materials for efficient distribution, and by keeping last-minute oral directions and answers to questions as brief as possible, the teacher can ensure that students have the maximum amount of time to work on it. Corresponding provisions for efficient collection of materials and advance notice to the students that all work must stop when time is called help to conclude the test on time and in an orderly fashion.

To aid the students in pacing themselves, it is helpful for the teacher to write a statement like this on the chalkboard near the beginning of the test.

**No more than____minutes remain for you to work on this test.
If you have not reached item____you are working too slowly.**

By changing the numbers entered in these statements every 10 or 15 minutes, the teacher can help the students find time to consider all questions.

During almost any test administration, some students are likely to feel the need of asking an occasional question. Questions such as those growing out of errors in the test copy or ambiguities in the directions or test questions require answers if the students are to respond properly. Teachers should help students understand the tasks but should stop short of giving clues to the answer. Sometimes the dividing line is hard to determine.

Such questions as those stimulated by obvious but noncritical typographical errors should not even be asked. Since the process of asking and answering a question during the course of an examination is always disturbing to others, even if it is done as quietly and discreetly as possible, and since the answer to one student's question might possibly give that individual an unfair advantage over the others, students should be urged to avoid all but the most necessary questions. Discussion of this point can well be undertaken prior to the day of the examination.

THE PROBLEM OF CHEATING

In addition to giving directions, answering questions, and helping students keep track of time, the instructor has at least one other major responsibility during the course of administering a test. That is to prevent cheating. This

1. The sidelong glance at a fellow student's answers
2. The preparation and use of a crib sheet
3. Collusion between two or more students to exchange information on answers during the test
4. Unauthorized copying of questions or stealing of test booklets in anticipation that they may be used again later on
5. Arranging for a substitute to take an examination
6. Stealing or buying copies of an examination before the test is given, or sharing such illicit advance copies with others

Although these various forms of cheating differ in seriousness, none can be viewed with indifference. The typical student has many opportunities to cheat. Some circumstances may even encourage examinees to cheat, but none justifies their doing so. Students may conclude, not without some justification, that the ethical standards of many of their fellow students are not very high, at least where cheating on examinations is concerned. They may go on to infer that this fact requires them to lower their own standards or justifies them in doing so. Whatever other conditions may contribute to it, cheating would not occur if all students were to recognize that it is always dishonest and usually unfair.

Some acts of cheating are no doubt motivated by desperation. The more extreme the desperation, the more ambitious and serious the attempt to cheat is likely to be. A major factor contributing to cheating is carelessness on the instructor's part in safeguarding the examination copy before it is administered and in supervising the students during the examination.

Emphasis on grades is sometimes blamed as a primary cause of cheating. But since grades are, or should be, symbols of educational achievement, we cannot indict grading as a cause of cheating without also indicting the goal of achievement in learning. Does anyone really want to do that? No doubt most students would find it easier to resist the temptation to cheat if no advantage of any consequence were likely to result from the cheating. But refusal to recognize and reward achievement may be as effective in reducing achievement as in reducing cheating. Such a price seems too heavy to pay.

Increased use of objective tests has also been cited as a cause of cheating. The mode of response to objective tests makes some kinds of cheating easier, but the multiplicity of questions makes other kinds of cheating more difficult. No form of test is immune to all forms of cheating. The quality of a test, however, may have a direct bearing on the temptation it offers to students to cheat. Demand for detailed, superficial knowledge encourages the preparation of crib sheets. If the examination seems to the students unlikely to yield valid measures of their real achievements, if it seems unfair to them in terms of the instruction they have received, if their scores seem likely to be determined by irrelevant factors anyway, the "crime" of cheating may seem less serious.

What cures are there for cheating? The basic cure is related to the basic cause. Students and their teachers must recognize that cheating is dishonest and unfair and that it deserves consistent application of appropriate penalties—failure in the course, loss of credit, suspension, or dismissal. Reports on the prevalence of cheating, no doubt sometimes exaggerated, should not be allowed to establish cheating as an acceptable norm for student behavior or to persuade instructors that cheating is inevitable and must be accommodated as gracefully as possible.

It is the responsibility of the instructor to avoid any conditions that make cheating easy—before, during, or after an examination. The security of the examination must be safeguarded while it is being written and duplicated and when it is stored. If the class is large and if students must sit in close proximity, alternate forms of the examination should be distributed to those sitting in adjacent seats. Alternate forms can easily be prepared by arranging the same questions in different order. Finally, instructors should take seriously the task of proctoring their examinations as part of their responsibility to the majority of students who will not cheat and who should not be penalized for their honesty.

Teachers have considerable authority in their own classroom. They should not overuse it under stress or underuse it when the situation demands it. If a teacher is satisfied beyond any reasonable doubt that a student is cheating, she or he needs no other justification for:

1. Collecting the examination materials and quietly dismissing the student from the room
2. Voiding the results of the examination, requiring an alternative make-up examination, or giving the student a failing grade on the examination
3. Bringing the incident to the attention of the school authorities if further action seems necessary

Honor Systems

One frequently mentioned proposal for dealing with the problem of cheating is the establishment of an honor system. Honor systems vary, but

Honor systems seem to work best in educational institutions whose moderate size and rich traditions encourage strong group identification and loyalties. The spirit of honor on which the system depends seldom arises or maintains itself spontaneously. It must be cultivated carefully and continuously. The things that must be done, or avoided, to maintain personal honor and the honor of the group are usually clearly defined in a code or by well-rehearsed tradition. The degree to which student experience with an honor system in such an environment cultivates a general and lasting spirit of personal honor in a world where no such system is in effect may be open to question. That such systems have worked to limit, or even eliminate, cheating in certain institutions seems beyond doubt. That they sometimes break down, disastrously, is also beyond doubt. What is moot however, is that adoption of the honor system is a feasible answer to the problem of cheating on examinations in almost any school or college.

Loss of Test Security

Instructors and administrators, especially at the college level, are occasionally beset by rumors that copies of this or that examination are "out" in advance of the scheduled administration of the examination. Sometimes the rumors are founded on fact. More often result from misinformation that anxious students are only too eager to pass along. Finally the rumor (not so identified, of course) reaches the ears of the instructor, often via one or a number of anonymous telephone calls. What is the instructor to do?

Clearly, the instructor must determine whether or not the rumor is founded on fact, a task that must be pursued with the most vigorous effort. If the instructor is ready to enlist the aid of the informants and if they are willing to help, even anonymously, the task may be possible. If the informants are unable or unwilling to supply any leads, then they should be told courteously but plainly that their information is worthless and their transmission of it harmful.

If verifiable evidence is obtained that some students have, or have seen, advance copies of the examination, the only reasonable course of action is to prepare a new examination, even if it means changing the form of the examination and possibly losing a night of sleep. But if such evidence cannot be obtained even by a thorough search, the rumor had probably best be allowed to die as quietly as it will.

Problems of this kind are most likely to arise and to cause most serious difficulties on college campuses, which is not to say that they are totally absent from high schools. Care in safeguarding examinations before they are given is the best preventative. But it is also helpful to be ready to respond wisely, and vigorously if the situation warrants, when the rumors that a test is out *do* begin to circulate, as they almost surely will sooner or later.

PROCEDURES FOR TEST SCORING

Student answers to objective test items may be recorded either on the test copy itself or on a separate answer sheet. Tests given in the elementary grades are almost always arranged so that the answers can be recorded in the test booklet. This avoids complicating the task of responding for the beginner. Cashen and Ramseyer found that the test scores of first-grade students were lowered substantially when they were required to record their answers on a separate answer sheet.[6] Scores of second-grade students were lowered somewhat, but those of third-grade students were affected very little. Recording answers in the test booklet lessens the danger of purely clerical errors and makes the corrected test copy easier to use for instructional purposes. The use of a separate answer sheet, on the other hand, makes the scorer's task much easier. It also makes possible the reuse of the test booklet. If a scoring machine is to be used, the answers must be recorded on an answer sheet that the machine is designed to handle.

If the answers are to be recorded on the test booklet, space for the answers should be provided near one margin of the test pages. To speed scoring and minimize the possibility of errors, the scorer may record correct answers on the columns of a separate answer key card, using one column for each page of answers and positioning the answers in the column so that they will match the answer spaces on the test copy.

In scoring the answers recorded in test booklets, the scorer may find it helpful to mark the answers, using a colored pencil. A short horizontal line through the student's response can be used to indicate a correct response. Sometimes it is advantageous to mark all responses using, in addition to the horizontal line for correct responses, an "X" to indicate an incorrect response and a circle around the answer space to indicate an omitted response.

[6] Valjean M. Cashen and Gary C. Ramseyer, "The Use of Separate Answer Sheets by Primary Age Children," *Journal of Educational Measurement*, 6 (1969), 155–58.

kind of marking is useful ...
of the test for class discussion.

Most classroom tests of educational achievement are scored by the instructor. If the test is in essay form, the skill and judgment of the instructor or of someone equally competent are essential. The task of scoring an objective test is essentially clerical and can often be handled by someone whose time is less expensive than an instructor's time and whose skill and energy are less in demand for other educational tasks.

Some school systems and colleges maintain central scoring services. Usually these services make use of small scoring machines, several of which are now available. But even if all the scoring is done by hand, a central service has the value of fostering the development of special skills that make for rapid, accurate scoring. Institutional test scoring services often provide statistical and test analysis services as well, and sometimes they even offer test duplication services that provide expert assistance in the special problems of test production and in the maintenance of test security.[8]

Instructors sometimes use the class meeting following the test for test scoring. Asking each student to check the answers of a classmate may on occasion be a reasonable and rewarding use of class time, but often the process tends to be slow and inaccurate. A difficulty encountered by one student on one test paper may interrupt and delay the whole operation. Most important, if the student scorers are concentrating on mechanical accuracy of scoring, as they probably should be, the circumstances will not favor much learning as a by-product of the scoring process.

But students can and usually should have the chance to learn from the mistakes they make on a test. Ordinarily the best occasion for this learning is *after* the tests have been scored and the answer sheets returned to the students. The correct answer to each item can be recorded on the blackboard, on a duplicated handout, or best of all, directly on the student's answer sheet. With this information students can satisfy themselves of the

[7] Vernon S. Gerlach, "Preparing Transparent Keys for Inspecting Answer Sheets," *Journal of Educational Measurement,* 3 (1966), 62.

[8] Robert L. Ebel, "Improving Evaluation of Educational Outcomes at the College Level," *Proceedings, 1953 Invitational Conference on Testing Problems* (Princeton, N.J.: Educational Testing Service, 1954).

accuracy with which their answers have been scored. Distributing copies of the test booklet will allow students to discover the nature of their mistakes and to clarify any misunderstandings. The teacher can prevent protracted arguments over the correctness of any particular answer by asking the protesting student to state his/her case in writing, with a promise of credit if the case seems to merit it. Discussions of this kind contribute to the feeling that students are being treated openly and fairly. Test reviews can also contribute enough to an increase in students' command of knowledge to be well worth the time required.

Scoring Machines

In recent years various small machines designed for classroom scoring of objective tests have appeared on the educational market. Most of them require the use of specially printed answer sheets or cards. Most of them use an optical system for sensing and an electronic system for counting right and wrong responses. The maximum number of five-alternative multiple-choice items that can be scored in one pass varies from 25 to about 100. The majority of these machines are equipped to print the score on the student's answer sheet, and some will mark wrong answers and provide data on item difficulty. The smallest is about the size of a portable typewriter; the largest about the size of a mimeograph machine. In cost they range from about $1,000 to about $3,000. In view of the time they can save the teacher, and the accuracy of the scores they yield, they are worthwhile investments for most schools.

Much larger, higher-capacity machines have been developed for use in large school systems, universities, and statewide or nationwide testing agencies.[9] Of course, they are much more expensive than the smaller machines. The output of these machines is often coupled to computers, which standardize and summarize the scores, print score distributions and listings, and provide complete analysis of the test data.[10] It is hard to exaggerate the contribution that machines like these can make to the efficient use of objective tests and to their progressive improvement through test analysis.

Correction for Guessing

Scores on objective tests are sometimes corrected for guessing. The purpose of such a correction is to reduce to zero the gain in score expected

[9] J. M. O'Malley and C. Stafford, "Scoring and Analyzing Teacher-made Tests with an IBM 1620," *Educational and Psychological Measurement,* 26 (1966), 715–17.

[10] C. D. Miller et al., "Scoring, Analyzing and Reporting Classroom Tests Using an Optical Reader and 1401 Computer," *Educational and Psychological Measurement,* 27 (1967), 159–64.

that of the second when, in fact, the two scores should be the same.

To correct the first student's score for guessing, it is necessary to subtract from that score an amount equal to the expected gain from blind guessing. Since on a true-false test the student can expect to answer one question wrongly for every question he/she answers correctly, the number of wrong answers is simply subtracted from the number of right answers. If the questions provided three equally likely answers instead of two, the student would expect to give two wrong answers to every right answer. In this case one would subtract one-half of the number of wrong responses from the number of right responses to correct for guessing. If multiple-choice items list five alternative possible answers to each question, only one of which is correct, the expected ratio of wrong to right answers is 4 to 1 and the guessing correction would call for subtracting one-fourth of the number of wrong answers from the number of right answers.

Logic of this kind leads to a general formula for correction for guessing

$$S = R - \frac{W}{N - 1} \qquad 10.1$$

where

S stands for the score corrected for guessing
R for the number of questions answered rightly
W for the number of questions answered wrongly, and
N for the number of possible alternative answers equally likely to be chosen in blind guessing.

It is easy to see that this formula becomes

$$S = R - W \qquad 10.2$$

in the case of two-alternative (true-false) items, or

$$S = R - \frac{W}{4} \qquad 10.3$$

in the case of five-alternative multiple-choice test items.

Instead of penalizing the student who guesses, one could correct for guessing by rewarding the student who refrains from guessing. That is, instead of subtracting 50 units from the score of the guesser, we could add 50 units to the score of the nonguesser. This too would eliminate the expected advantage from blind guessing. The assumption in this case is that if the nonguesser had guessed, she/he would have given the right answer to one-half of the true-false items. On three-alternative items the nonguesser would have been given correct answers to one-third of the items.

Logic of this kind leads to a second general formula for guessing correction

$$S' = R + \frac{O}{N}$$ 10.4

where

S' is the score corrected for guessing on the basis of items omitted
R is the number of items answered correctly
O is the number of items omitted, and
N is the number of alternative answers whose choice is equally likely on the basis of blind guessing.

Again, it is easy to see that this general formula becomes

$$S' = R + \frac{O}{2}$$ 10.5

in the case of true-false items, or

$$S' = R + \frac{O}{5}$$ 10.6

in the case of five-alternative multiple-choice test items.

If the same set of test scores is corrected for guessing in two different ways, by subtracting a fraction of the wrong answers and by adding a fraction of the omitted answers, two different sets of corrected scores will be obtained. But although the two sets of scores will differ in their average value (with the omit-corrected scores being higher in all cases) and in their variability (with the omit-corrected scores being more variable almost always), the two sets of scores will be perfectly correlated. If student A makes a higher score than student B when the appropriate fractions of their wrong responses are subtracted from the total of their right responses, A will also make a higher score than B when the appropriate fraction of their items omitted is added to the total of their correct responses.

corrected by addition ...,
value. But they are equally sound in relative value. With scores on tests of educational achievement, the absolute value is usually far less significant than the relative value.

It is also worth noting here that if no items are omitted, scores corrected for guessing by subtracting a fraction of the wrong responses correlate perfectly with the uncorrected scores, that is, with the numbers of right responses. This indicates that the magnitude of the effect of a guessing correction depends on the proportion of items omitted. Only if considerable numbers of items are omitted by at least some of the students will the application of either formula for correction for guessing have an appreciable effect.

Correction for guessing is sometimes misunderstood to mean that the effects of chance on test scores are eliminated or reduced, that the lucky guesser will, after his score is corrected, fare no better than the unlucky guesser. How far this is from truth is illustrated in Table 10–1. To make the illustration as simple as possible we have assumed that 32 students attempt all 10 items of a true-false test. Each student presumably knew the answers to 5 of the 10 questions. Hence the true score on this test of each

TABLE 10–1. SCORES OF 32 STUDENTS OF EQUAL ABILITY ON A 10-ITEM TRUE-FALSE TEST

| | *Frequency Distributions of Scores* | | |
Scale of Test Scores	True	Uncorrected	Corrected
10		1	1
9		5	
8		10	5
7		10	
6		5	10
5	32	1	
4			10
3			
2			5
1			
0			1

of the 32 students should have been 5, as indicated in the second column of the table.

But the students guess, and as usually befalls those who guess, some are luckier than others. The laws of probability indicate that one of the 32 would guess right on all five of the remaining questions, and thus get a total score of 10. Five of the 32 would be lucky on four of the five questions and get scores of 9. One poor soul would be completely unlucky and guess wrong on all five questions. His score would remain at 5, reflecting knowledge but no luck. These facts are tabulated in the third column.

Does the application of a guessing-correction formula improve the situation? Look at the fourth column of Table 10–1, which displays the scores obtained by applying equation 10.2. The differences due to chance have not been eliminated or even reduced. They have been magnified. Paraphrasing the words of the Bible: To him that hath luck a high score shall be given, even after correction for guessing. From him that hath not luck, even that score which is rightfully his shall be taken away!

Summary of Findings on Guessing Corrections

Should the scores on objective tests of educational achievement be corrected for guessing? Among the considerations that should influence the instructor's decision are these.

1. *Scores corrected for guessing will usually rank students in about the same relative positions as do uncorrected scores.*

Almost all experimental studies of the effect of announced correction for guessing on the reliability and validity of test scores have shown slight, if any, improvement attributable to the correction. Usually the correlation between corrected and uncorrected scores from the same test answers is in the high nineties—nearly perfect in terms of the standards of mental tests. Corrected scores may be slightly more reliable or slightly less reliable than uncorrected scores, depending on whether the correlation between number of items omitted and number answered correctly is positive or negative. Corrected scores may be slightly more valid than uncorrected scores if the correlation between number of items omitted and the criterion scores is positive. If not, they may be slightly less valid.

2. *The probability of getting a respectable score on a good objective test by blind guessing alone is extremely small.*

Suppose the objective test included 100 multiple-choice items, each of which offered five possible answers. A student who took many of such tests and always guessed blindly on every item in such a test would expect to

$$\frac{1}{1,268,000,000,000,000,000,000,000,000,000}$$

That is a rather small fraction. It means that in over one and a quarter *nonillion* sets of blindly guessed answers, one could expect to find only one perfect paper. If all of the people alive in the world today (say, four billion) had been doing nothing every day but making blind guesses on 100-item true-false tests (say, 10 tests per day) all year long, except Sundays and holidays (say, 3,000 tests per year), and had done so since the beginning of geologic time (say, three billion years ago) they would produce only 36,000,000,000,000,000,000,000 sets of answers. That number is too small by a factor of 40 million. Thus the kind of nonsense we have described— four billion people taking 3,000 true-false tests per year for three billion years, would have to go on in 35 million other worlds in order to produce one perfect answer sheet to a 100-item true-false test by blind guessing alone.

3. *Well-motivated examinees who have time to attempt all items guess blindly on few, if any, items.*

The data presented in Table 10–2 support this generalization. The number of guesses was obtained simply by asking the students to indicate any items on which they felt their responses were no better than blind guesses. In return for this information the students were promised at least a chance score on those items. That is, if less than half of their guesses were correct, they would be given credit for half of them as correct. Under this arrangement the students reported a total of 3,119 guesses out of a total of 56,550 responses, or about 1 in 18. As might be expected, some students reported no guesses at all. At the other extreme, a very few students reported that as many as 1 in 4 of their responses were no better than blind guesses.

Some who are concerned about the prevalence of guessing on objective tests would define any response made with less than complete certainty as a guess. Under this definition, naturally, the proportion of guesses would

TABLE 10–2. BLIND GUESSING ON FOUR TRUE-FALSE TESTS*

	Test 1	Test 2	Test 3	Test 4
Number of items	98	89	108	116
Number of students	158	158	121	121
Responses	15,484	14,062	13,068	14,036
Percent correct	76	72	76	71
Guesses	486	905	620	1,108
Guesses as percent of responses	3.1	6.4	4.7	7.9
Guesses correct	271	494	336	575
Percent of correct guesses	56	55	54	52
Test reliability	.79	.89	.79	.81

* Robert L. Ebel, "Blind Guessing on Objective Achievement Tests," *Journal of Educational Measurement*, 5 (Winter 1968), 321–25.

be much higher than that found in the study just reported. But we contend that informed guesses do give valuable indications of achievement. If one student's informed guesses turn out to be more frequently correct than another's, it is a good indication that the one has based his/her guesses on better information than the other.

4. *Ordinarily, no moral or educational evil is involved in the encouragement of students to make the best rational guesses they can.*

Guessing is regarded as an evil by those who see in it an attempt by examinees either to (1) deceive the examiner into thinking they know something they really don't or to (2) get by on the basis of slipshod learning. If learning were an all-or-none affair, with perfect mastery or total ignorance the only alternatives, these objections to guessing could carry considerable weight.

But in view of the fact that learning is usually a matter of more or less, it seems somewhat unreasonable to ask students to follow a rigid procedure of answering only those questions to which they can respond with certainty. Schools and colleges prepare for life, and life is seldom like that. Decisions on life's complex problems are seldom beyond question or doubt. Inevitably most of them require some degree of rational guessing, that is, acting on the basis of insufficient evidence. Decision making cannot be avoided when a question or problem arises, since the postponement of choice is itself a decision that may turn out well or badly. The most effective persons in life seem to be those whose informed guesses pay off most frequently.

5. *Students' rational guesses can provide useful information on their general level of achievement.*

a test probes a student's command of knowledge—the more it requires examinee to go beyond the recitation of facts and phrases committed to memory—the harder it may be to avoid some doubts about the correctness of one's choices. If a question is complex and difficult enough to challenge a student's command of knowledge, it is unlikely that the answer will be given with complete certainty. Nonetheless, uncertain responses can provide good evidence of competence, too. Two students may be uncertain to some degree about all the answers they give on a test, but the student of higher achievement is likely to respond correctly more often than is the poorer student.

6. *If a test is timed, a guessing correction removes the incentive for slower students to guess blindly.*

Students who work slowly or who lose track of time when taking a test may be unable to give a considered answer to each question, especially within narrow time limits. If such test scores are not corrected for guessing, students who run out of time can expect a higher score if they guess blindly than if they do not. Not all students are willing to guess blindly in such circumstances, even when directed to do so. Those who choose not to guess are placed at a disadvantage. Those who do guess blindly make their scores less reliable since the blind guessing adds nothing but random error to their test scores. Correcting test scores for guessing helps solve this problem by removing the incentive to guess blindly on those items the student does not have time to consider.

In some cases a better solution to this problem than correction for guessing may be encouragement of students to work rapidly enough to be able to answer all items. Most examinees could work faster than they do without serious loss of accuracy in their responses. If they are informed of the passage of time, most will adjust their rate of work accordingly. Their scores are then almost certain to be more reliable than if they had guessed blindly on some items, or if a guessing correction had been applied.

7. *Scores corrected for guessing may include irrelevant measures of the examinee's testwiseness or willingness to gamble.*

Contrary to what students sometimes seem to believe, the typical correction for guessing applies no special penalty to the one who guesses. It simply tends to eliminate the advantage of the student who guesses blindly in preference to omitting items. Testwise students know they have nothing to lose, and perhaps something to gain, by making use of every hunch and scrap of information in attempting an answer to every item. The test-naive student or the one who tends to avoid taking chances may be influenced by a guessing correction to omit many items on which his/her likelihood of correct response is well above the chance level.[11] To the degree that scores corrected for guessing give a special advantage to the bold or testwise student, their validity as measures of achievement may suffer.

DIFFERENTIAL SCORING WEIGHTS

One obtains all objective test scores by adding weighted response scores. The simplest system of scoring weights and the one most often used is $+1$ for the correct response to each test item and 0 for any response not correct. Correction for guessing involves a slightly more complex system of scoring weights, such as $+1$ for each correct response, -1, or -2, or -3, and so on, for each wrong response, and 0 for each omitted response.

Test constructors sometimes suggest that certain items carry more weight than others because they are thought to be more important items, items of better technical quality, more complex or difficult items, or more time-consuming items. For example, in a test composed of 50 true-false items and 25 multiple-choice items, the test constructor may decide that each multiple-choice item should be worth two points and each true-false item only one point.

Reasonable as such differential weights may seem to be on the surface, they seldom make the test to which they are applied a more reliable or valid measure. Nor do they ordinarily make the test a much worse measure. Like guessing corrections, to which they are closely related, they tend to have relatively small effects. Wilks concluded from a theoretical analysis of the problem that the method of weighting individual items matters little in a long test of intercorrelated items.[12] Aiken reached a similar conclusion.[13] Guilford and his co-workers reported this finding from an empirical study

[11] Glenn L. Rowley, and Ross E. Traub, "Formula Scoring, Number-Right Scoring and Test-Taking Strategy," *Journal of Educational Measurement,* 14 (Spring 1977), 15–22; and Robert Wood, "Inhibiting Blind Guessing: The Effect of Instructions," *Journal of Educational Measurement,* 13 (Winter 1976), 297–308.

[12] S. S. Wilks, "Weighting Systems for Linear Functions of Correlated Variables When There Is No Dependent Variable," *Psychometrika,* 3 (1938), 23–40.

[13] Lewis R. Aiken, Jr., "Another Look at Weighting Test Items," *Journal of Educational Measurement,* 3 (1966), 183–85.

time and offers fewer possibilities; in addition, the resulting raw scores are probably easier to interpret.[10]

If an achievement test covers two areas, one of which is judged to be twice as important as the other, then twice as many items should be written in relation to the more important area. This will result in more reliable and more valid measures than if an equal number of items is written for each area and those for the more important area are double-weighted.

Complex or time-consuming items should be made, if possible, to yield more than one response that can be independently scored as right or wrong. Very difficult items are likely to contribute less than moderately difficult items to test reliability. Giving the difficult items extra weight lowers the average effectiveness of the items and thus lowers the effectiveness of the test as a whole.

It has occurred to some test constructors that differential weighting of responses to test items might be useful in improving test reliability or validity. For example, in a question like the following:

A child complains of severe pain and tenderness in the lower abdomen, with nausea. What should the child's mother do?
  a. Give the child a laxative.
  b. Put the child to bed.
  c. Call the doctor.

Choice of the first response might result in a score of -1, of the second in a score of 0, and of the third in a score of $+1$. In this case the scoring weights were determined a priori. It has also been suggested that they might be determined experimentally, so as to maximize test reliability or validity.

[14] J. P. Guilford, Constance Lovell, and Ruth M. Williams, "Completely Weighted versus Unweighted Scoring in an Achievement Examination," *Educational and Psychological Measurement,* 2 (1942), 15–21.

[15] Alexander J. Phillips, "Further Evidence Regarding Weighted versus Unweighted Scoring of Examinations," *Educational and Psychological Measurement,* 3 (1943), 151–55.

[16] Darrell L. Sabers and Gordon W. White, "The Effect of Differential Weighting of Individual Item Responses on the Predictive Validity and Reliability of an Aptitude Test," *Journal of Educational Measurement,* 6 (1969), 93–96.

But in this case also the experimental results have been disappointing. Seldom have any appreciable, consistent gains in reliability or validity been found. It seems clear that to gain any real advantage by this means one would need to write items with this purpose specifically in mind. Most item writers, even skilled professionals, have enough difficulty writing items good enough for simple right-or-wrong scoring. To make them good enough for more finely graded differential weighting seems a formidable task. Test improvement via additional, good, simply scored items looks more promising to most item writers.

Exceptions will be found, of course, to the generalization that differential weighting of items, or of item responses, is not worthwhile in the scoring of classroom tests of educational achievement. But it is a good general guide to the constructor of an educational achievement test to settle for simple right-or-wrong scoring of individual items, with each item carrying the same weight as every other item, regardless of its importance, complexity, difficulty, or quality. Increasing the number of scorable units and making each unit as good as possible seem generally more effective than differential weighting of items or responses as a means of test improvement.

SUMMARY

Some of the principal ideas developed in this chapter are summarized in these 20 statements.

1. Students should be told well in advance when an important test is to be given.
2. Students should be taught essential test-taking skills.
3. The test constructor should avoid clues in the test items that enable an examinee to substitute testwiseness for command of knowledge.
4. Test anxiety is seldom a major factor in determining a student's score on a test.
5. The test administrator should help the student to adjust her/his rate of work on a test to the time available for it.
6. The instructor is responsible for the prevention or punishment of cheating on examinations.
7. The development of honor systems does not afford a generally promising solution to the problem of cheating on examinations.
8. The instructor is responsible for preventing students from gaining special advance copies of, or advance information about, any examination.

about the same order as uncorrected scores.

14. The probability is small of getting a respectable score on a good objective test by blind guessing alone.
— 15. Well-motivated examinees who have time to attempt all items do little blind guessing.
16. Students should be encouraged to make rational guesses on the answers to objective test items.
17. A guessing correction removes the incentive for slower students to guess blindly on the final items of a time-limited test.
18. Scores corrected for guessing may be influenced by the examinee's readiness, or reluctance, to gamble.
19. A guessing correction may complicate the scoring task and may lower scoring accuracy slightly.
20. Giving different weights to different items in a test, or to different correct or incorrect responses within an item, seldom improves score reliability or validity appreciably.

PROJECTS AND PROBLEMS

Project: Statement on Correction for Guessing

Anticipating an important objective test, a student asks whether or not the scores will be corrected for guessing. Write down the answer you would give and your justification for it (200–500 words).

11

Test Score Statistics

THE INTERPRETATION OF TEST SCORES

The score on a test usually is the sum of scores on the separate questions or items that comprise the test. For an objective test the score may be simply the number of questions answered correctly. For an essay test the reader may assign points to each answer indicating a subjective judgment of its adequacy. The size of an examinee's score in relation to the maximum possible score provides some indication of the quality of the individual performance. But it is also helpful to compare a particular score with the scores of other examinees, to examine the relationship of scores on this test with scores from the same group of students on other tests, and to investigate the intrinsic quality of the test. To obtain these kinds of information, we need the help of statistical methods.

Perhaps a concrete example will help to make clear the useful role that statistics can play in the interpretation of test scores. Exhibit 11–1 presents a sample test report of the sort that some instructors distribute to their students when they return the class's answer sheets. The test from which these data were obtained consisted of 25 true-false items dealing with ideas discussed in Chapters 2 and 3 of this text. The upper section on the left-hand side of the exhibit presents a frequency distribution of students' scores. Two students answered 24 or 25 items correctly; seventeen answered 22 or 23 correctly; sixteen answered 20 or 21 correctly; and so

n	=	59				
			0			
			9	41%	.37	
			15	51%	.46	

True Statements

3	5	6	7
8	9	12	15
21	22		

on. Fifty-nine students in all took this test. By means of this frequency distribution any student can rank his or her own performance in relation to those of fellow classmates.

In the upper right-hand portion of the exhibit, there are two numbers that summarize important characteristics of the distribution of scores. The first of these is the mean score. It is calculated by adding all 59 scores and then dividing the sum by 59. It indicates the average level of the scores for this group on this test. The second is the standard deviation. It indicates how widely the scores are dispersed about the mean score. Let us postpone for the moment a description of how the standard deviation is calculated. The third number in the upper right-hand portion of the exhibit indicates how accurately these 25 test items have assessed student achievement in this unit of study. How it is calculated and precisely what it means will be explained in Chapter 14, which discusses test reliability.

The lower left-hand section of the exhibit gives the numbers of those items that should have been marked true. The other fifteen statements should have been marked false. Four of the most difficult items in the test are identified in the section at the lower right. Each of these was missed by more than 40 percent of the students. Item 1, for example, was missed by 54 percent of the examinees. It had an index of discrimination of .28. This index is the difference in the proportions of correct answers between the 16 students who made highest scores on the whole test and the 16 who made lowest scores. Chapter 12 on item analysis will describe in more detail how these measures of item quality are obtained and what use can be made of them.

A teacher or any other user of tests who knows about frequency distributions, means, standard deviations, reliability coefficients, and indices of item difficulty and discrimination is better equipped to make good tests and to interpret test scores wisely than one who is ignorant of these things. One does not need to be a mathematical genius or a statistical wizard to gain usable knowledge of these important statistical tools. The task of this chapter and of Chapters 13 and 14 is to make the process of gaining that knowledge as easy and as rewarding as possible.

DESCRIBING SCORE DISTRIBUTIONS

The two most important characteristics of a distribution of test scores are (1) the average level of the scores and (2) the dispersion or variability of the scores. The statistics used most often to report the average level of scores are the *mean* and the *median*. To report dispersion, one is likely to use either the *standard deviation* or the *range*. Of these four, the mean and the standard deviation are by far the more common because they carry more information and are less subject to chance variations.

An example of the calculation of these statistics for a simple set of five test scores is presented in Exhibit 11–2. The given scores are 5, 4, 3, 2, and 1. Their sum is 15. To obtain the mean, we divide this sum by the number of scores. This yields 3. These operations are represented by the formula

$$M = \frac{\Sigma x}{n} = \frac{15}{5} = 3 \qquad\qquad 11.1$$

where

M is the mean score,
Σx is the sum total of all scores, and
n is the number of tests.

The median score, defined as the middle score, is also 3 in this particular

EXHIBIT 11–2. CALCULATION OF DISTRIBUTION STATISTICS

						Sum	Mean
Test scores	5	4	3	2	1	15	3
Squared scores	25	16	9	4	1	55	11
Score deviations	2	1	0	−1	−2	0	0
Squared deviations	4	1	0	1	4	10	2

Range = 5   Mean = 3   Median = 3   Variance = 2   Standard deviation = 1.414*

Mean of squared scores (11) minus the mean score squared (9) equals the variance (2).

* The standard deviation is the square root of the variance.

value is more indicative of *most* of the scores in the set, but that the mean more correctly estimates the value of *all* the scores.

Because the value of each score in the set affects the value of the mean, the mean tends to be a more stable measure of the average score level than does the median. That is, the mean is likely to vary less from one to another set of scores of the same kind than the median. Further, the mean is involved, directly or indirectly, in the calculation of many other statistics. Hence the mean is generally regarded by statisticians as a more precise and useful measure than is the median. To contrast the two statistics, suppose an instructor needs no more than an easily obtained estimate of the typical value of a set of scores. Then the median would be the measure to obtain. But if a fully representative estimate is desired and if other statistics are to be calculated, the mean will usually be preferred.

CALCULATING THE STANDARD DEVIATION

The process of calculating a standard deviation involves four steps.

1. Subtract the mean of the scores from each score in turn. The differences obtained by subtraction are called deviations.
2. Square each deviation (that is, multiply each deviation by itself) and add the squares. In our example the sum of the squared deviations is 10.
3. Divide this sum by the number of scores. This gives a quantity called the *variance*. In our example the variance is 2.
4. Find the square root of the variance. This quantity is the standard deviation. Since the square root of 2 is 1.414, the standard deviation of our set of five scores is 1.414.

The operations involved in finding the standard deviation may be represented by this formula:

$$\sigma = \sqrt{\frac{\Sigma(x - \bar{x})^2}{n}} = \sqrt{\frac{10}{5}} = \sqrt{2} = 1.414 \qquad\qquad 11.2$$

where

σ is the standard deviation,
Σ is a symbol meaning "the sum of,"
x is any individual score,
$\bar{x}$ is the mean score, and
n is the number of scores.

The square of a number, multiplied by itself, gives the number. Hence, if a number is divided by its square root, the answer (quotient) obtained will be the square root also. This is the basis of the "guess and divide" method of finding square roots. Let us apply this method to finding the square root of 2.

Since 1 times 1 equals 1, and 2 times 2 equals 4, the square root of 2 must be greater than 1 and less than 2. Suppose we guess 1.5 and divide 2 by 1.5. The answer we get is 1.33. Obviously, 1.5 is too large and 1.33 too small. Let us try 1.4. When we divide it into 2.0, we get 1.429. So, 1.4 is too small and 1.429 is too large. The average of those two is about 1.414. When this is used as the divisor, the quotient is 1.414. We have found the square root!

There are other, perhaps quicker methods of finding square roots. Some hand calculators give them directly. They can be looked up in tables of square roots. Or they can be calculated by more elegant arithmetical procedures. But if no better method is available, the guess and divide method will work.

The last statement in Exhibit 11–2 gives us an alternate way of calculating the variance. By simply subtracting the square of the mean score (in our example $3 \times 3 = 9$) from the mean of the squared scores ($55 \div 5 = 11$), we arrive at the same number as we obtained by working from the deviations. Since mean scores often include decimal fractions, they yield deviations that are not whole numbers either. Such deviations are tedious to square, to add, and to reduce to the square root. Hence, it is usually advantageous to avoid using deviations in calculating square roots and to work directly from the scores.

Standard deviations are used in defining standard test scores such as the College Board scores, in determining comparable or equivalent scores on two tests, in expressing the accuracy of a test score, and in controlling the weights of recitations, papers, and test scores in determining a grade. They are also used to define the grade interval in most widely used systems of grading.

Variances also, which so far have served only as means for calculating standard deviations, will help us to understand some aspects of test reliability. Knowing a little about variances and standard deviations, how they are determined and hence (in part) what they mean will enable you to

To test your understanding of score distribution statistics, start with a set of seven scores: 7, 6, 5, 4, 3, 2, and 1. Perform the required calculations to arrive at each of the following statistics: the range, mean, median, variance (two methods), and standard deviation

FREQUENCY DISTRIBUTIONS

To illustrate the calculation of score distribution statistics, we used a simple set of five scores. However, most test scores that teachers have to deal with not only involve much larger sets but the scores themselves are often two-digit numbers. Thus, we need to consider how teachers can deal with rather unwieldy numbers in a practical way.

Suppose two spelling tests of 100 words each have been given to a class of 25 students. The first test, List A, was dictated on Monday, and the second, List B, composed of entirely different words, on Wednesday. The students' test papers were scored by giving one unit of credit for each word correctly spelled. The scores obtained are shown in Table 11–1. How can these two sets of scores be described statistically? Consider first only the Monday test scores in List A.

Notice that the scores range from a high of 96 for Nathaniel to a low of 61 for Wendell. In order to include all the scores a range of 36 score units (96 − 61 + 1 = 36) is required. This range is used as one measure of the variability of the scores. To get a more complete picture of the students' scores on this test, a frequency distribution can be constructed.

Grouping the scores into score intervals simplifies the frequency distribution with no appreciable loss in accuracy. Each interval should include the same number of scores. That number depends on the range of scores.

The range of the List A spelling test scores is 36, which leads to a 3-unit score interval. Since the lowest score is 61, the bottom group is 61–63. The next is 64–66, and so on. On this basis the score intervals shown in the left column of Table 11–2 were set up.

TABLE 11–1. SCORES OF TWENTY-FIVE PUPILS ON TWO SPELLING TESTS

	List A, Monday	List B, Wednesday
Aaron	65	67
Barbara	75	72
Ben	66	72
Bud	88	92
Clyde	71	76
Donald	72	72
Dorothy	91	90
Eugene	82	80
Fay	84	80
Frank	76	81
Gary	69	64
Gladys	67	70
Jack	74	78
Jeff	80	77
Jerry	87	90
Joan	91	85
Melville	65	68
Nadine	77	78
Nathaniel	96	94
Patricia	93	87
Peggy	79	78
Perry	84	89
Richard	76	75
Shirley	73	78
Wendell	61	69

If the range is	Use an interval of
2–19	1
20–29	2
30–49	3
50–100	5

TABLE 11–2. FREQUENCY DISTRIBUTION OF TWENTY-FIVE SCORES ON LIST A

Interval	Scores	Frequency
94–96	96	1
91–93	91, 91, 93	3
88–90	88	1
85–87	87	1
82–84	82, 84, 84	3
79–81	80, 79	2
76–78	76, 77, 76	3
73–75	75, 74, 73	3
70–72	71, 72	2
67–69	69, 67	2
64–66	65, 66, 65	3
61–63	61	1
		$n = 25$

constructor an integrated, meaningful picture of the entire distribution of scores. It is also useful in showing how any particular score relates to all the other scores in the groups.

CALCULATIONS WITH DEVIATIONS

Frequency distributions can also be used to simplify calculations of the mean and the standard deviation. Instead of working with the original two digit scores, we work with single-digit class deviation numbers.

We begin by assigning deviation values (column 3) to each group of scores as follows. A score interval near the middle of the frequency distribution is chosen to be the zero interval. Successive intervals above the zero interval are numbered consecutively from 1 to (in this case) 6. Successive intervals below the zero interval are numbered consecutively from −1 to (in this case) −5.

The fourth column of Table 11–3 gives us the total deviation within each score interval. These figures were obtained by multiplying the frequency (column 2) by the deviation (column 3). The sum of these totals for the entire distribution is 6 (36 − 30). The mean of these deviation numbers is .24 (6 ÷ 25). The sum of the deviation numbers squared is 252, as is shown in the fifth column. Hence the mean of these deviation numbers squared is 10.08 (252 ÷ 25).

Recall that the variance is the mean of squared scores minus the square of the mean score. Hence the variance of these deviation numbers is 10.08 − .0576 (.24 × .24) or 10.0224.

To change the mean of the score interval deviations into the mean of the original scores, we must do two things:

1. Multiply the deviation mean by 3, since one of the deviation units is equal to three of the original score units. That is, .24 × 3 = .72
2. Add 77 to .72, since zero on the deviation scale corresponds to the mid-score 77, of the 76–78 score interval.

Thus the mean of this distribution of scores is 77.72.

TABLE 11–3. CALCULATIONS WITH DEVIATION UNITS

Group	Frequency (f)	Deviation (d)	fd	fd^2
94–96	1	6	6	36
91–93	3	5	15	75
88–90	1	4	4	16
85–87	1	3	3	9
82–84	3	2	6	12
79–81	2	1	2	2
76–78	3	0	0	0
73–75	3	−1	−3	3
70–72	2	−2	−4	8
67–69	2	−3	−6	18
64–66	3	−4	−12	48
61–63	1	−5	−5	25
Sum	25		6	252

Mean
Deviation units $\quad \dfrac{6}{25} = .24$

Score units $\quad 3 \times .24 + 77 = 77.72$

Variance
Deviation units $\quad \dfrac{252}{25} - .24^2 = 10.0224$

Score units $\quad 9 \times 10.0224 = 90.2016$

Standard deviation $\quad \sqrt{90.2016} = 9.50$

To change the variance of the score interval deviations into the variance of the original scores, we must multiply 10.0224 by 9. We are dealing with squared scores, and one deviation unit equals three original score units. Hence one deviation unit squared is equal to nine original score units squared. Thus the variance of the scores in this distribution is 90.2016. The standard deviation of these scores is the square root of 90.2016 or 9.50.

THE NORMAL DISTRIBUTION

Distributions of test scores frequently approximate a normal distribution, that is, a symmetrical, bell-shaped curve. For this reason, and because it is convenient to have a standard, idealized model as a point of reference when estimating the characteristics of any given distribution, we need to study the characteristics of the normal curve.

Some of the essential characteristics of the normal distribution are illustrated in Figure 11–1. It is a symmetrical curve, with the mean and median located in the same central position bisecting the area under the curve. The base line of the curve is marked in standard deviation units.

| | 1.65% | 4.41% | 9.19% | 14.98% | 19.15% | 19.15% | 14.98% | 9.19% | 4.41% | 1.65% | |
| -3σ | | -2σ | | -1σ | | 0 | | $+1\sigma$ | | $+2\sigma$ | $+3\sigma$ |

On Figure 11–1 ordinates (vertical lines from the curve to the base line) have been drawn at intervals of one-half of the standard deviation. Taking a convenient arbitrary length for the central ordinate and calling it 1.00, the other ordinates can be expressed as decimal values of the central ordinate (figures just above the curve). It is helpful to refer to the relative lengths of these ordinates when drawing replicas of the normal curve.

Percentages of the total area under the curve are also indicated for the area between each successive pair of ordinates. It is useful to remember that 68.26 percent of the total area lies between the ordinates located at $+1\sigma$ and -1σ; that 95.46 percent lies between the ordinates at $+2\sigma$ and -2σ, and 99.72 percent between the ordinates at $+3\sigma$ and -3σ. Detailed tables of ordinates and areas under the normal curve are available in good statistical references, such as Blommers and Lindquist, and Ferguson.[1] Moonan has published frequency distributions that approximate the normal distribution for various numbers of class intervals and for various numbers of measures.[2]

Theoretically, a normal curve extends without limit on either side of the mean. In practice, and for convenience, it is often considered to extend from three standard deviations below to three standard deviations above the mean, since 99.72 percent of the test scores or other measures comprising the distribution fall within those limits. But the distribution of scores from a class of, say, 30 students will not typically show a range from high score to low of six standard deviations. Hoel's figures indicate that the

[1] Paul Blommers and E. F. Lindquist, *Elementary Statistical Methods* (Boston: Houghton Mifflin Company, 1960); and George A. Ferguson, *Statistical Analysis in Psychology and Education* (New York: McGraw-Hill Book Company, 1959).

[2] William J. Moonan, "A Table of Normal Distribution Frequencies for Selected Numbers of Class Intervals and Sample Sizes," *Journal of Experimental Education*, 27 (March 1959), 231–35.

following ratio of range to standard deviation can be expected for samples of the sizes shown.[3]

Sample Size	Typical Range in Standard Deviation Units
10	3.0
50	4.5
100	5.0
1000	6.5

The typical values shown are averages. In some samples of the specified size the observed value of the ratio of range to standard deviation will be considerably more, and in other samples considerably less, than the value indicated. But it may be useful for the instructor to know that in a set of 25 test scores the highest score is more likely to be two than three standard deviations above the mean.

Another point worth noting is that the *points of inflection* of the curve occur at $+1\sigma$ and -1σ. As one follows the curve outward from the mean it is at these points that the slope of the curve stops increasing and starts to decrease. Exactly half of the area under the curve is located between ordinates at $+.6745\sigma$ and $-.6745\sigma$. When the normal curve is used to represent chance fluctuations in test scores due to errors of measurement, the value $.6745\sigma$ is referred to as the probable error of measurement. Half the errors are likely to be larger and half smaller than this value. The standard deviation of the normal curve is referred to as the standard error of measurement when the curve itself is used to indicate the expected distribution of errors of measurement. About 32 percent of the errors are likely to be larger and 68 percent smaller than the standard error of measurement.

While it is true, as pointed out at the beginning of this section, that many distributions of test scores do approximate the normal distribution, there is no compelling reason why they ought to. Indeed, to achieve highest reliability with a given number of test items, a flatter score distribution than the normal distribution is advantageous, one that has more scores at the extremes and fewer in the center. Rummel, working with a college-level mathematics test used to exempt some entering freshmen (about 50 percent) from a course in basic mathematical skills, found that item revisions that flattened the distribution of scores also reduced the errors made in exempting some freshmen and not exempting others.[4]

[3] Paul G. Hoel, *Introduction to Mathematical Statistics* (New York: John Wiley & Sons, Inc., 1947).
[4] Josiah Francis Rummel, "The Modification of a Test to Reduce Errors in the Classification of Examinees," unpublished dissertation, College of Education, The State University of Iowa, Iowa City, Iowa, 1950.

Sometimes tests yield as~~~~~ which the median score is much nearer the highest score than the lowest, or vice versa. Lord and Cook have reported studies of this phenomenon in actual distributions of test scores.[5] If this skewing is not attributable to a few outstandingly capable or incapable students in the group tested, it may be due to excessive ease, or difficulty, in the test itself. When the test is too easy, students of average achievement may receive scores almost as high as students of outstanding achievement. When it is too hard, students of average achievement may do little better than those of lowest achievement. In either case the distribution of scores is likely to be skewed, or asymmetric. Thus, lack of symmetry in the score distribution may indicate an inappropriate level of difficulty. But symmetry is not the same as normality.

PERCENTILE RANKS

Since the scores on different tests, when taken by different groups, can have widely different means, standard deviations, and distributions, it is useful to have some standard scale to which they all can be referred. One such scale is a scale of *percentile ranks*. Since this scale is useful in interpreting and working with the scores from classroom tests, it will be discussed in some detail.

The percentile rank of a given test score can be defined in three similar but significantly different ways. It is the percentage of the scores in a particular distribution of scores that:

1. falls below the given score, or
2. falls at or below the given score, or
3. falls below the midpoint of the given score interval.

[5] Frederic M. Lord, "A Summary of Observed Test-score Distributions with Respect to Skewness and Kurtosis," *Educational and Psychological Measurement*, 15 (1955), 383–89; and Desmond L. Cook, "A Replication of Lord's Study of Skewness and Kurtosis of Observed Test-score Distributions," *Educational and Psychological Measurement*, 14 (1959), 81–87.

Table 11–4 shows the effects of these different definitions on the percentile ranks of five hypothetical test scores. The highest score gets a percentile rank of only 80 under definition 1. The lowest score gets a percentile rank of 20 under definition 2. The average score gets a percentile rank of 40 under definition 1 and of 60 under definition 2. But under definition 3 the average score gets a percentile rank of 50, as it should in a symmetrical distribution of scores, and the highest and lowest scores are both the same distance from the extremes of the percentile scale, as they also should be in this situation. For these reasons, definition 3 is usually preferred.

There are three steps in the process of calculating the percentile rank equivalents of the scores in a particular set of scores.

1. Prepare a frequency distribution of the scores.
2. Add successive frequencies, starting with the lowest score, to obtain a column of cumulative frequencies.
3. Convert the cumulative frequencies into percentages of the last (highest) cumulative frequency.

Table 11–5 illustrates the calculation of percentile ranks for the List A spelling test scores (p. 215). Note that the scale extends from one score below the lowest score any student actually received to one score higher than any student received. Note too that the scale includes all possible scores between these extremes, even though no student actually received some of those scores. The number of students who received each of the possible scores is shown in the second column of the table.

The third column gives a cumulative frequency for each score on the scale. It is calculated by counting the number of scores lower than the scale score, and adding half the number of scores at that scale score point. Consider the scale score 75. There are 10 scores lower than 75, and one score of 75. So, we take the ten, add one half of the one and get a cumulative frequency of 10.5.

The fourth column of percentile ranks is obtained in this way: Divide the cumulative frequency for that score by the maximum cumulative fre-

TABLE 11–4. EFFECT OF DIFFERENT DEFINITIONS OF PERCENTILE RANKS

Score	Percentile Rank Under Definition		
	1	2	3
5	80	100	90
4	60	80	70
3	40	60	50
2	20	40	30
1	0	20	10

94			
93	1	23.5	94
92	0	23.0	92
91	2	22.0	88
90	0	21.0	84
89	0	21.0	84
88	1	20.5	82
87	1	19.5	78
86	0	19.0	76
85	0	19.0	76
84	2	18.0	72
83	0	17.0	68
82	1	16.5	66
81	0	16.0	64
80	1	15.5	62
79	1	14.5	58
78	0	14.0	56
77	1	13.5	54
76	2	12.0	48
75	1	10.5	42
74	1	9.5	38
73	1	8.5	34
72	1	7.5	30
71	1	6.5	26
70	0	6.0	24
69	1	5.5	22
68	0	5.0	20
67	1	4.5	18
66	1	3.5	14
65	2	2.0	8
64	0	1.0	4
63	0	1.0	4
62	0	1.0	4
61	1	0.5	2
60	0	0.0	0

quency. In this example that maximum is 25 because there are 25 scores in the set. If we had scores for 34 pupils, the maximum cumulative frequency would be 34. Then, having divided each score's cumulative frequency by the maximum cumulative frequency, multiply the quotient by 100.

Thus to find the percentile rank of any score in a set of scores you must know three things:

1. How many scores there were in the set
2. How many scores were lower than the given score
3. How many pupils got the given score

Consider the score of 52 in a set of 38 scores. If there is only one 52 and nine scores lower than 52, what is the percentile rank of 52? Well, the cumulative frequency for 52 is 9.5 (9 plus ½). If 9.5 is divided by 38, and multiplied by 100, the result is 25. So 25 is the percentile rank of a score of 52 in this set of scores.

Interpretation of Percentile Ranks

Test scores expressed as percentile ranks are sometimes confused with test scores expressed as percent correct. They are, of course, quite different. A percent correct score is determined by an examinee's performance relative to the content of the test. It expresses the relation between the number of points awarded to a specific examinee's paper and the maximum possible number of points for any paper. Usually the expectation is that few examinees in a group will receive percent correct scores less than some value near 70 percent, which is often set arbitrarily as the passing score. If the group as a whole does well on an examination, the percent correct scores will run higher than if the group as a whole does poorly.

A percentile rank, on the other hand, is determined solely by the relation between a specific examinee's score and the scores of other examinees in the group tested. Percentile ranks must necessarily range from near 0 to near 100, regardless of whether the group as a whole does well or poorly on the examination.

The insensitivity of percentile ranks to general level of group performance might seem to be a disadvantage. Yet in many cases the apparent level of group performance is largely determined by unintentional, and sometimes uncontrollable, variations in the difficulty of a test. It is unfortunately true that dependable standards of measurement are seldom provided by the examiner's a priori judgments of how difficult a question is likely to be, nor by judgments of how well the student has answered it, particularly with essay-type tests. The typical unreliability of measures obtained by these means has been demonstrated quite convincingly.

It is clear from this figure   .
differences near the middle of the distribution but reduce raw score differences toward the extremes. Stated in other words, a difference of 10
percentile rank units near the extremes corresponds to a much larger raw
score difference than does the same difference in percentile ranks near

FIGURE 11–2. *Relation Between Normal
and Rectangular Distributions*

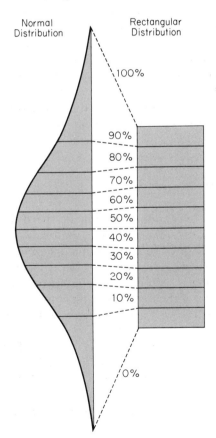

TABLE 11–6. RELATION OF SCORES TO PERCENTILE RANKS IN A NORMAL DISTRIBUTION

Equal Score Intervals		Equal Percentile Intervals	
Scores	Percentile Ranks	Percentile Ranks	Scores
100	100	100	100
80	96	80	60
60	73	60	53
40	27	40	47
20	4	20	40
0	0	0	0

the mean. Intuition suggests that the raw score distribution, approximately normal, is a more accurate reflection of the "true" distribution of abilities than is the rectangular distribution. But however plausible such an intuition may seem to be, it is difficult to verify by experiment or logical demonstration.

This relationship between raw test scores and percentile ranks is illustrated numerically in Table 11–6. This illustration was constructed so that the test scores would range from 0 to 100 with a mean of 50, the same as is true for percentile ranks. With equal score intervals, percentile rank differences are small at the extremes and large in the middle, as shown in the two columns on the left. With equal percentile rank intervals, raw score differences are large at the extremes and small in the middle. Thus when raw scores are converted to percentile ranks, differences in the middle are magnified and differences at the extremes are reduced. In the middle of the distribution of scores, a small score difference corresponds to a large percentile rank difference. At the extremes, a large score difference gives a much smaller percentile rank difference.

COEFFICIENTS OF CORRELATION

In dealing with test scores one frequently has need for an index of their relation to other measures. For example, the relation between scores on a reading readiness test given to pupils in the first grade and scores on a test of reading achievement given a year or two later may need to be determined. If the relation is high and if all pupils received the same kind of instruction regardless of their readiness test scores, the readiness test probably would be judged to be a good test because it accurately forecast later achievement.

Another illustration of the need for an index of the relation between sets of test scores is provided by the determination of some kinds of test reliability. If the same test is given twice to the same group, if two different but equivalent forms are given to the same group, or if a single test is split into two equivalent halves that are separately scored, we use an index of

TABLE 11-7. DATA FOR CORRELATION

| | Scores | | Products | | |
	First	Second	$F \times F$	$S \times S$	$F \times S$
Bill	5	5	25	25	25
Bob	6	8	36	64	48
Dick	9	7	81	49	63
Norm	5	7	25	49	35
Walt	8	9	64	81	72
	33	36	231	268	243

To calculate a coefficient of correlation by the best and most commonly used means, one needs six items of numerical information. From Table 11-7, they are

the number of pairs of scores (= 5)
the sum of the first scores (= 33)
the sum of second scores (= 36)
the sum of first scores squared (= 231)
the sum of second scores squared (= 268)
the sum of first times second scores (= 243)

How these numbers are combined to yield the coefficient of correlation is shown in Table 11-8. Using r as the symbol for the coefficient of corre-

TABLE 11-8. COMPUTATION OF CORRELATION

$$N \Sigma FS - \Sigma F \Sigma S = 5 \cdot 243 - 33 \cdot 36 = 1215 - 1188 = 27$$
$$N \Sigma F^2 - (\Sigma F)^2 = 5 \cdot 231 - 33 \cdot 33 = 1155 - 1089 = 66$$
$$N \Sigma S^2 - (\Sigma S)^2 = 5 \cdot 268 - 36 \cdot 36 = 1340 - 1296 = 44$$
$$\sqrt{66.44} = \sqrt{2904} = 54$$
$$27 \div 54 = .50 \qquad r = .50$$

lation, the upper-case Greek sigma (Σ) to indicate summation, and N to indicate the number of pairs we can express the operations in this formula

$$r = \frac{N\Sigma FS - \Sigma F \Sigma S}{[N\Sigma F^2 - (\Sigma F)^2][N\Sigma S^2 - (\Sigma S)^2]} \qquad 11.3$$

The example used here is extremely simple, intended only to show what a coefficient of correlation is and how it can be calculated. One would seldom want to calculate a "real" correlation coefficient, which might be based on 30 to 300 pairs of scores whose numerical values might range from a low of 50 to a high of 150, using this kind of paper and pencil computation. A desk calculator is almost the minimum equipment that would be required. A properly programmed computer is even better.

Rank Difference Correlation

Another formula for estimating a correlation coefficient is based on differences in rank between the two scores of each pair when the scores from each test have been ranked separately. A different symbol, the Greek letter rho, is used to indicate that this coefficient of correlation is somewhat different from the Pearson coefficient r. The formula is

$$\rho = 1 - \frac{6\Sigma d^2}{N(N^2 - 1)} \qquad 11.4$$

in which d^2 is the square of the difference between ranks for the scores of any pair and N is the number of pairs of scores.

To illustrate the use of this formula, let us apply it to the first ten pairs of spelling test scores from Table 11–1. Those scores are reproduced in the first two columns of Table 11–9. Columns three and four show the ranks of the scores. The highest score on List A, which is 91, is given the rank of 1. The second highest, 88, is given rank 2, and so on. There are two sets of tied scores on List B, two 80s and three 72s. If they had been slightly different, the two 80s would have occupied ranks 4 and 5. Since they are not different, they must be given the same rank. We use the average of 4 and 5, or 4.5. The next highest score is ranked 6. In the same way the three 72s, which if different would have been ranked 7, 8, and 9, are given the average of these three positions and all ranked 8. The next highest score to 72, a score of 71, gets ranked 10.

Column 5 in Table 11–9 shows the difference in ranks, and column six shows the squares of those differences. Adding column six gives us the Σd^2 required by the rank difference formula. This must be multiplied by 6, which is a constant. No matter how many pairs of scores are involved, the sum of the squared differences in rank is always multiplied by 6. In our example, 18.5 times 6 gives 111.

82	80	4	4.5	0.0	0.20
84	80	3	4.5	1.5	2.25
76	81	5	3	2	4
					18.5

The quantity in the denominator, $N(N^2 - 1)$, depends on the number of pairs of scores. In our example N is 10, so $N(N^2 - 1)$ is 10 times (100 − 1) or 990. Dividing 111 by 990, we obtain .11. Subtracting this from 1 gives .89, the rank difference coefficient of correlation for these ten pairs of scores. This coefficient is designated by the lower-case Greek letter rho ρ to distinguish it from the product-moment coefficient designated by r.

Correlations obtained from the rank difference formula usually will not agree perfectly with product-moment correlations from the same pairs of scores, but they are ordinarily quite close. Because they are much easier to compute than the product-moment correlations, classroom teachers are likely to give preference to them, as they should, when they need to estimate correlation coefficients.

Interpreting Coefficients of Correlation

If the scores in two sets were to be perfectly correlated in a negative sense, the correlation coefficient would be expressed as −1.00. This again is a virtually nonexistent phenomenon. However, for illustrative purposes we present the synthetic data in the middle third of Table 11–10. The four columns of variable 2 data show a perfect negative correlation with the variable 1 data at the left. Guard against the mistake of thinking or saying that a correlation of −1.00 is a low correlation—it is perfect correlation in a negative sense.

If the two sets of scores were to show no overall relation, the correlation coefficient would then be expressed by a minimum value of .00. This can happen, though it does not often happen with real test data. It has been

TABLE 11–10. EXAMPLES OF PERFECT AND ZERO CORRELATIONS

Variable 1	Variable 2			
	Perfect positive correlations			
	(r = 1.00)			
5	5	7	10	9
4	4	6	8	7
3	3	5	6	5
2	2	4	4	3
1	1	3	2	1

Variable 1	Variable 2			
	Perfect negative correlations			
	(r = −1.00)			
5	1	3	2	1
4	2	4	4	3
3	3	5	6	5
2	4	6	8	7
1	5	7	10	9

Variable 1	Variable 2			
	Zero correlations with variable 1			
	(r = .00)			
5	4	2	8	3
4	1	5	2	9
3	3	3	6	5
2	5	1	10	1
1	2	4	4	7

made to happen with the synthetic test data in the bottom third of Table 11–10. The column of scores at the left has zero correlation with each of the four columns of scores at the right. Thus the limits of possible coefficients of correlation are 1.00 and −1.00. If a calculation seems to indicate a correlation of 1.56 or of −3.20, it is certain that some mistake has been made.

It is sometimes helpful in interpreting a coefficient of correlation to relate it to the coefficients obtained in other more or less familiar situations. Scores on equivalent forms of a well-constructed educational achievement test, administered separately within a few days of each other, should show coefficients of correlation of 0.90 or higher. Scores on good tests intended to predict educational achievement correlate with subsequent good measures of achievement to the extent reflected in coefficients that average about 0.50 and range from about 0.30 to about 0.70, depending on the nature of the achievement, the quality of the measures of promise and of attainment, the interval between the measures, and many other factors. Coefficients of correlation between the scores on individual items of an objective test average about 0.10 but often range from about −0.30 to about 0.50.

If the process above is repeated to yield 50 or 100 pairs of scores, and if the coefficient of correlation between the X and Y scores is calculated, a value near 0.50 will be obtained. Instead of two dice, four might be used. If only one of the dice were rerolled to obtain the second score of each pair, a correlation of 0.75 would be expected. If three were rerolled, a correlation of 0.25 would be expected. Using 10 dice and rerolling only one of them should result in an expected coefficient of correlation of 0.90.

Thus when one encounters a correlation coefficient of, say, 0.83, it is reasonable to make the following kind of interpretation. If the related measures were determined by the combined effects of 100 independent, equally powerful factors, 83 of the 100 would have to be constant factors. That is, they would have to contribute the same value to each member of the pair of related measures to yield a coefficient of 0.83. The other 17 factors could vary.

Of course, this interpretation is merely suggestive and should not be taken too literally as a description of what actually happens. There is usually no evidence to suggest that the performance of students on any test is the result of the combined influence of a number of independent, equally powerful factors.

Coefficients of correlation are widely used in the study of test scores. If calculated accurately they provide precise estimates of the degree of relationship among the data on which they are based. One caution, however: when a coefficient obtained from one sample is used to estimate the correlation in another sample from the same population, or in the entire population, due note should be taken of the sample size. In general, small samples give inexact estimates of the correlation that would be obtained from other samples, or from the entire population.

SUMMARY

Some of the principal ideas developed in this chapter are summarized in the following 24 statements:

1. In order to do an adequate job of interpreting a set of test scores,

it is necessary to understand and use a variety of statistical tools: frequency distributions, standard scores, and measures of central tendency, variability, and correlation.

2. Students who took an objective test should be given a report of the score distribution, the correct answers, the score statistics, and statistics of difficult items.

3. The median is either the middle measure (if the number of measures is odd) or a point midway between the two middle measures (if the number of measures is even).

4. One finds the mean of a set of scores by adding all of the scores and dividing this amount by the total number of scores.

5. A few extremely high or low scores tend to pull the mean away from the median.

6. The variance of a set of scores is the sum of the squared deviations of the scores (from the mean of all scores) divided by the number of scores.

7. The standard deviation is the square root of the variance.

8. The square root of a number can be found by successive divisions until the quotient equals the divisor.

9. The variance of a set of scores can be found by subtracting the square of the mean from the mean of the squared scores.

10. Variances and standard deviations have many uses in the analysis and interpretation of test scores.

11. A frequency distribution of scores shows how many scores fall in each group, or at each level, along the score scale.

12. A frequency distribution is useful in showing how any particular score relates to all the other scores in the group.

13. One can sometimes simplify calculation of the mean and of the standard deviation by starting with the frequency distribution and by making use of a deviation scale whose unit is the class interval and whose zero is the midpoint of an interval near the middle of the distribution.

14. The normal curve is a theoretical, symmetric, bell-shaped curve that provides an idealized representation of the frequency distributions of some kinds of experimental data.

15. The larger the number of scores in a group, the greater the expected range of scores in standard deviation units.

16. One can give scores in any set a standard relative meaning by converting them into percentile ranks.

17. The percentile rank of a score is most appropriately defined as the percent of scores in a group that fall below the midpoint of the given score interval.

18. A complete set of percentile ranks yields a frequency distribution that is rectangular in shape.

pressing absence of relationship, to −1.00, expressing p
negative (inverse) relationship.

23. Correlation coefficients obtained from small or medium-sized samples are subject to large sampling errors.

24. If values of the two variables being correlated can be thought of as the result of influences of a number of independent, equally potent factors, then the correlation coefficient expresses the proportion of those factors making the same (rather than different) contribution to the values in each pair of variables.

PROJECTS AND PROBLEMS

Problem: Calculating the Mean and the Standard Deviation

This exercise is based on the two lists of spelling test scores presented in Table 11–1. In the example below, the frequency distribution, median, mean, variance, and standard deviation of the List A scores have been produced or calculated. Your task is to prepare a similar display based on the List B scores. Use the same class intervals, and make the calculated values as accurate as those shown here. Show some concern for the neatness of your work. You need not show details of your calculations.

I. Frequency Distribution

Class	Frequency		List A
94–96	6		96
91–93	5		91, 91, 93
88–90	4		88
85–87	3		87
82–84	2		82, 84, 84
79–81	1		80, 79
76–78	0		76, 77, 76
73–75	−1		75, 74, 73
70–72	−2		71, 72
67–69	−3		69, 67
64–66	−4		65, 66, 65
61–63	−5		61

II. Median   76

III. Mean
      Σx 1942
      Mean (ungrouped data)   77.68
      Σfd 6
      Mean (grouped data)   77.72

IV. Variance
      Σfd^2 252
      Variance (deviation scores)   10.0224
      Variance (raw scores)   90.2016

V. Standard Deviation   9.50

Problem: Calculating Percentiles

Prepare a chart like that shown in Figure 11–5 for computing the percentiles of the List B spelling test scores. Use the same method as was used with the List A scores. Prepare to turn in the chart.

Problem: Calculating a Correlation Coefficient

Compute the product-moment coefficient of correlation (Formula 11.3) and the rank-difference coefficient (Formula 11.4) using the second 10 pairs of scores (Gary-Patricia) in Table 11.1. The task will be much simpler if you convert the scores into deviations, using the equivalents shown in Table 11.3. Thus the scores for Aaron, 65 and 67, would become −4 and −3 respectively. Those for Barbara would become −1 and −2, and so on. Show your work in displays like those of Tables 11.8 and 11.9.

12

Marks and Marking Systems

THE PROBLEM OF MARKING

The problem of marking student achievement has been persistently troublesome at all levels of education. Hardly a month goes by without the appearance in some popular magazine or professional journal of an article criticizing current practices or suggesting some new approach. Progressive schools and colleges are constantly experimenting with new systems of marking, or sometimes of not marking. And still the problem persists.[1]

From some points of view, marking is even more complex and difficult a task than building a good test and using it properly. In an early classic of educational measurement, Thorndike explained some of the reasons why educational achievement is often difficult to measure.

Measurements which involve human capacities and acts are subject to special difficulties due chiefly to:
1. The absence or imperfection of units in which to measure.
2. The lack of constancy in the facts to be measured, and
3. The extreme complexity of the measurements to be made.[2]

Marks are, of course, measurements of educational achievement.

[1] Louise Witner Cureton, "The History of Grading Practices," *N.C.M.E. Measurement in Education*, Vol. 2, No. 4, May 1971.
[2] E. L. Thorndike, *Mental and Social Measurements* (2nd ed., New York: Teachers College, Columbia University, 1912), chap. 2.

A second reason why problems of marking are difficult to solve permanently is because marking systems tend to become issues in educational controversies. Odell noted that research on marking systems did not become really significant until after the turn of the century.[3] At about the same time, the development of objective tests was ushering in the somewhat controversial "scientific movement" in education. The rise of progressive education in the third and fourth decades of this century, with its emphasis on the uniqueness of the individual, the wholeness of mental life, freedom and democracy in the classroom, and the child's need for loving reassurance, led to criticisms of the academic narrowness, the competitive pressures, and the common standards of achievement for all pupils implicit in many marking systems. In the 60s and 70s, renewed emphasis on what is called "basic education" and on the pursuit of academic excellence has been accompanied by pleas for more formal evaluations of achievement and more rigorous standards of attainment.[4]

> Standards! That is a word for every American to write on his bulletin board. We must face the fact that there are a good many things in our national life which are inimical to standards—laziness, complacency, the desire for a fast buck, the American fondness for short cuts, reluctance to criticize slackness, to name only a few. Every thinking American knows in his heart that we must sooner or later come to terms with these failings.[5]

The shifting winds of educational doctrine blow unsteadily even at the same time. Some educational leaders espouse one philosophy, some another. Some teachers find it easy to accept one point of view, some another, even when they teach in the same educational institution. Since somewhat different marking systems are implied by each of these different philosophical positions, it is not surprising that differences of opinion, dissatisfaction, and proposals for change tend to characterize instructor reactions to marking systems.

A third reason why marking systems present perennial problems is that they require teachers, whose natural instincts incline them to be helpful guides and counsellors, to stand in judgment over some of their fellow human beings. This is not the role of friendship and may carry somewhat antisocial overtones.

"Forbear to judge, for we are sinners all," said Shakespeare, echoing the sentiments of the Sermon on the Mount: "Judge not, that ye be not

---

[3] C. W. Odell, "Marks and Marking Systems," in *Encyclopedia of Educational Research*, ed. Walter S. Monroe (New York: The Macmillan Company, 1950), pp. 711–17.

[4] Nelson A. Rockefeller et al., *The Pursuit of Excellence* (Garden City, N.Y.: Doubleday & Company, Inc., 1958), p. 49.

[5] John W. Gardner, *Excellence* (New York: Harper & Row, Publishers, 1961), pp. 158–59.

ing. The real need is not...

Odell observed in 1950 that, "Most of the writings since 1938 are so similar to earlier published material that little has been added to either research or opinion in this area."[6] Reviewing articles on marking problems and practices that were written a half century ago, one is struck by their pertinence to the present day. The same problems that were troublesome then are still troublesome. Some of the same remedies that were being proposed then are still being proposed.

Marking procedures, Hadley has pointed out, are about as good or as weak as the teachers who apply them.[7] Few teachers mark as well as they could, or should. Palmer has discussed candidly, but kindly, some of the failures of English teachers in marking the achievements of their students.[8] The more confident teachers are that they are doing a good job of marking, the less likely they are to be aware of the difficulties of marking, the fallibility of their judgments, and the personal biases they may be reflecting in their marks. Most teachers' marks, says Hadley, are partly fact and partly fancy. The beginning of wisdom in marking is to recognize these short-comings. The cultivation of wisdom is to work to improve them. Measurements and reports of achievement are essential in education, and no better alternative to marks seems likely to appear.

THE NEED FOR MARKS

Most instructors, at all levels of education, seem to agree that marks are necessary. Occasionally a voice is raised to cry that marks are educationally vicious, that they are relics of the dark ages of education.[9] However, as

[6] Odell, "Marks and Marking Systems," p. 711.

[7] S. Trevor Hadley, "A School Mark—Fact or Fancy?" *Educational Administration and Supervision*, 40 (1954), 305–12.

[8] Orville Palmer, "Seven Classic Ways of Grading Dishonestly," *The English Journal* (October 1962), pp. 464–67.

[9] Dorothy De Zouche, "The Wound Is Mortal': Marks, Honors, Unsound Activities," *Clearing House*, 19 (1945), 339–44; and H. B. Brooks, "What Can Be Done About Comparative Marks and Formal Report Cards?" *California Journal of Secondary Education*, 10 (1935), 101–6.

Madsen has pointed out, the claim that abolition of marks would lead to better achievement is, by its very nature, impossible to demonstrate.[10] If we forego measurements of relative achievement, what basis remains for demonstrating that one set of circumstances produces better educational results than another? Comparison of achievements between persons or between methods of teaching is inevitable, Madsen suggests. He concludes that it is the misuse of marks, not their use, that is in need of censure.

The uses made of marks are numerous and crucial. They are used as self-evaluative measures and also to report students' educational status to parents, to future teachers, and to prospective employers. They provide a basis for important decisions about educational plans and career options. Education is expensive. To make the best possible use of educational facilities and student talent, it is essential that each student's educational progress be watched carefully and reported as accurately as possible. Reports of course marks serve somewhat the same function in education that financial statements serve in business. In either case, if the reports are inaccurate or unavailable, the venture may become inefficient.

Marks also provide an important means for stimulating, directing, and rewarding the educational efforts of students. This use of marks has been attacked on the ground that it provides extrinsic, artificial, and hence undesirable stimuli and rewards. Indeed, marks are extrinsic, but so are most other tangible rewards of effort and achievement. Most workers, including those in the professions, are grateful for the intrinsic rewards that sometimes accompany their efforts. But most of them are even more grateful that these are not the only rewards. Few organized, efficient human enterprises can be conducted successfully on the basis of intrinsic rewards alone.

To serve effectively the purpose of stimulating, directing, and rewarding student efforts to learn, marks must be valid. The highest marks must go to those students who have achieved to the highest degree the objectives of instruction in a course. Marks must be based on sufficient evidence. They must report the degree of achievement as precisely as possible under the circumstances. If marks are assigned on the basis of trivial, incidental, or irrelevant achievements or if they are assigned carelessly, their long-run effects on the educational efforts of students cannot be good.

Some students and instructors minimize the importance of marks, suggesting that *what* students learn is more important than the *mark* they get. The conception rests on the assumption that there generally is not a close relationship between the amount of useful learning a student can demonstrate and the mark he or she receives. Others have made the same point by noting that marks should not be regarded as ends in themselves,

[10] I. N. Madsen, "To Mark or Not to Mark," *Elementary School Journal*, 31 (June 1931), 747–55.

rest with those who teach the courses and who assign the marks. From the point of view of students, parents, teachers, and employers there is nothing "mere" about the marking process and the marks it yields. Stroud has underscored this point.

> If the marks earned in a course of study are made to represent progress toward getting an education, working for marks is *ipso facto* a furtherance of the purposes of education. If the marks are so bad that the student who works for and attains them misses an education, then working for marks is a practice to be eschewed. When marks are given, we are not likely to dissuade pupils from working for them: and there is no sensible reason why we should. It simply does not make sense to grade pupils, to maintain institutional machinery for assembling and recording the gradings, while at the same time telling pupils marks do not amount to much. As a matter of fact they do amount to something and the pupil knows this. If we are dissatisfied with the results of working for marks we might try to improve the marks.[11]

Marks are necessary. If they are inaccurate, invalid, or meaningless, the remedy lies less in de-emphasizing marks than in assigning them more carefully so that they more truly report the extent of important achievements. Instead of seeking to minimize their importance or seeking to find some less painful substitute, perhaps instructors should devote more attention to improving the validity and precision of the marks they assign and to minimizing misinterpretations of marks by students, faculty, and others who use them.

Marks and Success

Those who question the value of marks often cite as evidence the low correlations that have been reported between marks and subsequent suc-

---

[11] James B. Stroud, *Psychology in Education* (New York: David McKay Company, Inc., 1946), p. 632.

cess in life.[12] High marks do not infallibly predict success. Low marks do not invariably foretell failure. But if these observations should lead us to conclude that learning has nothing to contribute to living or that marks cannot report amount of learning, we would be foolish indeed. Evidence that might seem to support such unreasonable propositions ought to be examined very closely.

There are at least four reasons why low correlations have been reported. One is that learning is not the only requirement for success in living. It is a necessary but not a sufficient condition. Other ingredients like ambition, opportunity, personality, and luck have much to do with success.

A second reason is the imperfection of our measures of achievement in learning. Some teachers do not have skill enough or take pains enough to measure and report student learning accurately. A third reason is the difficulty of defining success in living and of measuring it reliably. To the extent that our measures of learning and of living are unreliable, the correlation between those measures is bound to be low.

Finally, many of the studies purporting to show low correlations between school learning and subsequent success are small, poorly designed, and badly executed. The correlation coefficients that such unrepresentative samples yield are bound to be inaccurate. If the studies involve only small samples of individuals; if their marks report how hard they tried or how much trouble they caused as well as how much they learned; if good measures of vocational success were hard to get, as they usually are; should one be surprised that significant relationships often are not discovered?

Surely education is intended to contribute to success in life. Instructional programs are designed to help students learn what they must know in order to succeed. Marks should report how well students have learned what we have been trying to teach them. If those marks are only weakly related to later success, something must be wrong with the instructional program or with our assessments of what students learned from it or both. For marks to be unrelated to success is neither rational nor tolerable.

SHORTCOMINGS OF MARKS

The major shortcomings of marks, as they are assigned by many institutions, are twofold: (1) the lack of clearly defined, generally accepted, scrupulously observed definitions of what the various marks should mean and (2) the lack of sufficient relevant, objective evidence to use as a basis for

[12] Donald P. Hoyt, *The Relationship Between College Grades and Adult Achievement: A Review of the Literature.* Research Report No. 7, American College Testing Program, Iowa City, Iowa.

various marks should mean and ~~ ~
assigning them.[14] Odell reported,

> Where a typical five-letter system is used, the percents of the highest
> letter are likely to vary from 0 or near 0 to 40 or more; of the next
> to the highest from about 10 to 50 or more; and of the failure mark
> from 0 up to 25 or more.[15]

Some schools and colleges publish, for internal guidance and therapy,
periodic summaries of the marks assigned in various courses and departments. In one such unpublished study, instructors in one department were
found to be awarding 63 percent A's or B's whereas those in another
awarded only 26 percent A's or B's. Course X in one department granted
66 percent A's and B's, whereas Course Y in the same department granted
only 28 percent. Each of these two courses, incidentally, enrolled more
than 50 students.

The lack of clearly defined, uniform bases for marking and standards
for the meanings of various marks tends to allow biases to lower the validity
of marks. Often such extraneous factors as pleasantness of manner, willingness to participate in class discussions, skill in expressing ideas orally or
in writing, or success in building a self-image as an eager, capable student
will influence an instructor's assignment of grades. Some of these things
should not ordinarily be allowed to influence the mark a student receives.

Carter found that girls are somewhat more likely to get higher marks
than boys of equal ability and achievement.[16] Hadley reported that pupils
well liked by teachers tended to get higher marks than pupils of equal
ability and achievement who were less well liked.[17] These findings tend to

[13] James S. Terwilliger, "Individual Differences in Marking Practices of Secondary School
Teachers," *Journal of Educational Measurement*, 5 (1968), 9–15.

[14] Robert M. W. Travers and Norman E. Gronlund, "Meaning of Marks," *Journal of Higher
Education*, 21 (1950), 369–74.

[15] Odell, "Marks and Marking Systems," pp. 712–13.

[16] Robert S. Carter, "How Invalid Are Marks Assigned by Teachers?" *Journal of Educational
Psychology*, 43 (1952), 218–28.

[17] Hadley, "A School Mark—Fact or Fancy?"

support the accusations of students, and the guilt feelings of instructors, that accomplishment is not the pure and simple basis on which marks are assigned. Indeed, as Palmer has noted, some instructors deliberately use high marks as rewards and low marks as punishments for behavior quite unrelated to the attainment of educational objectives.[18]

The studies of Starch and Elliott on the unreliability of teachers' marks on examination papers are classic demonstrations of the instability of judgments based on presumably absolute standards.[19] Identical copies of an English examination paper were given to 142 English teachers, with instructions to score it on the basis of 100 percent for perfection. Since each teacher looked at only one paper, no relative basis for judgment was available. The scores assigned by the teachers to the same paper ranged all the way from 98 to 50 percent. Similar results were obtained with examination papers in geometry and in history.

Evidently marks such as Starch and Elliott collected for single examination papers are not highly reliable. How is it for composite semester marks? After surveying the evidence, Odell concluded that "the usual reliability of semester marks is indicated by a coefficient of from 0.70 to 0.80, perhaps even of from 0.80 to 0.90." With respect to the validity of marks, and on the basis of admittedly indirect and inadequate evidence, he suggested that "the degree of validity as a measure of mastery of subject matter is fairly high, probably on the average at least not below that represented by a coefficient of correlation of 0.70 and in many cases much higher."[20]

In assessing these estimates of reliability and validity it may be helpful to keep two things in mind. One is that semester marks are based on much more extensive and comprehensive observations of pupil attainments, perhaps as many as 80 hours of observation. One hour of intensive "observation" under the controlled conditions of a well-standardized test of achievement can yield measurements whose reliability may exceed 0.90.

The other thing to keep in mind is that a 0.70 coefficient of correlation does not really reflect very pure or precise measurements. In fact, if only half the observations summarized in the mark are completely relevant to the attainment being marked—and if the other half are completely irrelevant—the validity of the mark would be about 0.70 (assuming that each observation carries equal weight and that all observations are perfectly reliable). Hence if the summary values for the reliability and validity of semester marks reported by Odell do not suggest utter chaos, they do suggest that considerable room for improvement remains.

[18] Palmer, "Seven Classic Ways of Grading Dishonestly."

[19] Daniel Starch and E. C. Elliott, "Reliability of Grading Work in History," *School Review*, 21 (1913), 676–81; "Reliability of Grading Work in Mathematics," *School Review*, 21 (1913), 254–59; "Reliability of the Grading of High School Work in English," *School Review*, 20 (1912), 442–57.

[20] Odell, "Marks and Marking Systems," p. 713.

scholastic abilities of the students, along

scores on college admission tests seemed to contradict that explanation. Others claimed that research on teaching and long experience had taught professors how to teach more effectively. But few students or indeed professors found that explanation credible. Nor did employers who occasionally encountered barely literate applicants with B.A. or M.A. degrees.

There are other more plausible explanations. Most teachers find the task of assigning grades difficult and disagreeable, as we have said. Students often complain about low, but seldom about high grades. Nor does a high grade have to be defended with objective evidence. Hence the temptation for a teacher to avoid giving low grades is strong. Then, too, for college men during the middle decades of this century, getting high grades was a way of staying out of the army. Professors, particularly those unsympathetic with our military venture in Viet Nam were reluctant to give a low grade, however justifiable, that might terminate a college career or any career.

More recently colleges and even individual professors have been motivated by declining enrollments to compete for students. Giving higher grades for less demanding achievements is one means of attracting larger enrollments. Finally, those who are opposed to grades and grading on philosophical grounds can express their feelings and discredit the whole enterprise by giving everyone high grades.

Clearly grade inflation, like currency inflation, diminishes the value of high grades. If grades serve useful purposes in education, as most teachers believe, grade inflation ought to be controlled and corrected. How this can be achieved is the subject of the next section.

INSTITUTIONAL MARKING SYSTEMS

An obvious method for dealing with one of the major shortcomings of marks—the lack of a clearly defined, scrupulously observed definition of what the various marks should mean—is for a school faculty to develop, adopt, and enforce an institutional marking system. Ruch has stressed the

[21] Hildegard R. Hendrickson, "Grade Inflation," *College and University*, 52 (Fall 1976), 111–16.

point that marking schemes are essentially matters of definition.[22] Any marking system, he suggests, is somewhat arbitrary. "The adopted marking scheme must be defined. Its sole meaning and value rest upon its definition to pupils, teachers and parents alike."

Travers and Gronlund also emphasize the importance to an institution of clearly defining its marking system.[23] And Odell observes,

> ... when serious attention has been given to the matter and the general principles that should govern marking are agreed upon by a group of teachers, the marks the members of the group assign tend to form distributions much more similar than if this had not been done and their reliability is somewhat improved.[24]

If an institution lacks a clearly defined marking system or if instructors do not assign marks in conformity with the policies that define the system, then the marks will tend to lose their meaning and the marking system will fail to perform its essential functions. A marking system is basically a system of communication. It involves the use of a set of specialized symbols whose meanings ought to be clearly defined and uniformly understood by all concerned. Only to the degree that the marks do have the same meaning for all who use them is it possible for them to serve the purposes of communication meaningfully and precisely.

The meaning of a mark should depend as little as possible on the teacher who issued it or the course to which it pertains. This means that the marking practices of an instructor, of a department, or indeed of an entire educational institution are matters of legitimate concern to other instructors, other departments, and other institutions. It means that a general system of marking ought to be adopted by the faculty and the administration of a school or college. It requires that the meaning of each mark be clearly defined. General adherence to this system and to these meanings ought to be expected of all staff members. Such a requirement would in no way infringe the right of each instructor to determine which mark to give to a particular student. But it would limit the right of instructors to set their own standards or to invent their own meanings for each of the marks issued.

ABSOLUTE VERSUS RELATIVE MARKING

Two major types of marking systems have been in use in the United States since 1900. In the early years of the century almost all marking was in percents. A student who learned all that anyone could learn in a course,

[22] G. M. Ruch, *The Objective or New-type Examination* (Chicago: Scott, Foresman and Company, 1929), pp. 369–402.

[23] Travers and Gronlund, "Meaning of Marks."

[24] Odell, "Marks and Marking Systems," p. 715.

achievement. In the ~~.....~~

achievement is rewarded with a mark of A. A mark of B indicates ~~above~~ average achievement; C is the average mark; D indicates below average achievement; and F is used to report failure (that is, achievement insufficient to warrant credit for completing a course of study). Because a letter mark is intended to indicate a student's achievement relative to that of her/his peers, letter marking is sometimes characterized as "relative marking."

A popular term for one variety of relative marking is "grading on the curve." The "curve" referred to is the curve of normal distribution. One method for grading or marking on the curve, using five letter marks, is to determine from the ideal normal curve what proportion of the marks should fall at each of five levels and to follow these proportions as closely as possible in assigning marks. For example, the best 7 percent might get A's, the next best 23 percent get B's, and so on. Another process is to define the limits of the score intervals corresponding to various marks in terms of the mean and standard deviation of the distribution of achievement scores. Those whose scores are more than 1.5 standard deviations above the mean might get A's, those between .5 and 1.5 standard deviations above the mean get B's, and so on. This second process does not guarantee in advance that 7 percent of the students must get A's and 7 percent must fail. If the distribution of achievement is skewed, as it may be, or irregular, as it often is, these characteristics will be reflected in variations in the proportions of each mark assigned.

In the early decades of this century letter marking began to supersede percent marking. A clear majority of educational institutions now use letter marks. But percent marking is by no means dead. Some schools still use percents instead of letters in their marking systems. Others indicate percent equivalents of the various letter marks they issue. Official examining bodies still prefer to define passing scores in terms of percent, though they often transform test scores, or control the scoring process, to avoid any significant change in the ratio of failures to passes. The controversy that began when percent marking was first seriously attacked, and when the movement to substitute letter marks gained support, continues today. The issue of absolute versus relative marking is still a live one, particularly when relative marking is identified as "grading on the curve."

ACHIEVEMENT VERSUS ATTITUDE AND EFFORT

Studies such as those by Carter, Hadley, Travers and Gronlund, and others indicate that teachers often base the marks they issue on factors other than degree of achievement of the objectives of instruction. No doubt they will continue to do so, since marks can be useful instruments of social control in the classroom and since some degree of such control is essential to effective teaching. But the use of marks for these purposes must be limited, for it can easily be abused and tends to distort the intended meaning of the mark.

One of the important requirements of a good marking system is that the marks indicate as accurately as possible the extent to which the student has achieved the objectives of instruction in the particular course of study. If improving students' attitudes toward something or improving their willingness to put forth effort is one of the specific objectives of the course and if the instructor has planned specific educational procedures in the course to attain this goal, then it is quite appropriate to consider these things in assigning marks. But often this is not the case. Accordingly, attitude and effort probably should be excluded from consideration in determining the mark to be assigned.

Involving judgments of character and citizenship in marking is even more hazardous. Such judgments tend to be impressionistic evaluations rather than objective descriptions. If we like the behavior we call it straightforward, or perhaps thoughtful. If not, we are more likely to call it tactless, or perhaps indecisive. The countercharges of political leaders suggest that what looks like intelligent and courageous statesmanship to those in one party looks like incompetent bungling or spineless expedience to those in the other. Seldom are the traits of good character or good citizenship defined objectively, without the use of value-loaded and question-begging modifiers like "good," "desirable," "effective," or "appropriate."

The result of these difficulties is that valid assessments of character and citizenship are neither easy to secure nor in fact often secured. Odell confirmed our sentiments when he commented about marks reflecting character or citizenship, "In general, the conclusion seems justified that when a mark of this sort is given, it is not highly valid."[25]

Status or Growth

Some instructors have sought to improve the fairness of their marks by trying to base them on the amount of improvement a student has shown rather than on comparative level of achievement. Scores on a pretest, and other preliminary observations, are used to provide a basis for estimates of

[25] *Ibid.*, p. 715.

are appropriate and ... ...
between mean pretest and posttest scores as one measure of the effectiveness of instruction. But few educational tests are good enough to reliably
measure short-run gains in educational achievement for individual students.

From some points of view it may seem fairer to use growth rather
than final status as a measure of achievement. But, apart from the characteristic unreliability of growth scores just mentioned, there are other
problems. One is that for many educational purposes, knowledge that a
student is good, average, or poor when compared with his/her peers is
more important than knowledge that a particular individual changed more
or less rapidly than others did in a certain period of time. Another is that
students who get low scores on the pretest have a considerably greater
likelihood of showing subsequent large gains in achievement than their
classmates who earned higher initial scores. Students are not slow to grasp
this fact when their achievement is judged on the basis of gains. The course
of wisdom is for them to make sure that their pretest performance is not
so good as to constitute a handicap later on.

One rather strong incentive for marking students on the basis of
growth rather than status is to give all students a more nearly equal chance
to earn good marks. A student who achieves good marks on the basis of
status in one course is likely to do the same in other courses.[27] A student
whose marks are high one semester is likely to get high marks the next
semester.[28] However, the darker side of this picture is that status marking
condemns some students to low marks in most subjects, semester after
semester. Low marks discourage effort. Lack of effort increases the probability of more low marks. So the vicious cycle continues, bringing dislike
of learning and early withdrawal from school.

[26] Frederic M. Lord, "The Measurement of Growth," *Educational and Psychological Measurement*, 16 (1956), 421–37; and Paul B. Diederich, "Pitfalls in the Measurement of Gains
in Achievement," *School Review*, 64 (1956), 59–63.

[27] David Ohlson, "School Marks versus Intelligence Rating," *Educational Administration and
Supervision*, 13 (1927), 90–102.

[28] L. W. Ferguson and W. R. Crooks, "Some Characteristics of the Quality Point Ratio,"
Journal of General Psychology, 27 (1942), 111–18.

If students are taught to dislike school by constant reminders of their low achievement, the remedy probably is not to try to persuade them that rate of growth toward achievement is more important than status achieved, for that is a transparent falsehood. The remedy probably is to provide varied opportunities to excel in several kinds of worthwhile activities. Certainly this can be accomplished within a comprehensive program. It may even be done within a single classroom by an alert, versatile, dedicated teacher. When it is done, marking on the basis of status achieved will no longer mean that some students always win and others always lose. Instead individuals will be able to enjoy some of the rewards of excellence in their own specialties.

Finally, when reasonable care is taken to enroll students in courses appropriate to their level of ability and preparatory training, differences in initial status can be limited. In such cases the need to measure achievement in terms of change is also greatly reduced.

Marks Based on Criterion-Referenced Measures

Pupils will differ in the amount they learn under almost any course of instruction. The differences may, of course, be reduced through special effort, but teachers who attempt to impose on their pupils uniformity in amounts of learning probably will not succeed. In addition, they are likely to encounter sharp criticism from both pupils and parents. It may be a laudable goal to have all pupils attain a particular set of learning objectives, but unless the pupils are all of equal ability—or unless the objectives are entirely devoid of challenge—some pupils will attain more than others. Requiring the slower pupils to spend more time in learning may reduce the differences somewhat but is not likely to eliminate them.

Differences in ability and motivation among pupils will show up on criterion-referenced tests, just as they would on norm-referenced tests. These differences can be used as part of the basis for awarding marks. They ought to be so used if marks serve to motivate and reward efforts to learn. The notion that criterion-referenced testing will avoid problems of marking seems to be based on quite unrealistic expectations of uniform achievements in learning by all pupils. But programs of mastery learning cannot abolish individual differences in ability, interest, and determination.

SINGLE OR MULTIPLE MARKS

Achievement in most courses of study is a conglomerate of many factors. There is knowledge to be imparted, understanding to be cultivated, abilities and skills to be developed, attitudes to be fostered, interests to be encouraged, and ideals to be exemplified. Correspondingly, the bases used for determining marks include many aspects or indications of achievement: homework, class participation, test scores, apparent attitude, interest and specificity in what is marked.[30]

There is considerable merit in these suggestions, and under favorable conditions they can improve marking considerably. But they do involve problems. For one thing, they complicate rather than simplify the already irksome chore of marking. For another, they create additional problems of defining precisely what is to be marked and of distinguishing clearly among the different aspects of achievement. An even more serious problem is that of obtaining sufficient evidence, specific to each aspect of achievement, on which to base a reliable mark. Finally, and largely as a result of the preceding difficulties, the multiple marks exhibit considerable halo effect. That is, they seem to be determined more by the instructor's overall impression of the student than by careful analysis and independent measurement of various components of achievement.

Multiple marking is no panacea for the ills of marking. It may well call for more information than the instructor can readily obtain and more effort than the improvement it yields seems to warrant. It may try to tell students and their parents more than can be told clearly, perhaps even more than they really care to know. Multiple marking is not the only road to improvement in marking and probably not the best road currently available. Much can be done to make single marks more meaningful and more reliable. Perhaps those possibilities should be exploited before the more complex problems of multiple marking are tackled.

HOW MANY STEPS ON THE GRADE SCALE?

In general, letter marks and percent marks represent two extremes in terms of precision in grading. Those who advocated letter marks when they were first introduced suggested that the bases on which marks are usually determined are not reliable enough to justify the apparent precision

[29] Edward C. Bolmeier, "Principles Pertaining to Marking and Reporting Pupil Progress," *School Review*, 59 (1951), 15–24.

[30] Ann Z. Smith and John E. Dobbin, "Marks and Marking Systems," in *Encyclopedia of Educational Research*, ed. Chester W. Harris (3rd ed.; New York: The Macmillan Company, 1960), pp. 783–91.

of percent marking. They claimed that the best that most instructors can do is to distinguish about five different levels of achievement. Many instructors seemed to agree with this view.

Some proposals for improving marks have gone even further than the five-letter system in reducing marking categories. The use of only two marks such as S for satisfactory and U for unsatisfactory, P for pass and F for fail, or credit versus no credit has been suggested and adopted by some institutions.[31] Pass-fail grading enjoyed considerable popularity during the late 1960s, particularly on the more liberally inclined campuses. At the same time, however, there was increased interest in refining the grade scale by adding plus and minus signs to the basic letters, or decimal fractions to the basic numbers.

The notion that marking problems can be simplified and marking errors reduced by using fewer marking categories is an attractive one. Its weakness is exposed by carrying it to the limit. If only one category is used, if everyone is given the same mark, all marking problems vanish, but so does the value of marking. A major shortcoming of two-category marking, and to some degree of five-category marking as well, is this same kind of loss of information. To trade more precisely meaningful marks for marks easier to assign may be a bad bargain for education.

The use of fewer, broader categories in marking does indeed reduce the frequency of errors in marking. That is, with a few broad categories more of the students receive the marks they deserve because fewer wrong marks are available to give them. But each error becomes more crucial. The apparent difference between satisfactory and unsatisfactory, or between a B and a C, is greater than the difference between 87 percent and 88 percent. If a fallible instructor (and all of them, being human, are fallible) gives a student a mark of 86 percent when omniscient wisdom would have assigned a mark of 89 percent, the error has less consequence than if the instructor assigns a C when a B should have been given, or an "unsatisfactory" mark when the mark should have been "satisfactory." Hence the use of fewer categories is no royal road to more reliable marking. And, as noted previously, reducing the number of categories reduces the information conveyed by the mark.

Pass-Fail Grading

During the late 1960s successful efforts were made on a number of college campuses and in some public school systems to supplement or supplant conventional letter grades with a pass-fail grading system. Several pressures initiated and sustained these efforts: the pressure from faculty

---

[31] W. M. Stallings et al., "Pass-Fail Grading Option," *School and Society*, 96 (1968), 179–80; and M. R. Sgan, "First Year of Pass-Fail at Brandeis University: A Report," *Journal of Higher Education*, 40 (1969), 135–44.

Grades are poor predictors of later achievement.

3. Many instructors do such a poor job of grading that the grades they issue are almost without meaning.
4. The need to protect their grade-point average deters students from taking courses they want and ought to take outside their major field.
5. The pressure to make high grades forces students into bad study practices such as rote learning and all-night cramming, and drives some to cheat on examinations.
6. The threat of low grades destroys the love of learning that schools ought to foster.

There is some merit in these arguments, but there are also a number of flaws.

1. No individual, however successful, ever becomes immune to failure. Past success promises future success, but never can guarantee it.
2. Many personal qualities other than academic success contribute to success on the job. We should not expect the first to predict the second infallibly. Nor should we expect success or failure in appreciation of poetry to have much to do with success or failure in managing a grocery. But if, for example, there is no relation between the competence students show in their course work and their subsequent competence in the classroom, something is seriously wrong with the teacher training program.
3. The better remedy for poor grading practices is to eliminate such practices, not to throw out the grades themselves.
4. Students who are deterred from taking courses outside their major may be acting wisely if the courses they wish to take are in fact likely to be quite difficult for them to master. The fear of a low grade may be well justified by lack of adequate preparation. On the other hand, pass-fail grading may encourage students to take difficult courses, but it will not help them to master the material. However, if the course is one a student really needs and feels able

to handle satisfactorily, and if his/her grade point average is not already dangerously low, the possibility of a B or C should not deter that individual from taking it.

5. If grades are properly given they will not reward rote learning or cramming. Even if badly given they do not justify cheating.

6. Low achievement does more to destroy the love of learning than do the low grades that report low achievement. Most people come to love doing the things they know they can do well. The grades they get help them to know this.

In general, pass-fail grading may be attacked on the basis of two educationally sound principles:

1. Pass-fail grading removes much of the immediate motivation and reward for efforts to excel.

2. Pass-fail grading leaves students with an incomplete or an inaccurate record of their achievements.

The practical force of the first of these arguments is such that most systems of exclusive pass-fail grading tend to be short-lived. The force of the second is such that when a pass-fail option is offered to students, few of them decide to make use of it. They know that a transcript loaded with A's and B's will look better to a graduate school admission committee or to a prospective employer than one loaded with pass marks.

Almost every school or college offers some courses in which the aim is to provide certain experiences rather than to develop specific competencies. For such courses neither grades nor pass-fail decisions seem appropriate. Instead, students who attend enough course meetings to get a large proportion of the desired experience should simply be given credit for attendance. Courses in the appreciation of art, music, or literature, in recreational pursuits, in social problems, or in great issues may belong in this category of ungraded courses. But most other courses do not. Most courses do aim to develop competencies. Such courses call for assessments of achievement, and for them pass-fail grading is a poor substitute for more detailed and precise reporting of achievements.

Most of us want to be valued as persons. Most of us don't particularly want to be evaluated. But we can't enjoy the first without enduring the second. The weakness of pass-fail grading is that by doing a poor job of evaluating it keeps us from doing a good one of valuing.

Letters or Numbers

The successful revolt against percent marking was aided by the substitution of letter marks for numbers. Letters helped to emphasize the contrast between clearly relative marking and supposedly absolute percent

QUALITY CONTROL IN A MARKING SYSTEM

What a mark means is determined not only by how it was defined when the marking system was adopted, but also, and perhaps more importantly, by the way it is actually used. If an instructor assigns some A's, many B's, some C's, and very few lower marks, then B has become that grader's average mark, not C, as the marking system may have specified. Thus institutional control of marking requires surveillance of the results of the marking process and may require corrective action.

The temptations for instructors to depart from institutional policy in marking are many, and the rationalizations for doing so are not hard to find. Some instructors regard marking as the personal prerogative of the instructor. They may not distinguish between their very considerable freedom to determine which mark a particular student shall receive and their very considerable responsibility to make the meaning of their marks consistent with those of other instructors. To rationalize deviations from overall institutional policy in distribution of marks, they may claim unusual ability or disability in their students, special interest or aptitude in the subject of study, or (usually only by implication) exceptionally fine teaching.

Some instructors yield to the subtle pressures to give more high and fewer low marks. Perhaps they feel inclined to temper justice with mercy. Perhaps they wish to avoid controversy. An instructor seldom has to explain or justify a high mark or to calm the anger of the student who received it. Some instructors may feel that the favorable reputations of their courses among students depend on their generosity with high marks. Many good instructors like their students so much as persons that they find it difficult to disappoint any of them with a low mark, particularly if the student seems to have been trying to learn. These temptations to depart from standard marking practices are understandable as temptations, but most of them do not carry much weight as reasonable justifications. There are indeed some situations that do warrant departure from general institutional marking policies. But the determination of which situations those are probably cannot be left to the individual instructor, especially if uniformly meaningful marks are desired.

There are several things an educational institution can do to maintain the meaningfulness of the marks issued by its instructors. One is to publish each semester summary distributions of the marks issued in each course by each instructor. This is done systematically by some colleges and has been found quite effective. Another is to record alongside each individual grade report a set of numbers showing the distribution of marks to the student's classmates. The purpose of this is to make the relative meaning of the mark immediately apparent to all concerned.

A somewhat simpler variant of the procedure just described is to accompany each marking symbol by a fraction, the numerator of which shows what percent of the class received higher marks, while the denominator shows what percent received lower marks. These fractional interpretations may be required only when the instructor has exceeded or fallen short of specified limits for the proportion of marks above or below each category. Such a requirement tends to encourage observance of institutional regulations without preventing necessary exceptions.

Finally, an institution can return to the instructor a set of marks whose distribution among the marking categories is unsatisfactory and ask him or her to resubmit a revised set of marks.

SYSTEMATIC MARKING PROCEDURES

This and the next section are concerned with a particular set of systematic procedures for converting test scores, or composite numerical measures of achievement, into marks. The method is built around the five-unit scale of letter marks in use in most schools and colleges today.[32]

One of the purposes of any systematic method of assigning marks is to establish greater uniformity among instructors in their marking practices, and hence in the meaning of the marks they issue. A school or college faculty that adopts such a system will almost certainly improve the uniformity of marking practices and hence make the marks issued much more consistently meaningful. Another purpose is to make the systematic conversion of numerical measures into course marks simple enough to compete successfully with the unsystematic, hit-or-miss procedures that some instructors actually do use. To this end the procedures make use of statistics that are easy to determine or can be estimated with sufficient accuracy by short-cut methods.

---

[32] This method was developed in cooperation with Dean Dewey B. Stuit at the State University of Iowa. It was described in *Technical Bulletin No. 8* of the University Examinations Service, distributed to staff members of the College of Liberal Arts with the approval of the Educational Policy Committee in November 1954.

Acceptance of this assumption means that there can be no a priori certainty that expected percentages of A's, B's, or any other mark will be assigned. Indeed, in a particular class group there might be no A's or no F's at all. However, in large class groups (and, in the long run, in small class groups) the distribution of letter marks will ordinarily approximate a normal distribution.

The method makes use of the median score as the basic reference point or origin of the letter mark scale. Since there is seldom a meaningful *absolute zero* on any scale of academic achievement, it is almost always necessary to use some other reference point in setting the scale. The median or middle score provides a reference point that is reasonably easy to determine and reasonably stable from one sample to another. If the distribution of scores is skewed, the median is a more typical or representative measure than the mean.

When a five-unit scale is used for measuring achievement, the standard deviation of the test scores provides a unit of convenient size. The usual range of scores in a distribution of 20 to 40 scores equals about four or five standard deviation units. Although the standard deviation is tedious to calculate without a calculator, it can be estimated quite simply, with reasonable accuracy, for purposes of assigning marks (see p. 248).

Finally, the method of mark assignment here described makes provision for different distributions of marks in classes having different levels of average academic ability. The method does not require such differences, but it does permit faculties to take such variables into account—or to discount them. Probably most faculties would favor assigning more high marks in classes of high ability. But when they vote for this policy they also vote, whether explicitly or not, for giving lower than average marks in some other classes. There are both advantages and disadvantages in differentiating levels of marking to correspond with ability levels in various classes.

Mark adjustment data for classes at seven levels of ability, ranging from somewhat below to well above average, are presented in Table 12–1. The difference between successive levels in the lower limit of the A's is 0.2 standard deviation units. As a necessary but not easily demonstrable con-

TABLE 12–1. LETTER MARK DISTRIBUTION STATISTICS FOR CLASSES AT SEVEN LEVELS OF ABILITY

Ability Level	Lower Limit of A's	Percent of Marks					Ability Measures	
		A	B	C	D	F	GPA	Percentile
Exceptional	0.7	24	38	29	8	1	2.80	79
Superior	0.9	18	36	32	12	2	2.60	73
Good	1.1	14	32	36	15	3	2.40	66
Fair	1.3	10	29	37	20	4	2.20	58
Average	1.5	7	24	38	24	7	2.00	50
Weak	1.7	4	20	37	29	10	1.80	42
Poor	1.9	3	15	36	32	14	1.60	34

sequence of these lower limit differences, there are corresponding differences of 0.2 between successive levels in the grade-point averages. These differences seem sufficiently small, and the range of levels sufficiently wide, to accommodate most situations in which mark adjustments are needed. Of course the differences could be made smaller or larger, or the range of levels extended if either should seem necessary. The determining value in each row of the table is the first, which tells where the lower limit of the A's is located in standard deviation units above the mean. Given that value and tables of areas under the normal curve, all other figures in the row can be calculated.

Differentiating levels of marking requires uniform ability measures for the pupils in various classes. This could be provided either by scores on some test of academic aptitude or by grade-point averages in previous courses. Of course, the mark a particular student receives should not be directly affected by an aptitude test score or a previous grade-point average. Few instructors would argue that one student should get a higher mark than another simply because the first is thought to have more ability. Each student's achievement should determine the mark he/she gets. But since there is a substantial correlation between prior measures of ability and subsequent measures of achievement, it seems reasonable that the average mark in a class of more able students should be higher than the average mark in a class of less able students.

ASSIGNING LETTER MARKS

Four steps are involved in this process of assigning marks.

1. Select from Table 12–1 a distribution of marks appropriate to the level of ability of the class being graded.

ability levels. The last two columns, headed "ability measures, provide means for deciding which level is appropriate for a particular class. If the grade-point averages (GPA) of the class members in their previous course work is known, the mean of these GPA's indicates which ability level is appropriate for the class. If, for example, the class mean of those GPA's was found to be 2.24, the teacher could conclude that this class is slightly above average in ability, so that the level designated "fair" would be appropriate.

If grade-point averages are unavailable, inconvenient to use, or undesirable for some other reason, average aptitude test scores can be used in place of the grade-point averages. For this purpose, all the students in a particular school or college must have taken the same test or battery of tests. If the scores of those students are available in the form of local school percentile ranks, then the average of those percentile ranks could also be used to select the appropriate ability level. If, for the hypothetical class we have in mind, that average turned out to be 45, the instructor could conclude that these students are below average in ability and that the mark distribution for a "weak" class would be appropriate.

The five columns in the center of Table 12–1 indicate, for each ability level, what percent of the marks would be A's, B's, and so on if the distribution of numerical measures being converted to grades were perfectly normal. Since few distributions are likely to be perfectly normal, the percentage of each mark assigned in any actual case will usually differ somewhat from the norms indicated in Table 12–1. One could, of course, arrange the numerical measures in rank order and convert them to letter marks on the basis of the "ideal" percentages for a class of the specified level of ability. But, as suggested earlier, this process is open to more of the criticisms of grading on the curve than is the process being described here.

The second step in the process requires calculation of the median and the standard deviation. To calculate the median, you will recall that the following procedure is followed:

1. Arrange the scores in order from high to low.

2. If the number of scores is odd, the middle score is the median. The middle score in an odd number of scores is the score whose rank order is represented by the whole number just larger than half the number of scores. For example, in a set of 25 scores the median is the thirteenth score (13 is just larger than 12.5).

3. If the number of scores is even, the median is the average of the two scores closest to the middle of the distribution. For example, in a set of 26 scores the median is the average of the thirteenth and fourteenth scores.

To estimate the standard deviation this short-cut approximation is recommended.

1. Obtain the sums of those scores in the upper and in the lower sixth of the distribution.
2. Subtract the lesser sum from the larger.
3. Divide the difference by one-half the number of scores in the distribution.

Suppose we have 26 scores. The sum of the top four scores (upper one-sixth of the distribution) might be 137. The sum of the bottom four scores (lower one-sixth) might be 69. Then the estimated standard deviation would be

$$\frac{137 - 69}{13} = \frac{68}{13} = 5.23$$

The third step in the process, determining the lower score limits, makes use of the second column of Table 12–1, headed "lower limit of A's." The values in this column show how far the lower limit of the score interval for A marks lies above the median, in standard deviation units. In the case of a class of "fair" ability, the A mark interval begins 1.3 standard deviations above the median of the score distribution. In the case of a class of weak ability, the A mark interval begins 1.7 standard deviations above the median. Since the score interval that corresponds to each mark is one standard deviation in extent, once the lower limit of the A interval is determined, the lower limits of the B, C, and D intervals can be found by successive subtractions of the standard deviation from the lower limit of the A's.

To illustrate, consider a set of scores having a median value of 66.2 and a standard deviation of 6.5 for a class whose ability level is regarded by the teacher as "good." Table 12–1 indicates that the lower limit of the A mark interval should be 1.1 standard deviations (6.5) above the median (66.2). Hence this lower limit is 73.35. The lower limit of the B mark according to Table 12–1, the appropriate grade distribution would be "fair." Since there are 38 students in the class, the median is the average of the nineteenth and twentieth scores. The top and bottom sixths in a class of 38 include six scores each. Hence the six highest scores, from 100 to 112, are added to obtain the sum of 636. The sum of the six lowest scores, from 44 to 59, is 318. The difference between 636 and 318, divided by half the number of scores, gives the estimated standard deviation.

Using the lower limit factor of 1.3 (obtained from Table 12–1 for a "fair" class) in conjunction with a standard deviation of 16.7 and a median

EXHIBIT 12–1. SAMPLE PROBLEM IN LETTER MARK ASSIGNMENT

A. *Data for the problem*
   1. Class ability levels measures
      a. Mean GPA on previous years' courses: 2.17
      b. Mean percentile on aptitude test: 56.3
      c. Appropriate grade distribution (Table 12–1): fair
   2. Achievement scores (number of students = 38)

112	100	93	84	78	72	66	51
109	97	91	83	75	71	62	47
106	97	90	82	75	70	59	44
105	95	89	81	75	69	59	
104	95	84	80	74	68	58	

B. *Calculations from the data*

   1. Median $\dfrac{81 + 80}{2} = 80.5$

   2. Standard deviation $\dfrac{636 - 318}{19} = 16.7$

Marks	Lower Limits	Intervals	Number	Percent
A	$80.5 + 1.3 \times 16.7 = 102.2$	103–112	5	13
B	$102.2 - 16.7 = 85.5$	86–102	9	24
C	$85.5 - 16.7 = 68.8$	69–85	15	39
D	$68.8 - 16.7 = 52.1$	53–68	6	16
F		44–52	3	8
			38	100

of 80.5, it is determined that the lower limit of the A mark interval is 102.2. Successive subtractions of the standard deviation give the lower limits of the other mark intervals. From these lower limits the whole number score intervals are easily determined and the appropriate letter mark can be assigned to each numerical score. Note that the actual percentage of scores to which each mark was assigned differs somewhat from the ideal values of Table 12–1 reflecting the fact that the distribution of scores given in Exhibit 12–1 was not perfectly normal.

BASING MARKS ON COMPOSITE SCORES

When instructors determine a course mark, as they usually do, by combining marks on daily recitations, homework, term papers, and scores on quizzes and tests, each of the components carries more or less weight in determining the final mark. To obtain marks of maximum validity, instructors must give each component the proper weight, neither too much nor too little. How can they determine what those weights actually are and what they ought to be? And, if these two sets of figures are disparate, what can instructors do?

It is not easy to give a firm, precise answer to the question of how much influence each component ought to have in determining the final mark. But several guiding principles can be suggested.

In general, the use of several different kinds of indicators of competence is better than use of only one, provided that each of the indicators is relevant to the objectives of the course and provided also that it can be observed or measured with reasonable reliability.

Exclusive reliance on tests, for example, may give an unfair advantage to students who have special test-taking skills and may unfairly handicap students who give the best account of their achievements in discussions, on projects, or in other situations. But irrelevant accomplishments, such as mere glibness, personal charm, or self-assurance, should not be mistaken for solid command of knowledge. Nor should much weight be placed on vague intangibles or subjective impressions that cannot be quantified reliably.

If measures of each component aspect of achievement are highly correlated, the problem of weighting them properly is far less critical than if they are quite unrelated. For most courses the various measurable aspects of achievement are related closely enough so that proper weighting is not a critical problem. The natural "unweighted" weighting will give marks almost as valid as those resulting from more sophisticated statistical procedures.

The actual weight that a component of the final mark does carry depends on the variability of its measures and the correlations of those

section of the table displays the ~~~
Harry, on three tests X, Y, and Z, along with their total scores on the three tests. Dick has the highest total and Tom the lowest. The next section shows how the students ranked on the three tests. Each of them made the highest score on one test, middle score on a second, and lowest score on the third. But note, for future reference, that the ranks of their total scores on the three tests are the same as their ranks on Test Z.

The third section of the table gives the maximum possible scores (total points), the mean scores, and the standard deviations of the scores on the three tests. Test X has the highest number of total points. Test Y has the highest mean score. Test Z has scores with the greatest variability.

On which test was it most important to do well? On which was the payoff for ranking first the highest, and the penalty for ranking last the heaviest? Clearly on Test Z, the test with the greatest variability of scores. Which test ranked the students in the same order as their final ranking,

TABLE 12–2. WEIGHTED TEST SCORES

Tests	X	Y	Z	Total
Student scores				
Tom	53	65	18	136
Dick	50	59	42	151
Harry	47	71	30	148
Student ranks				
Tom	1	2	3	3
Dick	2	3	1	1
Harry	3	1	2	2
Test characteristics				
Total points	100.0	75	50	225.0
Mean score	50.0	65	30	145.0
Standard Deviation	2.5	5	10	6.5
Weighted scores	×4	×2	×1	
Tom	212	130	18	360
Dick	200	118	42	360
Harry	188	142	30	360

based on total scores? Again the answer is Test *Z*. Thus the influence of one component on a composite depends not on total points or mean score but on score variability.

Now if the three tests should have carried equal weight, they can be made to do so by weighting their scores to make the standard deviations equal. This is illustrated in the last section of the table. Scores on Test *X* are multiplied by 4, to change their standard deviation from 2.5 to 10, the same as on Test *Z*. Scores on Test *Y* are multiplied by 2, to change their standard deviation to 10 also. With equal standard deviations the tests carry equal weight, and give students having the same average rank on the tests the same total scores.

When the whole possible range of scores is used, score variability is closely related to the extent of the available score scale. This means that scores on a 40-item objective test are likely to carry about four times the weight of scores on a 10-point essay test question, provided that scores extend across the whole range in both cases. But if only a small part of the possible scale of scores is actually used, the length of that scale can be a very misleading guide to the variability of the scores.

In view of the difficulty of determining precisely how much weight each component *ought* to carry, the problem of determining precisely how much weight each component *does* carry seems less serious as an obstacle to valid marks. Further, as we have noted, if the components are quite highly related, the difference between optimum and accidental weighting may be hard to detect, as it affects the validity of the marks. But if instructors find a serious discrepancy between what they think the component weights ought to be and what they in fact are, two alternatives present themselves.

One is to multiply the underweighted components by some weighting factor to increase their variability and hence increase the weight they carry. The other is to increase the number of observations of the underweighted component, or the precision with which it is measured, and hence also to increase the weight it carries. Of the two methods, the first is likely to be more convenient. The second is likely to yield the more reliable, and in this case the more valid, marks.

If an instructor has promised a class, for example, that the final mark will be based on five components, weighted as follows:

Contributions in class	15%
Daily assignments	20%
Term paper or project	15%
Midterm test	20%
Final test	30%

then she or he should plan to obtain enough independent scores on marks, record these in the grade book, and then reconvert the letter marks to numbers for purposes of calculating the final average. A better procedure is to record the test scores and other numerical measures directly. These can be added, with whatever weighting seems appropriate, to obtain a composite score which can then be converted into the final mark.

Not only does the recording of scores rather than letters usually save time in the long run, it also contributes to accuracy. Whenever a range of scores, some higher, others lower, is converted to the same letter mark, information is lost. Usually this information is not retrieved when the letter marks are changed back to numbers so they can be added or averaged. Each B, whether a high B or a low B in terms of the score on which it was based, is given the same value in the reconversion. Hence to avoid the loss of score information it is usually desirable to record the raw scores, not the scores after conversion to letter marks.

SUMMARY

Some of the principal ideas developed in this chapter are summarized in these 25 statements:

1. Marking systems are frequent subjects of educational controversy because the process of grading is difficult, because different educational philosophies call for different marking systems, and because the task is sometimes disagreeable.
2. Measurements and reports of achievement are essential in education, and no better means than marks seems likely to appear.
3. To serve effectively their purposes of stimulating, directing, and rewarding student efforts to learn, marks must be valid and reliable.
4. There is nothing wrong with encouraging students to work for high marks if the marks are valid measures of achievement.
5. Though they cannot possibly predict success in life, school marks

can report accurately a student's success in learning the knowledge that is essential to success.

6. The major shortcomings of marks are attributable to a lack of clearly defined and scrupulously observed meanings for the marks and also to the lack of sufficient good evidence to use as a basis for assigning marks.

7. Marking standards often vary from instructor to instructor and from institution to institution.

8. Recent trends toward more high and fewer low marks (grade inflation) can be and should be reversed.

9. Marks will tend to lose their meaning if the institution lacks a clearly defined marking system or does not require instructors to mark in conformity with the system.

10. In a majority of the educational institutions in this country, relative marking systems, which make use of letter marks such as A, B, C, D, and F, have replaced presumably absolute marks, which make use of percentages.

11. Evidence of the unreliability of percentage marks, obtained by Starch and Elliott early in this century, was largely responsible for the shift toward letter marking.

12. Marks should ordinarily be based exclusively on achievement and should not attempt to indicate attitude, effort, or deportment.

13. Marks measuring status tend to be more reliable, more meaningful, and educationally more constructive than marks measuring growth.

14. The discouraging effects of consistently low marks can be more effectively counteracted by providing students with diverse opportunities to excel than by basing marks on growth.

15. The use of multiple marks on various aspects of achievement can improve marking but may cost more in extra effort than the improvement is worth.

16. The more marks available in the system to indicate different levels of achievement, the more reliable the marks will be, but the less convenient the system may be to use.

17. Pass-fail marks cannot do the job that marks are supposed to do as well as more finely graded marks.

18. A return to numerical marks would emphasize their use as measurements and would simplify the calculation of grade-point averages.

19. Publication of distributions of marks, course by course, is essential to quality control of the marking system.

20. Relative marking that divides the score scale into equal intervals is an alternative to strict marking on the curve.

24. The weight carried by
    the composite depends on the variability of the component scores.
25. Precise weighting of the components on a numerical basis is not
    crucial to the quality of the marks assigned.

PROJECTS AND PROBLEMS

Problem: Assigning Letter Marks

The problem in this exercise is to assign letter marks and stanines to
the achievement scores given below for a class at the indicated level of
ability. Use the methods starting on page 248 of chapter 12. Show your work
in the form used in the lower half of exhibit 12–1. You need not include the
data for the problem, as given below, on the paper you prepare to turn in.

1. Class ability level measures:
   a) Mean G.P.A. on previous year's courses: 2.44
   b) Mean percentile on aptitude test: 63
2. Achievement scores (number of students $= 25$)

190	176	157	151	137
181	173	157	147	133
180	164	155	147	133
180	162	152	144	132
177	157	151	138	130

*The construction of solid and reliable tests requires consideration
of quantitative information regarding the difficulty and
discriminating power of each test exercise, or item, that is
proposed for use. Such information is provided by
item-analysis data.*

FREDERICK B. DAVIS

13

How to Improve Test Quality Through Item Analysis

THE VALUE OF ITEM ANALYSIS DATA

The analysis of student response to objective test items is a powerful tool
for test improvement. Item analysis indicates which items may be too easy
or too difficult and which may fail for other reasons to discriminate clearly
between the better and the poorer examinees. Item analysis sometimes
suggests why an item has not functioned effectively and how it might be
improved. A test composed of items revised and selected on the basis of
item analysis data is almost certain to be much more reliable than one
composed of an equal number of untested items. Finally, teachers who
utilize item analysis are likely to improve their skills in test construction
much more rapidly than those who do not.

THE PROCESS OF ITEM ANALYSIS

Item analysis begins after the test has been administered and scored. Many
different processes of item analysis and many different indices of item
quality have been developed.[1] A procedure simple enough to be used

[1] Frederick B. Davis, "Item Analysis in Relation to Educational and Psychological Testing,"
Psychological Bulletin, 49 (1952), 97–121; and William W. Turnbull, "A Normalized Graphic
Method of Item Analysis," *Journal of Educational Psychology*, 37 (1956), 129–41.

3. Count the number of times each possible response to each item was chosen on the papers of the upper group. Make a separate listing of the same data for the papers of the lower group.
4. Record these response counts opposite the responses they refer to on a copy of the test.
5. Add the counts from the upper and lower groups to the keyed correct response. Subtract this sum from the maximum possible sum, that is, the sum of the number of papers in upper and lower groups, and divide the difference by that maximum possible sum. Express the quotient as a percentage; that is, multiply the decimal fraction by 100. The result is an index of item difficulty.
6. Subtract the lower group count of correct responses from the upper group count of correct responses. Divide this difference by the maximum possible difference, that is, the number of papers in the upper (or lower) group. This quotient, expressed as a decimal fraction, is the index of discrimination.

An Example of Item Analysis

An illustration of the data obtained by this process for one item is presented in Exhibit 13–1. This item was constructed for a test of under-standing of contemporary affairs in 1946. Answer sheets were available for 178 students, so the upper and lower groups consisted of the 48 papers having highest and the 48 having lowest scores. The best answer is marked with an asterisk. The figures in the parentheses following each response

EXHIBIT 13–1. ILLUSTRATION OF ITEM ANALYSIS DATA

26%   What change in life expectancy (number of years a person is likely to live) has been occurring?
.48
     *a. It has been increasing (47–24)
     b. It has been declining due to rising rates of cancer and heart disease (0–10)
     c. It has increased for young people but decreased for older people (0–5)
     d. It has remained about the same (1–7)
     (Omits 0–2)

indicate how many of the upper group students (first figure) and how many of the lower group students (second figure) chose each response. Of the 48 upper group students, 47 chose the first (correct) response and one chose the fourth response. Of the 48 lower group students, 24 chose the first response, 10 the second, 5 the third, and 7 the fourth. Evidently two of the lower group students failed to respond to the item.

The moderate degree of difficulty of the item is indicated by the 26 percent of incorrect response in the two groups combined, calculated as follows:

a. Add the numbers of correct responses (choice of response 1) from upper and lower groups:

$$47 + 24 = 71$$

b. Subtract this number from total number of students in both groups:

$$(48 + 48) - 71 = 25$$

c. Divide this difference by the total number of students:

$$25 \div 96 = 0.26$$

d. Convert this decimal to a percent:

$$0.26 \times 100 = 26\%$$

The reasonably good level of discrimination is indicated by the difference of 0.48 in proportions of correct response between upper and lower groups $[(47 - 24) \div 48 = 0.48]$. Each of the distracters functioned well since each attracted some responses, largely from students in the lower group.

SELECTION OF THE CRITERION GROUPS

Step 3 in the process of item analysis called for the counting of responses in upper and lower 27 percent groups. Why 27 percent? Why not upper and lower fourths (25 percent), thirds (33 percent), or even halves (50 percent)? The answer is that 27 percent provides the best compromise between two desirable but inconsistent aims: (1) to make the extreme groups as large as possible and (2) to make the extreme groups as different as possible. Truman Kelley demonstrated that when extreme groups, each greater. In each case the supposed advantage is slightly more than offset by the opposing disadvantage. The optimum value is 27 percent.

Use of an Internal versus
an External Criterion

The type of item analysis we describe in this chapter, like most such procedures, makes use of an internal criterion for the selection of groups of high and low achievement. That is, the total score on the test to be analyzed is used as the criterion rather than some other independent (external) measure of achievement. In order to conclude that an item showing high discrimination is a good item, one must assume that the entire test, of which that item is a part, is a good test.

Such an assumption is ordinarily quite reasonable. Most test constructors come close enough to the mark on their first attempt to make the total score a fairly dependable basis for distinguishing between students of high and low achievement. However, it must be conceded that item analysis using an internal criterion can only make a test a better measure of *whatever it does measure*. To make the test a better measure of what it *ought* to measure, one would need to use some better criterion than the total score on the test itself. Obviously this would be an external criterion. Yet an external criterion has no real advantage over an internal criterion unless it is truly a better measure than the test of whatever the test is supposed to measure. Ryans found the available external criteria to be of limited value in validating the items of a professional information test.[3]

The use of total test score as a basis for selecting upper and lower groups for item analysis has two important advantages. The first is relevance. Within limits set by the wisdom and skill of the test constructor, the score on a teacher-made test does come closer than any other measure is

[2] Truman L. Kelley, "The Selection of Upper and Lower Groups for the Validation of Test Items," *Journal of Educational Psychology*, 30 (1939), 17–24.

[3] David G. Ryans, "The Results of Internal Consistency and External Validation Procedures Applied in the Analysis of Test Items Measuring Professional Information," *Educational and Psychological Measurement*, 11 (1951), 549–60.

likely to come to measuring what that person wished to measure. The second is convenience. The total score on the test whose items are being analyzed is always readily available.

The selection of highly discriminating items, using total test score as the criterion, results in a test whose items are valid measures of what the whole test measures. In this sense, item analysis is a technique of item validation. But the kind of analysis and selection we have been considering does not demonstrate, and might not even improve, the validity of the test as a whole. What it can do to the test as a whole, and this is no small thing, is to make the test more reliable, and thus probably more valid too.

Counting the Responses

The counting of responses to the items is likely to be the most tedious and time-consuming part of the analysis. However, for many classroom tests the number of papers in each group will be less than 10, which makes the task seem less formidable. If paid clerical help is not available, student volunteers may do the work. It is quite possible to obtain the response counts by a show of hands in class, as Diederich has suggested, or to circulate tally sheets within upper, middle, and lower thirds of the class and have the students record their own responses.[4] Some machines designed for the scoring of classroom tests produce edge-markings of correct or incorrect responses that can be used to get the most essential item analysis data. More complex machines can be programmed to calculate and print the desired indices.

THE INDEX OF DISCRIMINATION

The index of discrimination that results from step 6 was first described by Johnson.[5] Since then it has attracted considerable attention and approval.[6] It is usually designated by the capital letter D. It is simpler to determine and to explain than such other indices of discrimination as the biserial coefficient of correlation, the tetrachoric coefficient of correlation, Flanagan's coefficient, and Davis's coefficient.[7] It has the very useful property,

[4] Paul Diederich, "Short-cut Statistics for Teacher-made Tests," *Evaluation and Advisory Service Series No. 5* (Princeton, N.J.: Educational Testing Service, 1960), p. 44.

[5] A. Pemberton Johnson, "Notes on a Suggested Index of Item Validity: The U-L Index," *Journal of Educational Psychology,* 62 (1951), 499–504.

[6] Max D. Engelhart, "A Comparison of Several Item Discrimination Indices," *Journal of Educational Measurement,* 2 (1965), 69–76.

[7] John C. Flanagan, "General Considerations in the Selection of Test Items and a Short Method of Estimating the Product-Moment Coefficient from the Data at the Tails of the Distributions," *Journal of Educational Psychology,* 30 (1939), 674–80; and Frederick B. Davis, "Item Analysis Data," *Harvard Education Papers No. 2,* Graduate School of Education, Harvard University, 1946.

Item discrimination indices of all types are subject to considerable sampling error.[8] The smaller the sample of answer sheets used in the analysis, the larger the sampling errors. An item that appears highly discriminating in one small sample may appear weak or even negative in discrimination in another sample. The values obtained for achievement test items are also sensitive to the kind of instruction the students received relative to the item. Hence the use of refined statistics to measure item discrimination seldom seems to be warranted.

But even though one cannot determine the discrimination indices of individual items reliably without using large samples of student responses, item analysis based on small samples is still worthwhile as a means of overall test improvement. How much better a revised test composed of the most discriminating items can be expected to be will depend on how large the samples and how small the sampling errors are.

THE INDEX OF ITEM DIFFICULTY

Historically, two measures of item difficulty have been used. One, which is slightly easier than the other to calculate but slightly more confusing to interpret, defines the index of difficulty of a test item as the proportion of a defined group of examinees who answer it correctly. Under this definition the larger the numerical value of the index of discrimination, the *easier* the item. This definition is somewhat illogical and has led some English test specialists to refer to the index as an index of facility (ease) rather than as an index of difficulty. Another way of avoiding the confusion is to define the index of difficulty as the proportion of the group who do not answer the item correctly. This is the definition that will be used in this book.

The index of difficulty of a test item is not solely the property of that item. It reflects also the ability of the group responding to the item. Hence, instead of saying, "The index of difficulty for this item is 56 percent," it

[8] Fred Pyrczak, "Validity of the Discrimination Index as a Measure of Item Quality," *Journal of Educational Measurement,* 10 (Fall 1973), 227–31.

would be better to say, "When this item was administered to that particular group, its index of difficulty was 56 percent."

The estimation of item difficulty from the responses of only the upper and lower groups, disregarding the middle group, involves some bias. Omitting the information provided by the middle group also has the effect of reducing the size of sample on which the difficulty index is based. This in turn tends to increase sampling errors somewhat. However, the use made of difficulty indices in classroom testing is seldom crucial enough to justify high precision in their determination.

It is sometimes suggested that item-difficulty indices should be corrected for chance success (or guessing) so that the percent reported would indicate what proportion of the group *knew* the answer, instead of including also those who just luckily happened to get it right. Even if such a correction were logically defensible, which is by no means clear, the refinement might be hard to justify in consideration of the use typically made of item-difficulty indices in classroom test construction.

Ordinarily such indices are used primarily to analyze low discrimination items in terms of their extreme ease or difficulty. Of course, if the results of the test are used for diagnosis of pupil difficulty or of inadequate teaching, the indices of item difficulty will have added significant uses.

DISTRIBUTION OF ITEM DIFFICULTY VALUES

It is quite natural to assume, and many test constructors do assume, that a good test intended to discriminate well over a fairly wide range of levels of achievement must include some easy items to test the poorer students and some difficult items to test the better students. But the facts of educational achievement testing seldom warrant such an assumption. The items in most achievement tests are not like a set of hurdles of different heights, all of which present essentially the same task and differ only in level of difficulty. Achievement test items do differ in difficulty, but they differ also in the kind of task they present.

Suppose a class of 20 students takes a test on which 12 of the students answer item 6 correctly but only 8 answer item 7 correctly. A reasonable assumption is that any student who answered the harder question (item 7) correctly should also answer correctly the easier question (item 6). Anyone who missed the easier question would also be expected to miss the harder. But such assumptions and expectations are often mistaken when applied to educational achievement tests.

Table 13–1 presents data on the responses of 11 students to six test items. A plus (+) in the table represents a correct response, a zero (0) an incorrect response. In this exhibit the students have been arranged in order of ability, and the items in order of difficulty. Note that the item missed by good student B was not one of the most difficult items. Poor student J missed all of the easier items but managed correct answers to two of the more difficult items.

It is possible to imagine a test which would give highly consistent results across items and across students when administered to a particular group. Results would be called consistent if success by a particular student on a particular item practically guaranteed success on all other items in the test that were easier for the group than that item. Correspondingly, failure on a particular item would almost guarantee failure on all harder items if student responses were highly consistent. But a test showing such a degree of consistency among the responses would also be characterized by much higher reliability than ordinarily obtained with the same number of items. Such tests can be imagined but are seldom met with in practice. This is another reason why specifications requiring that the test include items ranging widely in difficulty are seldom warranted.

Most item writers produce some items that are ineffective (nondiscriminating) because they are too difficult or too easy. Efforts to improve the accuracy with which a test measures, that is, to improve its reliability, usually have the effect of reducing the range of item difficulty rather than increasing it. The differences in difficulty that remain among items highest in discrimination are usually more than adequate to make the test effective in discriminating different levels of achievement over the whole range of abilities for which the test is expected to be used.

Some data from a simple experimental study of the relation between spread of item difficulty values, on the one hand, and spread of test scores and level of reliability coefficients, on the other, are presented in Figure 13–1.

Three synthetic tests of 16 items each were "constructed" by the selection of items from a 61-item trial form of a contemporary affairs test. This trial form had been administered to over 300 college freshmen and an item analysis performed to yield indices of difficulty and discrimination for each item. The items constituting the three 16-item tests were selected so as to yield tests differing widely in difficulty distributions.

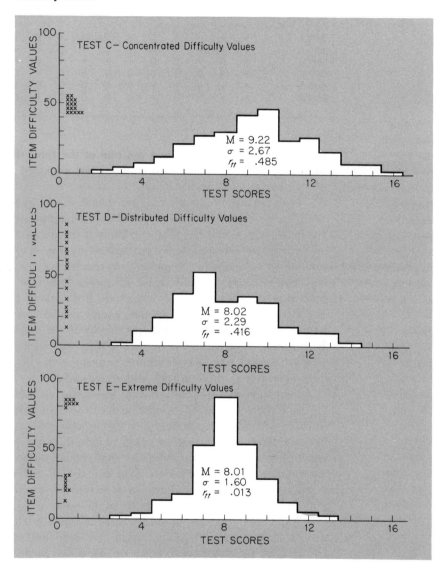

In Test C, the items selected were *concentrated* in difficulty values as near the middle of the entire distribution of difficulty values as possible.

In Test D, the items selected were *distributed* in difficulty values as uniformly as possible over the entire range of available difficulty values.

the spread of test scores. The wider the dispersion, ... more concentrated the distribution of test scores. Note, too, the very low reliability of scores on the test composed only of very easy and very difficult items and the somewhat higher reliability of the scores from those tests composed of items more nearly in the mid-range of difficulty. In short, the findings of this study support the recommendation that items of middle difficulty be favored in the construction of achievement tests.

ITEM SELECTION

One of the two direct uses that can be made of indices of discrimination is in the selection of the best (that is, most highly discriminating) items for inclusion in an improved version of the test. How high should the index of discrimination be?

Experience with a wide variety of classroom tests suggests that the indices of item discrimination for most of them can be evaluated in these terms:

Index of Discrimination	Item Evaluation
0.40 and up	Very good items
0.30 to 0.39	Reasonably good but possibly subject to improvement
0.20 to 0.29	Marginal items, usually needing and being subject to improvement
Below 0.19	Poor items, to be rejected or improved by revision

It probably goes without saying that no special effort should be made to secure a spread of item discrimination indices—the higher each item discrimination index, the better. Of two tests otherwise alike, the one in which the average index of item discrimination is the highest will always be the better, that is, the more reliable.

A simple relation can be shown to exist between the sum of the indices of discrimination for the items of a test and the variance of the scores on the test.[9] It is expressed in the formula:

$$\sigma^2 = \frac{(\Sigma D)^2}{6}$$

This formula indicates that score variance (σ^2) is directly proportional to the square of the sum of the discrimination indices (ΣD^2). Since it is true in general that the larger the score variance for a given number of items, the higher the reliability of the scores, the formula also indicates that the greater the average value of the discrimination indices, the higher the test reliability is likely to be.

ITEM REVISION

The second, and perhaps the more constructive, of the two direct uses that can be made of indices of item discrimination is in the revision of the test items. Lange, Lehmann, and Mehrens[10] have argued persuasively for this use. Five items illustrating the process of revision on the basis of analysis data are presented and discussed here. These items were written for a test of background knowledge in natural science and were intended for use by high school students. They were administered to a representative group of students in a preliminary tryout. The responses of good and poor students to these items were analyzed, and those items whose analysis data were most satisfactory were selected for the final form of the test. Among the items that were rejected there appeared to be some that might be salvaged by revision. When revisions had been made, the items were tried out with another representative group of students and reanalyzed. Results of the tryouts before and after revision for five selected items are indicated in the following paragraphs.

The first item deals with the distinction between the terms *climate* and *weather*.

63%   What, if any, is the distinction between climate and weather?
0.13
    a. There is no important distinction. (1–6)
    b. Climate is primarily a matter of temperature and rainfall, while weather includes many other natural phenomena. (33–51)
  c. Climate pertains to longer periods of time than weather. (43–30)
    d. Weather pertains to natural phenomena on a *local* rather than a *national* scale. (23–13)

This item is somewhat too difficult for the group tested (only 73

---

[9] Robert L. Ebel, "The Relation of Item Discrimination to Test Reliability," *Journal of Educational Measurement,* 4 (Fall 1967), 125–28.

[10] Allan Lange, Irwin J. Lehmann, and William A. Mehrens, "Using Item Analysis to Improve Tests," *Journal of Educational Measurement,* 4 (1967), 125–28.

the better students in the group, and
a more obviously incorrect response. The revised item (revisions in upper-
case letters) reads:

38%   What, if any, is the distinction between climate and weather?
0.58

        a. There is no important distinction. (2–22)
        b. CLIMATE IS PRIMARILY A MATTER OF RAINFALL, WHILE
           WEATHER IS PRIMARILY A MATTER OF TEMPERATURE. (3–
           25)
     c. Climate pertains to longer periods of time than weather. (91–33)
        d. WEATHER IS DETERMINED BY CLOUDS, WHILE CLIMATE IS
           DETERMINED BY WINDS. (4–20)

Analysis data of the revised item reveal that the revisions were effec-
tive. The changed item is much easier and much more highly discriminat-
ing than the original. Only nine of the good students chose distracters.
Equally important is the fact that these revisions did not appreciably in-
crease the number of poor students choosing the correct response. It is
interesting to note that on the second tryout the number of poor students
who chose response *a* increased markedly, even though this response had
not been altered.

The next item deals with the common misconception that meteors are
"falling stars."

64%   Do stars ever fall to the earth?
0.35

        a. Yes. They may be seen often, particularly during certain months.
           (12–28)
        b. Yes. There are craters caused by falling stars in certain regions
           of the earth. (30–43)
        c. No. The earth moves too rapidly for its gravitational force to act
           on the stars. (5–11)
     d. No. The falling of a single average star would destroy the earth.
           (53–18)

This item again is somewhat too difficult, though its discriminating
power is fairly good. The item might be made somewhat easier by revising
the response *b*. This response can be legitimately criticized as "tricky"

because there are *meteor* craters. Hence in the revision, this response alone was changed.

58%   Do stars ever fall to the earth?
0.56

     a. Yes. They may be seen often, particularly during certain months. (20–68)
     b. NO. PLANETS LIKE THE EARTH HAVE NO ATTRACTION FOR STARS. (1–4)
     c. No. The earth moves too rapidly for its gravitational force to act on the stars. (9–14)
    *d. No. The falling of a single average star would destroy the earth. (70–14)

The change obviously spoiled the attractiveness of the second response. Again it is interesting to note that this change did not increase the proportion of poor students choosing the correct answer but apparently shifted most of their choices to response *a* which had not been changed in the revision.

The next item attempted to get at the notion, important in "dry farming," that cultivation of the soil surface helps to conserve soil moisture.

77%   Under which of the following conditions is subsoil moisture most
0.09   likely to come to the surface and evaporate during dry weather?

     a. When the temperature of the soil is high (12–26)
     b. When the soil is cultivated regularly (56–40)
     c. When the air pressure is high (5–16)
    *d. When the soil is closely packed (27–18)

This item is much too difficult and is low in discrimination. The chief offender in response *b*. Not only was it attractive to a great many students, but it was even more attractive to the good students than to those of low ability. Since this response to the stem of the item reveals acceptance of an idea exactly opposite to that for which we were testing, the data should probably have been interpreted to mean that the item could not be salvaged. However, an attempt was made by writing a new second response.

87%   Under which of the following conditions is subsoil moisture most
0.02   likely to come to the surface and evaporate during dry weather?

     a. When the temperature of the soil is high (59–25)
     b. WHEN THE AIR ABOVE THE SOIL IS MOTIONLESS (15–33)
     c. When the air pressure is high (12–30)
    *d. When the soil is closely packed (14–12)

This revision improved the performance of the second response but

a. Removal of natural plant cover allowing faster run-off into streams (17–13)
b. Increased demands for water in homes, businesses, and industry (15–26)
c. Neither *a* or *b* (12–22)
d. Both *a* and *b* (56–39)

This item is of appropriate difficulty but is not highly discriminating. In this case it appeared that the fault might lie with the design of the item itself. The question was framed in such a way that there were two important, correct answers, and hence it was necessary to include each of these as a single, supposedly incorrect response and to make "both" the correct response. This approach is apparently somewhat confusing. Furthermore, no opportunities are provided for the use of bona fide distracters. In the revision one of the correct responses was placed in the stem of the item and three bona fide distracters were provided as follows:

47%   WHAT FACTOR, OTHER THAN INCREASED WATER USE, HAS BEEN
0.62   RESPONSIBLE FOR WATER SHORTAGES IN MANY LOCALITIES?

a. RESTRICTION OF STREAM FLOW BY HYDROELECTRIC DAMS (3–22)
b. DISTURBANCE OF NORMAL RAINFALL BY ARTIFICIAL RAIN-MAKING (3–18)
c. INTENSIVE FARM CULTIVATION, WHICH PERMITS MOST RAINFALL TO SOAK INTO THE GROUND (10–38)
d. REMOVAL OF NATURAL PLANT COVER ALLOWING FASTER RUN-OFF INTO STREAMS (84–22)

The item was made somewhat easier and much more discriminating. In this case, the revision process worked in a way that gladdened the heart of the item writer.

The final item in this illustrative series deals with mechanical advantage of a single fixed pulley.

88%   What is the maximum mechanical advantage obtainable with a sin-
0.21   gle fixed pulley and a rope that will break under a load of 500
        pounds?
        a. 1 (22–1)
         b. 2 (20–30)
         c. 500 (38–40)
         d. 1,000 (20–29)

This item appeared to discriminate marginally, but it was far too difficult. The item writer assumed that the principal difficulty lay in the abstract nature of the concept of the mechanical advantage. Hence he attempted to rephrase the item using a concrete situation.

61%   A WORKMAN LIFTS PLANKS TO THE TOP OF A SCAFFOLD BY
−0.07 PULLING DOWN ON A ROPE PASSED OVER A SINGLE FIXED PUL-
        LEY ATTACHED TO THE TOP OF THE SCAFFOLD. THE ROPE WILL
        BREAK UNDER A LOAD OF 500 POUNDS, AND THE WORKMAN
        WEIGHS 200 POUNDS. WHAT IS THE HEAVIEST LOAD THE WORK-
        MAN CAN LIFT WITH THE PULLEY?
         a. 100 pounds (1–6)
        b. 200 pounds (35–42)
         c. 400 pounds (32–23)
         d. 500 pounds (32–29)

The item in this form was considerably easier, but it turned out to have negative discriminating power. The correct response to the revised item was much more obvious to the poor students than was the correct response in the original item and only somewhat more obvious to the good students. It appears that the problem situation, though completely defensible scientifically, is just complex enough to mislead the good students, while being fairly simple on a superficial basis to the poor students.

The foregoing items do not illustrate all the possible ways in which item analysis data may be interpreted to aid in item revision. What they do indicate is the general nature of the process and the fact that it *may* be highly successful.

Analysis of Items in a Criterion-Referenced Test[11]

A criterion-referenced test is made up of clusters of items, each of which is intended to measure the attainment of a separate objective. If each of these clusters is considered to be a separate test, one can calculate item discrimination indices on the basis of total scores on each cluster. One must recognize, however, that the indices obtained from such short tests

[11] Kevin D. Crehan, "Item Analysis for Teacher-Made Mastery Tests," *Journal of Educational Measurement*, 11 (Winter 1974), 255–62.

Some of the principal ideas developed
these 12 statements.

1. Item analysis is a useful tool in the progressive improvement of a teacher's classroom tests.
2. Item analysis begins with the counting of responses made by good and poor students to each of the items in a test.
3. It is convenient and statistically defensible to consider as "good" students those whose scores place them in the upper 27 percent of the total group and to consider as "poor" students those whose scores place them in the lower 27 percent of the total group.
4. Responses may be counted by hand tally, by show of hands in class, or by machine.
5. A convenient and satisfactory index of discrimination D is simply the difference between upper and lower 27 percent groups in the proportion of correct responses.
6. While logical objections can be made to the use of the total score on a test as a criterion for analyzing the items in the test, the practical effect of these shortcomings is usually small, and the practical convenience of disregarding them is great.
7. The proportion of incorrect responses to an item in upper and lower 27 percent groups combined provides a satisfactory measure of item difficulty.
8. For most classroom tests it is desirable that all of the items be of middle difficulty, with none of them extremely easy or extremely difficult.
9. In general, the wider the distribution of item difficulty values in a test, the more restricted the distribution of test scores and the lower the reliability of those scores.
10. Good classroom test items should have indices of discrimination of 0.30 or more.
11. The reliability coefficient of a test can be predicted from the number of items in the test and the mean index of discrimination.
12. Data on the response choices of good and poor students can be used as a basis for item revision and improvement.

A very convenient conception is that of the "reliability coefficient"
of any system of measurements for any character. By this is
meant the coefficient between one half and the other half of
several measurements of the same thing.

C. SPEARMAN

14

How to Estimate, Interpret, and Improve Test Reliability

THE IMPORTANCE OF RELIABILITY

For most tests of educational achievement, the reliability coefficient provides the most revealing statistical index of quality that is ordinarily available. If the scores yielded by any educational achievement test were all perfectly accurate, true scores with no errors attributable to the particular sample of questions used, to alertness, anxiety, fatigue, or other factors that might affect examinee performances, to lucky guesses or unlucky slips, and with no errors caused by the mistakes or biases of the person scoring the test, then the test would have perfect reliability, reflected by a reliability coefficient of 1.00. No educational achievement test, no other type of mental test, and indeed no physical measurement has ever achieved this degree of perfection. Error is unavoidably involved in any measurement, but the goal of measurement specialists in all fields is to reduce these inevitable errors of measurement to a reasonable minimum.

Expertly constructed educational achievement tests often yield reliability coefficients of 0.90 or higher. In contrast, the achievement tests used in many elementary, secondary, and college classrooms often show reliability coefficients of 0.50 or lower. One of the ways of making test scores more reliable is to lengthen the test on which they are based, that is, to include more questions or items in it. But a test having a reliability coefficient of 0.50 would need to be increased to nine times its original length other potential merits it may have are blurred and may be largely lost. Only to the degree that test scores are reliable can they be useful for any purpose whatsoever.[1]

Reliability is important to students whose grades are often heavily dependent on the scores they make on educational achievement tests. If they were clearly aware of the importance of test reliability to them, it is likely that they would ask for evidence that the tests used to measure their achievement are not only fair in terms of the purposes of the course, but also are of sufficient technical quality to yield reliable scores.

Reliability is important also to teachers who are aware that their examinations have shortcomings and who seek to improve them. Estimates of the reliabilities of teacher-made tests would provide the essential information for judging their technical quality and for motivating efforts to improve them. Lengthening an unreliable test is not the only way, and may not be the best way, to improve its reliability. If modern knowledge and techniques of test construction are applied, most educational achievement tests can be made to yield scores having reliability coefficients that at least approach 0.90.

AN OPERATIONAL DEFINITION OF TEST RELIABILITY

> *The reliability coefficient for a set of scores from a group of examinees is the coefficient of correlation between that set of scores and another set of scores on an equivalent test obtained independently from the members of the same group.*

Three aspects of this definition deserve comment. First, it implies that reliability is not a property of a test in itself but rather when that instrument is applied to a particular group of examinees. The more appropriate a test

[1] Robert L. Ebel, "The Value of Internal Consistency in Classroom Examinations," *Journal of Educational Measurement*, 5 (1968), 71–73.

is to the level of abilities in the group, the higher the reliability of the scores it will yield. The wider the range of talent in a group, the higher the reliability of the scores yielded by a test of that talent.

Second, the operational definition specifies the use of a correlation coefficient as a measure of reliability. One of the properties of the correlation coefficient is that it provides a relative, rather than an absolute, measure of agreement between pairs of scores for the same persons. If the differences between scores for the same person are small relative to the differences between scores for different persons, then the test will tend to show a high reliability. Conversely, if the differences between scores for the same person are large relative to the differences between persons, then the scores will show low reliability.

Third, the operational definition calls for two or more independent measures, obtained from equivalent tests of the same trait for each member of the group. This is the heart of the definition. From this it follows that the various means of obtaining independent measurements of the same achievement will provide the basis for several distinct methods for estimating test reliability.

METHODS OF OBTAINING INDEPENDENT SCORES ON EQUIVALENT TESTS

At least five methods have been used for obtaining the independent measurements necessary for estimating test reliability. These methods yield reader reliability, test-retest, equivalent forms, split-halves, Kuder-Richardson, or analysis of variance coefficients.

Reader Reliability

Essay tests, whose scores depend appreciably on the expert judgment of a reader, are sometimes scored independently by two or more readers. The correlation between, or among, the multiple sets of ratings for a single set of student examination papers provides a measure of the reliability with which the papers were read.[2]

However, these coefficients of *reader* reliability should not be confused with coefficients of *examinee* reliability or coefficients of *test* reliability. A coefficient of reader reliability simply indicates how closely two or more readers agree in rating the same set of examination papers. A coefficient of examinee reliability indicates how consistently examinees perform on the same set of tasks. A coefficient of test reliability, on the other hand,

---

[2] Robert L. Ebel, "Estimation of the Reliability of Ratings," *Psychometrika*, 16 (December 1951), 407–24.

Perhaps the simplest ~~~~ measures for the same individuals of the same ability is to give ~~~ ~~ test twice. This would provide two scores for each individual tested. The correlation between the set of scores obtained on the first administration of the test and that obtained on the second administration yields a test-retest reliability coefficient.

A number of objections have been raised to the test-retest method. One is that the same set of items is used in both sets. Since this set of items represents only one sample from what is ordinarily a very large population of possible test items, the scores on the retest provide no evidence on how much the scores might change if a different sample of questions was used. Another is that students' answers to the second test are not independent of their answers to the first. Their responses on the retest will undoubtedly be influenced to some degree by recall, and possibly also by student discussion and individual or joint effort to learn the material in the interval between tests. A third objection is that if the interval between the test and the retest is long, errors of measurement may get confused with real changes in student ability as a result of learning. Finally, readministration of the same test simply to determine how reliable it is does not appeal to most students or teachers as a very useful way of spending educational time. Lack of interest on the student's part may sometimes make the second test a much poorer measure than the first, even though the actual test is the same in both cases.

Equivalent Forms

If two or more parallel forms of a test have been produced in such a way that it seems likely that the scores on these alternate forms will be equivalent and if each student in the group is given both forms of the test, then the correlation between scores on the two forms provides an estimate of their reliability. The major drawback to this approach is that teachers do not ordinarily prepare alternate forms of educational achievement tests, particularly those designed for classroom use. Even if parallel forms were available, there would be some valid objections from students to duplicate testing simply for the purpose of obtaining a reliability coefficient.

Split-Halves

The difficulties associated with determination of test-retest and equivalent-forms reliability coefficients encouraged the search for more practical alternatives. In one of these, a single test was split into two reasonable equivalent halves. These independent subtests were then used as a source of the two independent scores needed for reliability estimation. One common method of splitting a test has been to score the odd-numbered items and the even-numbered items separately. Then the correlation between scores on the odd- and even-numbered items is calculated. Of course, splitting a test in this way means that the scores whose reliability is determined have been obtained from half-length tests. To obtain an estimate of the reliability of the total test it is necessary to correct, or step up, the half-test correlation to the expected full-length value. This is done with the help of the Spearman-Brown formula.

The general Spearman-Brown formula, which may be used to predict the increase in reliability resulting from lengthening a test by the addition of similar items, is:

$$r_n = \frac{nrs}{(n-1)rs + 1}$$

14.1

This formula should be read as follows: "The reliability, r_n, of a test n times as long as a shorter test of known reliability, rs, is equal to n times the reliability of the shorter test, divided by $(n-1)$ times the reliability of the shorter test, plus 1." If, for example, a given test has a reliability of 0.50 and if its length is increased to nine times the original length by the addition of equivalent items, the formula may be applied as follows:

$$r_n = \frac{9 \times .50}{(9-1).50 + 1} = \frac{4.50}{5} = .90$$

The lengthened test has a reliability of 0.90.

When we need only to predict the reliability of a test twice as long as a given test, as in the case of reliability estimation by the split-half method, the formula is somewhat simpler.

$$r_2 = \frac{2rs}{rs + 1}$$

14.2

If, for example, the correlation between the odd-numbered items and the even-numbered items in a particular test should be 0.82, then the formula indicates that the reliability of the total test should be given by 1.64 divided by 1.82, which is approximately 0.90.

where

k is the number of items in the test

Σ is the symbol for "the sum of"

p is the proportion of correct responses to a particular item

q is the proportion of incorrect responses to that item (so that p plus q always equals 1), and

σ^2 represents the variance of the scores on the test.

This formula requires that the proportion of correct responses to each item be determined and that this decimal be multiplied by the proportion of incorrect responses. These individual products are then added, and that sum is divided by the variance (square of the standard deviation of the test scores) and subtracted from 1. This gives us the term in brackets, which we now multiply by the number of items in the test (k) and divide by $k -$ 1. The resulting reliability figure is applicable only to tests scored by giving one point to each item answered correctly and zero to those answered incorrectly. If the scores of the tests are corrected for guessing or if other forms of weighted scoring are used, more complex variations of the formula must be employed.

Here is a simple illustration of the use of Kuder-Richardson formula 20 (K-R20) to estimate the reliability of a six-item test taken by ten students. The distributions of student scores and of item scores are shown in Table 14–1.

The distribution of student scores shows that one student answered all six items correctly; one answered five correctly; two answered four correctly; and so on. The distribution of item scores shows that one item was answered correctly by eight students; one item answered correctly by seven students; two items answered correctly by five students, and so on. The number of students is indicated by $n = 10$. The number of items is indicated by $k = 6$. The variance of the student scores is $\sigma^2 = 2.01$. The sum of the item variances is $\Sigma pq = 1.35$. If these values are substituted in the K-R 20 formula, the reliability coefficient obtained is .40.

[3] G. F. Kuder and M. W. Richardson, "The Theory of the Estimation of Test Reliability," *Psychometrika*, 2 (September 1937), 151–60.

TABLE 14–1. DATA FOR CALCULATING THE RELIABILITY (K-R 20) OF A SIX-ITEM TEST

Student Scores		Item Scores		Item Variances		
Score	Frequency	Score	Frequency	p	q	pq
6	1	8	1	.8	.2	.16
5	1	7	1	.7	.3	.21
4	2	6	0	.6	.4	.00
3	3	5	2	.5	.5	.50
2	2	4	2	.4	.6	.48
1	1		–			——
$n =$	10	$k =$	6		$\Sigma\,pq =$	1.35

$$\Sigma x = 33 \qquad \Sigma x^2 = 129 \qquad \sigma^2 = \frac{129}{10} - \frac{33}{100} = 12.90 - 10.89 = 2.01$$

The top row of figures shows that one student answered all six items correctly, and one item was answered correctly by eight students. Since there were ten students, the proportion of correct responses was .8, and the proportion of incorrect responses .2.

LEARNING EXERCISE

Verify the calculations of score variance and of the sum of item variances shown in Table 14–1. Recall that the variance is given by subtracting the square of the mean score from the mean of the squared scores. Recall that the variance of an item (scored 1 or 0) is the proportion correct multiplied by the proportion not correct. Then verify the calculation of the K-R 20 coefficient.

Use of Kuder-Richardson formula 20 requires information on the difficulty (proportion of correct responses) of each item in the test. If the items do not vary widely in difficulty, a reasonably good approximation of the quantity Σpq can be obtained from information on the mean test score, M, and the number of items in the test, k.

This formula, K-R 21, is:

$$r = \frac{k}{k-1}\left[1 - \frac{M(k-M)}{k\sigma^2}\right] \qquad\qquad 14.4$$

One limitation of the K-R 21 is that it always gives an underestimate of the reliability coefficient when the items vary in difficulty, as they almost always do. If a test includes many items or questions on which the average score is either near perfect or near zero, this underestimate could be quite large. If most of the items have average scores of more than 30 percent but less than 70 percent of the maximum possible score, the underestimate is much smaller.

tests by only 4.2 percent on the average estimated the K-R 20 coefficients by 16.1 percent. The coefficients obtained from the adjusted formula also showed a slightly higher correlation with the K-R 20 values ($r = .935$) than did those obtained from the usual formula ($r = .930$). In only seven of the 101 examinations did the K-R 21' overestimate the K-R 20 coefficients. Thus K-R 21' combines convenience in calculation with satisfactory accuracy of estimation. Its use is recommended.[4]

LEARNING EXERCISE

Apply formulas K-R 21 and K-R 21' to the data of Table 14–1. Compare both reliability estimates with that obtained from K-R 20.

THE RELIABILITY OF CRITERION-REFERENCED TESTS

Reliability is as important for criterion-referenced tests as it is for conventional norm-referenced tests, and it can be determined in much the same way. The notion that "classical" test theory and "traditional" methods of test analysis are inappropriate for criterion-referenced tests is based on a misconception, namely, that scores on a criterion-referenced test show no variability because all who take the test make perfect scores, answering all the questions correctly. While this is a theoretical possibility, it almost never actually happens. One could "rig" a test to make it happen, but such a test would serve no useful educational purpose. The only reason for giving a criterion-referenced test is to identify students who have, and who have not, achieved a certain educational objective.[5]

[4] Pamela A. Wilson, Steven M. Downing, and Robert L. Ebel, "An Empirical Adjustment of the Kuder-Richardson 21 Reliability Coefficient to Better Estimate the Kuder-Richardson 20 Coefficient." Unpublished manuscript, 1977.

[5] Richard Shavelson, et al., "Criterion-Referenced Testing: Comments on Reliability," *Journal of Educational Measurement*, 9 (Summer 1972), 133–37.

The same procedures that are used to estimate the reliabilities of norm-referenced tests—that is, test-retest, equivalent forms, split-halves, or Kuder-Richardson—can also be used to estimate the reliabilities of criterion-referenced tests. There is, of course, one important difference. The reliability of a norm-referenced test applies to the total test score; that of a criterion-referenced test applies to a single cluster of items, since each cluster is intended to measure the attainment of a different objective. Indeed, the use of multiple reliability coefficients for the criterion-referenced test is the only device that makes sense.

In a typical criterion-referenced test, the clusters intended to measure attainment of a particular objective include only a few items. One might expect the reliabilities of such short tests to be quite low. In practice they often turn out to be surprisingly high. The explanation is found in the homogeneity of the item clusters. Since each item in the cluster is intended to measure the same objective, correlations between items tend to be high, which indicates a highly reliable cluster score.

RELIABILITY OF ESSAY TEST SCORES OR RATINGS

A version of Kuder-Richardson formula 20 that is useful in estimating the reliability of essay test scores or of multiple ratings of the same performance is:

$$r = \frac{k}{k-1}\left[1 - \frac{\Sigma \sigma_i^2}{\sigma_i^2}\right]$$ 14.6

where

k represents the number of separately scored essay test questions or independent ratings of a performance
σ_i^2 is the variance of student scores on a particular question or from a particular rater
$\Sigma \sigma_i^2$ is the sum of these question or rater variances for all questions or all raters, and
σ_i^2 is the variance of the total essay test scores, or the sums of the ratings from all raters.

The application of this formula to scores of five students on the four questions of an essay test is shown in Exhibit 14–1. These scores might also be regarded as the ratings by four judges of the performances of five students. In either case the calculation of a reliability estimate would proceed in the same way.

The five students are identified by letters A through E in the row across the top; the four questions (or raters) by numbers 1 through 4 in

2. Squares of Scores and Totals

		Student				
Question	A	B	C	D	E	Total
1	4	36	9	36	36	529
2	1	16	4	9	16	196
3	1	25	1	9	16	196
4	9	36	1	9	9	256
Total	49	441	49	225	289	1177

3. Sums of Squared Scores and Totals

20 question scores squared	283
5 student totals squared	1053
4 question totals squared	1177

4. Variances

Total score $\quad \sigma_i^2 = \dfrac{1053}{5} - \dfrac{67^2}{5^2} = 210.6 - 179.6 = 31.0$

Sum of item $\quad \Sigma\sigma_i^2 = \dfrac{283}{5} - \dfrac{1177}{5^2} = 56.6 - 47.1 = 9.5$

5. Reliability

$$r = \frac{k}{k-1}\left[1 - \frac{\Sigma\sigma_i^2}{\sigma_t^2}\right] = \frac{4}{3}\left[1 - \frac{9.5}{31.0}\right] = 1.33 \times 0.69 = \boxed{0.92}$$

the column at the left. Figures in the body of sections 1 and 2 of the exhibit are the question scores or ratings. Totals for each question, and those totals squared, are shown in the two right-hand columns of these sections. The rows entitled "total" give the sum of scores for each student, the sum of the question sums (and student sums), and the sum of the squared question sums.

Section 3 of the exhibit shows the squared scores or ratings, the squared student sums, and the sums of the squared question scores. If the squared individual ratings, 4, 36, 9, and so on (20 in all), are added, the sum is 283. If the five squared student totals, 49, 441, 49, 225, and 289, are added, the sum is 1053. If the four squared question totals (529, 196, 196, and 256) are added, the sum is 1177.

How these values plus those in the top two sections are used to calculate the total score variance and the sum of item variances is shown in the sections 4 and 5. Section 4 shows the calculation of the total score variance, $\sigma_t{}^2$, and the sum of the item or question variances. In the fifth section these variances are combined according to the Kuder-Richardson formula 20 to obtain the reliability coefficient. Because, in this example, the variation in scores *between* students is relatively great in comparison to the variation *within* students, the reliability coefficient is unusually high. Essay test scores and performance ratings are not normally as reliable as this example might suggest.

RELIABILITY AND ERRORS OF MEASUREMENT

A reliability coefficient, as has been said, is an estimate of the coefficient of correlation between one set of scores on a particular test for a particular group of examinees and an independent set of scores on an equivalent test for the same examinees. The higher this coefficient, the more consistently the test is measuring whatever it does measure. Perfect reliability, never actually obtained in practice, would be represented by a coefficient of 1.00. Although reliability coefficients of 0.96 or higher are sometimes reported, most test constructors are reasonably well satisfied if their tests yield reliability coefficients in the vicinity of 0.90. The reliability coefficients ordinarily obtained for teacher-made tests tend to fall considerably short of this goal.

Another way of interpreting a reliability coefficient is to say that it is an expression of the ratio of the variance of true scores to the variance of obtained scores. One obtains the variance of a set of scores by finding how much each score differs from the mean of the set of scores, squaring those differences, adding them, and dividing by the number of scores. By the *hypothetical true score* of an individual on a test is meant the average of a very large number of scores that might be obtained on similar tests, under similar conditions, for the same individual. The difference between the true score and an obtained score is called an *error of measurement*. It is assumed that in a very large number of obtained scores for the same person, the errors of measurement will tend to cancel each other, so that the average of a very large number of obtained scores closely approximates the true score for that person.

Table 14–2 illustrates how the true score for a specific student on a specific test might be estimated and how that estimate might be used to calculate the error of measurement in each obtained score, and the overall error variance. If student John Doe takes ten 100-word spelling tests, he

8	69	. .
9	65	0
10	66	+1
	650	0

Mean $= \dfrac{650}{10} = 65$ (True Score)

Error variance $= \dfrac{124}{10} = 12.4$

---

might get the scores shown in the second column of the table. The mean of these scores is 65. This is our estimate of his true score. It leads to the determination of the errors of measurement shown in the third column. The mean error is zero. The variance of the errors, which one obtains by squaring each error, adding all ten of them and dividing by ten, is 12.4. This 12.4 is the error variance for John Doe on 100-word dictation spelling tests of this type. If we should similarly determine true scores for each of the other students on 100-word spelling tests, we could calculate the variance of their true scores. From this, and the variance of their obtained scores whose calculation was described earlier, we could obtain an estimate of the reliability of the spelling test scores, using the formula

$$r = \frac{\sigma_t^{\,2}}{\sigma_o^{\,2}} \qquad\qquad 14.7$$

in which r stands for the coefficient of reliability, $\sigma_t^{\,2}$ represents the variance of the true scores, and $\sigma_o^{\,2}$ the variance of the obtained scores. But this approach, which requires the giving of a number of tests to all students in the class in order to estimate their true scores, is obviously not a very popular one. The main reason we have discussed it as a hypothetical possibility is because it can shed light on the interpretation of reliability coefficients.

The relation between obtained scores, true scores, and errors of measurement that we have just discussed can be expressed in the formula:

$$X = \overline{X} + e \qquad\qquad 14.8$$

in which X stands for any test score, $\overline{X}$ for the average of a very large number of similar scores, and e for an error of measurement.

It is ordinarily assumed that errors of measurement are uncorrelated with true scores. In other words, the size of the error of measurement is assumed to be unrelated to the size of the true score. If this is true, the variance of the obtained scores equals the variance of the true scores plus the variance of the errors of measurement. This can be expressed in a formula as follows:

$$\sigma_o{}^2 = \sigma_t{}^2 + \sigma_e{}^2 \qquad\qquad 14.9$$

in which $\sigma_o{}^2$ stands for the variance of the obtained scores, $\sigma_t{}^2$ for the variance of the true scores, and $\sigma_e{}^2$ for the variance of the errors of measurement.

Some of these relations are illustrated numerically in Table 14–3 where the true scores, the errors of measurement, and the obtained scores for five students are displayed. Note that for each student, the obtained

TABLE 14–3. RELIABILITY AND ERRORS OF MEASUREMENT

Students	True Scores	Errors of Measurement	Obtained Scores
Arline	18	−2	16
Dan	9	+1	10
Jean	15	+2	17
John	21	+1	22
Victor	12	−2	10
Mean	15	0	15
Variance	18	2.8	20.8

$$\text{Reliability} = \frac{18}{20.8} = 0.865$$

$$\sigma_e = \sqrt{2.8} = 1.67 \quad \text{(direct calculation)}$$

$$\sigma_e = \sqrt{20.8\,(1 - 0.865)}$$

$$= 4.56 \times 0.367$$

$$= 1.67 \quad \text{(from formula)}$$

are unknown and the error of measure~~~~~
score is also unknown. However, given the standard deviation of the distribution of obtained scores and the reliability coefficient of those scores, one can estimate the standard deviation of the errors of measurement. This quantity is called the *standard error of measurement*. By combining equations 14.7 and 14.9 to eliminate the expression for the variance of the two true scores, and then by solving the resulting combined equation for the variance of errors of measurement and taking the square root of both sides, this expression is obtained for the standard error of measurement.

$$\sigma_e = \sigma_o \sqrt{1 - r} \qquad\qquad 14.10$$

When the values for σ_o and r shown in Table 14–3 are substituted in this formula, the value $\sigma_e = 1.67$ is obtained. Note that this is identical with the value obtained when the standard deviation of the errors of measurement is calculated directly. This shows that an estimate of the standard deviation of the errors of measurement can be obtained from the standard deviation and reliability of the obtained scores, without any information about the individual errors of measurement.

The standard error of measurement provides an indication of the absolute accuracy of the test scores. If, for example, the standard error of measurement for a set of scores is 3, then for slightly more than two-thirds of the obtained scores (about 68 percent of them) the errors of measurement will be three points or less. For the remainder of scores, of course, the errors of measurement will be greater than three score units.

Another way of expressing the absolute accuracy of test scores is to use the probable error of measurement. For half the scores in any given set of scores, the errors of measurement will be no greater than the probable error of measurement for that set. The other half, of course, will have errors greater than the probable error of measurement. The probable error of measurement is somewhat smaller than the standard error of measurement. It is, in fact, 0.6745 times the standard error of measurement.

One of the shortcomings of the reliability coefficient is that its magnitude is not solely dependent upon the quality of the test. It depends also on the variability of the group to which the test is applied. Since the standard error of measurement is affected very little by the variability of the group tested, it has sometimes been proposed to substitute it for the ordinary reliability coefficient. Unfortunately, the standard error of measurement has shortcomings of its own. For tests using a given type of item, the standard error of measurement is almost entirely dependent upon the number of items in the test and hardly at all upon their quality. This point has been demonstrated by Lord and supported by Swineford.[6]

IMPROVING TEST RELIABILITY

The coefficient of reliability of a set of test scores is related to a number of other characteristics of the test and of the group tested. Typically the reliability coefficient will be greater for scores:

1. from a longer test than from a shorter test
2. from a test composed of more homogeneous items than from a more heterogeneous test
3. from a test composed of more discriminating item than from a test composed of less discriminating items
4. from a test whose items are of middle difficulty than from a test composed mainly of quite difficult or quite easy items
5. from a group having a wide range of ability than from a group more homogeneous in ability
6. from a speeded test than from one all examinees can complete in the time available

The Spearman-Brown formula (equation 14–1, p. 278) indicates the theoretical relation between test reliability and test length. The effect of successive doublings of the length of an original five-item test, the reliability of which was assumed to be 0.20, is shown in Table 14–4. The same data are shown graphically in Figure 14–1.

As the table and the figure indicate, the higher the reliability of the test, the smaller the increase in reliability with added test length. Adding 60 items to a 20-item test could increase its reliability from 0.50 to 0.80. But adding 80 more items to the 80-item test would raise its reliability only from 0.80 to 0.89. To achieve perfect reliability, an infinite number of

---

[6] Frederic M. Lord, "Do Tests of the Same Length Have the Same Standard Error of Measurement?" *Educational and Psychological Measurement*, 17 (1957), 501–21; Frederic M. Lord, "Tests of the Same Length Do Have the Same Standard Error of Measurement," *Educational and Psychological Measurement*, 19 (1959), 233–39; and Frances Swineford, "Note on 'Tests of the Same Length Do Have the Same Standard Error of Measurement,'" *Educational and Psychological Measurement*, 19 (1959), 241–42.

| 640 | 0.97 |
| ∞ | 1.00 |

items would have to be used, which of course means that perfect reliability cannot be attained by lengthening any unreliable test.

Two assumptions, one statistical, the other psychological, are involved in the use of the Spearman-Brown formula. The statistical assumption is that the material added to the original test to increase its length has the same statistical properties as the original test. That is, the added items should have the same average difficulty as the original items and their

FIGURE 14–1. *Relation of Test Length to Test Reliability*

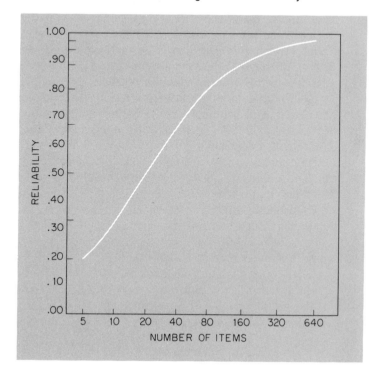

addition to the test should not change the average intercorrelation among the test items. The psychological assumption involved is that lengthening the test should not change the way in which the examinees respond to it. If practice on items like those in the test facilitates correct response, if fatigue or boredom inhibits it, or if any other factors make the examinees respond quite differently to the lengthened test, reliability predictions based on the Spearman-Brown formula could be erroneous.

Homogeneity of test content also tends to enhance test reliability. A 100-item test in American history is likely to be more reliable than a 100-item test covering all aspects of achievement in high school. Also the subject matter in some courses, such as mathematics and foreign languages, is more tightly organized, with greater interdependence of facts, principles, abilities, and achievements, than is the subject matter of literature or history. This is another aspect of test content homogeneity that makes high reliability easier to achieve in tests of mathematics and foreign languages than in some other tests of educational achievement.

The items in homogeneous tests also tend to have higher indices of discrimination than items in tests covering more diverse content and abilities. But item discrimination is also heavily dependent on the technical quality of the item—on the soundness of the idea underlying the item, the clarity of its expression, and—in the case of multiple-choice items—the adequacy of the correct response and the attractiveness of the distracters to examinees of lower ability. The nature and determination of indices of discrimination and their relation to test reliability was discussed in greater detail in the previous chapter. For the present it will be sufficient to say that the relation is close and important. Working to improve the discrimination of the individual items in most classroom tests is probably the most effective means of improving test reliability and, hence, test quality.

The difficulty of a test item affects its contribution to test reliability. An item that all examinees answer correctly, or all miss, contributes nothing to test reliability. An item that just about half of the examinees answer correctly is potentially capable of contributing more to test reliability than an item that is either extremely easy or extremely difficult. Of course, such an item could also be totally nondiscriminating. Items of intermediate difficulty, that is, from 25 to 75 percent correct responses, are all capable of contributing much to test reliability. Items that more than 90 percent or fewer than 10 percent of the examinees answer correctly cannot possibly contribute as much. Contrary to popular belief, a good test seldom needs to include items that vary widely in difficulty.

The reliability coefficient for a set of test scores depends also on the range of talent in the group tested. If an achievement test suitable for use in the middle grades of an elementary school is given to pupils in the fourth, fifth, and sixth grades, the reliability of the complete set of scores

Classroom tests are sometimes constructed and scored so that the range of scores obtained is much less than that which is theoretically available. For example, an essay test with a 100-point maximum score may be graded with a view to making 75 a reasonable passing score. This usually limits the effective range of scores to about 30 points. A true-false test, scored only for the number of items answered correctly, has a useful score range of only about half the number of items. A multiple-choice test, on the other hand, may have a useful score range of three-fourths or more of the number of items in the test. Hence a 100-item multiple-choice test is usually more reliable than a 100-item true-false test.

The dependence of test reliability on score variability is illustrated with hypothetical data for three kinds of tests in Figure 14–2. The essay test was assumed to consist of 10 questions, each worth a maximum of 10 points, with a score of 75 on the entire test set in advance as the minimum passing score. The other two tests consist of one hundred items each and are scored by giving one point of credit for each correct answer. There is no "correction for guessing" by a subtraction of a fraction of the wrong answers. Each multiple-choice answer is assumed to offer four alternative answers, so that the expected chance score on it is 25. The expected chance score on the true-false test is, of course, 50.

The data at the bottom of Figure 14–2 show the expected difference among the tests in average score (mean), in variability (standard deviation), in effective range, and in reliability. While these are hypothetical data, based on deductions from certain assumptions, they are reasonably representative of the results teachers typically achieve in using tests of these types.

It is possible to construct a 100-item multiple-choice test whose reliability coefficient will be above 0.90, but it is not easy to do and relatively few instructors succeed in doing it. Again, 100-point essay tests can be handled so that their reliability will be as satisfactory as that of a 100-item multiple-choice test. But this also is not easy to do, and few of those who prepare and score classroom tests succeed in doing it without taking special pains.

FIGURE 14–2. Hypothetical Score Distributions for Three Tests

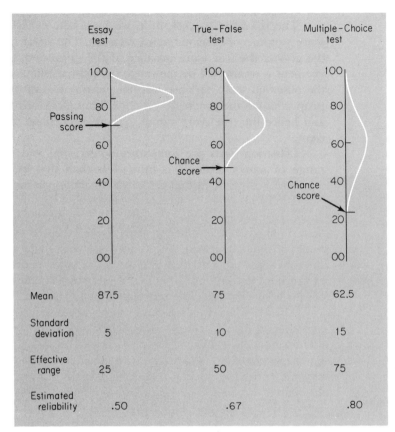

	Essay test	True–False test	Multiple–Choice test
Mean	87.5	75	62.5
Standard deviation	5	10	15
Effective range	25	50	75
Estimated reliability	.50	.67	.80

Scores from a test given to a group under highly speeded conditions will ordinarily show a higher reliability coefficient than would be obtained for scores from the same test given to the same group with time limits generous enough to permit all examinees to finish. But most of the increased reliability of speeded test scores is spurious, an artifact of the method of estimating reliability. If, instead of estimating reliability from a single administration of the speeded test, we were to administer separately timed equivalent forms of the test under equally speeded conditions, the correlation between scores on these equivalent forms would be less than that estimated from a single administration. Hence the apparent increase in reliability that results from speeding a test is usually regarded as a spurious increase.

Here is what causes the trouble. Scores on a speeded test depend not only on how many items examinees can answer, but also on how fast they can work to answer them. Thus to estimate the reliability of scores on a test score reliability can be obtained from only if the speed at which examinees work is not an important factor in determining their scores.

In this chapter, we have stressed the importance of test reliability as a factor in test quality. How can test constructors make more reliable tests? By taking advantage of the factors affecting reliability that are under their control. This means writing, revising, and selecting test items so that they will discriminate as clearly as possible between relatively greater versus less achievement of those things the test is intended to measure. Choosing items of high discrimination will result automatically in choosing items of middle difficulty—that is, items that between 25 and 75 percent of the examinees can answer correctly. Test builders will also include as many items as possible in the test, so as to make the test as long as possible. When the time available for testing is limited, as it usually is, test constructors should favor items that are least time-consuming individually.

SUMMARY

Some of the principal ideas developed in this chapter are summarized in these 14 statements:

1. Educational tests always are less than perfectly reliable because of item sampling errors, examinee performance errors, and scoring errors.
2. Test reliability may be defined operationally as the coefficient of correlation between scores on two equivalent forms of a test for a specified group of examinees.
3. Separate coefficients of test reliability, examinee reliability, and scoring reliability may be obtained.
4. The coefficient of correlation between scores on two reasonably equivalent halves of a test can be corrected by using the Spearman-Brown formula to obtain a good estimate of test reliability.
5. The Kuder-Richardson formulas yield estimates of test reliability

from data on the variability of test scores and item scores and the number of items in the test.

6. The more widely the items in a test vary in difficulty, the more seriously the Kuder-Richardson formula 21 may underestimate reliability.

7. A reliability coefficient may be interpreted as a ratio of the variance of true (error-free) scores to the variance of obtained (error-affected) scores.

8. The standard error of measurement is an estimate of the general magnitude of errors expressed in test score units.

9. The standard error of measurement is found by multiplying the standard deviation of the scores by the square root of the difference between the reliability coefficient and 1.

10. Longer tests composed of more discriminating items are likely to be more reliable than shorter tests composed of less discriminating items.

11. Homogeneous tests are likely to be more reliable than heterogeneous tests.

12. Scores obtained from heterogeneous groups are likely to be more reliable than scores obtained from homogeneous groups.

13. The more variable the scores obtained from a test, the higher its reliability is likely to be.

14. Reliability coefficients obtained from speeded tests tend to be spuriously high.

PROJECTS AND PROBLEMS

Problem: Calculation of a Reliability Coefficient

Using the data given below, calculate a split-halves, a Kuder-Richardson 20, and a Kuder-Richardson 21 reliability coefficient.

Note: The easiest and most accurate way to get the quantity Σpq need for K-R. 20 is to multiply the number of right answers to an item by the number of wrong answers. Add these products for all 10 items and divide by 225. In this problem,

$$p = \frac{R}{15} \quad q = \frac{W}{15} \quad \text{so} \quad pq = \frac{R \times W}{225}$$

8	3	3 3 3 3 3	3 3 4 3 3	3 1 1 1 3
9	2	1 2 2 3 2	2 2 2 1 2	1 2 2 4 2
10	2	2 2 4 2 2	1 1 2 1 2	1 1 2 1 1

Problem: Reliability of Essay Test Scores

Eight students receive the scores shown below on the five questions of an essay test. Using the procedures described on pages 282–84, estimate the reliability of the eight scores. Show your work in a table like that of Exhibit 14-1.

Table B

Question	A	B	C	D	E	F	G	H	*Sum*
				Student					
1	6	4	6	4	3	6	6	8	43
2	6	0	7	4	2	7	3	4	33
3	7	5	5	2	0	2	7	5	33
4	2	4	6	4	4	5	3	5	33
5	7	2	4	7	4	2	7	3	36
Total	28	15	28	21	13	22	26	25	178

Examinations comprise a crucial aspect of the whole educational process, since they represent willy-nilly what all the fine words have been about. Moreover examinations furnish practically the only objective evidence of the value of a course of instruction. A published examination (and examinations are always published, whether officially or unofficially) presents a fair statement of the course objectives. All else that is said about the course may be summarily classified in the category of "pious hopes."

M. W. Richardson

15

The Validity of Classroom Tests

THE PROBLEM OF VALIDITY

One of the most frequent charges laid against tests used to assess achievement, to select personnel, or to certify competence is that they lack validity. Surely some tests deserve to be found guilty as charged. However, in some cases the claim that a test lacks validity simply helps an examinee to explain away his or her poor performance on the test. In other cases the charge expresses a general dislike and mistrust of all tests. Often those who make such charges cannot say clearly just what is wrong with the tests or what could be done to correct the alleged defect(s). Perhaps they should not be criticized too strongly on this account, however. Even test specialists have difficulty in coming to agreement on what validity means and how it should be demonstrated. One aim of this chapter is to provide some sensible, practical bases for answering the kinds of questions about test validity that are most frequently asked.

Solid evidence supporting the validity of most educational tests is very difficult to obtain. Possibly because of this, test specialists have worried a great deal about the validity problem and have written many articles about it. By contrast, physical scientists, who probably do a better job of measuring than do psychologists and educators, seem to be relatively indifferent to, even unaware of, the validity problem. They tend to worry more about how accurate or useful their measurements are than about such basically criterion to which we can appeal for a ~~decision~~

With respect to the first question, our behavior is more like that of the typical scientist: We define the measurements, develop their properties, and use whichever is more appropriate or convenient in a specific situation. With respect to the second, we withhold full confidence in either test, in the hope that someone will find an answer to the essentially unanswerable question we have asked. Yet neither central tendency nor intelligence is a meaningful quantitative concept apart from some specific operations for calculation or some specific testing procedures.

Some examples of tests and measurements used in the physical sciences, on the athletic field, by the bookkeeper, or by the statistician may be instructive at this point. Why are questions seldom if ever raised about the validity of the Babcock Test for measuring the proportion of butterfat in cream? Is it because the processes of the test *guarantee* that it measures what it is intended to measure? Sulfuric acid is added to the cream to dissolve the protein and liberate the fat globules. Then by centrifuging they are caused to rise into the neck of the bottle, where they are easily measured. If every test *must* have some kind of validity, this would have to be called intrinsic or self-evident validity. But why get involved with validity or validation at all in this case? Why not concede that some tests and measurements need not be validated?[1]

The National Collegiate Athletic Association has approved a certain arrangement for measuring how high a person can vault with the aid of a pole. How much validity does it have? An automobile owner adds the charges on her credit card slips to measure how much she has spent on gasoline in a month. How much validity does this measurement have? A statistician measures the variability of a set of test scores by calculating their standard deviation. How much validity does this measurement have?

Perhaps the point is clear. If the process of measurement itself defines quantitatively the thing to be measured, the question of validity need never arise. Only when one variable is measured in order to make inferences about some other presumably related variable, or about some underlying,

[1] Robert L. Ebel, "Must All Tests be Valid?" *American Psychologist,* 16 (1961), 640–47.

and hence unobservable determinant of a particular kind of behavior, do real questions of validity arise.

Have we been led astray by too easy assent to the proposition that validity is the most important quality any test can have, and that therefore every test must be validated? Surely any test ought to do what it was intended to do. But that statement is tautological and not really helpful in the absence of any means for determining how well it does what it should do.

Instead of this probably futile pursuit of validity for every test, perhaps we should shift our attention in some cases to the quality of the operational definition embodied in the test. We can accept or reject that definition, but we cannot validate it. We can get a group of expert judges to review it, to suggest improvements, and ultimately to approve it. This might give us reasonable assurance that the test would do what it was intended to do.

If a panel of experts does indeed deem our test a good standard of evaluation, is it then valid? We might call it so. But why? Surely this kind of validity bears only a faint resemblance to that based on correlation with a criterion. Clarity of thinking is not helped by using the same words, validity and validation, to refer to such different qualities and processes. Is not our compulsion to find some basis for calling every test valid an illustration of what Stuart Chase called "the tyranny of words"?[2] Why not simply claim that it is a good test? Instead of claiming that we have validated it, why not simply claim that it was developed with care and expertness?

Thus, one reasonable and satisfactory conclusion with respect to test validation is that while some tests need it very much, others may be quite effective operationally and yet cannot be proven valid without resort to semantic sleight of hand.

CONVENTIONAL WISDOM AND SOME ALTERNATIVES

What has just been said does not represent the conventional views of test specialists on the subject of test validity. A substantial part of that wisdom can be expressed in these five propositions.

1. Validity is the most important quality any test can have.
2. Validity refers to the effectiveness of a test in measuring what it is intended to measure.
3. Validity has many different facets, takes many different forms, and has been defined in many different ways.
4. Validity can be demonstrated best by tryout after the test has been constructed.

[2] Stuart Chase, *The Tyranny of Words* (New York: Harcourt Brace Jovanovich, Inc., 1938).

complained that we cannot see."

Looking at validity from a somewhat different perspective, one may think of some alternatives to the conventional wisdom. One set of them can be expressed in these five propositions.

1. Validity is not so much a property of a test as it is of the inferences and decisions made with the help of the test. That is, it is not the test itself but the use made of the test scores that has more or less validity.
2. Validity, if defined as the extent to which real test scores correlate with ideal criterion measures, is unimportant for classroom tests and many other kinds of tests.
3. Valid test use requires good tests which are
   (a) based on clear specifications of test content, and
   (b) capable of yielding reliable (that is, reasonably precise) scores.
4. What a test measures can be defined most clearly by describing the tasks that compose it, not by naming some trait or characteristic it is supposed to measure.
5. Rational methods are likely to be more effective than statistical methods in defending the validity of the use of scores from a particular test in a particular situation.

An elaboration and defense of these propositions will be presented in the next several sections.

Test Content or Test Use?

We have long known that validity depends on the purposes for which a test is used, the group with which it is used, and the circumstances in which it is used. If a test is used for different purposes, it is likely to have a different validity for each different purpose. Equally true, though less often mentioned, is the use of test scores as only one of several sources of information for drawing inferences and making decisions about a person. In such situations there is no clear one-to-one relation between the test and some more general criterion of competence or success. Hence it seems more reasonable to focus concerns for validity, not on the test itself, but on the use that is made of it.

Viewed in this light, validity depends on the appropriateness of the selected test to the intended use. It depends not only on the quality of the test, but on how the test was used and on decisions reached on the basis of the test scores. Choosing a valid test is less important than using it validly.

The responsibility of the test developer is to be as clear as possible about what is being measured and to produce a test that measures as accurately as possible. The responsibility of the test user is to make valid decisions using the test scores and all other relevant information that is available. Sometimes (usually in classroom testing) the user is also the developer. That one person then has all three responsibilities: to be clear, to measure accurately, to use validly. In any case, we speak more precisely if we refer to the "valid use of test scores" rather than to "valid tests."

Correlations or Definitions

A very commonly held view is that validity is determined by substantial correlation between the test scores and some "true" or "ideal" criterion measures of the same ability. But few tests can be validated by that means because the necessary criterion measures do not exist. To produce them, we would have to do exactly the same things we did to get the test scores. If we did a good job of test construction, the test scores themselves are the best criterion measures we know how to get of the abilities we are trying to measure.

But there is a more fundamental and direct means than correlation with some external criterion of showing that the test measures what it should measure. That is to build the test on the basis of an *operational definition* of the ability or competence it is intended to measure. An essential characteristic of a measurable property, as Cook has pointed out, is that it must be clearly defined and unambiguous.[3] "So long as we stick to operational definitions in discussing and thinking about the abstract concepts used in educational measurements," says Cureton, "we will be on safe ground."[4] To be operationally defined, an achievement must be defined in terms of tasks that will differentiate between those having more and those having less of that achievement.

There is no better way of making clear what one means by achieve-

[3] Walter W. Cook, "Tests: Achievement," in *Encyclopedia of Educational Research*, ed. Walter S. Monroe (rev. ed.; New York: The Macmillan Company, 1950), p. 1464.

[4] E. E. Cureton, "Validity," in *Educational Measurement*, ed. E. F. Lindquist (Washington, D.C.: American Council on Education, 1951), p. 625.

be tested. If anxiety, for example, produces characteristic reactions
to standard test situations that differentiate more anxious from less anxious
persons, there would be far less concern about the validity of an anxiety
test. The same statement can be made about practically all other traits or
achievements that instructors would like to test. The persistent difficulties
that plague our efforts to measure some outcomes of education are less
attributable to limitations of measurement than to uncertainty about what
is to be measured.

Validity and Goodness

The term *validity* has been used often simply to mean goodness. But
if validity is essentially a question of test usage, another term is needed to
designate the quality of the test. What better word than *goodness,* provided
we specify what constitutes a good test?

Perhaps we can agree that a good test is one built on the basis of
specifications that clearly define the test content—that is, the kinds of tasks
to be included in it and the outcomes of learning they are to demonstrate.
Further, and most important, it is a test that yields reliable scores.

Questions concerning the validity of such a test should never arise.
What the test measures is the examinee's ability to do tasks like those
included in the test. It measures what it measures. Only when the scores
are used to make particular inferences and decisions in particular situations
do questions of the validity of those inferences or decisions arise. Let us
speak, then, not of valid *tests,* but of valid *uses* of test scores.

Tasks or Traits

A test developer may claim no more for a test than that it measures
how successfully an examinee can handle the type of tasks that compose
it. If the developer does this, questions about the test's validity are unlikely
to arise. Concern for validity usually is expressed when there appears to
be a difference between what a test is supposed to measure and what it
appears to measure. Is this a test of scientific understanding as its title

claims, or is it really an intelligence test? Is that a test of intelligence, or is it really only a reading test?

If one is willing to accept as a definition of what a test is measuring a simple description of the tasks that the test requires a student to perform, then what a test appears to measure and what it really does measure will be practically identical. For example, the question, "What is the sum of $1/5$ and $1/6$?" appears to measure, and really does measure (beyond an ability to read), the student's ability to add two particular common fractions. The tasks in most classroom tests of educational achievement can be described as obviously and sensibly as this if one is willing to settle for an obvious, commonsensical description.

But some test builders are not. They prefer to name their tests and describe what their tests are measuring, not in terms of the tasks they present, but in terms of the traits they presumably measure. So we have tests of intelligence, persistence, empathy, rigidity, creativity, anxiety, tolerance, perceptiveness, reasoning, and many other traits. For tests like these, the question of whether the test really measures what it claims to measure does arise, as indeed it should. Does the task of completing a figure analogy measure intelligence? Does ability to suggest unconventional uses for a brick measure creativity? Does ability to repeat a series of digits in reverse order measure memory?

Unfortunately, when such questions do arise, it is usually impossible to find satisfactory answers to them. For the traits these tests are supposed to measure are so highly generalized and so variable from one situation to another than a primary, intrinsically valid trait-defining test is seldom available for them. In the absence of such direct measures of the traits in question, it is well-nigh impossible to establish the validity of tests that claim to measure the traits *indirectly*.

Statistical or Judgmental Decisions

The use of test scores almost always involves statistical procedures. Over the years these procedures have been refined and elaborated enormously. To adapt the treatment of real data to ideal mathematical models, simplifying assumptions need to be made and nuisance variables tend to be ignored. The aim is to produce a dependable formula that will generate valid answers automatically. The numerical precision and rigorous logic of mathematics looks like an attractive substitute for fallible and possibly biased human judgment. A great deal of effort has gone into attempts to develop a practically useful science of human behavior.

Progress has been disappointingly slow. The situations in which decisions affecting people need to be made are too complex, too unique, and too ephemeral to be dealt with adequately by any reasonably simple and stable formulas. There are too many variables to consider, and their influ-

or a jury in cases of law or equity. The decision usually must be reached in the same way, by marshalling evidence, weighing it for accuracy and relevance and adding it all up to make a judgment. No routine methodology is likely to be generally effective.

CONTENT VALIDITY

In our usual parlance, the kind of validity classroom tests of achievement in learning are supposed to have is *content validity;* that is, they are supposed to sample representatively and adequately the content of the course of instruction.

If we want to define validity precisely, and to limit it to situations in which

1. inferences are drawn from observations of one set of behaviors about a quite different set of behaviors, and
2. our concern is with the relative accuracy of those inferences

then many applications of content validity do not really involve inferential validity at all. When test behaviors do in fact sample representatively a population of criterion behaviors, or when they constitute the only kind of criterion behaviors that are available for observation, the question of validity need never arise. The accuracy of our measurements of what was intended to be measured is indicated as well as it can be indicated by a coefficient of reliability. Perhaps instead of content validity we should call it content reliability, or job sample reliability. Verbal habits, unfortunately, are not that easy to change. We are no doubt fated to live with the somewhat imprecise term *content validity,* and with the confused thinking about test quality it may continue to spawn.

Are we dismissing the notion of validity as applied to content too hastily and on superficial grounds? Test behavior, after all, is not necessarily identical with non-test behavior. And test items do not always measure in fact what they were intended to measure. Do not these considerations argue for retention of the concept of content validity?

Hypothetically, yes. Practically, no. Only if non-test behavior can be quantified satisfactorily, which it seldom can be, does that aspect of content validity become practically useful. Only if what an item is intended to measure can be quantified independently of what it measures in fact (which it seldom can be), does the other aspect of content validity become practically useful. This is not to say that the test developer can safely ignore the relation between test and non-test behaviors, or between what an item is intended to measure and what it does measure. It is only to say that these questions can be dealt with more simply and clearly as matters of concrete operational definition than of hypothetical validity.

Tests of spelling ability provide instructive examples of the points we have been trying to make. A multiple-choice test of spelling error recognition (having as a stem, "Which of the following words, if any, is misspelled?") might be judged good or poor as a test of ability to recognize misspelled words on the basis of the reliability of the scores it yields. The question of its validity need not arise, because the test itself operationally defines the characteristic being tested. If such a question should be raised, it could not be answered empirically. To say that the test is intrinsically valid or invalid is to pay lip service to a conceptual deity who has no power for good or evil in this domain.

If we wish to use scores from the multiple-choice test to estimate scores on a dictation (free-response) spelling test, the question of validity does indeed arise, and can indeed be given an empirical answer. Going a step further, should we validate the dictation spelling test scores against criterion scores obtained by counting errors in the person's free writing. I think not. For the one measures how well the person *can* spell. The other measures how well she or he ordinarily *does* spell. If a person is adroit in avoiding hard-to-spell words, the "does spell" score may be much better than the "can spell" score. It may be interesting to explore this relationship, but it is unreasonable to use the correlation between the two (that is, the concurrent validity coefficient) as a measure of the quality of either test. The validity coefficient does not indicate how good the test is, but only how useful as a basis for estimates of some other measures.

Content validity (so called) is indeed distinctly different from criterion-related validity. Some would say that content validity is inferior to, or less scientifically respectable, than criterion-related validity. This view is mistaken in my opinion. Content validity is the only basic foundation for any kind of validity. If the test does not have it, the criterion measures used to validate the test must have it. And one should never apologize for having to exercise judgment in validating a test. Data never substitute for good judgment.

Those who reject rational judgment as a basis for test validity often to determine grades and test were any good or not. Part of the trouble is that teachers' grades often are not highly reliable. Another part is that the grades usually do, and usually ought to, reflect pupil achievements that the test could not or was not intended to measure. One could reasonably expect students who get grades of A in a biology course to make a higher average score on a biology achievement test than students who get grades of B. But it would be unreasonable to expect every A student to make a higher score on the test than any B student. Further, one could probably show that the average score of A students in biology on an intelligence test was higher than the average score of the B students. Would this then validate the intelligence test as a biology test?

PREDICTIVE VALIDITY

Consider next the matter of prediction, which is sometimes viewed as the principal, if not the exclusive purpose for testing, at least by many test theorists. Those who use tests, however, generally seek to obtain evidence that will be useful as a guide to intelligent action.

But, some may say, does not intelligent action always imply prediction? In a trivial sense, perhaps, it does. But there is an enormous difference between a general's use of information about the strength and movements of enemy forces in order to defeat the enemy, and his possible, but most improbable, use of the same information to predict which army was likely to be victorious.

In our involvements in human affairs we are not passive observers, not predictors of outcomes over which we have no control. We are active participants who have some measure of influence over events, and some measure of responsibility for outcomes. We do well to use the information we can get to direct action toward desirable outcomes, not to predict inevitable results.

Let us cite a concrete example. Those who direct the National Teacher Examinations for the Educational Testing Service do not claim that it will predict success in the classroom. What they do claim is that it will indicate how much the applicant knows about the job of teaching. They claim that this knowledge is a necessary but certainly not a sufficient condition for effective classroom performance. They defend the examination on logical grounds, contending that it does not need to be defended experimentally—indeed that such an experiment would be virtually impossible to carry out. None of these experts believe that a correlation between ratings of classroom effectiveness and NTE scores can shed more than a feeble and uncertain light on how well the test was doing the job it was intended to do; yet, at the same time, none of them doubt that knowing how to do a job usually facilitates doing it.

Several years ago graduate students at a major university began to raise questions about why their professors were still testing them and grading them. Had not the professors predicted success when the students were selected? Had they no faith in their own predictions? The answer here is nearly the same as in the case of the NTE. Ability to do graduate work is a necessary, but not a sufficient condition for success in graduate study. There is hard work to be done. There are challenges to be met. There is growth to be demonstrated. The use of test scores and other information about the applicants was to guide the hopefully intelligent action of the faculty in choosing which of them to try to teach, not to predict their inevitable success in learning.

So let us leave off saying that the main purpose of testing is prediction. Predict an eclipse? Yes. Predict the tides in Barnegat Bay? Yes. Predict a thunderstorm over Bowling Green? As well as may be. But the success of a person in school or on a job depends to a considerable extent on the efforts of the person. It depends on unforeseen contingencies and on a multitude of unmeasured variables. The best predictions we can make are often crude and imprecise. Nor need we labor incessantly to make them more precise. In education and in employment the best use that can be made of a test score is to encourage rather than to predict success.

CONSTRUCT VALIDITY

The term *construct validity* was introduced into the literature on test validity by Cronbach and Meehl in 1955.[5] They defined a construct as a postulated (that is, assumed or hypothetical) attribute of people that underlies and determines their overt behavior. If the behavior can be directly observed, or if the trait can be operationally defined, it is not a construct in this sense.

Much effort has gone into the scientific study of underlying, or latent, traits. Much creative, not to say fanciful, imagination has been applied to

[5] L. J. Cronbach and P. E. Meehl, "Construct Validity in Psychological Tests," *Psychological Bulletin*, 52 (1955), 281–302.

problems with algebra, calculus, or computers; these are not the kind of latent traits Cronbach and Meehl had in mind. We would speak more sensibly, I think, if we did not call them constructs.

Any domain of knowledge, any skill or ability can, of course, be *called* a construct. What cannot be done is to show that a test of this knowledge, skill, or ability possesses construct validity of the kind Cronbach and Meehl described.

The basic procedure of construct validation involves two steps. First, hypothesize the relations that should exist between scores on the test to be validated and measures of certain other abilities or traits. Second, collect data to test the hypotheses. To the extent that the hypotheses are confirmed, the test is validated. Now if the hypotheses were exact, quantitative hypotheses, and if they were derived from a rational quantitative theory of human behavior, these procedures could indeed establish the validity of the test. The trouble with construct validation as it is ordinarily practiced is that the hypotheses to be tested are not exact quantitative hypotheses, and they are not derived from any quantitative theory of human behavior, because no such theory exists. In ordinary practice a spelling test is claimed to have construct validity as a test of spelling ability if sixth graders make higher scores on it than fourth graders. What bothers one about this inference is that sixth graders will do better than fourth graders on almost any test. One author suggested that a test of study skills can be shown to have construct validity if overachievers make higher scores on it than do underachievers. Again, one might suspect that overachievers will make higher scores than underachievers on almost any test. The best way of determining whether a test of study skills actually measures study skills is by looking at the tasks that compose it.

ANSWERING QUESTIONS ABOUT VALIDITY

What do classroom teachers and other test users need to know about validity? They need to know enough to give honest, informative answers to questions likely to be asked about the tests being used. Here are some common questions along with the appropriate answers that teachers might use to defend their tests.

Is This a Valid Test?

If validity refers simply to goodness or quality, the answer is "yes." Speaking more precisely, one can say that valid use is being made of a good test. It is a good test for two reasons: first, because the kind of tasks included in it and the elements of knowledge they deal with have been clearly defined in the test specifications; and second, because it yields reliable scores. In addition, it is being used validly because what it requires the students to do is precisely what the course of instruction has been trying to teach them how to do.

Has This Test Been Validated?

If validating a test requires evidence of high correlation between these test scores and some "true" or "ideal" measure of the same ability, the answer must be "no." Tests of this kind cannot be validated in that way, because the necessary true or ideal measures do not exist and cannot be produced. The test scores themselves are the best measures we know of to judge the abilities we are trying to measure. However, the quality of the test has been assured by these means.

1. What the test was intended to measure was defined clearly and in detail in the test specifications.
2. The test was built so as to conform strictly to the specifications.
3. Analysis of the test scores showed a very satisfactory level of reliability.

High reliability is a necessary condition for high validity. The other necessary condition is that the test measure what such a test ought to measure. Thus this test was "validated" by building relevance into the tasks and by demonstrating reliability in the scores. Strictly speaking, of course, the validity depends on the use made of the test scores, not just on the definiteness and accuracy of the scores. Even a good test used inappropriately is likely to result in invalid inferences and decisions.

Is This Test Biased?

Scores on this test indicate what any examinee, regardless of race or sex or social condition, can do (or chooses to do) with tasks like these under conditions of a test. Some might do much better on a different test covering

The main conclusions to be drawn from the discussion presented in this chapter can be summarized in the following 13 propositions:

1. For many tests it is unnecessary to provide evidence of a close relationship between test scores and criterion measures.
2. Physical scientists show less concern than psychologists and educators for the validity of their measurements.
3. It is often difficult and seldom essential to conclude definitively which of two procedures provides the more valid measure of a particular characteristic.
4. Validity is much more a characteristic of test use than it is of test content.
5. Valid test use requires good tests, which are those conforming to a clear specification of test content and yielding reliable scores.
6. What a test measures is defined more clearly by the tasks included in it than it could be by the name of a trait it is supposed to measure.
7. Valid decisions involving the use of test scores are more likely to be made judgmentally than statistically.
8. The exercise of judgment is inescapable in the process of making valid inferences and decisions. No impersonal, wholly empirical means are available.
9. Content validity (so called) involves an operational definition of the thing being measured.
10. Course grades usually do not provide satisfactory criteria for the empirical validation of classroom tests of educational achievement.
11. In education the best use that can be made of a test score is to produce success, not to predict it.
12. Construct validity is of little use in defending the quality of educational tests.
13. The importance of validity as a desirable characteristic of educational tests has been vastly overrated.

By weighing we know what things are light and what heavy.
By measuring we know what things are long and what short.
The relations of all things may be thus determined, and it is of the
greatest importance to measure the motions of the mind. I beg
your majesty to measure it.

SENECA (335 B.C.)

16

Standardized Achievement Tests and Testing Programs

WHAT IS A STANDARDIZED ACHIEVEMENT TEST?

The term *standardized test* originally meant, and still means when used precisely, a test that:

1. has been carefully, expertly constructed, usually with tryout, analysis, and revision;
2. has explicit instructions for uniform (standard) administration; and
3. has tables of norms (standards) for score interpretation derived from administration of the test to a defined sample of students.

Used loosely, the term can refer to almost any published test or inventory, whether standardized in the manner just described or not. In this section, *standardized test* will be used in its more restricted sense, and attention will be limited to the characteristics, values, and limitations of standardized tests of achievement. Consideration will be given to standard test scores and norms in the next chapter.

Most standardized achievement tests are composed of objective test items. It would be almost impossibly difficult to standardize the scoring of anything but an objective test. As a matter of fact, objective test items were invented to meet the needs of the wide-scale survey testing that led to the

students. This effect has been particularly apparent in recent years.
and more the offerings of test publishers have tended to concentrate on tests of general knowledge rather than on those of specific course content. There are numerous tests of intelligence, numerous batteries of tests of general educational development, numerous tests of reading and of arithmetic. But the more specialized the subject and the more advanced the level, the more limited the potential market, and thus the fewer the offerings.

Some of those who develop and publish tests argue that this trend is educationally desirable. They contend that it is general educational development that is important, not a student's knowledge of the subject matter of specific courses. No doubt they are honestly persuaded that this is so, despite the obvious fact that the belief serves well to support large volume sales of general tests. But they must be mistaken.

In most walks of life where knowledge is used, general knowledge is not adequate. What the doctor or the lawyer or the editor or the artisan needs is specific knowledge. The English teacher may claim that her students studying *King Lear* or *Silas Marner* or *The Catcher in the Rye* are learning to understand and interpret and appreciate literature in general. But what one learns mostly in studying *King Lear* is that particular play. Under a competent teacher, one learns what Shakespeare perceived and expressed about particular aspects of human frailty or nobility evoked by a specific situation. The quotations one remembers are specific quotations. The general ability we speak of probably consists entirely of an organized and integrated body of particulars.

Another factor that has caused a reduction in the variety of tests offered by publishers is persistent criticism from test specialists of the inadequacies of some of the "standardized" tests that were published in such abundance, and so hurriedly, during the early days of the testing movement. Critics pointed to inadequate research to determine appropriate content, inadequate item tryout and editorial review, inadequate norms, inadequate validity studies, and meager manuals. They succeeded in improving the general level of test quality, but at the cost of restricting those tests more and more to fields where large-volume sales could be anticipated.

In these circumstances it is legitimate to wonder if the critics have really served education well. Is there not a place, is there not a need, for tests that cover smaller units of instruction; tests that can be supported with smaller volume sales because they are less ambitiously conceived and less elaborately developed; tests that may even lack alternate forms, or norms, or validity studies? Perhaps some test publisher could perform an educational service by selecting, cataloging, and editing the best of the many good tests that are produced around the country by expert teachers who are also skillful in test construction. Published tests of achievement need not be limited to those that have been painstakingly standardized, and they ought not to be limited to subjects where volume of sales is certain to be large.

ACHIEVEMENT TEST BATTERIES

Standardized tests of educational achievement are often developed, published, and administered in coordinated sets known as test batteries. The number of tests, or subtests, in a battery may vary from four or less to ten or more. The number of items per test may vary from 35 or fewer to 100 or more; and the time per test ranges from 10 minutes to more than an hour. The administration of a battery like the Iowa Tests of Educational Development requires three or four half-day sessions.

A test battery can provide comprehensive coverage of most of the important aspects of achievement at the elementary school level, many at the secondary level, and some at the college level. The more uniform the educational programs of the students, the more suitable is a uniform test battery for all of them. Such a battery can be planned to avoid duplication in the content covered by the several tests and to minimize the number of serious omissions.

Use of a battery of tests that was developed as an integrated whole thus offers substantial advantages. The only significant disadvantage is the lack of flexibility. The battery may include some tests that are of little interest to particular users and may omit others they would have preferred. But this is part of the price that must be paid for the advantages of convenience in use, comprehensiveness of coverage, and comparability of scores. Test developers quite naturally seek to minimize the disadvantages of batteries, and they are usually quite successful in doing so.

The coordination of achievement tests within a battery has another important advantage: It makes possible the provision of comparable scores and norms. This is important if a student's achievement in one area is to be compared with his/her achievement in another. If uncoordinated tests are used, a student might seem to do better on Test A than on Test B shown in Exhibit 16–1. The horizontal lines on the chart represent various percentile ranks. They are spaced as they would be if scores on the vertical scale were normally distributed. There is a vertical line on the chart for each test in the battery. The percentile ranks shown across the top of the chart are marked as dots on each vertical scale, and connected by lines to form the profile. Larry Hill is about average, overall. (His percentile rank for the total test is 52.) His best achievements are in reading, vocabulary, and work-study skills. His poorest are in language and mathematics.

In using profiles, it is important to remember that small differences could result from errors of measurement. A slightly higher score on one test than another does not necessarily indicate higher achievement in that area. On the other hand, if a student's score is 52 on Test A and 53 on Test B, it is slightly more probable that the examinee's achievement in B is actually higher than in A. Slightly less probable is the hypothesis that the student is actually better at A than at B. It is highly unlikely that this individual is equally good in both areas of achievement.

These observations are not intended to minimize the importance of errors of measurement. Nor are they intended to suggest that much confidence can be placed in any one of the hypotheses just mentioned. But they are intended to challenge the beliefs, sometimes expressed, that small score differences are totally devoid of significance or that they signify identity of achievement. Just as too much significance can be attached to these differences, so also too little significance, or the wrong significance, can be attached to them.

Percentile Bands

Some test publishers stress the fact that test scores are subject to error by refusing to report an exact percentile equivalent for each raw test score. Instead they report a range of values within which the true percentile equivalent probably lies. This range of percentiles is often referred to as a percentile band. For example, the manual may indicate that the equivalent percentile rank for a test score of 37 is some value between 28 and 57;

EXHIBIT 16–1. EXAMPLE OF PUPIL PROFILE CHART

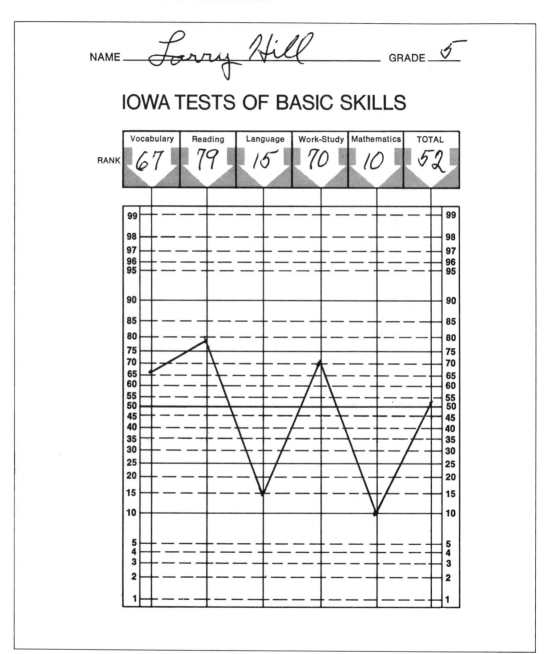

NAME *Larry Hill*   GRADE *5*

IOWA TESTS OF BASIC SKILLS

	Vocabulary	Reading	Language	Work-Study	Mathematics	TOTAL
RANK	67	79	15	70	10	52

One use of percentile bands in a battery of tests is to indicate whether or not a difference between any two scores is significant. If percentile bands should overlap, the manual suggests, then there is probably no significant difference between achievements in the two areas. But if they do not overlap, the interval between bands may be regarded as indicative of a true difference in achievement.

These suggestions guard against the danger of attaching too much importance to score differences that might be due to errors of measurement. But they invite two other misinterpretations. One is that differences below a somewhat arbitrary critical value have no significance at all. The other is that as the differences increase toward the critical value they change suddenly and categorically from insignificant to significant. The fact is, however, that insignificance does not end and significance begin at any particular size of score value. The larger the difference in scores, the more confidently one can believe in a corresponding difference in achievement. These facts are illustrated in Figure 16–1, in which a statistically defensible relation between size of a difference and confidence in it is contrasted with that implied by the use of percentile bands in the way just described.

These two misinterpretations limit and distort the essential meaning of test scores. In reducing the possibility of overly exact interpretation, they reduce the amount of information to be interpreted. And they complicate the process of score interpretation by requiring the test user to deal with two percentiles—neither of which is a good indication of the probable meaning of the score—instead of with a single percentile representing the most probable meaning. For these reasons the value of percentile bands in improving score interpretation seems open to question.[1]

[1] P. Kenneth Morse, "Reporting Test Results: Percentile Bands vs. Percentile Ranks," *Journal of Educational Measurement*, 1 (1964), 139–42.

FIGURE 16-1. Confidence in a Score Difference.

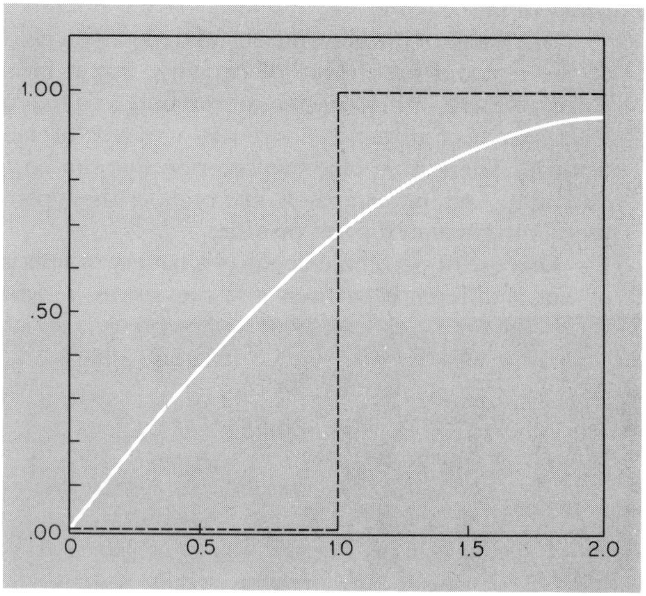

Horizontal Scale: Score difference divided by its standard error. Vertical Scale: Confidence the score difference is real. Solid Curve: Relation indicated by sampling theory. Dotted Lines: Relation implied by percentile bands.

Subtest Scores

Just as tests that constitute a test battery provide separate measures of different aspects of achievement, so it is possible to subdivide a single complex test into separately scored parts to obtain measures of several different aspects. The desire to obtain as much information as possible from a test sometimes leads the test developer to offer a large number of part scores, each of which is based on only a few test items. There are two limitations to this process. One is that as the number of part scores is increased, the reliability of each diminishes. On many tests, a part score based on as few as 10 or 15 items may report more error of sampling than true achievement. The other drawback is that increasing the number of scores a test yields complicates the process of using it without producing a corresponding gain in value. Often all the test users really want, and all they have time to use effectively, is a single overall measure of achievement in an area. On a standard test of achievement, therefore, the provision of a number of part scores should be viewed more with skepticism than with acclaim.

inform students, teachers, school administrators, and the effectiveness of their educational efforts.

Schools have often been criticized for setting up testing programs, giving and scoring the tests, and then doing nothing with the test scores except to file them in the principal's office. If the school faculty and the individual teachers do not study the test results to identify levels and ranges of achievement in the school as a whole and within specific classes; if they do not single out students of high and low achievement; and if the scores are not reported and interpreted to students, parents, and the public, these criticisms are justifiable. But if they mean that no coherent program of action triggered specifically by the test results and designed to "do something" about them emerged from the testing program, then the criticisms probably are not justified.

What a good school faculty "does" about standardized test scores is something like what good citizens do with the information they glean from a newspaper. Having finished the evening paper, they do not lay it aside and ask themselves, "Now what am I going to do about all this, about the weather, the accidents, the crimes, the legislative decisions, the clothing sales, the stock market reports, the baseball games won and lost, and all the rest?" They may, of course, plan specific actions in response to one or two items. But most of what is memorable they simply add to their store of latent knowledge. In hundreds of unplanned ways it will affect the opinions they express later, the votes they cast, the other decisions they make. Information can be very useful ultimately, even when it triggers no immediate response.

Educators who properly deplore judging teacher competence solely on the basis of pupil test scores sometimes fail to see that it is equally unwise to take action on school or pupil problems solely on the basis of those same test scores. Seldom do standardized test scores by themselves provide sufficient guidance for wise and effective educational actions. It follows that these test scores should be regarded primarily as sources of useful information, not as stimuli and guides to immediate action.

The ultimate, and occasionally immediate, actions that are taken on the basis of standardized achievement test scores fall into two general classes, instructional and evaluative. If the tests are given at the start of or during a specific course they can serve as learning exercises or problems, or as guides to

1. placement in differentiated instructional "tracks"
2. individualized instruction
3. remedial instruction

The fall testing programs that have become popular in recent decades are intended to serve primarily these purposes.

If the tests are given at the end of a course or unit of instruction they function primarily as evaluators of the pupils' success, of the teachers' effectiveness, of the curriculum's adequacy. To argue that terminal evaluations come too late to do any good is to ignore the fact that pupils are likely to continue to study in other courses, that teachers are likely to continue teaching in other classes, and that the curriculum or some revision of it will be used in the future. Past successes and failures are useful guides to future improvements. In life there is no such thing as an absolutely final examination.

A school faculty or teacher who sees the need and has the opportunity should not hesitate to develop a program for action based partly on the scores provided by standardized tests of achievement. But neither should feel that the testing was a waste of time unless such a program is developed. The immediate purpose to be served by standardized test scores is the provision of information, information that can *contribute* to the wisdom of a host of specific actions stimulated by other educational needs and developments.[2]

DIAGNOSTIC TESTING

Like several other concepts in education, diagnostic testing is more cherished as an ideal than effectively demonstrated in practice. Taking their cue from medicine, and noting that some pupils seem to be ailing educationally, the advocates of diagnostic testing propose to identify the causes of educational ailment and to correct them. In the early days of objective testing, diagnostic tests in a number of school subjects proliferated. Now, outside the fields of elementary reading and arithmetic, few standardized diagnostic tests are available. Even in these two fields, it is being recognized that diagnostic tests are no clear indicators of the sources of a student's

---

[2] G. D. Moore and Leonard Feldt, "Positive Approach to the Use of Test Results," *National Elementary Principal*, 42 (1963), 65–70; and William A. Mehrens, "The Consequences of Misusing Test Results," *National Elementary Principal*, 47 (1967), 62–64.

Another reason for this lack of ~~success~~ effective diagnosis and remediation take a great deal more time than most teachers have, or most pupils would be willing to devote. The diagnosis of reading difficulties is a well-developed skill, and remedial treatments can be very effective. Because reading is so basic to other learning, the time required for diagnosis and remediation is often spent ungrudgingly. But where the subject of study is more advanced and more specialized, the best solution to learning difficulties in one area, say algebra, physics, economics, or German, is to leave off study in that area and cultivate learning in other areas that present fewer problems.

Any achievement test can provide "diagnostic" information of value to individual pupils if they are told which items they missed. With the teacher's help, these pupils can then correct the mistakes or misconceptions that led them astray. Highly specific "diagnosis" and "remediation" of this sort can be effective and ought to be encouraged. Good diagnosis and remediation also take place informally in the give-and-take of recitation and discussion. This too ought to be encouraged. But more general, more formal and elaborate efforts at diagnosis through testing seldom have been effective. Nor do they give promise of effectiveness in the foreseeable future.

SCHOOL TESTING PROGRAMS

Local schools and school systems frequently supplement teacher-made classroom achievement tests with school-wide testing, in order to:

1. provide information needed for instruction and guidance
2. evaluate local school achievement against external standards
3. stimulate and direct continuing efforts to improve curriculum and instruction in the local school

Sometimes these school testing programs are well planned and competently handled,[3] sometimes the results are put to good use, and sometimes the

[3] Robert H. Bauernfeind, *Building a School Testing Program* (Boston: Houghton Mifflin Company, 1969); and Arthur E. Traxler, "15 Criteria of a Testing Program," *The Clearing House*, 25 (September 1950), 3–7.

testing program is strongly supported by the faculty and the community. Unfortunately, these desirable conditions do not always exist. Sometimes a school's testing program is imposed by an administration that believes all good schools have such programs, without knowing very clearly what educational purposes they serve. In that situation the school's testing program is not likely to be very good—or very popular or well used either.

The chief justification of a school testing program should be the use made of the scores obtained.[4] To give tests, obtain scores, and record each on the pupil's cumulative record card does not ordinarily constitute sufficient use to justify the testing. On the other hand, it is a mistake to develop such an elaborate program for "using" the test scores—for example, in teachers' meetings, conferences with pupils and parents, and various other kinds of action programs—that the testing program begins to absorb more than its share of the school's time and budget.

Developing a School Testing Program

Most educators now agree that a school testing program should not be imposed by administrative fiat on an unprepared and hence possibly unwilling school staff. But to democratize the approach by appointing a committee of teachers and administrators to plan the testing program may develop into a classic illustration of the stumbling efforts of the blind to lead the blind. The first requirement of a good school testing program is not that it be democratically planned, but that it be *competently* planned. Of course the teachers who must administer the testing program and use its results should be helped to understand what is to be done, and why. Their support for the program should be sought. However, support for the program will be easier to secure if it is competently, rather than haphazardly, planned.

A school planning to adopt or to modify its testing program has two options. One is to tailor a program to fit its own needs and purposes. This is an attractive alternative if the school has teachers, counselors, and administrators who know enough about tests and testing programs to plan a good one. The other is to participate in a cooperative interscholastic testing program such as the Iowa Testing Programs, the Michigan School Testing Service, or the Educational Records Bureau.

The main advantage of the local program lies in its specific fit to local conditions. Its main disadvantages are that it needs more expertness and time to plan and operate than the cooperative program requires and that

---

[4] Arthur E. Traxler, "Use of Results of Large-scale Testing Programs in Instruction and Guidance," *Journal of Educational Research,* 54 (October 1960), 59–62; and G. D. Moore and L. Feldt, "Positive Approach to the Use of Test Results," *National Elementary Principal,* 42 (1963), 65–70.

viewed in the perspective of other educational costs and of the educational value received, they are by no means high. A school that absolutely cannot afford a good testing program can hardly afford to operate at all.

Whether a school elects to develop its own testing program or to participate in an established, cooperative program, and regardless of the number of its staff who have some competence in testing, it will usually benefit greatly from the appointment of a specialist to manage all of its testing activities. Such a staff member can be given responsibility for efficient performance of a multitude of tasks associated with the program. He can also handle the administration of tests in other programs involving pupils of the school. If qualified to do so, he can serve as a consultant to teachers on their own evaluation problems. Unfortunately, the supply of talent in this area is less than abundant. Perhaps colleges of education have not done as much as they could and should to train easily identifiable specialists in school testing.

REPORTING TEST SCORES

The most basic use to be made of test scores is simply to report them to all who need to know, along with a simple interpretation of what they mean.[5] They should be reported to the students, and usually to the parents as well. Teachers should receive the scores for initial review and should keep them at hand for ready reference on future occasions. Summaries of the score distributions should be reported to the school authorities and to the community. If these communications are made, many other important uses of the test scores will occur spontaneously. It is no more necessary to develop a comprehensive, formal program for using test scores than for using a dictionary or a typewriter. If the scores are at hand, along with a guide to their interpretation, they will be used whenever the occasion arises.

School officials have sometimes been negligent about reporting the

[5] Robert L. Ebel, "How to Explain Standardized Test Scores to Your Parents," *School Management,* 5 (March 1961), 61–64.

results of their testing programs. Sometimes they have been unnecessarily cautious. Most test scores are not especially difficult to understand. When understood, they are almost never dangerous. A school should seldom, if ever, require all pupils to take a test whose results are not to be reported to them or their parents. Pupils and parents are partners with teachers and administrators in the educational process. The process works best if they are admitted to full partnership. In many states educational authorities have ruled that parents have a right to know their children's test scores and any other information on file about them. The decision upset some educators who had grown accustomed to working with confidential files, but it seems fully justifiable on educational grounds. It is hard to imagine information that teachers need to know about a pupil which should not also be accessible to his/her parents.

JUDGING TEACHER COMPETENCE

Should the results of standardized tests of student achievement given in a school program be used to evaluate the competence of teachers? The popular answer from teachers and most professional educators is a resounding No! Surely test results can never tell the whole story of a teacher's effectiveness. A superintendent who notes low achievement test scores for a particular class and who concludes solely on the basis of this evidence that the teacher is incompetent would be no wiser than a physician who notes a patient's complaint of pains in the lower abdomen and summarily concludes that the patient's appendix must be removed. Fortunately not many superintendents and not many physicians are foolish enough to jump to conclusions like these.

But would it not be equally foolish to deny, a priori and in all cases, that poor pupil achievement *might* be the result of poor teaching—just as we cannot preclude the possibility of pain in the lower abdomen being caused by appendicitis. If we agree that quality of teaching influences the quality of educational achievement, then we must also agree that good measures of that achievement have something to contribute to the complex process of evaluating teacher competence. If we do not agree that good learning requires good teaching, why try to hire good teachers or even to train them in the first place?

Now it is quite proper to call attention to the limitations of standardized tests as measures of pupil achievement, and to their additional limitations as bases for inferring teacher competence. Exhibit 16–2 lists some of the limitations of both uses. But these limitations are by no means so serious, so inherent, and so unavoidable as to completely deny any relationship with pupil achievement or teacher competence. However, those who object most strongly to the use of standardized tests for these purposes would

a. Pupil ability ~~~~~
b. School, family, and community support ~~~ ~~~~~~~
c. Quality of educational curricula and instructional materials
2. Insensitivity to the teacher's contributions that do not directly foster learnings
   a. Motivation
   b. Guidance
   c. School morale
   d. Direction of co-curricular activities
3. Imperfection as measures of student achievement

probably object with equal vigor to any other definite bases for measuring achievement or competence. It is more the fact that judgments are being made than the basis on which they are made that causes concern.

Yet despite the difficulty of the task and the uncertain quality of the result, judgments of teacher competence do have to be made. Almost every school and college has, and uses, procedures for differentiating the better from the poorer teachers. Teachers do differ in effectiveness. The pupils of good teachers learn more important things, and learn them better, than do the pupils of poor teachers. Hence, standard test scores do provide one kind of evidence of teacher effectiveness. They never tell the whole story, but they do reveal one important facet. They should never be used exclusively or blindly, but neither should any other evidence of a teacher's competence or lack of it. The indications they can give should not be denied or disregarded.

ADMISSION AND SCHOLARSHIP PROGRAMS

Testing programs for college admission and scholarship awards are usually designed and operated by independent agencies. Since they are of interest to the college-bound—who often constitute the major part of a school's enrollment—they necessarily concern staff members, who must arrange for their administration and sometimes for the interpretation of their scores. Yet these programs are not under the effective control of the schools, and are not integral parts of their educational offerings.

With the increasing popularity of higher education, which has forced some colleges to become increasingly selective in admissions, and with increasing use of scholarships to help capable students of limited means, participation in these programs has increased rapidly in recent years. The number of such programs has also increased. These developments have led to complaints from school administrators[6] and to responses from test specialists.[7] Some of the objections raised to external testing programs, and answers to the objections, are summarized here.

Objection:	The different programs of this type serve similar purposes, use similar tests, and yield similar scores for the same student. The repeated testing involves needless duplication, needless testing time, and needless expense to all concerned.
Answer:	Multiple testing gives the student multiple opportunities and options. Though similar, the tests are not identical and give somewhat different indications of abilities. Taking each test is likely to be a useful learning experience for the student.
Objection:	The tests ordinarily emphasize particular kinds of verbal and numerical skills to the exclusion of certain other kinds of special talents. They thus narrow the possibilities of college admission to the "all-around" students.
Answer:	The scope of verbal and numerical skills is broad. Together these skills encompass much that is fundamental to achievement in most areas of learning. Colleges are free to admit students with relatively low scores on admission tests if they give other indications of promise.
Objection:	Truly creative intellects are penalized by multiple-choice tests because they often choose and can justify one of the "wrong" answers on the basis of brilliant insights that the test makers overlooked.
Answer:	There is no empirical evidence to support this objection, partly because there is no obviously valid means of measuring the "true creative ability" of an intellect. On the other hand, there is ample evidence, which Chauncey and Hilton[8] have summarized, that aptitude tests *are* valid for the highly able.
Objection:	Emphasis on aptitude test scores for college admission and scholarship awards encourages intensive coaching to do well

[6] Joint Committee on Testing, *Testing, Testing, Testing* (Washington, D.C.: American Association of School Administrators, Council of Chief State School Officers, National Association of Secondary-School Principals, 1962), p. 32.

[7] Frank B. Womer, "Pros and Cons of External Testing Programs," *The North Central Association Quarterly*, 36 (Fall 1961), 201–10; Robert L. Ebel, "External Testing: Response to Challenge," *Teachers College Record*, 64 (December 1962), 190–98; and Paul L. Dressel, "Role of External Testing Programs in Education," *Educational Record*, 45 (1964), pp. 161–66.

[8] Henry Chauncey and Thomas L. Hilton, "Are Aptitude Tests Valid for the Highly Able?" *Science*, 140, No. 8 (1965), 1297–1304.

cooperate in these programs, even though the demands on staff cooperation and school facilities may seem heavy at times. With good guidance,
students will avoid registration for tests that are unlikely to help them. The
indirect influence of these testing programs on school morale, through the
recognition and rewards they offer for effective learning, can more than
repay the efforts the school expends in cooperation. Finally, if the school
has a staff specialist who is assigned responsibility for managing the school's
involvement in the program, the job is likely to be done well without
unreasonable demands on other staff members.

CERTIFICATION OF COMPETENCE

The numerous testing programs that are operated to aid in the certification
of professional or technical competence are generally of little direct concern
to the schools, except for technical high schools in a few instances. It is
interesting to speculate on reasons why the teaching profession makes less
use of written tests in the certification of competence to practice than
almost any other profession, except perhaps the ministry. Let it be granted
without argument that no written test can assess *all* aspects of skill or
competence in the practice of a profession. The best it can do is to indicate
whether examinees know enough about the work they hope to do to be
intellectually qualified. It cannot reveal how skillfully, or with what wisdom,
they will use the knowledge at their command. But the aspects of competence that written tests can assess *are* important, and written tests can do
an efficient, valid job of assessing them. Some of the arguments that
teachers use against written tests of professional competence are self-serv-
ing, defensive evasions. Neither the profession nor the public should tolerate them indefinitely.

Those who are responsible for the development of tests to be used in
certifying competence should themselves be highly competent test devel-

[9] John W. French and Robert E. Dear, "Effects of Coaching on an Aptitude Test,"
Educational and Psychological Measurement, 14 (1959), 319–30.

opers. In some cases they are; in many they are not. Usually, and quite understandably, they are first and foremost experts in the profession or trade in which competence is to be examined and certified. They may work under the supervision of a specialist in testing, and they may gradually acquire through experience some sophistication in methods of testing. However, lacking special training for the job they are asked to do, they may sometimes show less than the desired competence in doing it. Across the country and around the world there are many untrained or poorly trained test constructors doing their very limited best to handle some very important responsibilities. Universities that offer training in educational measurement ought to do much more than they have done in the past to provide good pre-service or in-service training for these workers.

Tests used to certify competence ought to be highly valid tests. To many this suggests that the tests ought to be validated against "appropriate" criterion measures. Unfortunately, as pointed out in Chapter 15, the problem of obtaining valid criterion measures is no easier to solve than that of getting valid test scores. Whether the test is validated directly, or indirectly via some criterion, there is no escape from the exercise of expert judgment in determining what ought to be measured and how it ought to be measured. The frequent absence of this kind of expert judgment in test development is a more serious weakness of many tests of professional competence than is the lack of "adequate validation" of the developed test.

In recent years concern has been expressed that certification tests and other ability tests may be biased against minority group members.[10] Sometimes evidence is cited that applicants from these groups tend to make lower scores on the certification tests than do other applicants. But to the extent that the certification test is a relevant test, such score differences simply indicate that minority group applicants tend to be less well qualified than the other applicants. Society may decide that to help right old wrongs a preferential bonus should be added to the test scores of minority group applicants. War veterans have often been shown that kind of preference on civil service selection tests. And surely those who develop or use tests for certification of competence should try to get tests of the highest possible validity. But they should view with skepticism the claim that written tests are less valid for minority group members than for others.[11] In most situations valid written tests are less subject to racial, religious, or personal bias than any other aid to selection or certification.

[10] APA Task Force, "Job Testing and the Disadvantaged," *American Psychologist*, 24 (1969), 637–50.

[11] Julian C. Stanley and Andrew C. Porter, "Correlation of Scholastic Aptitude Test Score with College Grades for Negroes versus Whites," *Journal of Educational Measurement*, 4 (1967), 199–218; and T. Anne Cleary and Thomas L. Hilton, "An Investigation of Item Bias," *Educational and Psychological Measurement*, 28 (1968), 61–75.

general education rather than to specific subjects.

3. Achievement test batteries provide for comprehensive coverage of achievements and for comparable scores in different areas of achievement.

4. Profiles of test scores indicate both the pupil's general level of achievement and his/her specific strengths and weaknesses.

5. Percentile bands call attention to the lack of precision in educational measurements at the cost of complicating those measurements and distorting their interpretation somewhat.

6. Subtest scores may be too unreliable to use effectively.

7. The primary and essential use of standardized achievement test scores is to provide information to all concerned with the educational process.

8. Standardized test scores are useful in facilitating instruction and in evaluating its results.

9. Except in the fields of elementary reading and arithmetic, diagnostic testing has proved to be of little educational value.

10. The chief justification of a local school testing program is the use the school makes of the test scores obtained.

11. If scores obtained from a testing program are reported and interpreted to teachers, pupils, and parents, no other formal or elaborate program for using them is necessary.

12. Standard test scores provide information that can *contribute* to evaluations of teacher competence, but such scores should never be used as the sole basis for evaluating teachers.

13. It is more important for a school testing program to be *competently* planned than to be democratically planned.

14. In general, locally designed testing programs are likely to be somewhat more relevant to local needs, but somewhat less expertly designed than external testing programs.

15. External testing programs designed to serve admission and scholarship purposes have been criticized as needlessly duplicating each other, emphasizing only verbal and quantitative skills, penalizing creative thinkers, and making test-passing instead of learning the

focus of a teacher's efforts. There is only limited validity to any of these charges.

16. The essential functions served by tests of technical or professional competence would be better served if those who develop such tests were better trained and paid more attention to the problems of test validity.

17. Valid tests are less likely to be biased against minority group members than any alternative means of selection or certification.

PROJECTS AND PROBLEMS

Project: Notes On A Published Test

Choose from your instructor's files a published test that seems likely to be useful to you in your work. Prepare a concise summary of the principal features of the test, following the outline given below.

A. Identifying information
   1. Name of the test
   2. Publisher (and address)
   3. Date of publication
   4. Authors (and their positions)
B. Descriptive information
   1. Types and numbers of items
   2. Fields of knowledge sampled
   3. Means for recording and scoring answers
   4. Scores provided
   5. Time required
   6. Cost per pupil tested
C. Interpretive information
   1. Type and adequacy of norms
   2. Score reliability and measurement errors
   3. Data on item difficulty
   4. Evidence for test validity
D. Evaluative information
   1. Readability and attractiveness of test and answer sheets
   2. Readability and completeness of directions for administering, scoring, and interpreting
   3. Favorable and critical comments from other reviewers (Buros or periodicals)
   4. Summary of your own evaluation

17

Standard Scores, Norms,
and the Passing Score

One of the distinguishing marks of a standardized test is the provision of norms to aid in score interpretation. For standard achievement tests these norms are usually in the form of a table of equivalents between raw scores (number right, sometimes corrected for guessing) and some type of derived score, such as

> grade equivalent scores
> age equivalent scores
> standard scores
> percentile ranks
> stanines

Effective use of standardized tests requires an understanding of these derived scores, and the ability to interpret them.[1] The first part of this chapter is intended to foster this ability.

GRADE AND AGE NORMS

Grade and age norms are most appropriate for elementary school subjects like reading and arithmetic, which are studied continuously at increasing levels of complexity and skill over a long period of time. To obtain a table

[1] Robert L. Ebel, "How to Explain Standardized Test Scores to Your Parents," *School Management*, 5 (1961), 61–64.

of equivalents the test must be given to a substantial number of pupils in each of the grades for which it is intended. Then the median raw score of pupils in each grade, or of each age, is determined. The numerical designation of the grade, or the age in years, is considered to be the grade equivalent (or age equivalent) of that particular raw score. Both grade and age equivalents are usually indicated to tenths of a unit, each tenth corresponding roughly to one month of schooling in a school year of approximately ten months.

One usually obtains the actual equivalents reported in the table graphically by plotting the median test scores against grade or age scores, drawing a smooth curve through the points, and reading the score equivalents for each grade or age value from the curve. Suppose, for example that a reading test is given to one large and representative sample of pupils in grades 3 through 8 at the beginning of December, and another large sample about five months later at the end of April. The median scores for each grade might look something like those shown in Table 17–1.

These data have been plotted in Figure 17–1. Note that the median score for the third grade in the December testing is plotted as Grade 3.3 (third grade, plus three months). Similarly, the other December test medians are plotted as 4.3 (for grade 4), 5.3, 6.3, 7.3, and 8.3. The April medians are plotted as 3.8, 4.8, and so on. A smooth curve has been drawn to approach the points as closely as possible. Table 17–2 presents the grade equivalents of some of the raw test scores. These were obtained from Figure 17–1 by reading straight across from the test score value to the curve and then straight down to the corresponding grade level.

Age equivalents are obtained similarly, though since the age data are less uniform than the grade data, more points are usually plotted for age equivalents. Often only four age levels per year are recognized, indicated, for example, by the numbers 11.0, 11.3 (three months past eleventh birthday), 11.6, and 11.9.

Although grade and age norms are easy to interpret, they are also subject to misinterpretations. Both grade and age equivalent scores involve

TABLE 17–1. MEDIAN READING TEST SCORES IN GRADES 3–8		
	Median Raw Score	
Grade	December	April
3	33	42
4	45	57
5	59	64
6	72	74
7	77	81
8	82	85

TABLE 17–2. GRADE EQUIVALENTS OF READING TEST SCORES			
Score	Grade	Score	Grade
85	8.8	55	4.8
80	7.6	50	4.5
75	6.8	45	4.1
70	6.2	40	3.8
65	5.6	35	3.4
60	5.2	30	2.8

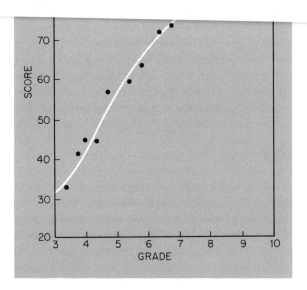

the assumptions that the subject tested is studied consistently, year after year, and that a student's rate of increase in competence is reasonably constant from year to year. They also assume that the test in question samples adequately what is being taught at all of the grade or age levels for which scores are reported. These assumptions are quite often violated. When they are, the grade or age scores can be quite misleading.

If a bright fifth-grade boy gets a grade equivalent score of 7.4 on an arithmetic test, his parents (perhaps even his teacher!) may feel that he should skip from the fifth- to the seventh-grade arithmetic class. This would be a mistake. His score does not mean that he knows as much about arithmetic overall as the typical seventh grader. How could he, since he hasn't had a chance to learn the new things normally taught in the sixth and seventh grades? All his grade equivalent score of 7.4 means is that he understands whatever arithmetic the test covers about as well as a seventh grader does. No doubt he is good for his grade, but whether he is ready for a more advanced grade is quite a different question.

Grade and age equivalents have many of the same characteristics and tell much the same story. In many schools grade grouping is essentially age grouping. In some, however, where there are frequent cases of grade skipping, or of failure and retention in grade, the age variation within a grade may be substantial. The older pupils in such a grade tend to make lower test scores and the younger pupils to make higher scores. Some test publishers report different norms for each age level within a grade, but the accurate establishment of such norms requires that enormous numbers of students be tested.

Further, the more highly differentiated these equivalents are, the less meaningful they become as standards of attainment. Overage students in the fourth grade may typically read less well than their classmates who have not been retained, but this does not make their poor reading satisfactory, even for them. High school girls may do less well than boys in the study of algebra, but this does not mean that a poorer performance from them is just as satisfactory as a better performance from the boys.

NORMS AND STANDARDS

Norms, which report how students actually do perform, should not be confused with *standards*, which reflect estimates of how well they should perform. The standard of correctness in arithmetic problems is 100 percent. The norm of pupil achievement on any given test may be only 70 percent. Yet this percentage functions as a kind of standard on which to base comparisons of an individual with his/her peers. Few students are regarded as failures in an area of study if their performance is above the norm. Few are regarded as successes if their performance is below it. It is in this context that highly differentiated norms lose much of their significance. If the differentiation were carried far enough, the only reason why individual students would not score at the norms appropriate for them would that that their scores include some error of measurement.

STANDARD SCORES AND PERCENTILES

A third kind of norm is provided by the various types of standard scores. Raw scores are usually transformed into standard scores on the basis of the raw score means and standard deviations. If X represents a student's raw score on a given test, M_x the mean score on that test in the norm or reference group, and σ_x the standard deviation of the scores in that group, then the student's standard z score would be found from the formula:

$$z = \frac{X - M_x}{\sigma_x}$$

17.1

To convert to a ~~~~
Educational Development, simply multiply the z score by five and add 15.

$$\text{ITED score} = 5z + 15 \qquad 17.4$$

Finally, to arrive at a stanine standard score (linear transformation), use this formula.

$$\text{Stanine} = 2z + 5 \text{ (rounded to the nearest whole number)} \qquad 17.5$$

The characteristics of these scales are summarized in Table 17–3.

To say that in some cases the transformation of raw scores to standard scores is linear means that if the pairs of corresponding values, raw score and standard score, were plotted on a graph they would all fall on a single straight line. This also means that the shape of the distribution of standard scores is identical with the shape of the raw score distribution, and that the asymmetry and irregularities of the raw score distribution are faithfully reproduced in the distribution of standard scores.

Perhaps they should be. On the other hand, these irregularities may be due more to peculiarities of the test itself than to any essential characteristics of the thing being measured. If one wishes to assume that what is being measured is distributed normally, in a smooth, symmetrical fashion,

TABLE 17–3. SUMMARY OF CHARACTERISTICS OF STANDARD SCORES

Characteristic	z	T	Type of Score CEEB	ITED	Stanine
Mean	0.0	50	500	15	5
Standard deviation	1.0	10	100	5	2
Maximum	+3.0	80	800	30	9
Minimum	−3.0	20	200	0	1
Negative values	Yes	No	No	No	No
Decimals	Yes	No	No	No	No
Transformation	Linear	Linear*	Linear	Linear*	Linear*

* In other, better forms of T-scores, ITED scores, and stanines, the transformation is not linear. Instead, the form of the distribution of scores is adjusted to make it approximately normal.

it is possible to transform the raw scores nonlinearly so that the distribution of standard scores is normal. Such a normalizing transformation, sometimes called an area transformation, involves three steps.

1. The distribution of raw scores is converted into percentile ranks. (A method for doing this was described in Chapter 11.)
2. From a table of percentile ranks for normally distributed z scores, read the normalized z score corresponding to each raw score percentile. A few selected points from such a table are shown here:

Percentile	99.9	97.7	84.1	50.0	15.9	2.3	0.1
z Score	3.0	2.0	1.0	0.0	−1.0	−2.0	−3.0

3. Convert the z scores into the desired T scores or stanines, using one of the formulas just given.

The normative meaning of these standard scores is not so obvious or so easily explained as that of the grade and age scores, or of the percentile ranks. To understand it requires some knowledge of score distributions and of the descriptive statistics related to them—the mean and the standard deviation. They are more often used to provide a common, clearly defined scale for reporting and comparing the results from different tests. But they do have substantial normative meaning that can be useful if one knows about it and looks for it.

The calculation and interpretation of the other major type of normative score, the percentile rank, was discussed in Chapter 11. Percentiles offer the best all-around means of presenting normative information. They are precise and easy to interpret. More and more test authors and publishers are turning to the use of percentiles in their test manuals.

THE BASIS FOR TEST NORMS

To be accurate, test norms must be based on the test scores of large and representative samples of examinees who have been tested under standard conditions, and who take the test as seriously, but no more so, as will other students to be tested later for whom the norms are needed. That complex sentence outlines a very complex and difficult process.

Norms obviously must be obtained from pupils in schools that are willing to take time out from their other responsibilities to help with the norming administration. That very willingness may make them somewhat atypical of the population of schools and pupils generally. To get enough cooperation to provide a reasonably large norm sample is hard enough. To make it a representative sample is even harder. First one must decide what population it is supposed to represent. Then one must decide what different schools cannot provide simple reasons, as Flanagan has pointed out, for considering the school, not the pupil, as the unit to be sampled in obtaining test norms.[2] At least, one must consider *both* the number of schools and the number of pupils represented in the test norms to judge their adequacy.

The administration of tests to obtain normative data can take significant amounts of time away from the school's other important activities. The occasional reluctance of schools to cooperate is easy to understand, but it would be quite wrong for them to believe that test administration has no direct educational value for the students who participate in it. They learn while thinking about answers to the questions. If scores are reported they may learn from these too. A school that "doesn't have time" to cooperate in the tryout or norming of a standardized test must have a phenomenal program, and must be making amazingly good use of pupil and teacher time doing things that are more important.

But some schools do find the time requirement a deterrent. To reduce it, some test developers have broken down a test into smaller units so that items as well as pupils can be sampled. Lord[3] and other workers[4] have described procedures for doing this that seem to work quite well in situations where the more usual techniques of tryout and norming would take too much school time.

A serious error that some test users have made is to use norms for individual pupil scores in interpreting school average scores. Although the mean of the school averages must be the same as the mean for the individual pupil scores, the school averages are likely to be far less variable than the pupil scores. The *average* score in a truly excellent school may be lower than the scores made by one-third of the pupils from all schools, and the average score in very poor school may be better than the scores of one-third of all pupils. Thus when school averages are evaluated in terms

[2] John C. Flanagan, "Units, Scores and Norms," in *Educational Measurement*, ed. E. F. Lindquist (Washington, D.C.: American Council on Education, 1951), pp. 741–42.

[3] Frederic M. Lord, "Estimating Norms by Item Sampling," *Educational and Psychological Measurement*, 22 (1962), 259–67.

[4] Thomas R. Owens and Daniel L. Stufflebeam, "An Experimental Comparison of Item Sampling and Examinee Sampling for Estimating Test Norms," *Journal of Educational Measurement*, 6 (1969), 75–83.

of norms for pupil scores, degrees of excellence or of deficiency are likely to be badly underestimated. The only proper basis for evaluation of school averages is a separate table of norms for school averages.

Clearly, in order for norms to provide valid standards for evaluating achievement, a test must always be given under the same conditions as when the norming scores were obtained. The directions, time limits, and pupil motivation should be the same. Any other circumstances that would affect the test performance, except the abilities of the particular students tested, should be the same.

This is no small order. No wonder it is sometimes done badly. No wonder test reviewers frequently complain about inadequate or inaccurate norms. No wonder some test specialists, comparing the great difficulty of getting good norms with their limited relevance and durability, have begun to wonder if the prize is worth the struggle.

There is also a subtle and indirect, but persuasive, influence on test authors and publishers to develop norms that will make the test user's pupils, and the school's educational program, look good. It is highly unlikely that deliberately falsified norms have ever been published. However, in the process of developing the norms, scores of decisions must be made, and these may affect the severity or leniency of the standards implied by the norms. Decisions that, taken individually, seem reasonable may have the cumulative effect of lowering normative standards substantially.[5] As a consequence, when test users shift from one test battery to another, they sometimes find that their pupils seem miraculously to have gained (or lost) a year or more of educational development.

The better test publishers have worked hard to overcome some of these problems and limitations of test norms, not only in their own tests but also in the whole enterprise of standardized testing. Standard populations of pupils have been proposed. A common "anchor test" to use as a basis for adjusting norms from different populations has been proposed. But none of these remedies has seemed feasible enough or potentially useful enough to be widely used.

The moral of this discussion is that test users should incline more toward critical rather than unquestioning acceptance of test norms. Before interpreting students' scores according to norms, they should always ask what population was sampled and how it was sampled to get the norms reported.

Alternatives to National Norms

Because accurate national norms are difficult to get and of limited relevance in many local situations, some test specialists have suggested that they should be abandoned in favor of purely local norms. These are

---

[5] Jason Millman and John Lindolf, "The Comparability of Fifth-grade Norms of the California, Iowa and Metropolitan Achievement Tests," *Journal of Educational Measurement*, 1 (1964), 135–37.

association of schools was conceived and guided during its formative years by Dr. Ben Wood. Its operations were managed with high professional competence for many years by Dr. Arthur Traxler. During the 1969–1970 school year, over 900 independent schools and public schools were associated with it.

In addition to providing an economical source of supply for a carefully selected list of standardized tests, with directions for uniform administration, and with a central, economical scoring and reporting service, the Bureau provides its members with extensive and detailed norms for the tests. It reports the results of numerous research studies and holds an annual conference on testing and educational problems for its member schools. The Bureau has long been a constructive influence in American education.

Not every association of schools for the purposes of educational cooperation needs to be as large and as elaborate as the Educational Records Bureau. However, the Bureau does provide a model that deserves to be copied more widely. It solves the most difficult problems of getting accurate, relevant test norms and simplifies the problems of designing, operating, and using a school testing program. Moreover, it provides for the in-service education of teachers and school administrators in effective educational measurement.

DETERMINATION OF THE PASSING SCORE

There is a widespread popular belief that any person who takes a test either passes or fails it. For tests used to measure amount of achievement, this is patently false. However, it is substantially true of one kind of test, namely, those used to certify competence to practice in the trades and professions.

A second popular belief is that when a test is used to pass or fail examinees, the distinction between the two outcomes is clear-cut and unequivocal. This is almost never true. Determination of a minimum acceptable performance always involves some rather arbitrary and not wholly satisfactory decisions.

There are several approaches to the problem of setting a passing score. One is to decide on the minimum essentials of competence—what every practitioner must know, or be able to do, in order to practice effectively and safely. Tasks designed to test whether the applicant possesses this knowledge and these abilities are developed to constitute the test.

Theoretically, the passing score on such a test should be a perfect score. In practice, of course, to insist on a perfect score as the minimum passing score would be almost to guarantee that no one would pass. First, minimum essentials are not matters of consensus; second, the item writer's ability to test them unequivocally is also not perfect; and finally the examinee's performance is not flawless enough to make a perfect score a reasonable minimum score. There needs to be some margin for errors on all counts.

A second approach is to broaden the scope of the ability to be tested somewhat, replacing the "minimum essentials" concept with the concept of "important fundamentals." Test construction is handled in the same manner, but the passing score is set somewhat below 100 percent correctness. Conventionally, passing scores on such tests have been 75 percent, 70 percent, or even 65 percent correct.

This approach is more satisfactory than the first, but it has two weaknesses. The first is that the "conventional" passing score is an arbitrary percentage with no clearly rational justification. This weakness can be overcome to some degree by using this line of reasoning:

1. On a well-constructed objective test no examinee, however weak, should actually get a score less than the expected chance score on that test, but one or two should get close to the expected chance score.
2. On a well-constructed objective test the very best examinees should get scores at or near the maximum possible score.
3. Hence, the ideal mean score on such a test falls at a point midway between the maximum possible score and the expected chance score.
4. The passing score might then be defined as a point midway between the ideal mean score and the expected chance score.

How this reasoning applies to two hypothetical tests is shown in Table 17–4.

If the test does not meet the criteria of goodness expressed by points 1 or 2—that is, it is too easy or too difficult to give a mean score near the ideal mean and insufficiently discriminating to give a low score near the expected chance score—a better estimate of the passing score might be obtained by these modifications of the foregoing procedures.

2. Average the actual mean score and the ideal mean score.
3. Define the passing score as a point midway between the two averages.

If the divergence between ideal and actual values is extreme, it might be advisable to forget the ideal values and define the passing score as the point midway between the mean score and the lowest score.

The second weakness of the definition of the passing score as some percentage of the total score is that it still leaves substantial elements of chance in determination of the passing score. The items may be more difficult, or less difficult or less discriminating, than the test constructor intended. Whether an examinee passes or fails a specific test may be determined by the questions in the test rather than by his or her level of professional competence.

The second weakness of this approach can be overcome to some degree by determining the passing percentage from a subjective analysis of the relevance and difficulty of each item in the test. Table 17–5 illustrates four categories of relevance and three categories of difficulty, and gives the expected percentages of passing for items in each category. These expected percentages are what would be expected of a minimally qualified (barely passing) applicant.

Suppose, for example, that the number of items in a 100-item test falling in each category when the ratings of five judges are pooled were as shown in the second column of Table 17–6. Multiplying each of these

TABLE 17–5. RELEVANCE, DIFFICULTY, AND EXPECTED SUCCESS ON TEST ITEMS

Relevance Categories	Difficulty Levels		
	Easy	Medium	Hard
Essential	100%	—	—
Important	90	70%	—
Acceptable	80	60	40%
Questionable	70	50	30

TABLE 17–6. PASSING SCORE ESTIMATED FROM ITEM CHARACTERISTICS

Item Category	Number of Items*	Expected Success	Number × Success
Essential	94	100	9400
Important			
Easy	106	90	9540
Medium	153	70	10710
Acceptable			
Easy	24	80	1920
Medium	49	60	2940
Hard	52	40	2080
Questionable			
Easy	4	70	280
Medium	11	50	50
Hard	7	30	210
	500		37130

$$\frac{37130}{500} = 74.26 \text{ or } 74\% = \text{passing score}$$

* Actually the number of placements of items in the category by all five of the judges.

numbers by the expected proportion of correct answers gives the products shown in the fourth column of Table 17–6. The sum of these products divided by 500 gives an estimate of the appropriate passing score.

A third approach assumes that competence is essentially a relative term, and that the task of a certification test is simply to select the most competent and to reject those who are less competent. The test is still based on important fundamentals, but the passing score is not defined as some proportion of correct answers. Instead, it is defined as that score above which 50 percent, or 66 percent, or 90 percent of all scores fall. This means that the poorest one-half, one-third, or one-tenth of the applicants fail regardless of the absolute value of their scores.

The obvious drawback of this approach is that it allows the passing score to vary according to the general level of competence of the examinees at a specific testing. If that general level is high, some fairly well qualified applicants may fail. If is it low, some poorly qualified applicants may pass.

Whether the passing score should be defined as a percent of the total score or as a percent of applicants to be passed probably should depend on the expected stability of the examinations in level of difficulty compared to the expected stability of the group of examinees in levels of ability. If an examiner is more confident of the stability of examination difficulty than of examinee group ability, he or she may choose the percent of total score and the score 80 percent of the examinees exceed. The figures used in this example, 75 percent of the items, and 60 percent and 80 percent of the examinees, are simply illustrative. Depending on circumstances, an examining authority might want to raise or lower any of them. The object in setting these values is to keep the amount of content knowledge, and the proportion of passes and failures, within what seem to be reasonable bounds while making reasonable allowance for the unavoidable errors of measurement. This fourth alternative has not been widely used, but would seem to have considerable merit as a rational solution to a difficult problem.

A fifth approach uses the performance of certified practitioners as a basis for setting the passing score. It requires the certification test to be given to a large and representative sample of professionals who have been approved to practice and who are actually practicing. A decision is made by the certifying authority that any applicant who scores above the lowest quarter, lowest fifth, or lowest tenth of those actually practicing the profession deserves to be certified to practice it also. If the supply of applicants is good, and if the profession is seeking to upgrade itself rapidly, it may set the passing score fairly high on the scale of actual practitioner performances.

One problem with this fifth approach, of course, is getting the scores of a sufficient sample of practitioners, and of getting them to take the test conscientiously. A solution to this problem might be to break the test into representative sets of 15 to 25 items, asking each respondent to answer only those in one set. From their performances on these sets synthetic score distributions of the entire test could be constructed. This procedure, by limiting the proportion of the test exposed to any one person, would help to safeguard test security. Two other steps might also be desirable:

1. Getting practitioner responses to the items in several forms of the test at the same time. The fewer items in any single form that a person sees, the less test security is threatened.
2. Reminding practitioners who respond to the items of the importance to the profession and to themselves of safeguarding item security.

From the preceding paragraphs it is clear that a variety of approaches can be used to solve the problem of defining the passing score. Unfortunately, different approaches are likely to yield different results. Anyone who expects to discover the "real" passing score by any of these approaches, or any other approach, is doomed to disappointment, for a "real" passing score simply does not exist. All any examining authority can hope for, and all any of their examinees can ask, is that the basis for defining the passing score be stated clearly, and that the definition be as rational as possible.

SUMMARY

The main ideas developed in this chapter can be summarized in the following 12 statements.

1. Grade and age norms are most appropriate for elementary school subjects that are studied continuously over a long period of time.
2. A grade equivalent score in arithmetic of 7.4 for a fifth-grade boy does not ordinarily mean that he is ready for seventh-grade arithmetic.
3. Norms report what is, standards what ought to be, but national norms inevitably function as a kind of local standard.
4. The basic standard score is the z-score, in which a given raw score is expressed as a plus or minus difference from the mean in standard deviation units.
5. Normalized standard scores can be obtained by converting raw scores to percentile ranks and then entering a table which gives z-score equivalents of the percentile ranks.
6. To be accurate test norms must be based on large and representative samples of examinees, tested under standard conditions.
7. The adequacy of test norms depends on both the number of pupils and the number of schools represented in them.
8. Pupil norms are not appropriate for the interpretation of school averages.
9. Similar schools that cooperate in administering the same tests can secure highly relevant and useful norms.
10. The passing score may be defined as some fraction of the total test score, as some fraction of applicants to be passed, or as a score higher than that made by some fraction of certified practitioners.
11. The passing score may be defined on the basis of the pooled judgments of experts on the relevance and difficulty of each item in the test.
12. Passing scores cannot be discovered. They must be defined, but the definition should be as clear and as rational as possible.

1. What raw scores, grade equivalents, percentiles, and stanines mean. (These tests were not corrected for guessing. The standard error of measurement of the grade equivalent scores is about 0.4.)
2. Why local percentiles differ from publishers' percentiles, and what the differences indicate in this case.
3. What the scores indicate about the achievements of Roland, in general and more specifically.

BASIC SKILLS TEST SCORES FOR ROLAND ELKINS

Test	Raw Score	Grade Equivalent	Publisher's Percentile	Local Percentile	Local Stanine
Vocabulary	21	5.3	46	46	
Reading	37	5.3	46	37	
Language	78	5.7	55	49	
Study skills	57	5.3	48	42	
Arithmetic	27	4.2	16	9	
Composite	—	5.2	45	37	

18

Intelligence and Aptitude Tests

A very important group of published tests is composed of those designed to measure intelligence. From the early years of this century up to the present many teachers, perhaps a majority of them, have regarded intelligence testing as an essential part of a good school testing program. Many of them believe that each of us has a definite amount of intelligence, measured by our IQ (intelligence quotient), and that this was given to us at birth and remains essentially intact for our entire life. They feel that it is important for a teacher to be aware of each student's IQ, so that all can be educated to their "capacity"—yet without demanding from any, more than that person is able to do.

THE NATURE OF INTELLIGENCE

Despite widespread acceptance of the idea that intelligence exists, no one seems to have a very clear idea of what it is. Presumably it has a biological basis in neuroanatomy or in brain physiology. A few types of gross mental deficiency have been identified with severe metabolic defects.[1] In an interesting popular article, Shultz has summarized evidence on the relation of

[1] H. Eldon Sutton, "Human Genetics: A Survey of New Developments," *The Science Teacher*, 34 (1967), 51–55.

When psychologists are asked ~~...~~ variety of answers, none of which is very specific.[3] One calls it ability to learn, that is, to do the work of the school. The lack of this ability is what Alfred Binet was interested in detecting in his early tests.[4] Another characterizes it as ability to reason, to solve problems, and use the "higher mental processes." Still another emphasizes original thinking and the ability to adapt to novel situations.

These different conceptions of the nature of intelligence have contributed to the development of a wide diversity of tasks for testing it. Examples of some of the better known types are presented in the next section.

KINDS OF TASKS USED TO TEST INTELLIGENCE

I. Verbal

1. *Synonyms (or antonyms)*

   Identify the pair of words in each set that are either synonyms or antonyms.

   a. accident   *b.* bad   *c.* evil   *d.* worry

   a. accept   *b.* make   *c.* object   *d.* order

2. *Verbal analogies*

   snow: flake: *a.* cloud: fleecy   *b.* hail: storm

               c. icicle: eaves   *d.* rain: drop

3. *Commands*

   The task is to obey simple commands.

   "Give me the pencil."

   "Put the book on the shelf."

---

[2] Gladys Denny Shultz, "The Uninsulted Child," *Ladies Home Journal*, 73 (1956), 60–63.

[3] "Intelligence and Its Measurement: A Symposium," *Journal of Educational Psychology*, 12 (1921), 123–47, 195–216.

[4] Alfred Binet, "Nouvelles recherches sur la mesure du niveau intellectuel chez les enfants d'ecole," *Année Psychologique*, 17 (1911), 145–201.

4. *Sentence completion*

While most teachers agree that educational tests are useful, one occasionally hears the suggestion that education could go on perfectly well, perhaps much better than in the past, if tests and testing were _____.

a. abolished   *c.* criticized   *e.* praised

b. continued   *d.* investigated

5. *Sentence interpretation*

Given sentence: The date must be advanced one day when one crosses the International Date Line in a westerly direction.

Interpretive question: If a ship approaches the International Date Line from the east on Tuesday, what day is it on board the ship after the line has been crossed?

II. Quantitative

6. *Digit span*

The examiner says a series of numbers and asks the subjects to repeat them, forward or backward. The maximum number the student can repeat is his digit span.

7. Number series

1	3	5	7	9	?
1	2	3	5	8	?

8. *Arithmetic computation*

Add 23 to 66.

Divide 96 by 16.

9. *Arithmetic reasoning*

How many 5¢ candy bars can be bought with 30¢?

If concrete is to be made with 4 parts of sand to 1 part of cement, how many shovels of cement should be put with 16 shovels of sand?

10. *Relative magnitudes*

How much larger than $1/3$ is $1/2$?

A dollar is how many times as much as a dime?

11. *Water jar problems*

If you have a 7-quart jar and a 3-quart jar how can you get exactly 8 quarts of water?

III. Information

12. *General*

How many legs does a dog have?

What is the special name for a doctor who takes care of teeth?

13. *Common sense*

Why are street lights turned off in the morning?

Why do houses have windows?

14. *Absurdities*

What is foolish about these statements?

"The fish I tried to catch got away, but it made a delicious meal."

Given several pictures in a set, the examinee is asked to indicate which best illustrates the meaning of a particular word.

18. *Picture completion*
    Tell me what part of this picture is missing.

19. *Figures analogies*
    A: B:: C:?

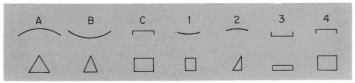

20. *Matrix progression*
    What figure belongs in the blank space?

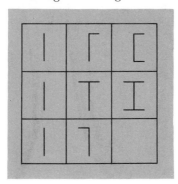

21. *Maze tracing*
    The task is to find a clear path through a maze of lines.

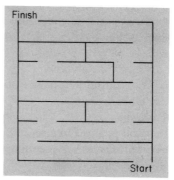

22. *Figure drawing*
    Draw a picture of a man.

V. Abstract Process

23. *Similarity (and difference)*
    Which of these is most like a calf?
    (a) a colt   (b) a cat   (c) a pony
    In what way is a tennis ball different from a baseball?

24. *Classification*
    The examinee is directed to sort a set of words, objects, or symbols into a given set of categories.

25. *Sequence*
    Arrange the following words in the proper order:

afternoon	morning
daybreak	noon
evening	sunrise
midnight	twilight

26. *Coding*
    Given a simple code, the task is to translate a set of symbols into the code.

    Code

———	+	X	————	=
1	2	3	4	5

    Task

X	X	+	=	———	+

to measure intelligence. This approach has also been tried. It has shed much light on the extent to which proficiency on certain tasks tends to be related to, or independent of, proficiency on other tasks. But it has provided no compelling definition of intelligence. Each practitioner interprets its finding somewhat differently. One finds a common, general intellectual factor.[5] Another finds seven primary mental abilities.[6] Still another finds an elaborate multidimensional structure of intellect.[7] The tasks used to measure intelligence can be grouped as coarsely or subdivided as finely as one chooses. But none is excluded from the comprehensive definition, and the dimensions or elements of mental ability are no more discrete and distinguishable than the segments of a line.

DESIGNING INTELLIGENCE TESTS

Educational and Environmental Tasks

A few of the tasks used to test intelligence, for example, giving synonyms, interpreting sentences, computing, and solving problems, are objects of specific instruction in schools. Hence, almost identical tasks are likely to be found in general achievement test batteries. Ability to handle other tasks such as analogy problems, recognition of absurdities, and problems of classification and sequence is usually learned incidentally at home, at play, in school, or elsewhere.

It is sometimes assumed that what a student succeeds in learning incidentally is a better indication of intelligence than the person's success in learning what he or she has been taught. The assumption may be justified, but the evidence and logic needed to justify it are not obvious. Teaching does indeed assist learning, but it does not make learning automatic nor does it eliminate the need for effort and ability on the part of students. Intelligence contributes to learning in school as well as out of it.

[5] Charles E. Spearman, *The Abilities of Man* (New York: The Macmillan Company, 1927).
[6] L. L. Thurstone, "Primary Mental Abilities," *Psychometric Monographs*, No. 1 (1938).
[7] J. P. Guilford, "Intelligence: 1965 Model," *American Psychologist*, 21 (1966), 20–25.

Obviously, if we wish to compare the intelligence of children who have been to school with those who have not, we should not use tasks that the school tries to teach. As a general principle, if we seek to infer basic ability to learn from measurements of success in learning, we must first try to equalize opportunities to learn and then select as test items only problems to which all children have probably been exposed. Yet, as Coleman and Cureton point out, even if opportunities for in-school learning were equalized, there would still remain great differences in the availability of incidental learning.[8] These differences in environments and life styles among different families, different neighborhoods, and different regions of the country cannot, and probably should not, be eliminated.

Nonverbal and Culture-Fair Tests

Some intelligence tests attempt to minimize, or to eliminate altogether, the influence of verbal ability on test scores. The tasks are based on objects, drawings, or figures that require assembly, classification, arrangement, selection, manipulation, or some other response. Sometimes even the instructions involve no words, but are given in pantomime.

These tests are useful if students who speak different languages must be tested with the same test, or if a student with a severe language handicap must be tested. They appeal to those seeking measures of basic intelligence, uncontaminated by learning, particularly language learning. But there is no good reason to believe that these nonverbal tests get any closer to basic native intelligence than do the verbal tests. Ability to do well on them can also be learned. And since verbal facility is so important an element in school learning, and in most areas of human achievement, what the nonverbal tests succeed in measuring usually seems to have little practical usefulness.

Most intelligence tests not only require some degree of adeptness with a particular language, but also assume familiarity with a specific culture. This quality limits their usefulness in other cultures. It even casts some doubt on their purity as measures of basic, abstract intelligence. However, attempts to build culture-free tests have failed because testing requires communication and communication is impossible in the absence of culture: its concepts, symbols, and meanings.

Attempts to build culture-fair tests by eliminating items that discriminate between different cultures have been no more successful. If carried far enough, they result in eliminating all the items. There is no difference between individuals in their response to any test item that cannot be attributed to differences in culture, if culture is defined inclusively enough. Each of us lives in a somewhat different culture. Not only Eskimos and

[8] William Coleman and Edward E. Cureton, "Intelligence and Achievement: the 'Jangle Fallacy' Again," *Educational and Psychological Measurement*, 14 (1954), 347–51.

Those who conceive of intelligence as an abstract ability to think are likely to favor tasks that present novel problems, such as number series, water-jar problems, figure analogies, matrix progressions, or maze tracing. So long as the task is a problem requiring thought, so long as it is novel, its exact nature is relatively unimportant. Since the ability being tested is presumably a unitary, generally applicable ability, any novel problem will do. Nor is a diversity of problem tasks in the test deemed necessary. The assumption is that the examinee's success with any of them will depend not on the problem but only on the examinee's ability to reason.

But thinking is always based on content. What examinees have or have not learned does make a difference in their ability to handle these tasks that supposedly involve only abstract reasoning. A little judicious coaching can often prove a great boon. In addition, however, the influence of relevant incidental learning is a factor that cannot be discounted. Thus the claim that these tasks measure abstract intelligence is also open to question.

Individual and Group Intelligence Tests

The earliest tests of intelligence were administered individually. Later, tests that could be administered simultaneously to all individuals in a group were developed. Both are still in use, because each has special advantages and limitations.

EXHIBIT 18–1. COMPARISON OF INDIVIDUAL AND GROUP INTELLIGENCE TESTS

Aspect	Individual	Group
Task presentation	Oral	Written
Range of task types	Wider	Less wide
Dependence on reading	Minimal	Substantial
Mode of response	Oral, free	Multiple-choice
Flexibility in testing	High	Low
Age suitability	Younger	Older
Scoring	Semiobjective	Objective
Time required	Longer	Shorter
Cost	Higher	Lower
Reliability	High	High
Validity (where suitable)	Satisfactory	Satisfactory

Some of the differences between individual and group intelligence tests are summarized in Exhibit 18–1. As a result of their special properties, individual intelligence tests are usually administered to young children, to those with reading disabilities, and to other special cases. Group tests, because they are economical of time and money, are generally used for routine testing of older children. There is no important difference between the two types in reliability or validity.

TESTS OF SPECIAL APTITUDES

Somewhat related to tests of general intelligence, but often sounder conceptually and more useful practically, are tests of special aptitudes. They are sounder conceptually because what is to be measured is more restricted and more clearly defined. Fewer assumptions about the origin of the aptitude or its changelessness are made. They are more useful practically because their purposes are more specific and more readily attainable.

Some tests of special aptitude, such as academic aptitude, are quite comprehensive. Others, such as those of engine lathe aptitude, are rather specific. Often aptitude tests are grouped into batteries to provide for measurement of diverse aptitudes or to permit differential predictions of aptitudes for diverse activities. Texts by Cronbach,[9] Anastasi,[10] and Thorndike and Hagen[11] describe various aptitude tests and test batteries in some detail. In general, they are of high quality, although as Super's[12] classic reviews indicated, they are subject to further improvement.

Aptitude tests are sometimes criticized for seeking to predict success in training programs rather than on the job. A medical aptitude test, for example, is judged to be valid if it assigns the highest scores to those who do best in medical schools, but success in medical school does not always forecast success in the practice of medicine. Yet we must not forget that criteria of success in training programs are easier to define and to measure than criteria of on-the-job success, and also that short-range predictions can be made with greater accuracy and assurance than can long-range predictions. Both of these arguments would seem to support aptitude tests as they are presently constituted. If there is evidence of unreasonable disparity between competence in training and competence on the job, it

[9] Lee J. Cronbach, *Essentials of Psychological Testing* (3rd ed.; New York: Harper & Row, Publishers, 1970).

[10] Anne Anastasi, *Psychological Testing* (3rd ed.; New York: Crowell, Collier and Macmillan, 1968).

[11] Robert L. Thorndike and Elizabeth Hagen, *Measurement and Evaluation in Psychology and Education* (3rd ed.; New York: John Wiley & Sons, Inc., 1969).

[12] Donald E. Super, *The Use of Multifactor Tests in Guidance* (Washington, D.C.: American Personnel and Guidance Association, 1958).

general mental ability, he suggested that steps be taken to "kill the IQ."

The apparent simplicity of the IQ concept is one reason for its popularity and for the misunderstandings associated with it. It is calculated from the formula:

$$IQ = 100 \times \frac{\text{Mental age}}{\text{Chronological age}} \qquad 18.1$$

Since the pioneer work of Alfred Binet, most mental test scores have been expressed as years and months of mental age. If a student taking an intelligence test answers correctly as many of the questions asked as does the average child who is 11 years and 3 months of age, then the student's mental age is reported as 11 years 3 months, or 135 months. But if the student's actual chronological age is only 10 years 6 months (126 months) his IQ is

$$100 \times \frac{135}{126} = 107$$

The IQ ratio is easy to understand in terms of its calculation and meaning. But like many other simple generalizations, it fits the facts none too well.

To begin with, if it is a measure of some permanent quality of the mind, it ought to remain constant as the years pass. This means that mental age ought to increase as steadily as does chronological age, and at a constant rate of increase. The person of exceptional intellect who has an IQ of 150 based on a mental age of 15 at age 10 should have a mental age of 30 when he reaches 20 years, a mental age of 75 at 50 years, and a mental age of 120 at 80 years. Of course, nothing like this can be demonstrated. In fact, it is virtually impossible to devise a test of general intelligence on which the average 25-year-old does much better than the average 16-year-old.

[13] William Stern, *The Psychological Methods of Testing Intelligence*, trans. Guy M. Whipple (Baltimore: Warwick, 1914).

We may explain this fact in several ways. For one, we may assume that general mental ability stops developing at about age 16. This is not unreasonable in relation to the general pattern of physical growth, although it should be noted that physical growth shows little of the constant rate of increase from year to year that the IQ assumes to be characteristic of mental growth. Nor does physical development necessarily cease even at age 20, for many persons take up new sports well into middle age.

Another, different explanation for the apparent halt of mental development at about age 16 is that the educational experiences that most children share in schools, in homes, and at play—experiences that provide the background for answering intelligence test questions—stop occurring to all children in essentially the same way at about that age. Henceforth, fewer new experiences are encountered. Those that do occur are likely to differ more from person to person. The common experiences formerly provided in school, at home, and at play are replaced by a multiplicity of experiences on the job and in various spheres of activity. Tests of *general* mental ability have no place for tasks based on *special* experiences. Finally, as Owens has reported, for those whose occupations or social positions involve them in verbal, quantitative, or other tasks like those represented on the tests, intelligence test scores continue to increase in adult life.[14]

Judged in the light of facts like these, the famous statement that Americans are, intellectually speaking, a nation of 12-year-olds—a statement based on intelligence test results for World War I draftees—is seen to be more a reflection on the contents of the intelligence test than on the abilities of those tested. Walter Lippman discussed this and other apparent flaws in the concept of general intelligence in his debate with Lewis Terman in the pages of *The New Republic*.[15]

If the measurement of intelligence is limited to the years below 16, as it usually is in school practice, the logical difficulties with ratio IQs are less troublesome. But some remain. Assuming that an individual's intelligence is a constant characteristic, one would expect that the proportion of the population with IQs above 116 or below 84, for example, ought to be the same for each age group. But it is difficult to build an intelligence test that shows this kind of stability.

To make IQs generally applicable to all groups in society, many test developers have shifted from ratio IQs to deviation IQs. At each age a score one standard deviation above the mean score for the age group is taken to represent an IQ of 116[16] in that group. A score one standard

---

[14] William A. Owens, Jr., "The Retest Consistency of Army Alpha after 30 Years," *Journal of Applied Psychology,* 38 (1954), 154; and by the same author, "Age and Mental Abilities: A Second Adult Followup," *Journal of Educational Psychology,* 57 (1966), 311–25.

[15] Walter Lippman, "Intelligence Tests," *The New Republic,* 32 (1922), and 33 (1923).

[16] Some test makers use 115. Others have used other values near 116. But 116 is the value recommended in the booklet on test standards published by the American Psychological Association.

seems to regard these numbers as sacrosanct indicators of "intelligence." The fact that different tests are based on quite different tasks is glossed over by the use of the same kind of unit to express the measurements obtained. Were it not for this apparent generality of mental ability, and for the apparent simplicity of its measurement, the concept of abstract intelligence probably would not have gained so strong a following in the educational establishment.

Achievement Quotients and "Underachievement"

The success and popularity of the IQ encouraged the development of other quotients in the early days of standardized testing. One of these was the Educational Quotient (EQ), defined as:

$$EQ = 100 \times \frac{\text{Educational age}}{\text{Chronological age}} \qquad 18.2$$

Another was the Achievement Quotient (AQ)

$$AQ = 100 \times \frac{\text{Educational age}}{\text{Mental age}} \qquad 18.3$$

But both of these depend on assumptions that are even more questionable than those involved in the IQ. They are subject to even greater errors and ambiguities, and hence they have fared much less well. Indeed they are now both generally discredited, for the following reasons.

To determine a pupil's educational age, one must administer a test for which age equivalent scores are available. An age equivalent for a given number of right answers is the age level for which that number of right answers is the average score. To determine age equivalent scores for a test of educational achievement is troublesome and costly, and of questionable value. If all pupils studied the same topics in the same sequence over a range of grades, that is, if all of them followed the same curriculum, reporting levels of educational achievement at age levels would make some sense. But curricula are not the same, textbooks are not the same, tests are not the same. To use the average test performance of pupils following diverse curricula as a basis for measuring the achievement of a specific pupil who has been following a specific curriculum is not particularly reasonable.

There are a number of additional difficulties with the achievement quotient, as Conrad has pointed out.[17] Educational ages and mental ages are abstractions that carry the implication that their values are independent of the particular tests used. This is not true. Further if the "ages" are determined by using different samples of the population, the quotients may be systematically biased upward or downward, or biased differently at different points along the scale. Finally, of course, errors of measurement in each of the two ages tend to be compounded in the quotient calculated from them.

Because their untrustworthiness is widely recognized, and because the necessary age scores are difficult to obtain, achievement quotients have fallen into disfavor and disuse. But the notions of underachievement and overachievement, which involve the same questionable assumptions and the same operational difficulties, are still popular. Thorndike has discussed some of the limitations of these notions.[18] Education is more likely to gain than to lose if the concepts of over- and underachievement are consigned to the same oblivion that has overtaken achievement quotients.

THE INHERITANCE OF INTELLIGENCE

One particular aspect of the nature of intelligence has been the focus of controversy for more than a century. To what extent is it a native, inborn characteristic? To what extent is it acquired? It was Galton's interest in intelligence as an inheritable trait that opened up the modern era of scientific study of intelligence.[19] Since his time, hundreds of scholars have both theorized and contributed research data in an effort to end the controversy.

Studies of descendants of the same parents have seemed to show mental ability or lack of it to run in families. Further, comparisons of the intelligence of identical twins, fraternal twins, and siblings have pointed toward a correlation between degree of genetic similarity and degree of similarity in intelligence. On the other hand, studies of children reared in

[17] Herbert S. Conrad, "Norms," *Encyclopedia of Educational Research*, ed. Walter S. Monroe (rev. ed., New York: The Macmillan Company, 1950).

[18] Robert L. Thorndike, *The Concepts of Over- and Underachievement* (New York: Teacher's College Press, 1963).

[19] Francis Galton, *Inquiries into Human Faculty and Its Development* (London: Macmillan, 1883).

that determines intelligence and that could be subject to the laws
of heredity
2. The impossibility of isolating the influences of heredity and environment and of controlling and manipulating them sufficiently to
obtain unequivocal results

Few are inclined to challenge the statement that a particular individual's
intelligence has an inherited biological base, or that individuals differ in
the quality of that base. Extreme cases of mental deficiency are often either
inherited or result from prenatal conditions. In other instances, disease or
accident may act to damage some part of the brain or nervous system.
However, among normal individuals it is difficult to find cause-result evidence to link specific qualities of the biological base with corresponding
differences in developed intelligence.

In this respect mental intelligence may be analogous to physical health.
Just as one person may be born with physical deformities or physiological
deficiencies that impair health throughout life, so another may be born
with anatomical or physiological deficiencies of the brain and nervous
system that impair intelligence throughout life. For the vast majority of
human beings, however, both physical health and mental intelligence depend almost entirely on what happens to us, and above all on what we
ourselves do with the capabilities we inherit.

To make an analogy with computer technology, we are computers of
the same model that were designed to have identical capacities and, save
for accidental flaws, do have identical capacities. What differentiates the
work we do is what we have been programmed to do. Yet our analogy
cannot be carried to the extreme, for obviously human beings have a hand
in writing the programs that guide their thoughts and actions.

Three events in recent years have fanned the flames of controversy
over the influence of heredity on intelligence. One was the publication of
Arthur Jensen's[20] review of research which led him to conclude that much

[20] Arthur R. Jensen, "How Much Can We Boost I.Q. and Scholastic Achievement," *Harvard
Education Review*, 34 (1969), 1–123.

of a person's intelligence was inherited, and to suggest the possibility that there might be substantial racial differences in intelligence. Some scholars supported Jensen.[21] Others disagreed, as did many socially concerned citizens.[22] On several occasions those who opposed "Jensenism" demonstrated the depth of their feelings (and their limited support for freedom of speech) by disrupting public meetings at which he or William Shockley had been invited to speak.

A second was the CBS television broadcast in April 1975 of a documentary entitled "The IQ Myth," narrated by Dan Rather. Though both proponents and critics of the IQ concept, and of intelligence testing, were given a hearing, its critics were presented in a more favorable light. The narrator concluded the program with these words:

> Finally, it would be well to keep in mind that all this is true, not just for your own children, but for your neighbors'. Black or white, rich, middle-class or poor—for all of them, IQ is no natural talent, no godly gift, but something their family and their community have given them or denied them.

A third event was the publication in 1976 of charges[23] that Sir Cyril Burt, father of British educational psychology, had reported false data and invented facts to support his belief that intelligence is largely inherited. Burt was charged with having:

> Guessed at the IQs of parents he interviewed, but later used these guesses as hard data
> Named as research collaborators persons who may never have existed
> Produced identical answers, accurate to three decimal places, from different sets of data
> "Proved" his hypotheses by working backward to calculate data that would confirm them

Jensen has defended Burt, calling the charges "trumped up" and "bizarre." Acknowledging that Burt did make some errors, he nonetheless discounts them as trivial, and concludes that even if all Sir Cyril's data were

---

[21] Richard Herrnstein, "I.Q.," *Atlantic*, September 1971, p. 43; and William Shockley, "Heredity, Environment, Race, I.Q.," *Phi Delta Kappan*, 53 (January 1972), 297–312.

[22] Among those educators who registered a strong protest were Jerome S. Kagan, "Inadequate Evidence and Illogical Conclusions," *Harvard Educational Review*, 34 (1969), 274–77; J. McV. Hunt, "Has Compensatory Education Failed? Has It Been Attempted?" *Harvard Educational Review*, 34 (1969), 278–300; and Lee J. Cronbach, "Heredity, Environment and Educational Policy," *Harvard Educational Review*, 34 (1969), 338–47.

[23] Leon J. Kamin, *The Science and Politics of I.Q.* (New York: John Wiley & Sons, Inc., 1974); and Oliver Gillie, "Did Sir Cyril Burt Fake his Research on Heritability of Intelligence?" *Phi Delta Kappan*, 58 (February 1977), 469–70.

intelligence is there all right, but just inaccessible. Another assumption is that it doesn't exist in any real sense until it has been developed.

The intelligence of infants has been measured and studied extensively.[24] One salient finding is that early measurements correlate poorly with later measurements of the same individuals. Again, one can assume that the apparent instability is due to inadequate measurements, or that it is due to actual changes in the developing intelligence. Those who emphasize hereditary factors as determinants of intelligence will choose one explanation. Those who emphasize learning and experience will prefer the other. Whatever the explanation, the measurements are not good predictors of subsequent educational development.

Intelligence and Teaching

It is obvious that individuals display different degrees of ability to learn. Since these differences are self-evident, why they exist might seem to be a matter of purely academic interest that should hardly concern the classroom teacher. Yet a teacher's hypotheses about the source and nature of the differences can have important consequences in his/her teaching. If a teacher believes such differences reflect inherited capacities that set limits to what a given person can learn, she or he may "waste" little time trying to teach those whose capacities are limited. And if inherited capacity rather than acquired background knowledge is viewed as the main determinant of future learning, the classroom may become a sort of educational quarry where the stones of hidden talent are sorted for polishing. By contrast, if teachers believe that there are no effective biological limits to learning, they will not despair of helping anyone to learn more, and they will concentrate on developing ability rather than prospecting for it.

Teachers who see intelligence as an inherent characteristic that limits the learning of some pupils have tended to use IQ scores more to explain why some pupils do not learn than to help all pupils to learn more. They

---

[24] Nancy Bayley, "Mental Growth During the First Three Years," *Genetic Psychology Monographs*, 14 (1933), 1–92.

have tended to explain away intelligence as just another characteristic in which races differ. Instead of using intelligence test scores to ensure equality of educational opportunity, they have used them to deny it. This is why some school systems have dropped intelligence tests from their testing programs.[25]

If there were clear evidence that important biological differences in learning ability existed among schoolchildren, that these differences accounted to a significant degree for variations in school achievement, and that intelligence tests could measure these biological differences, then we ought to accept that evidence and take it into account in our teaching practices. But the evidence is far from clear or conclusive. We do well not to imagine barriers to learning where none exist, or to assume that brightness gives easy access to all knowledge.

SUMMARY

What conclusions can we draw from the foregoing discussion with respect to a school's use of intelligence tests?

1. Schools should not try to determine each child's IQ, first, because intelligence per se is too abstract a concept, and, second, because it cannot be quantified with any real accuracy.
2. They should not spend time and money on individually administered intelligence tests, even with very young pupils, except in unusual cases.
3. Teachers should regard intelligence tests as useful measures of general ability in school learning, an ability that is based on prior learning.
4. Underachievers or overachievers should not be identified on the basis of intelligence test scores.
5. Administrators should prefer verbal to nonverbal intelligence tests, and tests that emphasize abilities developed in school, not as a result of incidental learning.
6. Intelligence tests should not be regarded as *essential* to a good school testing program.
7. Tests that try to measure abstract intelligence, abstract mental abilities, or "the higher mental powers" should be avoided.
8. Instead of choosing tests that purport to be "culture free" or "culture fair," schools should choose tests whose content is relevant to the learning tasks of the school.

[25] J. O. Loretan, "The Decline and Fall of Group Intelligence Testing," *Teachers College Record*, 67 (1965), 10–17.

19

Personality, Attitudes, and Interests

PERSONALITY TESTS

Published tests of personality are relatively abundant. In the *Seventh Mental Measurements Yearbook*,[1] the number of entries in each of four major categories was:

Achievement	535
Personality	147
Intelligence	131
Other	347
	1160

Personality tests range from rather comprehensive personality inventories and temperament surveys to rather specific tests designed to assess, for example, hypnotic susceptibility in children or the dimensions of alcohol addiction in adults.

Despite the number and variety of personality tests, their usefulness in the process of education is open to question. Not only are some person-

[1] Oscar N. Buros, *The Seventh Mental Measurements Yearbook* (Highland Park, N.J.: The Gryphon Press, 1972).

beauty, and so on. Clearly we are not likely to get a single meaningful measure of "how much a person has" of such a complex mixture of characteristics. Instead we must measure aspects of the total personality.

But this trait approach does not solve the problem, even if we limit ourselves to the behavioral aspects of personality. Traits we have semantically differentiated—friendliness, tolerance, integrity, loyalty, ambition, determination, optimism, and so on ad infinitum—overlap and and interact so that it is difficult to define any of them clearly. Traits that cannot be defined clearly can never be measured precisely.

For ages human beings have sought to discover the underlying elements of behavior. The ancients thought they had it in their theory of the four humors—blood, phlegm, yellow bile, and black bile—which they envisioned as contributing warmth, inertia, anger, and melancholy, respectively, to a person's temperament. Jung, Kretschmer, and others have tried to identify and distinguish a limited number of types of personality.[2] Currently, factor analysts are engaged in a search for some simple structure of basic determiners of behavior—so far without apparent success.

It is not even clear that personality traits can be properly regarded as causes of observed behavior. Perhaps they are only names for the behavior, which itself is the consequence of previous experience(s) interacting with a given present situation. Do some high school students refuse to study *because* of lack of motivation? Or is lack of motivation simply the term we use to describe their behavior, which is in fact the result of many previous experiences and current competing interests? We call generous a man who drops a $20 bill in the collection plate on Sunday. Does he do this *because* he is generous, or does the word *generosity* simply name a class of similar behaviors? If personality traits are not causes of behavior, perhaps educators should not waste too much time trying to measure them. If in fact trait names only *describe* behavior, then why measure traits at all—except to name a behavior or set of behaviors that the individual *has already* exhibited?

[2] Carl G. Jung, *Psychological Types: Or the Psychology of Individuation* (London: Routledge, 1959); Ernst Kretschmer, *Physique and Character: An Investigation of the Nature of Constitution and the Theory of Temperament* (London: Routledge, 1936).

Motivation

One of the personality traits that teachers most often wish to measure is motivation. They see some of their students studying hard and others avoiding study as much as possible. They explain the difference by saying that some students are well and others poorly motivated. But is motivation a cause, or is it simply a description of the observed result? Is motivation a mysterious spiritual essence, or is it the result of a complex interaction of beliefs, values, and choices? Can it be measured apart from its manifestation in how hard the student actually works at learning?

The fact that motivation is more a consequence than a cause, and that it probably can never be "measured" effectively by any paper-and-pencil test, does not mean that teachers or students can ignore it. Hard work is essential to learning, and getting students to work hard is an essential part of teaching. We will not here undertake a study of the techniques of motivation—suffice it to say that they are varied and their results are not wholly predictable. Often the essential motivational factors are out of the teacher's reach, even out of the school's. Sometimes, however, they are not. Some teachers are generally successful in motivating students. With some students they may be outstandingly successful. But it is a safe bet that their arsenal of secret weapons does not include a paper-and-pencil test of motivation. Motivation, like most other personality traits, is less a cause than a consequence.

Personality Tests in Educational Programs

If schools had systematic, rational programs for personality development, it would be essential to include personality tests in the school's total program of evaluation. But few schools have such programs, and the limited versions that a few schools have tried, designed to develop such personality traits as ambition, honesty, patriotism, and piety, have not been notably successful. Nor are there any clear guides as to the directions personality development should take. Surely the world would be a poorer place to live if all of us had the same "good" personality. Some of us have "difficult" personalities, difficult for our families and friends and even for ourselves. But if one were to eliminate from the list of the world's great men and women those who had serious personality defects of one kind or another, only a handful would remain.

This does not mean that the schools can ignore the serious personality problems some of their students face. For the student's sake, as well as for the order, effectiveness, and harmony of the school, these problems need to be solved as well as possible. But personality development probably cannot and should not replace cognitive development as the central mission of the school.

are really related ...

matter how disguised or presented, a paper-and-pencil test remains for the examinee essentially a cognitive task. The emotion that plays so large a part in responses that reflect personality is largely absent from the responses to a paper-and-pencil test.

A final problem with personality tests involves the matter of invasion of privacy.[3] Personality tests cause more trouble on this score by far than either aptitude or achievement tests. Those who design personality tests often ask questions about intimate personal or family affairs, questions that may embarrass respondents (Do you ever wet the bed?) or irk their parents (Do your parents quarrel?). Even if it could be proved that knowing these facts enables test administrators to help students with their personal problems, the probing might still be resisted. But in the virtual absence of any such proof, it is almost universally resented.

In summary, these difficulties arise with the use of personality tests in schools:

1. Personality traits are difficult to define because they probably do not exist as distinct entities.
2. The essentially cognitive nature of the tasks presented by paper-and-pencil tests, plus their susceptibility to faking, makes them poorly adapted to the measurement of personality traits.
3. Personality tests that seek to uncover basic causes of maladjustments are likely to probe sensitive areas of concern, and thus are likely to be resented.

In view of these problems, and because most schools are not ordinarily equipped to carry out systematic programs of personality development, personality tests probably have no place in their systematic testing programs. This does not, of course, rule out selective, clinical use of adjustment inventories or problem checklists to aid counselors helping troubled students. But no one concerned in this process—counselor, student, teachers,

[3] George K. Bennett, "Testing and Privacy," *Journal of Educational Measurement*, 4 (1967), 7–10.

or parents—should expect a personality test to reveal much of a person's basic structure of personality. Indeed the very notion of such a structure is probably something of an illusion. Nor should anyone expect a personality test to contribute very much to the solution of the problem.

Personality Tests In Selective Admissions

Those who are responsible for selecting students for admission to a particular college, or to training for the professions, often seek to supplement tests of cognitive ability with tests of personality. They recognize the crucial importance of personality to effective performance in training, and even more to subsequent success and happiness. In the past, such institutions allocated hundreds of thousands of dollars to develop, try out, and evaluate diverse approaches to the measurement of aspects of personality. But as of this writing, no major selective testing program is making operational use of any personality test. Such tests have been used quite extensively by private agencies concerned with the selection of executives, but these practices have been criticized sharply—and with considerable justification.[4]

There are two reasons why personality tests are little used in responsible selection programs. One is the almost insurmountable difficulty we have mentioned of making good, useful personality tests. The other is real concern over the wisdom and the ethics of using them. It is not always, perhaps not even usually, the normal, happy, well-adjusted person who makes the greatest contribution to human welfare. History is replete with records of great men and women who suffered agony of spirit during their developing years. Geniuses are not all mad, but the line between madness and genius is often not at all clear. Denial of advanced education to a capable student who seems maladjusted or somewhat odd might be an extremely shortsighted policy. It might also be quite unfair to reject an otherwise well qualified applicant simply because that person adopts a rather singular life style. The directors of selection testing programs are properly cautious about the use of personality tests.

WHAT ARE ATTITUDES?

Attitudes constitute one aspect of an individual's personality. The concept of an attitude, like that of personality, is not easy to define precisely. It may be defined very generally as "the sum total of a man's inclinations and feelings, prejudice or bias, preconceived notions, ideas, fears, threats, and

[4] William H. Whyte, Jr., *The Organization Man* (New York: Simon and Schuster, Inc., 1956).

unfavorably. Bias is commonly deplored. Its opposites—open-mindedness, tolerance, fairness—are approved. But to remain open-minded, a person must leave questions undecided. It is good to stay open-minded, to give a fair hearing to all sides of a question, if no immediate action is required. It is not good to use open-mindedness as an excuse for evasion of responsibility when hard choices must be made. Remaining open-minded is not always possible or good. We like others to be open-minded to our ideas, but not to be easily persuaded when contrary ideas are presented.

Some attitudes involve mainly feelings. These are sometimes the results of conditioning. A child is conditioned to fear thunderstorms by the anxious behavior of a fearful mother. Another may be conditioned to fear small dogs by the aggressive playfulness of a puppy. A third may be conditioned to love reading by the pleasant experience of being read to at bedtime.

Other attitudes are primarily cognitive generalizations. A political leader's words and actions, or what we know about that person's friends and supporters, may cause us to like and to trust him/her. If we do, we are probably generalizing on the basis of a limited number of observations or even from hearsay testimony. Suppose a church states a position or takes an action that seems wrong to us; again we may conclude, on rather scanty evidence, that its whole influence is bad.

Cognitive attitudes are closely related to knowledge. The difference between them is chiefly in how universally they are accepted, or how easily they can be shown to be true. What we believe is made up of our knowledge and our attitudes. Those propositions that most informed persons regard as true constitute knowledge. Those on which significant differences of opinion exist we term attitudes. In other words, attitudes are personal beliefs.

Several other terms that we commonly use in describing personality

[5] L. L. Thurstone and E. J. Chave, *The Measurement of Attitude* (Chicago: University of Chicago Press, 1929), pp. 6–7.

[6] R. L. Thorndike and E. Hagen, *Measurement and Evaluation in Psychology and Education* (3rd ed.; New York: John Wiley & Sons, Inc., 1969), p. 382.

represent specific kinds of attitudes. Self-concepts are attitudes of a person toward him or herself; interests are attitudes of desire for certain activities; ideals are attitudes of desire for the attainment of certain goals; and values are attitudes of approval of specific things or accomplishments.

Why Different People Have Different Attitudes

There are several reasons why the beliefs that we call attitudes differ from person to person. One is that they involve broad generalizations, with much relevant and occasionally contradictory evidence. Another is that they deal less with things as they are than with things as they ought to be. Personal goals and values affect them. Consider these examples:

Earl Warren was an outstanding Chief Justice.
Communism is evil.
Pollution of our air and water must be stopped.
Our most urgent problem in the United States today is reestablishment of respect for law and order.

These propositions are all more or less debatable. They are too general and too loaded with value judgments to be *proved* true or false. But individuals and governments, after reflection and deliberation, will decide to act as if they were either true or false. Despite their somewhat limited justifiability, attitudes are powerful determiners of action.

Attitudes have a noteworthy self-sustaining and reinforcing property. Once people develop an attitude toward something, once they arrive at an emotional feeling or a cognitive generalization about it, further experience is more likely to support than to weaken it. This is because human beings tend to observe and to remember selectively. They notice and believe incidents that support the correctness of their attitudes and ignore or discredit incidents that seem to call the attitudes into question. The vulnerability of a person's attitudes, the fact that they are not universally believed or easily shown to be true, makes one who holds them use every opportunity to strengthen and defend them.

A well-established attitude is very difficult to dislodge. Seldom can one person induce another to change an attitude, however ill founded it may seem. If a change comes—and attitudes do change—it is likely to be as result of a voluntary, internal decision. If evidence against an attitude accumulates, or if clinging to it entails penalties, the holder may gradually soften and ultimately reverse it.

How Are Attitudes Measured?

Attitudes affect behavior and thus can be measured by observers making use of rating scales. However, the difficulties of finding qualified observers and of finding sufficient relevant incidents to observe usually are being made to aid the student in making sound decisions about his/her own future, the probability that the responses will be faked approaches zero. Efforts to minimize faking by disguising the purpose of the test have generally proved ineffective. Usually the disguise introduces an inordinate amount of error as a result of indirect measurement.

Instruments used to measure attitudes are usually referred to as attitude scales. Although many elaborate techniques of scale construction have been developed, including scalogram analysis (Guttman),[8] unfolding (Coombs),[9] and latent structure analysis (Lazarsfeld),[10] only two have come into wide use. These methods involve either scaled statements (Thurstone)[11] or scaled responses (Likert).[12]

In the Thurstone technique a large set of statements describing varying attitudes toward something like an institution (for example, established religion) or a development (for example, urbanization) is assembled or written. Judges are asked to sort these statements into groups that fall in equally spaced intervals along the attitude continuum from highly favorable to highly unfavorable. Statements that different judges place at widely separated points on the continuum are discarded. From those that remain a smaller set representing the entire continuum as well as possible is selected. These statements constitute the attitude scale.

Each statement carries a scale value determined by the average of its placements by the several judges along the original continuum. The student whose attitude is to be measured is given the scaled statements in random

[7] H. P. Longstaff, "Fakeability of the Strong Interest Blank and the Kuder Preference Record," *Journal of Applied Psychology*, 32 (1948), 360–69.

[8] Louis Guttman, "The Basis for Scaleogram Analysis," in *Measurement and Prediction*, ed. Samuel Stouffer et al. (Princeton, N.J.: Princeton University Press, 1950), pp. 60–90.

[9] C. H. Coombs, *A Theory of Data* (New York: John Wiley & Sons, Inc., 1964), p. 585.

[10] Paul F. Lazarsfeld, "Latent Structure Analysis," in *Psychology: A Study of a Science*, ed. S. Koch (New York: McGraw-Hill Book Company, 1959), Vol. III, pp. 476–542.

[11] L. L. Thurstone and E. J. Chave, *The Measurement of Attitude* (Chicago: University of Chicago Press, 1929).

[12] R. Likert, "A Technique for the Measurement of Attitude," *Archives of Psychology*, 22, No. 140 (1932), 1–55.

order and asked to indicate which statements she or he can accept. The individual's score is the average of the scale values of those statements.

Statements like the following might appear in a scale of attitudes toward permissiveness in child rearing.

	Scale Value
Children should be free to do as they please with their own playthings.	9.5
Decisions on matters of conduct should be made by parent and child jointly.	6.3
In modern times children are being allowed too much freedom.	3.5

The Likert technique also starts with a set of statements, though usually not so many are required. Further, instead of expressing a number of different degrees of favorableness or unfavorableness, each statement is intended to be clearly favorable or unfavorable. Neutral statements are avoided. Examinees respond to each item on a five-point scale of agreement:

	Numerical Scores	
	Favorable	Unfavorable
Strongly agree	5	1
Agree	4	2
Uncertain	3	3
Disagree	2	4
Strongly disagree	1	5

Their score on the item depends, as indicated above, on the extent to which they agree with statements favoring the attitude and disagree with statements opposing it.

Here are three statements that might appear on a scale of political liberalism:

Unemployment insurance tends to encourage idleness.
Government serves the businessman better than it serves the laborer.
A family can live quite comfortably on welfare.

Items that discriminate best between those receiving highest and those receiving lowest scores on the total scale are retained for the final form of the scale.

The Likert technique is easier to use in developing an attitude scale than the Thurstone technique, and gives almost equally good results. It is currently the most widely used technique.

The number of attitudes that could be measured is almost infinite.

never is a serious attempt made to measure the extent to which such objectives have been achieved.

Beyond question, schooling does lead to attitude changes. Many of these changes are results of the acquisition of new knowledge that calls old attitudes into question. Many are the results of conditioning. For example, a teacher who radiates enthusiasm for his/her subject and also demonstrates a genuine interest in students as individuals will probably foster an enduringly favorable attitude toward that field of study. On the other hand, a poorly managed school may condition students to dislike the whole process of education.

Regardless of how attitudes are changed, it seems very doubtful that a teacher or a school should set out deliberately to inculcate certain systems of belief. It seems even more doubtful that an institution designed for the education of a free people should use techniques of conditioning to inculcate the attitudes it approves. Clearly, attitudes accepted as a result of conditioning have not been freely chosen on their merits, as those of a member of a free society ought to be.

What this means is that a teacher or a school should not make the cultivation of a particular set of attitudes one of its explicitly stated and publicly announced primary objectives. Inevitably good teachers will have personal attitudes that they believe to be both good and true. Inevitably these attitudes will affect the knowledge they choose to teach and perhaps even their manner of teaching. Inevitably these and other attitudes will get talked about in good class discussions. The teacher's attitudes will not remain hidden from the students. But under no circumstances should students be required to accept the teacher's attitudes as a condition of satisfactory achievement. What they should be expected to do is to gain command of knowledge and upon this basis form their own attitudes.

Such a procedure is not only the educationally ethical one, it is also likely to be the most effective pedagogically. A frontal attack on other people's attitudes is likely only to strengthen their commitment to them.

[13] Mervin E. Shaw and Jack M. Wright, *Scales for the Measurement of Attitudes* (New York: McGraw Hill Book Company, 1967).

But if attitudes are recognized as theirs to hold or to change, if they are challenged to examine their attitudes critically—that is, in the light of relevant knowledge, if resources relevant to them are increased, they may find personal satisfaction in adopting new attitudes. Attitude modification by indirection is probably the best strategy.

Neither this strategy nor any other will guarantee adoption by students of a single "ideal" set of attitudes, but this lack of certainty is more to be applauded than deplored. If the propositions that constitute our attitudes are uncertain knowledge, it is good to have different ones held and defended. Efforts to defend them, plus the test of time, are quite likely to lead ultimately to knowledge, which can then properly replace the uncertainty of attitudes. And if we must live with some degree of error in our beliefs, as we inevitably must, it is best that such error not be universally accepted as truth.

Thus, the fact that attitudes are almost impossible to measure as educational achievements is no serious loss. We shouldn't include them among our explicit objectives, and we shouldn't try to teach them in any case. The fact that they are very difficult to measure as outcomes of instruction, however, has probably helped to keep the feet of idealistic teachers in paths of virtue.

HOW ARE INTERESTS MEASURED?

Interests have also been measured by asking subjects directly what they like or would like to do. Here again two somewhat different approaches have been used. The Strong Vocational Interest Blank[14] uses brief designations of such things as occupations, amusements, and activities, and asks respondents to indicate whether they like, dislike, or are indifferent to them. The Kuder Preference Record presents triads of activities and asks examinees to choose which they like most and least of each triad.[15]

Another significant difference between these two approaches has to do with the standards against which examinee interests are measured. Scoring weights for alternative responses to items in the Strong test were derived from the responses of successful individuals in each occupation. By contrast, the developers of the Kuder Preference Record assigned items to various interest scales on the basis of student responses that led to a clustering of interest groups. Some of these clusters included activities that were mainly musical, clerical, scientific, and so on. Thus, the scores reported indicate interests in types of activities rather than in particular occupations.

[14] Edward K. Strong, Jr., *Vocational Interests of Men and Women* (Stanford, Calif.: Stanford University Press, 1943).

[15] G. F. Kuder, "The Stability of Preference Items," *The Journal of Social Psychology*, 10 (1939), 41–50.

What it does mean is that *if* that person succeeds he or she will probably be happy in that career.

SUMMARY

The principal ideas developed in this chapter can be summarized in the following 11 propositions:

1. The concept of personality is broad and the factors that influence its development are complex.
2. Personality trait names are more useful in describing behavior than in explaining it.
3. It is unlikely that paper-and-pencil tests of motivation will prove useful to the teacher.
4. The central mission of the school is cognitive development rather than personality development.
5. Personality tests are resented more often and more deeply as unwarranted invasions of privacy than are tests of cognitive achievements.
6. Personality tests have not been used effectively, and probably should not be used at all, in selective admission to educational programs.
7. Attitudes are generalizations whose validity is open to question.
8. A person's attitudes tend to be self-reinforcing.
9. The two principal techniques of attitude measurement are those developed by Thurstone and by Likert. Thurstone's technique uses scaled statements. Likert's technique uses scaled responses.
10. The two principal techniques of interest measurement are those developed by Strong and by Kuder. Strong's technique calls for expressions of liking, indifference, or dislike for particular activities. Kuder's technique calls for choice among alternative activities.
11. Schools probably should not set out to develop directly certain desired attitudes in their students.

Vague and insignificant forms of speech, and abuse of language, have so long passed for mysteries of science; and hard or misapplied words with little or no meaning have, by prescription, such a right to be taken as deep learning and height of speculation, that it will not be easy to persuade either those who speak or those who hear them, that they are but the covers of ignorance and hindrance of true knowledge.

JOHN LOCKE

Glossary of Terms Used in Educational Measurement

This glossary of 125 terms used in educational measurement is intended primarily to aid the reader who encounters an unfamiliar term. An effort has been made to make them conform to general usage by specialists in educational measurement. Other useful glossaries of measurement terms by Gerberich, Lyman, Lennon, and by the California Test Bureau are available.[1]

Absolute Marks are based on teacher judgment of the adequacy of a pupil's achievement, without reference to the achievements of other pupils in the group.

An **Achievement Test** is one designed to measure a student's grasp of some body of knowledge or proficiency in certain skills.

Affective outcomes of education involve feelings more than understandings. A person's likes and dislikes, pleasures and annoyances, satisfactions and discontents, confidence and diffidence, pride and humility, ideals and values are some of the affective outcomes that education may develop.

Analytic Scoring requires preparation of a scoring guide which lists elements of quality or defects that may appear in the product to be scored. The guide may also indicate how many points to award or subtract for each degree of quality or deficiency.

An **Aptitude Test** is one given to determine the

---

[1] J. Raymond Gerberich, *Specimen Objective Test Items* (New York: David McKay Co., Inc., 1956), pp. 392–412; Howard B. Lyman, *Test Scores and What They Mean* (Englewood Cliffs, N.J.: Prentice-Hall, Inc., 1963), pp. 194–205; Roger T. Lennon, "A Glossary of 100 Measurement Terms," *Test Service Notebook, No. 13* (New York: Harcourt Brace Jovanovich, Inc., 1956); *A Glossary of Measurement Terms* (Los Angeles, Calif.: California Test Bureau, 1964), pp. 1–16.

objective test item that was not determined in any way by the content of the item, and which reflects a purely random selection among the alternatives offered.

The **Central Tendency** of a set of test scores is some average value, such as the mean or the median.

Comparable Scores are expressed on the same scale and have the same relative meaning within some common reference group. If scores on different tests are comparable, a particular numerical score represents the same level of proficiency or deficiency regardless of the subject matter of the test.

Conditioning is the process of changing the behavior of an organism by manipulation of stimuli (classical conditioning) or of responses (operant conditioning).

The **Construct Validity** of a test is the accuracy with which it presumably measures some hypothetical, operationally undefined personal characteristic such as intelligence, motivation, or creativity.

The **Content Validity** of an educational achievement test is determined by the extent to which the items in the test adequately sample the areas of subject matter and the abilities that a course of instruction has aimed to teach.

A **Correlation Coefficient**, limited by the values plus 1 and minus 1, expresses the degree of relationship between two sets of test scores or other measurements of each of the individuals in a group.

Creativity is a presumed faculty that enables some to excel in originating ideas (Aristotle), theories (Newton), poems (Keats), plays (Shakespeare), symphonies (Beethoven), and so on.

A **Criterion** is a standard of judging. In test development it usually refers to a characteristic or ters of items, each of which is intended to indicate whether or not some particular objective of instruction has or has not been achieved.

Cross-Validation is a process of testing the quality of a test item, a test, or a test battery using data independent of that used originally to select or revise the items for the test.

A **Culture-Fair** test is intended to indicate how much general intelligence or other basic aptitude a person has, regardless of the kind of educational or cultural experience that may have developed (or failed to develop) the aptitude.

A **Cumulative Frequency** is a number obtained from a frequency distribution of scores that shows for any given score interval the number of the scores in the distribution that lie below and in that interval.

A **Decile** is any one of nine points that divide the score scale into 10 intervals, each of which includes one-tenth of the total frequency.

The **Deviation** of a test score is the difference between that score and some point of reference, such as the mean, the median, or an arbitrary reference point.

A **Diagnostic Test** is designed to reveal specific weaknesses or failures to learn in some subject of study, such as reading or arithmetic.

The **Difficulty Index** of a test item is based on the proportion of examinees in a group who do not answer the test item correctly. The most common index of difficulty is the percent of incorrect response, though difficulty indices on other scales are sometimes encountered.

A **Discrimination Index** is a measure of the extent to which students who are judged to be good in terms of some standard succeed on the item and those who are judged to be poor on the same standard fail it. A commonly used index of discrimination is simply the difference in a proportion of correct responses between the group of those scoring in the top 27 percent on the total test and the group scoring in the bottom 27 percent on the same test. Other indices of discrimination are based on the coefficient of correlation between success on the item and total score on the test.

A **Distracter** is any of the incorrect answer options in multiple-choice test items.

A **Distribution of Scores** is a tabulation or enumeration of the frequency of occurrence of each score in a given set of scores.

The items in **Equivalent Forms** of a test are the same in type, cover the same content, have the same distribution of difficulty values, and yield scores having the same mean, variability, and reliability.

An **Error of Measurement** is the difference between an obtained score and the corresponding true score.

The **Error Variance** in a set of test scores is the mean of the squared errors of measurement for each score in the set.

An **Essay Test** presents one or more questions or other tasks that require extended written responses from the person being tested.

An **Evaluation** is a judgment of merit, sometimes based solely on measurements such as those provided by test scores, but more frequently involving a synthesis of various measurements, critical incidents, subjective impressions, and other kinds of evidence.

An **Examinee** is a person who takes an examination or test.

In an **Expectancy Table** the rows ordinarily correspond to score intervals on some predictor of achievement, and the columns correspond to score intervals on some measure of actual achievement. The figures in each cell of such a double-entry table indicate the relative frequency with which an individual having a given score on the predictor will receive a given score on the criterion of achievement.

An **External Examination** is one chosen or prepared by someone other than the classroom teacher for administration to the students in that classroom. The tests used in statewide or nationwide testing programs, and sometimes those used in local testing programs, are external examinations.

A test possesses **Face Validity** if the questions in it appear to measure the knowledge or ability the test is intended to measure.

Factor Analysis seeks to identify a small number of hypothetical characteristics that will account for the correlations between scores on a much larger number of tests for the individuals in a particular group.

A **Free Response Test** requires the examinee to provide an answer to the test question. It does not allow him to choose among several suggested answers.

A **Frequency Distribution** consists of a sequence of score intervals, opposite each of which is recorded the number of scores in the total group falling in that interval.

Global Quality Scaling of a student's answer to an essay test question is based on the reader's general, overall estimate of its quality. This kind of scaling is an alternative to analytic scoring.

A **Grade Equivalent Score** reports a student's performance on a test in terms of the school grade level for which that level of performance is typical. A pupil whose grade equivalent score on a reading test is 6.3 reads as well as the typical pupil who has completed three months in the sixth grade.

A student's **Grade Point Average** is obtained by adding the numerical values of each of the grades and dividing by the number of grades. Often the grade values are weighted according to the number of credits awarded for completion of the course to which the grade refers.

A **Guessing Correction** is a factor that is added to or subtracted from the number of items correctly answered. The purpose of this correction is to make the score a student could expect to get by guessing blindly on certain questions no higher than the score of a student who omits those items in preference to guessing blindly on them.

Halo Effect describes a bias in ratings arising from the tendency of a rater to be influenced in his rating of specific traits by his general impression of the person being rated.

Intelligence is the capacity to apprehend facts and propositions and their relationships, and to reason about them.

An **Internal Criterion** is applied in judging the

Item Analysis involves the counting of responses to objective test items to determine the difficulty and discriminating power of the item.

The **Item Stem** of a multiple-choice test item is the introductory question or incomplete statement. The examinee chooses an answer to or a completion of the item stem from among the options provided in the remainder of the item.

An **Item-Test Correlation** is the coefficient of correlation between scores on the item and scores on the test as a whole.

Knowledge is a structure of concepts and relations built by reflective thought out of information received. Any experience of participation, observation, reading, or thinking *can* become part of a person's knowledge. It *will* become part of that knowledge if he or she thinks about it, makes sense of it, understands it.

A **Marking System** in a school or college lists the marks a teacher may issue and describes what each mark is intended to mean.

A **Mastery Test** is not intended to indicate how much a student has achieved relative to other students, but only whether or not he or she has achieved enough to satisfy the minimum requirements of the teacher or the examining agency.

A **Matching Exercise** consists of two lists of statements, terms, or symbols. The examinee's task is to match an item in one list with the one most closely associated with it in the other.

The **Mean** is a measure of the average numerical value of a set of scores. It is calculated by adding all of the scores and dividing the sum by the number of scores.

Measurement is a process of assigning numbers to the individual members of a set of objects or persons for the purpose of indicating differences among them in the degree to which they possess the characteristic being measured.

statement, and two or more options, consisting of answers to the question or completions of the statement.

A **Normal Distribution** is an ideal frequency distribution defined by a mathematical formula. It is represented by a symmetrical, bell-shaped curve characterized by scores concentrated near the middle and tapering toward each extreme.

Normalized Standard Scores are derived in a way that makes the distribution of scores approximately normal, regardless of the shape of the distribution of raw scores on which they were based.

A pupil's score on a **Norm-Referenced Test** indicates how the pupil's performance on the test compares with that of other pupils in some appropriate reference group.

The **Norms** for a test indicate how the members of a particular reference group or groups scored on the test.

An **Objective Test** is one that can be provided with a simple predetermined list of correct answers, so that subjective opinion or judgment in the scoring procedure is eliminated.

Objectivity is characteristic of statements that can be verified by an independent observer or judge.

Operational Definitions of quantitative concepts (variables) describe how the amount of the variable can be determined.

Overachievement is indicated when a pupil's score on an achievement test is higher than would have been predicted on the basis of the pupil's intelligence or aptitude test score.

Pass-Fail marks indicate only whether a pupil did or did not complete a course of study satisfactorily.

A **Percentile Band** is a range of percentiles within which a particular student's true percentile rank on the test is likely to fall. The use of percentile bands serves to emphasize the uncertainty associated with any test score, but it does this at the cost of precise information on the individual's most probable percentile rank.

The **Percentile Rank** of a particular score in a given distribution of scores is a number indicating the percentage of scores in the whole distribution that fall below the point at which the given score lies.

In a **Performance Test** the subject is required to demonstrate his or her skill by manipulating objects or instruments.

Personality refers to the complex of characteristics that gives a particular person identity, distinguishing him or her from other persons. A person's appearance, habits, attitudes, interests, values, and knowledge all contribute to personality. How that personality is perceived by others depends mainly on the individual's behavior in social situations.

A **Population** of persons, test items, or other objects is the whole number of all who belong to a particular set or collection. Some part of a population becomes a sample.

The **Predictive Validity** of a test indicates how accurately some earlier measure of ability can forecast some later measure of performance.

The **Probable Error** of a set of test scores is the median error of measurement, in absolute value. Half the errors of measurement are larger and the other half smaller than the probable error of measurement.

The **Product-Moment** (or Pearson) coefficient of correlation is the mean for all pupils of the product of their standard scores on the two measures being correlated.

A **Profile** is a graphic representation of the relative magnitude of a student's scores on several tests. In order for such a profile to be meaningful, the scores on all of the tests must be comparable scores, based on the same standard scale.

A **Proposition** is a sentence that can be said to be either true or false.

A **Quality Scale** consists of a series of typical specimens of such things as handwriting, composition, or drawings of a particular subject, arranged in an order of merit, usually with a numerical value assigned to each. Such a scale is then used as a standard of comparison for rating the quality of work of other examinees.

The **Quantification** of anything requires the specification of operations by means of which appropriate numbers can be attached to various amounts of the characteristic or property. A written test is often used to quantify achievement in a particular course of study. No measurement of anything is possible until some process for quantifying the attribute to be measured has been worked out.

A **Quartile** is one of three points along the score scale of a frequency distribution that divide the distribution into four parts of equal frequency.

A **Random Sample** is selected in such a way as to guarantee equal probability of selection to all possible samples of this size that could be formed from the members of the universe involved. It is also true that each element in the universe has equal probability of being included in a random sample.

A **Range of Scores** is the smallest interval on the score scale that will include all the measures in the distribution.

A **Raw Score** is the number first obtained in scoring the test, before any transformation to a standard score or other derived score.

In a **Rectangular Distribution** successive equal intervals along the score scale include the same number of scores.

The **Relevance** of a task in a test is the extent to which it contributes to the purposes of the test by virtue of the abilities it calls into play.

The **Reliability Coefficient** is the estimate of the coefficient of correlation between the scores for students in a particular group on two equivalent forms of the same test. Reliability is sometimes defined also as the proportion of total score variance that is not error variance.

The **Representative Sample** is one chosen in such a way as to make it more likely than a random sample to exhibit the same characteristics as the population.

A **Response Count** for an objective test item indicates the frequency with which one or more of the answer options were chosen by examinees in a particular group.

A **Response Set** is a predisposition on the part of an examinee to resolve uncertainty in answering sample value of some statistic and the value obtained when calculated on the basis of the entire population.

A **Scatter Diagram** is a device for displaying the relationship between scores on two tests for the individuals in a group. Scores on one test are represented on the vertical dimension, those on the other along the horizontal dimension. A tally mark is entered on the diagram to reflect the pair of scores for a particular individual.

A **Score** is a number assigned to an examinee to provide a quantitative description of his or her performance on a particular test.

A **Scoring Formula** indicates how the raw score on the test is to be obtained from the number of correct, incorrect, or omitted responses. The simplest scoring formula is "Score equals number right." Other formulas provide corrections for guessing.

A **Scoring Key** indicates the correct answer to each item.

A **Short Answer Test** requires the examinee to produce a word, phrase, or number that answers the test question.

A **Situational Test** is based upon descriptions—verbal or pictorial or both—of specific situations, real or imagined. The examinee's task is to respond to some problem in, or question about, the situation.

A **Skewed Distribution** is an asymmetrical distribution in which most of the scores are closer to one end of the distribution than they are to the other. If the longer tail of the distribution extends toward the lower end of the score scale, the distribution is said to be negatively skewed. If the longer tail extends to the higher end of the score scale, the distribution is said to be positively skewed.

The **Spearman-Brown Formula** is used to predict

be true than false.

Speededness of a test is the extent to which an examinee's score on it depends on quickness in working through it. It is sometimes measured by the proportion of examinees who *do not* reach and answer the last item in the test.

A **Split-halves Reliability Coefficient** is obtained by using half the items on the test, sometimes the odd-numbered items, to yield one score for an examinee and the other half of the items to yield another, independent score. The correlation between the scores on these two half-tests, corrected with the aid of the Spearman-Brown Formula, provides an estimate of the reliability of the total test.

The **Standard Deviation** is a measure of variability, dispersion, or spread of a set of scores around their mean value. Mathematically, the standard deviation is the square root of the mean of the squared deviations of the scores from the mean of the distribution of scores.

The **Standard Error of Measurement** is an estimate of the standard deviation of the errors of measurement associated with the test scores in a given set. The standard error of measurement is estimated by multiplying the standard deviation of the scores by the square root of one minus the reliability coefficient.

A **Standard Score** is one derived from a raw score so that it can be expressed on a uniform standard scale without seriously altering its relationship to other scores in the distribution. A simple type of standard score is the *z-score*, which expresses each raw score as a positive or negative deviation from the mean of all raw scores on a scale in which the unit is one standard deviation.

A **Standardized Test** is one that has been constructed in accord with detailed specifications, one for which the items have been selected after tryout for appropriateness in difficulty and discriminating power, one which is accompanied by a manual giving definite directions for uniform administration and scoring, and one which is provided with relevant and dependable norms for score interpretation.

A **Stanine Score** (from *stan*dard *nine*) is a single-digit standard score on a nine-unit scale. The distribution of stanine scores in the population from which they were derived has a mean of 5 and standard deviation of 2.

A **Statistic** is a number used to describe or characterize some aspect of a sample. For example, the number of cases in the sample, the mean value of the measures in the sample, the standard deviation of those measures, and the correlation between two sets of measures for the members of the sample are statistics.

A **Table of Specifications** includes a test outline that specifies what proportion of the item shall deal with each content area and with each type of ability. It may also include other specifications, such as number of items in the test, time to be allowed for its administration, and description of kinds of items that will or will not be included in the test.

A **Taxonomy** is an orderly classification, originally of plants and animals, arranged according to their presumed natural relationships. Taxonomies of cognitive and affective educational objectives have been prepared.

A **Test** is any kind of device or procedure for measuring ability, achievement, interest, and other traits.

A **Test Item** is the smallest independent unit of a test. Each statement to be judged true or false, each question to which an answer is to be selected, each incomplete statement to which a completion is to be selected, each blank in a sentence or paragraph to be filled in is a separate test item.

Test-retest Reliability is calculated by correlating scores for the same students on two administrations of the same test.

Testwiseness enables an examinee to do full justice to himself, or to outwit an inept examiner.

A **Trait** is any attribute of a person that is possessed in differing amounts by different members of a group or class. It is a physical characteristic or a relatively stable mode of behavior. Such things as height, intelligence, quality of handwriting, or understanding of chemical principles are traits.

A **True-false Item** consists of a statement that the examinee is asked to judge to be either true or false.

A **True Score** is an idealized error-free score for a specific person on a specific test. It may also be defined as the mean of an infinite number of independent measurements of the same trait, using equivalent forms of the test.

The **Validity** of a test is often defined as the degree to which it measures what it purports to measure, or as the extent to which a test does the job for which it is intended. For some types of tests for which good independent criterion measures are available, statistical coefficients of validity can be obtained. These are coefficients of correlation between scores on the test and the criterion measures.

The **Variance** is a measure of the dispersion of scores about their mean. The variance is the mean of the squared deviations of the scores from their mean.

In **Weighted Scoring** the number of points awarded for a correct response is not the same for all items in the test. In some cases, weighted scoring involves the award of different numbers of points for the choice of different responses to the same item.

A **z-score** is a standard score. Raw scores are converted into z-scores by subtracting the mean from the raw score and dividing the difference by the standard deviation. Thus, z-scores are equally likely to be positive or negative. They ordinarily range from about -3 to about $+3$.

Ayres, Leonard P., 21

Barnes, Elinor J., 60
Bauernfeind, Robert H., 319
Bayley, Nancy, 359
Beers, F. S., 49
Bennett, George K., 365
Betts, Gilbert L., 55
Binet, Alfred, 345
Bishop, Carol H., 182
Blommers, Paul, 211
Bloom, Benjamin S., 37, 50, 82, 86
Board, Cynthia, 141
Boaz, George, 35
Bolmeier, Edward C., 241
Bridgman, Donald S., 227
Brody, William, 59
Brooks, H. B., 229
Buros, Oscar K., 362
Burt, Sir Cyril, 358

Carter, Ralph E., 102
Carter, Robert S., 233
Cashen, Valjean, 188
Chase, Stuart, 298
Chauncey, Henry, 324
Chave, E. J., 367, 369
Ciardi, John, 135
Cleary, T. Anne, 326
Coffman, William E., 56,95
Cohen, Morris R., 45
Coleman, William, 350
Collet, LeVerne S., 137
Conrad, Herbert S., 356
Cook, Desmond L., 75, 137, 213
Cook, Walter W., 300

Cromack, Theodore R., 90
Cronbach, Lee J., 306, 352
Crooks, W. R., 239
Cureton, Edward E., 300, 350
Cureton, Louise Witmer, 227
Curtis, F. D., 102
Curtis, H. A., 178

Davis, Frederick B., 258, 262
Dear, Robert E., 325
DeZouche, Dorothy, 229
Diederich, Paul B., 239, 262
Dobbin, John E., 241
Downing, Steven M., 281
Dressel, Paul L., 82, 324
Dyer, Henry S., 63

Ebel, Robert L., 39, 49, 77, 111, 117,
    150, 171, 182, 189, 268, 275, 276,
    281, 297, 321, 324, 329
Elliott, E. C., 99, 234
Engelhart, Max D., 262
Eurich, Alvin C., 75

Feldt, Leonard, 318, 320
Ferguson, George, A., 211
Ferguson, L. W., 239
Finlayson, D. S., 99
Fitzgibbon, Thomas J., 1
Flanagan, John C., 262, 335
Franklin, Benjamin, 36
French, John W., 325
Frisbie, David, 115
Frost, Robert, 12

381

Subject Index